PLUTARCH'S "LIVES"

SELECTED AND EDITED

JOHN S. WHITE, LL.D.

WITH FORTY-FIVE
ILLUSTRATIONS

BIBLO AND TANNEN

ISBN 0-8196-0174-8

CONTENTS.

	PAGE
LIFE OF THESEUS	3
LIFE OF ROMULUS	28
COMPARISON OF THESEUS AND ROMULUS	47
LIFE OF LYCURGUS	49
LIFE OF SOLON	73
LIFE OF THEMISTOCLES	88
LIFE OF CAMILLUS	106
LIFE OF PERICLES	136
LIFE OF DEMOSTHENES	168
LIFE OF CICERO	190
COMPARISON OF DEMOSTHENES AND CICERO	229
LIFE OF ALCIBIADES	233
LIFE OF CORIOLANUS	260
COMPARISON OF ALCIBIADES AND CORIOLANUS	284
LIFE OF ARISTIDES	288
LIFE OF CIMON	306
LIFE OF POMPEY	326
THE ENGINES OF ARCHIMEDES; FROM THE LIFE OF MARCELLUS	370
DESCRIPTION OF CLEOPATRA; FROM THE LIFE OF ANTONY	375
ANECDOTES FROM THE LIFE OF AGESILAUS	380
THE BROTHERS; FROM THE LIFE OF TIMOLEON	383
THE WOUND OF PHILOPŒMEN	386
A ROMAN TRIUMPH; FROM THE LIFE OF PAULUS ÆMILIUS	388
THE NOBLE CHARACTER OF CAIUS FABRICIUS; FROM THE LIFE OF PYRRHUS	393
FROM THE LIFE OF QUINTUS FABIUS MAXIMUS	396
THE CRUELTY OF LUCIUS CORNELIUS SYLLA	398
THE LUXURY OF LUCULLUS	401

CONTENTS.

	PAGE
FROM THE LIFE OF SERTORIUS THE ROMAN, WHO ENDEAVORED TO ESTABLISH A SEPARATE GOVERNMENT FOR HIMSELF IN SPAIN	406
THE SCROLL; FROM THE LIFE OF LYSANDER	410
THE CHARACTER OF MARCUS CATO	411
THE SACRED THEBAN BAND; FROM THE LIFE OF PELOPIDAS	416
FROM THE LIFE OF TITUS FLAMININUS, CONQUEROR OF PHILIP	418
LIFE OF ALEXANDER THE GREAT	420
THE DEATH OF CÆSAR	446
WEIGHTS, MEASURES, ETC., MENTIONED BY PLUTARCH; FROM THE TABLES OF DR. ARBUTHNOT	440
A CHRONOLOGICAL TABLE, FROM DACIER AND OTHER WRITERS	450
INDEX FOR REFERENCE AS TO THE PRONUNCIATION OF PROPER NAMES	459

LIST OF ILLUSTRATIONS.

	PAGE
TEMPLE OF THESEUS AT ATHENS	2
PORTICO OF TEMPLE OF HERCULES AT ATHENS	7
THE ISLAND OF NAXOS	15
GIRL PLAYING AT DICE	62
GIRL OF TANAGRA WEARING THE CHITON	63
YOUTH WITH CHLAMYS AND HAT	64
YOUTH WITH CHLAMYS AND HAT	65
THE GULF OF SALAMIS	75
MILTIADES	89
THEMISTOCLES	94
THEMISTOCLES RECEIVING THE TROPHY OF VICTORY	98
EXILE OF THEMISTOCLES	100
RESTORATION OF THE WEST END OF THE ACROPOLIS	136
ATHENS FROM MOUNT HYMETTUS	137
ATHENS FROM THE ROAD TO ELEUSIS	146
THE PARTHENON IN THE TIME OF PERICLES	149
TEMPLE OF HERCULES	150
TEMPLE OF MINERVA AT ÆGINA	163
RUINS OF THE PARTHENON	167
DEMOSTHENES	170
THE CAPITOL	217
WRITING IMPLEMENTS	228
ALCIBIADES	233
SPHACTERIA AND PYLOS FROM NAVARINO	241
MOUNTS OLYMPUS AND OSSA FROM THE PLAIN OF THESSALY	305
PLAIN OF MARATHON	308

LIST OF ILLUSTRATIONS.

	PAGE
GROVES OF THE ACADEMY	318
GATE OF LIONS AT MYCENÆ	325
POMPEY	327
COIFFURES OF ROMAN LADIES	348
ARCH OF CONSTANTINE	350
HARBOR OF BRUNDUSIUM	353
RIVER PENEUS, LOOKING TOWARD MOUNT PINDUS	362
LADY OF TANAGRA WITH CHITON AND HAT	376
GREEK WARRIOR	380
GREEK WARRIOR	381
WINE JUGS OR OINOCHOI	390
MIXING BOWLS OR KROTERES	391
WALL DECORATIONS FROM POMPEII	402
GATE OF LIONS AT MYCENÆ (RESTORED)	417
ALEXANDER THE GREAT	423
THERAMENES DRAGGED FROM THE ALTAR BY ORDER OF CRITIAS	428
TEMPLE OF POSEIDON AT PAESTUM	445
THEATRICAL MASKS	448

INTRODUCTION.

"WHAT! a book for girls as well as boys?" Well, is it not high time, when almost every wholesome book made for young folks in the score of years just past has been dedicated to the boys alone?

I am afraid most of you will say right here—"*I* always skip the introduction to a book; it is so stupid!" But if I could only sketch so boldly for you this sweet and Christ-like pagan that the picture would afford you a little of the pleasure the study of his works has brought to me, you would fain read the last word. Plutarch wrote a hundred books and was never dull. Most of these have been lost, but the portions which remain have found, with the exception of Holy Writ, more readers through eighteen centuries than the works of any other writer of ancient times. Besides the fifty "lives" and about twenty "comparisons" which are still extant, we have five large octavo volumes of essays, conversations, and dialogues, covering a vast range of topics. Lamprius, who is commonly thought to have been Plutarch's son, and who was himself something of a philosopher, has left us a catalogue of his father's writings; but, as Dryden capitally said, "you cannot look upon the list without the same emotions that a merchant must feel in perusing a bill of freight after he has lost his vessel." The writings which no longer exist are these—a marvel in themselves of human talent and industry:

The Lives of Hercules, Hesiod, Pindar, Crates, and Daïphantus, with a Parallel; Leonidas, Aristomenes, Scipio Africanus Junior, and Metellus, Augustus, Tiberius, Claudius,

Nero, Caligula, Vitellius, Epaminondas and the Elder Scipio, with a Parallel.
Four Books of Commentaries on Homer.
Four Books of Commentaries on Hesiod.
Four Books to Empedocles, on the Quintessence.
Five Books of Essays.
Three Books of Fables.
Three Books of Rhetoric.
Three Books on the Introduction of the Soul.
Two Books of Extracts from the Philosophers.
Three Books on Sense.
Three Books on the Great Actions of Cities.
Two Books on Politics.
An Essay on Opportunity, to Theophrastus.
Four Books on the Obsolete Parts of History.
Two Books of Proverbs.
Eight Books on the Topics of Aristotle.
Three Books on Justice, to Chrysippus.
An Essay on Poetry.
A Dissertation on the Difference between the Pyrrhonians and the Academicians.
A Treatise to prove that there was but one Academy of Plato.

Plutarch was born about the year 50, A.D., at Chæronea, in Bœotia—a little town, but of good repute, in which he spent nearly the whole of his three score years and ten, being loth, as he said, "to make it less by the withdrawal of even one inhabitant." He learned philosophy under Ammonius at Athens. He traveled much and made many friends. But for his visit to Egypt we should know little or nothing of the worship of Isis and Osiris, and the Egyptian mysteries. Twice he went to Italy, apparently upon public business, and, while in Rome, lectured in the Greek language and taught philosophy. He appears to have learned the Latin tongue later on at his own home. We know very little else of his life except

INTRODUCTION.

that he was married, and was the father of five children, two of whom survived to manhood. We may judge from his occasional allusions to his private life that it was supremely happy; "exhibiting," he writes in a letter to his wife, "scarcely an erasure, as in a book well-written." But the pity is that, like Shakspeare, whom Plutarch greatly resembles in the universality of his genius, the story of his life was never told. Four centuries after his death Agathias wrote this memorable epitaph to be engraved upon a statue erected by the Romans to his memory:

> Chæronean Plutarch, to thy deathless praise
> Does martial Rome this grateful statue raise,
> Because both Greece and she thy fame have shared—
> Their heroes written, and their lives compared.
> But thou thyself couldst never write thy own;
> Their lives have parallels, but thine has none!

It is remarkable that Plutarch never mentions in his writings the names of his great contemporaries,—Tacitus, Quintilian, Seneca, and both the Plinys, Martial, Suetonius, and Juvenal, nor, on the other hand, would you discover from their writings that such a man as Plutarch ever lived. But the greatest writers through all the years since the second century have told his praises and drawn at will from his ceaseless fountain of wisdom. Taurus calls him a man of the most consummate learning; in the language of Sardianus he is the "divine Plutarch"; and when Theodorus Gaza, a learned classical scholar three hundred years ago, was asked what author he would save, if learning must suffer a "general shipwreck," he replied, "Plutarch," because in preserving him he should secure the best substitute for all other books.

Nobody ever read human nature with a juster eye, and weighed character and merit in finer scales than our own Emerson. He chats most delightfully of Plutarch:—"No poet could illustrate his thought with more novel or striking similes or happier anecdotes. I do not know where to find a book—to borrow a phrase of Ben Jonson's—'so rammed with life.' His style is realistic, picturesque, and varied; his sharp objective eyes seeing everything that moves, shines, or threatens in nature or art, or thought or dreams. Indeed, twilights, shadows, omens, and spectres have a charm for him. He believes in witchcraft and the evil eye, in demons and ghosts—but prefers, if you please, to talk of these in the morning. His vivacity and abundance never leave him to loiter or pound on an incident. I admire his rapid and crowded style, as if he had such store of anecdotes of his heroes that he is forced to suppress more than he recounts, in order to keep up with the hasting history."

The sentiment of Plutarch, like his heart, was always pure. "Truth," he says, "is the greatest good that man can receive, and the goodliest blessing God can give." He was very plain-spoken, as were all the Greek and Roman authors, writing only for men to read. Not until women were educated to read, and think, and write, did literature become elevated and refined from impurity of subject and expression. In the selections from the Lives which I have given you, I have pruned away whatever seemed indelicate for the young reader, or tedious; some of the least interesting biographies I have, for lack of space, omitted altogether. But the selections are given as nearly as possible in Plutarch's own words, following pretty closely the quaint but generally vivid translation called "Dryden's," made by many different scholars, corrected and revised a few years ago by Professor Clough, of London.

In reading the Essays of Plutarch, the wonder constantly grows that his knowledge could be so extensive and so scientific. He gives a lucid and correct explanation of the cause of the rainbow; he discusses the principles of gravitation as a subject of common information, so skilfully that Sir Isaac Newton must yield the palm of originality as to the discovery that all matter attracts all other matter. His discourse

"Concerning the face that appeareth in the orb of the moon" evidences a marvelously profound understanding of astronomy, beyond which the science of the present day has made little advance. And Dr. Holmes himself will confess to you that in this same Plutarch of eighteen hundred years ago you may discover a veritable "Autocrat of the Breakfast-table." Among the subjects of which he discourses are: "Brotherly Love," "Bashfulness," "Chattering," "How to know a Flatterer from a Friend," "That Brutes make use of Reason," "Whether Sleep or Death appertains to the body or the soul," "On the Cure for Anger," and a vast number of others touching upon almost every sphere of human knowledge, and illustrated and adorned with a wealth of figure and anecdote that admit us unintentionally but surely into the very heart of the ancient home life.

Horace bids the pin-feathered poet "study to be unstudied," and Plutarch in his sphere deems it the highest object of ambition to be a philosopher without seeming to be one. In his essay "Of Man's Progress in Virtue," he considers it "an argument of a generous and truly brave disposition in a scholar not to assume the name and character of one, and as some do, to put 'philosopher' among his titles; but if any, out of respect, chance to give him that appellation, to be surprised, blush, and with a modest smile, answer him in the words of the poet:

> "'You compliment your friend: he whom you commend
> Must needs be more than man—far more than I pretend.'" *

Plutarch believes heartily in the reasoning power of brutes. He loves animals, and his writings are full of tender allusions to instances of affection and sagacity among them that evidence the closest acquaintance with their habits and history.

In the Conversation "Whether Water or Land Animals are the more Sagacious," occurs this anecdote:—

---

* *Odyssey*, XVI. 187.

"It happened that King Pyrrhus, traveling one day, found a dog watching over the carcass of a person slain; and hearing that the dog had been there three days without meat or drink, yet would not forsake his dead master, he ordered that the man should be buried, but that the dog should be preserved and brought to him. A few days after there was a muster of the soldiers, so that they were forced to march all in order by the king, with the dog quietly lying by him for a good while. But when he saw the murderers of his master pass by him, he flew upon them with a more than ordinary fury, barking and baying and tearing their throats, and ever and anon turning about to the king; which did not only rouse the king's suspicion, but the jealousy of all that stood about him. Upon which the men were presently apprehended; and though the circumstances were very slight which otherwise appeared against them, yet they confessed the fact and were executed."

There is nothing in the extant writings of Plutarch to indicate that he had any knowledge of the Christian religion, although the purity and humility of his life, his fearless championship of the right, and his broad humanity peculiarly adapted him to be a follower of the Great Teacher. His profound faith in divine Providence and in the immortality of the soul everywhere illuminates his pages, and I cannot give you a truer key to his heart and a closer acquaintance with the man himself whose Lives you are about to read than by quoting a few of the words from his beautiful " Letter of consolation to Apollonius upon the death of a gifted son":

"That virtuous men die in the prime of their years by the kindness of the gods, to whom they are peculiarly dear, I have already told thee in the former part of my discourse, and will give a short hint of it now, bearing witness to that which is so prettily said by Menander, 'He whom the gods do love dies young.' Thy Apollonius died in the beautiful flower of his years, a youth in all points perfect, who gained the love and provoked the emulation of all his contemporaries. He was dutiful to his father and mother, obliging to his domestics, was a scholar, and (to comprehend all in a word) he was a lover of mankind. He had a veneration for the old men that were his friends as if they had been his parents; he had an affection for his companions and equals, reverenced his instructors, was hospitable and mild to guests and strangers, gracious to all and beloved by all, as well for his attractive countenance as for his lovely affability. Therefore, being accompanied with the applauses of thy piety and his own, he hath only made a digression from this mortal life to eternity, as if he had withdrawn from the entertainment before he grew absurd, and before the staggerings of drunkenness came upon him, which are incident to a long old age. Now if the sayings of the old philosophers and poets are true, as there is probability to think, that honors and high seats of dignity are conferred upon the righteous after they are departed this life, and if, as it is said, a particular region is appointed for their souls to dwell in, you ought to cherish very fair hopes that your son stands numbered among these blest inhabitants.

"Of the state of the pious after death, Pindar discourseth after this manner:

"'There the sun shines with an unsullied light,
When all the world below is thick with night.
There all the richly scented plants do grow,
And there the crimson-colored roses blow;
Each flower blooming on its tender stalk,
And all these meadows are their evening walk.
There trees peculiarly delight the sense
With their exhaled perfume of frankincense;
The boughs their noble burdens cannot hold,
The weight must sink them when the fruit is **gold.**
* * * * *
Death its efforts on the body spends;
But the aspiring spirit upward tends—
Nothing can damp that bright and subtile **flame,**
Immortal as the Gods, from whence it came.'"

TEMPLE OF THESEUS AT ATHENS.

THESEUS.

As geographers, Sosius,* crowd into the edges of their maps parts of the world which they do not know about, adding notes in the margin to the effect that beyond this lies nothing but sandy deserts full of wild beasts, unapproachable bogs, Scythian ice, or a frozen sea, so, in this work of mine, in which I have compared the lives of the greatest men with one another, after passing through those periods which probable reasoning can reach to and real history find a footing in, I might very well say of those that are farther off, Beyond this there is nothing but prodigies and fictions; the only inhabitants are the poets and inventors of fables; there is no credit, or certainty any farther. Yet, after publishing an account of Lycurgus the lawgiver and Numa the king, I thought I might, not without reason, ascend as high as to Romulus, being brought by my history so near to his time. Considering therefore with myself

> Whom shall I set so great a man to face?
> Or whom oppose? who's equal to the place?

(as Æschylus expresses it), I found none so fit as he who peopled the beautiful and far-famed city of Athens, to be set in opposition with the father of the invincible and renowned city of Rome. Let us hope that Fable may, in what shall follow, so submit to the purifying processes of Reason as to take the character of exact history. We shall beg that we may meet with candid readers, and such as will receive with indulgence the stories of antiquity.

Theseus seemed to me to resemble Romulus in many par-

---

* Sosius Senecio, Plutarch's friend at Rome, whom he addresses.

ticulars. Both of them had the repute of being sprung from the gods.

> Both warriors; that by all the world's allowed.

Both of them united with strength of body an equal vigor of mind; and of the two most famous cities of the world, the one built Rome, and the other made Athens be inhabited Neither of them could avoid domestic misfortunes nor jealousy at home; but towards the close of their lives are both of them said to have incurred great odium with their countrymen, if, that is, we may take the stories least like poetry as our guide to the truth.

Theseus was the son of Ægeus and Æthra. His lineage, by his father's side, ascends as high as to Erechtheus and tne first inhabitants of Attica. By his mother's side he was descended of Pelops, who was the most powerful of all the kings of Peloponnesus.

When Ægeus went from the home of Æthra in Trœzen to Athens, he left a sword and a pair of shoes, hiding them under a great stone that had a hollow in it exactly fitting them; and went away making her only privy to it, and commanding her that if, when their son came to man's estate, he should be able to lift up the stone and take away what he had left there, she should send him away to him with those things with all secrecy, and with injunctions to him as much as possible to conceal his journey from every one; for he greatly feared the Pallantidæ, who were continually mutinying against him, and despised him for his want of children, they themselves being fifty brothers, all sons of Pallas, the brother of Ægeus.

When Æthra's son was born, some say that he was immediately named Theseus, from the tokens which his father had *put** under the stone; others that he received his name afterwards at Athens, when Ægeus *acknowledged** him for his son.

---
* Thĕsis, putting; Thesthai, to take to oneself, to adopt or acknowledge, as a son.

He was brought up under his grandfather Pittheus, and had a tutor and attendant set over him named Connidas, to whom the Athenians, even to this time, the day before the feast that is dedicated to Theseus, sacrifice a ram, giving this honor to his memory upon much juster grounds than to Silanio and Parrhasius, for making pictures and statues of Theseus. There being then a custom for the Grecian youth, upon their first coming to man's estate, to go to Delphi and offer first-fruits of their hair to the god, Theseus also went thither, and a place there to this day is yet named Thesea, as it is said, from him. He clipped only the fore part of his head, as Homer says the Abantes did. And this sort of tonsure was from him named Theseis. The Abantes first used it, not in imitation of the Arabians, as some imagine, nor of the Mysians, but because they were a warlike people, and used to close fighting, and above all other nations accustomed to engage hand to hand; as Archilochus testifies in these verses:

> Slings shall not whirl, nor many arrows fly,
>   When on the plain the battle joins; but **swords**,
> Man against man, the deadly conflict try,
>   As is the practice of Euboea's lords
> Skilled with the spear.——

Therefore, that they might not give their enemies a hold by their hair, they cut it in this manner. They write also that this was the reason why Alexander gave command to his captains that all the beards of the Macedonians should be shaved, as being the readiest hold for an enemy.

Æthra for some time concealed the true parentage of Theseus, and a report was given out by Pittheus that he was the son of Neptune; for the Troezenians pay Neptune the highest veneration. He is their tutelar god, to him they offer all their first-fruits, and in his honor stamp their money with a trident.

Theseus displaying not only great strength of body, but

equal bravery, and a quickness alike and force of understanding, his mother Æthra, conducting him to the stone, and informing him who was his true father, commanded him to take from thence the tokens that Ægeus had left, and to sail to Athens. He without any difficulty set himself to the stone and lifted it up; but refused to take his journey by sea, though it was much the safer way, and though his mother and grandfather begged him to do so. For it was at that time very dangerous to go by land on the road to Athens, no part of it being free from robbers and murderers. That age produced a sort of men, in force of hand, and swiftness of foot, and strength of body, excelling the ordinary rate, and wholly incapable of fatigue; making use, however, of these gifts of nature to no good or profitable purpose for mankind, but rejoicing and priding themselves in insolence, and taking the benefit of their superior strength in the exercise of inhumanity and cruelty, and in seizing, forcing, and committing all manner of outrages upon everything that fell into their hands; all respect for others, all justice, they thought, all equity and humanity, though naturally lauded by common people, either out of want of courage to commit injuries or fear to receive them, yet no way concerned those who were strong enough to win for themselves. Some of these Hercules destroyed and cut off in his passage through these countries, but some, escaping his notice while he was passing by, fled and hid themselves, or else were spared by him in contempt of their abject submission; and after that Hercules fell into misfortune, and, having slain Iphitus, retired to Lydia, and for a long time was there slave to Omphale, a punishment which he had imposed upon himself for the murder. Then, indeed, Lydia enjoyed high peace and security, but in Greece and the countries about it the like villanies again revived and broke out, there being none to repress or chastise them. It was therefore a very hazardous journey to travel by land from Athens to Peloponnesus; and Pittheus, giving him an exact account of each of these robbers and villains, their strength, and the cruelty they used to all strangers, tried to persuade Theseus to go by sea. But he, it seems, had long since been secretly fired by the glory of Hercules, held him in the highest estimation, and was never more satisfied than in listening to any that gave an account of him; especially those that had seen him, or had been present at any action or saying of his. So that he was altogether in the same state of feeling as, in after ages, Themistocles was, when he said that he could not sleep for the trophy of Miltiades; entertaining such admiration for the virtue of Hercules that in the night his dreams were all of that hero's actions, and in the day a continual emulation stirred him up to perform the like. Besides, they were related, being born of own cousins. For Æthra was daughter of Pittheus, and Alcmena of Lysidice; and Lysidice and Pittheus were brother and sister, children of Hippo-

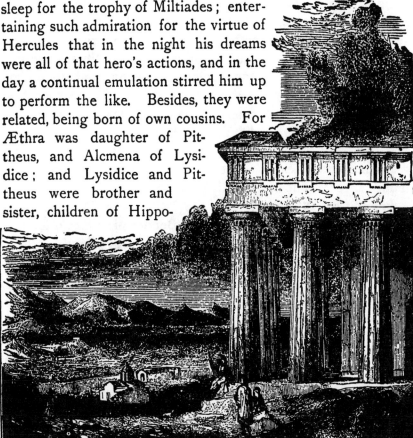

PORTICO OF TEMPLE OF HERCULES AT ATHENS.
(It is erroneously called Temple of Theseus in W. Gr.)

damia and Pelops. He thought it therefore a dishonorable thing, and not to be endured, that Hercules should go out everywhere, and purge both land and sea from wicked men, and he himself should fly from the like adventures that actually came in his way; not showing his true father as good evidence of the greatness of his birth by noble and worthy actions, as by the tokens that he brought with him, the shoes and the sword.

With this mind and these thoughts, he set forward with a design to do injury to nobody, but to repel and revenge himself of all those that should offer any. And first of all, in a set combat he slew Periphetes, in the neighborhood of Epidaurus, who used a club for his arms, and from thence had the name of Corynetes, or the club-bearer; who seized upon him, and forbade him to go forward in his journey. Being pleased with the club, he took it, and made it his weapon, continuing to use it as Hercules did the lion's skin, on whose shoulders that served to prove how huge a beast he had killed; and to the same end Theseus carried about him this club; overcome indeed by him, but now, in his hands, invincible.

Passing on further towards the Isthmus of Peloponnesus, he slew Sinnis, often surnamed the Bender of Pines, after the same manner in which he himself had destroyed many others before. And this he did without having either practiced or ever learnt the art of bending these trees, to show that natural strength is above all art. This Sinnis had a daughter of remarkable beauty and stature, called Perigune, who, when her father was killed, fled, and was sought after everywhere by Theseus; and coming into a place overgrown with brushwood, shrubs, and asparagus-thorn, there, in a childlike, innocent manner, prayed and begged them, as if they understood her, to give her shelter, with vows that if she escaped she would never cut them down nor burn them. But Theseus calling upon her, and giving her his promise that he would use her with respect, and offer her no injury, she came forth. Whence it is a family usage amongst the people called Ioxids, from the name of her grandson, Ioxus, both male and female, never to burn either shrubs or asparagus-thorn, but to respect and honor them.

The Crommyonian sow, which they called Phæa, was a savage and formidable wild beast, by no means an enemy to be despised. Theseus killed her, going out of his way on purpose to meet and engage her, so that he might not seem to perform all his great exploits out of mere necessity; being also of opinion that it was the part of a brave man to chastise villanous and wicked men when attacked by them, but to seek out and overcome the more noble wild beasts. Others relate that Phæa was a woman, a robber full of cruelty, that lived in Crommyon, and had the name of Sow given her from the foulness of her life and manners, and afterwards was killed by Theseus. He slew also Sciron, upon the borders of Megara, casting him down from the rocks, being, as most report, a notorious robber of all passengers, and, as others add, accustomed, out of insolence and wantonness, to stretch forth his feet to strangers, commanding them to wash them, and then while they did it, with a kick to send them down the rock into the sea.

In Eleusis he killed Cercyon, the Arcadian, in a wrestling match. And going on a little farther, in Erineus, he slew Damastes, otherwise called Procrustes, forcing his body to the size of his own bed, as he himself was used to do with all strangers; this he did in imitation of Hercules, who always returned upon his assailants the same sort of violence that they offered to him; sacrificed Busiris, killed Antæus in wrestling, and Cycnus in single combat, and Termerus by breaking his skull in pieces (whence, they say, comes the proverb of "a Termerian mischief"), for it seems Termerus killed passengers that he met by running with his head against them. And so also Theseus proceeded with the punishment of evil men, who underwent the same violence from him which they had inflicted upon others, justly suffering after the manner of their own injustice.

As he went forward on his journey, and was come as far as the River Cephisus, some of the race of the Phytalidæ met him and saluted him, and, upon his desire to use the purifications, then in custom, they performed them with all the usual ceremonies, and, having offered propitiatory sacrifices to the gods, invited him and entertained him at their house, a kindness which, in all his journey hitherto, he had not met.

On the eighth day of Cronius, now called Hecatombæon, he arrived at Athens, where he found the public affairs full of all confusion, and divided into parties and factions, Ægeus also, and his whole private family, laboring under the same distemper; for Medea, having fled from Corinth, was living with him. She first was aware of Theseus, whom as yet Ægeus did not know, and he being in years, full of jealousies and suspicions, and fearing everything by reason of the faction that was then in the city, she easily persuaded him to kill him by poison at a banquet, to which he was to be invited as a stranger. He, coming to the entertainment, thought it not fit to discover himself at once, but, willing to give his father the occasion of first finding him out, the meat being on the table, he drew his sword as if he designed to cut with it; Ægeus, at once recognizing the token, threw down the cup of poison, and, questioning his son, embraced him, and, having gathered together all his citizens, owned him publicly before them, who, on their part, received him gladly for the fame of his greatness and bravery.

The sons of Pallas, who before were quiet, upon expectation of recovering the kingdom after Ægeus's death, who was without issue, as soon as Theseus appeared and was acknowledged the successor, highly resenting that Ægeus first, an adopted son only of Pandion, and not at all related to the family of Erechtheus, should be holding the kingdom, and that after him, Theseus, a visitor and stranger, should be destined to succeed to it, broke out into open war. And, dividing themselves into two companies, one part of them marched openly from Sphettus, with their father, against the city; the other, hiding themselves in the village of Gargettus, lay in ambush, with a design to set upon the enemy on both sides. They had with them a crier of the township of Agnus, named Leos, who discovered to Theseus all the designs of the Pallantidæ. He immediately fell upon those that lay in ambuscade, and cut them all off; upon tidings of which Pallas and his company fled and were dispersed.

From hence they say is derived the custom among the people of the township of Pallene to have no marriages or any alliance with the people of Agnus, nor to suffer the criers to pronounce in their proclamations the words used in all other parts of the country, Acouĕtĕ Leoi (Hear ye people), hating the very sound of Leo, because of the treason of Leos.

Theseus, longing to be in action, and desirous also to make himself popular, left Athens to fight with the bull of Marathon, which did no small mischief to the inhabitants of Tetrapolis. And having overcome it, he brought it alive in triumph through the city, and afterwards sacrificed it to the Delphinian Apollo. The story of Hecale, also, of her receiving and entertaining Theseus in this expedition, seems to be not altogether void of truth; for the townships round about, meeting upon a certain day, used to offer a sacrifice, which they called Hecalesia, to Jupiter Hecaleius, and to pay honor to Hecale, whom, by a diminutive name, they called Hecalene, because she, while entertaining Theseus, who was quite a youth, addressed him, as old people do, with similar endearing diminutives; and having made a vow to Jupiter for him as he was going to the fight, that, if he returned in safety, she would offer sacrifices in thanks of it, and dying before he came back, she had these honors given her by way of return for her hospitality, by the command of Theseus, as Philochorus tells us.

Not long afterwards came the third time from Crete the collectors of the tribute which the Athenians paid them upon the following occasion. Androgeus having been treacherously murdered in the confines of Attica, not only Minos, his father, put the Athenians to extreme distress by a perpetual war, but the gods also laid waste their country; both famine and pestilence lay heavy upon them, and even their rivers were dried up. Being told by the oracle that if they appeased and reconciled Minos, the anger of the gods would cease and they should enjoy rest from the miseries they labored under, they sent heralds, and with much supplication were at last reconciled, entering into an agreement to send to Crete every nine years a tribute of seven young men and as many virgins, as most writers agree in stating; and the most poetical story adds that the Minotaur destroyed them, or that, wandering in the Labyrinth, and finding no possible means of getting out, they miserably ended their lives there; and that this Minotaur was (as Euripides hath it)

> A mingled form, where two strange shapes combined,
> And different natures, bull and man, were joined.

Now when the time of the third tribute was come, and the fathers who had any young men for their sons were to proceed by lot to the choice of those that were to be sent, there arose fresh discontents and accusations against Ægeus among the people, who were full of grief and indignation that he, who was the cause of all their miseries, was the only person exempt from the punishment; adopting and settling his kingdom upon a foreign son, he took no thought, they said, of their destitution and loss of their lawful children. These things sensibly affected Theseus, who, thinking it but just not to disregard, but rather partake of, the sufferings of his fellow-citizens, offered himself for one without any lot. All else were struck with admiration for the nobleness, and with love for the goodness, of the act; and Ægeus, after prayers and entreaties, finding him inflexible and not to be persuaded, proceeded to the choosing of the rest by lot. Hellanicus, however, tells us that the Athenians did not send the young men and virgins by lot, but that Minos himself used to come and make his own choice, and pitched upon Theseus before all others; according to the conditions agreed upon between them, namely, that the Athenians should furnish them with a ship, and that the young men who were to sail with him should carry no weapon of war; but that if the Minotaur was destroyed the tribute should cease.

On the two former occasions of the payment of the tribute, entertaining no hopes of safety or return, they sent out the ship with a black sail, as to unavoidable destruction; but now, Theseus encouraging his father and speaking greatly of himself, as confident that he should kill the Minotaur, he gave the pilot another sail, which was white, commanding him, as he returned, if Theseus were safe, to make use of that; but if not, to sail with the black one, and to hang out that sign of his misfortune. Simonides says that the sail which Ægeus delivered to the pilot was not white, but

> Scarlet, in the juicy bloom
> Of the living oak-tree steeped.

The lot being cast, and Theseus having received out of the Prytaneüm those upon whom it fell, he went to the Delphinium, and made an offering for them to Apollo of his suppliant's badge, which was a bough of a consecrated olive tree, with white wool tied about it.

Having thus performed his devotion, he went to sea, the sixth day of Munychion, on which day even to this time the Athenians send their virgins to the same temple to make supplication to the gods. It is farther reported that he was commanded by the oracle at Delphi to make Venus his guide, and to invoke her as the companion and conductress of his voyage, and that, as he was sacrificing a she goat to her by the seaside, it was suddenly changed into a he, and for this cause that goddess had the name of Epitragia.

When he arrived at Crete, as most of the ancient historians as well as poets tell us, having a clue of thread given him by Ariadne, who had fallen in love with him, and being instructed by her how to use it so as to conduct him through the windings of the Labyrinth, he escaped out of it and slew the Minotaur, and sailed back, taking along with him Ariadne and the young Athenian captives. Pherecydes adds that he bored holes in the bottoms of the Cretan ships to hinder their pursuit. Demon writes that Taurus, the chief captain of Minos, was slain by Theseus at the mouth of the port, in a naval combat, as he was sailing out for Athens. But Philochorus gives us the story thus: That at the setting forth of the yearly games by King Minos, Taurus was expected to carry away the prize, as he had done before; and was much grudged the honor. His character and manners made his power hateful, and he was accused, moreover, of too near familiarity with Pasiphae, for which reason, when Theseus desired the combat, Minos readily complied. And as it was a custom in Crete that the women also should be admitted to the sight of these games, Ariadne, being present, was struck with admiration of the manly beauty of Theseus, and the vigor and address which he showed in the combat, overcoming all that encountered with him. Minos, too, being extremely pleased with him, especially because he had overthrown and disgraced Taurus, voluntarily gave up the young captives to Theseus, and remitted the tribute to the Athenians.

There are yet many traditions about these things, and as many concerning Ariadne, all inconsistent with each other. Some relate that she hung herself, being deserted by Theseus. Others that she was carried away by his sailors to the isle of Naxos, and married to Œnarus, priest of Bacchus; and that Theseus left her because he fell in love with another,

For Ægle's love was burning in his breast.

Now Theseus, in his return from Crete, put in at Delos, and,

THE ISLAND OF NAXOS.

having sacrificed to the god of the island, dedicated to the temple the image of Venus which Ariadne had given him, and danced with the young Athenians a dance that, in memory of him, they say is still preserved among the inhabitants of Delos, consisting in certain measured turnings and returnings, imitative of the windings and twistings of the Labyrinth. And this dance, as Dicæarchus writes, is called among the Delians, the Crane. This he danced round the Ceratonian Altar,* so called from its consisting of horns taken from the left side of the head. They say also that he instituted games in Delos, where he was the first that began the custom of giving a palm to the victors.

When they were come near the coast of Attica, so great was the joy for the happy success of their voyage, that neither Theseus himself nor the pilot remembered to hang out the sail which should have been the token of their safety to Ægeus, who, in despair at the sight, threw himself headlong from a rock, and perished in the sea. But Theseus, being arrived at the port of Phalerum, paid there the sacrifices which he had vowed to the gods at his setting out to sea, and sent a herald to the city to carry the news of his safe return. At his entrance, the herald found the people for the most part full of grief for the loss of their king, others, as may well be believed, as full of joy for the tidings that he brought, and eager to welcome him and crown him with garlands for his good news, which he indeed accepted of, but hung them upon his herald's staff; and thus returning to the seaside before Theseus had finished his libation to the gods, he stayed apart for fear of disturbing the holy rites, but, as soon as the libation was ended, went up and related the king's death, upon the hearing of which, with great lamentations and a confused tumult of grief, they ran with all haste to the city. And from hence they say, it comes that at this day, in the feast of Oschophoria

---

* Kĕras, a horn.

the herald is not crowned, but his staff, and all who are present at the libation cry out *eleleu, iou, iou,* the first of which confused sounds is commonly used by men in haste, or at a triumph, the other is proper to people in consternation or disorder of mind.

Theseus, after the funeral of his father, paid his vows to Apollo the seventh day of Pyanepsion; for on that day the youth that returned with him safe from Crete made their entry into the city. They say, also, that the custom of boiling pulse at this feast is derived from hence; because the young men that escaped put all that was left of their provision together, and, boiling it in one common pot, feasted themselves with it, and ate it all up together. Hence, also, they carry in procession an olive branch bound about with wool (such as they then made use of in their supplications), which they call Eiresione, crowned with all sorts of fruits, to signify that scarcity and barrenness was ceased, singing in their procession this song:

> Eiresione bring figs, and Eirsione bring loaves;
> Bring us honey in pints, and oil to rub on our bodies,
> And a strong flagon of wine, for all to go mellow to bed on.

The ship wherein Theseus and the youth of Athens returned had thirty oars, and was preserved by the Athenians down even to the time of Demetrius Phalereus, for they took away the old planks as they decayed, putting in new and stronger timber in their place, insomuch that this ship became a standing example among the philosophers, for the logical question as to things that grow; one side holding that the ship remained the same, and the other contending that it was not the same.

Now, after the death of his father Ægeus, forming in his mind a great and wonderful design, he gathered together all the inhabitants of Attica into one town, and made them one people of one city, whereas before they lived dispersed, and were not easy to assemble upon any affair for the common interest. Nay, differences and even wars often occurred between them, which he by his persuasions appeased, going from township to township, and from tribe to tribe. And those of a more private and mean condition readily embracing such good advice, to those of greater power he promised a commonwealth without monarchy, a democracy, or people's government, in which he should only be continued as their commander in war and the protector of their laws, all things else being equally distributed among them;—and by this means brought a part of them over to his proposal. The rest, fearing his power, which was already grown very formidable, and knowing his courage and resolution, chose rather to be persuaded than forced into a compliance. He then dissolved all the distinct state-houses, council halls, and magistracies, and built one common state-house (the Prytaneüm) and council hall on the site of the present upper town, and gave the name of Athens to the whole state, ordaining a common feast and sacrifice, which he called Panathenæa, or the sacrifice of all the united Athenians. He instituted also another sacrifice, called Metœcia, or Feast of Migration, which is yet celebrated on the sixteenth day of Hecatombæon. Then, as he had promised, he laid down his regal power and proceeded to order a commonwealth, entering upon this great work not without advice from the gods. For having sent to consult the oracle of Delphi concerning the fortune of his new government and city, he received this answer:

> Son of the Pitthean maid,
> To your town the terms and fates
> My father gives of many states.
> Be not anxious nor afraid:
> The bladder will not fail to swim
> On the waves that compass him.

Which oracle, they say, one of the sibyls long after did in a manner repeat to the Athenians, in this verse,

The bladder may be dipt, but not be drowned.

Farther yet designing to enlarge his city, he invited all strangers to come and enjoy equal privileges with the natives, and it is said that the common form, *Come hither all ye people*, was the words that Theseus proclaimed when he thus set up a commonwealth, in a manner, for all nations. Yet he did not suffer his state, by the promiscuous multitude that flowed in, to be turned into confusion and be left without any order or degree, but was the first that divided the commonwealth into three distinct ranks, the noblemen, the husbandmen, and artificers. To the nobility he committed the care of religion, the choice of magistrates, the teaching and dispensing of the laws, and interpretation and direction in all sacred matters; the whole city being, as it were, reduced to an exact equality, the nobles excelling the rest in honor, the husbandmen in profit, and the artificers in number. And that Theseus was the first, who, as Aristotle says, out of an inclination to popular government, parted with the regal power, Homer also seems to testify, in his catalogue of the ships, where he gives the name of *People* to the Athenians only.

He also coined money, and stamped it with the image of an ox, either in memory of the Marathonian bull, or of Taurus, whom he vanquished, or else to put his people in mind to follow husbandry; and from this coin came the expression so frequent among the Greeks, as a thing being worth ten or a hundred oxen. After this he joined Megara to Attica, and erected that famous pillar on the Isthmus, which bears an inscription of two lines, showing the bounds of the two countries that meet there. On the east side the inscription is,—

> Peloponnesus there, Ionia here,

and on the west side,—

> Peloponnesus here, Ionia there.

He also instituted the games, in emulation of Hercules, being ambitious that as the Greeks, by that hero's appointment, celebrated the Olympian games to the honor of Jupiter, so, by his institution, they should celebrate the Isthmian to the honor of Neptune. At the same time he made an agreement with the Corinthians, that they should allow those that came from Athens to the celebration of the Isthmian games as much space of honor before the rest to behold the spectacle in as the sail of the ship that brought them thither, stretched to its full extent, could cover; so Hellanicus and Andro of Halicarnassus have established.

Concerning his voyage into the Euxine Sea, Philochorus and some others write that he made it with Hercules, offering him his service in the war against the Amazons, and had Antiope given him for the reward of his valor; but the greater number, of whom are Pherecides, Hellanicus, and Herodorus, write that he made this voyage many years after Hercules, with a navy under his own command, and took the Amazon prisoner, —the more probable story, for we do not read that any other, of all those that accompanied him in this action, took any Amazon prisoner. Bion adds, that, to take her, he had to use deceit and fly away; for the Amazons, he says, being naturally lovers of men, were so far from avoiding Theseus when he touched upon their coasts, that they sent him presents to his ship; but he, having invited Antiope, who brought them, to come aboard, immediately set sail and carried her away. An author named Menecrates, that wrote the History of Nicæa in Bithynia, adds, that Theseus, having Antiope aboard his vessel, cruised for some time about those coasts, and that there were in the same ship three young men of Athens, that accompanied him in this voyage, all brothers, whose names were Euneos, Thoas, and Soloon. The last of these fell desperately in love with Antiope; and, escaping the notice of the rest, revealed the secret only to one of his most intimate acquaintance, and employed him to disclose his passion to Antiope. She rejected his pretences with a very positive denial, yet treated the matter with much gentleness and discretion, and made no complaint to Theseus of anything that had happened; but Soloon, the thing being desperate, leaped into a river near the seaside and drowned himself. As soon as Theseus was acquainted with his death, and his unhappy love that was the cause of it, he was extremely distressed, and, in the height of his grief, an oracle which he had formerly received at Delphi came into his mind; for he had been commanded by the priestess of Apollo Pythius, that, wherever in a strange land he was most sorrowful and under the greatest affliction he should build a city there, and leave some of his followers to be governors of the place. For this cause he there founded a city, which he called, from the name of Apollo, Pythopolis, and, in honor of the unfortunate youth, he named the river that runs by it Soloon, and left the two surviving brothers intrusted with the care of the government and laws, joining with them Hermus, one of the nobility of Athens, from whom a place in the city is called the House of Hermus; though by an error in the accent it has been taken for the House of Hermes, or Mercury, and the honor that was designed to the hero, transferred to the god.

This was the origin and cause of the Amazonian invasion of Attica, which would seem to have been no slight or womanish enterprise. For it is impossible that they should have placed their camp in the very city, and joined battle close by the Pnyx and the hill called Museum, unless, having first conquered the country round about, they had thus with impunity advanced to the city. That they made so long a journey by land, and passed the Cimmerian Bosphorus when frozen, as Hellanicus writes, is difficult to be believed. That they encamped all but in the city is certain, and may be sufficiently confirmed by the names that the places thereabout yet retain, and the graves and monuments of those that fell in the battle. Both armies being in sight, there was a long pause and doubt on each side which should give the first onset; at last Theseus, having sacrificed to Fear, in obedience to the command of an oracle he had received, gave them battle, in which action a great number of the Amazons were slain. At length, after four months, a peace was concluded between them by the mediation of Hippolyta (for so this historian calls the Amazon whom Theseus married, and not Antiope), though others write that she was slain with a dart by Molpadia, while fighting by Theseus's side, and that the pillar which stands by the temple of Olympian Earth was erected to her honor. Nor is it to be wondered at, that in events of such antiquity, history should be in disorder. This is as much as is worth telling concerning the Amazons.

The celebrated friendship between Theseus and Pirithoüs is said to have been begun as follows: The fame of the strength and valor of Theseus being spread through Greece, Pirithoüs was desirous to make a trial and proof of it himself, and to this end seized a herd of oxen which belonged to Theseus, and was driving them away from Marathon, and, when news was brought that Theseus pursued him in arms, he did not fly, but turned back and went to meet him. But as soon as they had viewed one another, each so admired the gracefulness and beauty, and was seized with such a respect for the courage of the other, that they forgot all thoughts of fighting; and Pirithoüs, first stretching out his hand to Theseus, bade him be judge in this case himself, and promised to submit willingly to any penalty he should impose. But Theseus not only forgave him all, but entreated him to be his friend and brother in arms; and they ratified their friendship by oaths. After this Pirithoüs married Deidamia, and invited Theseus to the wedding, entreating him to come and see his country, and make acquaintance with the Lapithæ; he had at the same time invited the Centaurs to the feast, who, growing hot with wine and beginning to be insolent and wild, the Lapithæ took immediate revenge upon them, slaying many of them upon the place, and afterwards, having overcome them in battle, drove the whole race of them out of their country, Theseus all along taking the part of the Lapithæ, and fighting on their side.

Theseus was now fifty years old, as Hellanicus states, when he carried off Helen, who was yet too young to be married. Some writers, to take away this accusation of one of the greatest crimes laid to his charge, say that he did not steal away Helen himself, but that Idas and Lynceus brought her to him, and committed her to his charge, and that, therefore, he refused to restore her at the demand of Castor and Pollux; or, indeed, they say her own father, Tyndarus, had sent her to be kept by him, for fear of Enarophorus, the son of Hippocoön, who would have carried her away by force when she was yet a child. But the most probable account, and that which has most witnesses on its side, is this: Theseus and Pirithoüs went both together to Sparta, and, having seized the young lady as she was dancing in the temple of Diana Orthia, fled away with her. There were presently men in arms sent to pursue, but they followed no farther than to Tegea; and Theseus and Pirithoüs being now out of danger, having passed through Peloponnesus, made an agreement between themselves, that he to whom the lot should fall should have Helen to his wife, but should be obliged to assist in procuring another for his friend. The lot fell upon Theseus, who conveyed her to Aphidnæ, not being yet marriageable, and delivered her to one of his allies, called Aphidnus, and having sent his mother, Æthra, after to take care of her, desired him to keep them so secretly that none might know where they were; which done, to return the same service to his friend Pirithoüs, he accompanied him in his journey to Epirus, in order to steal away the king of the Molossians' daughter. The king, his own name being Aidoneus, or Pluto, called his wife Proserpina, and his daughter Cora, and a great dog which he kept Cerberus, with whom he ordered all that came as suitors to his daughter to fight, and promised her to him that should overcome the beast. But having been informed that the design of Pirithoüs and his companion was not to court his daughter, but to force her away, he caused them both to be seized, and threw Pirithoüs to be torn to pieces by the dog, and put Theseus into prison, and kept him.

About this time Menestheus, the son of Peteus, grandson of Orneus, and great-grandson to Erechtheus, the first man that is recorded to have affected popularity and ingratiated himself with the multitude, stirred up and exasperated the most eminent men of the city, who had long borne a secret grudge to Theseus, conceiving that he had robbed them of their several little kingdoms and lordships, and, having pent them all up in one city, was using them as his subjects and slaves. He put also the meaner people into commotion, telling them, that, deluded with a mere dream of liberty, though indeed they were deprived both of that and of their proper homes and religious usages, instead of many good and gracious kings of their own, they had given themselves up to be lorded over by a newcomer and a stranger. Whilst he was thus busied in infecting the minds of the citizens, the war that Castor and Pollux brought against Athens came very opportunely to further the sedition he had been promoting, and some say that he by his persuasions was wholly the cause of their invading the city. At their first approach they committed no acts of hostility, but peaceably demanded their sister Helen ; but the Athenians returning answer that they neither had her there nor knew where she was disposed of, they prepared to assault the city, when Academus, having, by whatever means, found it out, disclosed to them that she was secretly kept at Aphidnæ. For which reason he was both highly honored during his life by Castor and Pollux, and the Lacedæmonians, when often in after times they made incursions into Attica, and destroyed all the country round about, spared the Academy for the sake of Academus.

Hercules, passing by the Molossians, was entertained in his way by Aidoneus the king, who, in conversation, accidentally spoke of the journey of Theseus and Pirithoüs into his country, of what they had designed to do, and what they were forced to suffer. Hercules was much grieved for the inglorious death of the one and the miserable condition of the other. As for Pirithoüs, he thought it useless to complain; but begged to have Theseus released for his sake, and obtained that favor from the king. Theseus, being thus set at liberty, returned to Athens, where his friends were not yet wholly suppressed, and dedicated to Hercules all the sacred places which the city had set apart for himself, changing their names from Thesea to Heraclea, four only excepted, as Philochorus writes. And wishing immediately to resume the first place in the commonwealth, and manage the state as before, he soon found himself involved in factions and troubles; those who long had hated him had now added to their hatred contempt; and the minds of the people were so generally corrupted, that, instead of obeying commands with silence, they expected to be flattered into their duty. He had some thoughts to have reduced them by force, but was overpowered by demagogues and factions. And at last, despairing of any good success of his affairs in Athens, he sent away his children privately to Eubœa, commending them to the care of Elephenor, the son of Chalcodon; and he himself, having solemnly cursed the people of Athens in the village of Gargettus, in which there yet remains the place called Araterion, or the place of cursing, sailed to Scyros, where he had lands left him by his father, and friendship, as he thought, with those of the island. Lycomedes was then king of Scyros. Theseus, therefore, addressed himself to him, and desired to have his lands put into his possession, as designing to settle and to dwell there; though others say that he came to beg his assistance against the Athenians. But Lycomedes, either jealous of the glory of so great a man, or to gratify Menestheus, having led him up to the highest cliff of the island, on pretence of showing him from thence the lands that he desired, threw him headlong down from the rock and killed him. Others say he fell down of himself by a slip of his foot, as he was walking there, according to his custom.

after supper. At that time there was no notice taken, nor were any concerned for his death, but Menestheus quietly possessed the kingdom of Athens. His sons were brought up in a private condition, and accompanied Elephenor to the Trojan war, but, after the decease of Menestheus in that expedition, returned to Athens, and recovered the government. But in succeeding ages, beside several other circumstances that moved the Athenians to honor Theseus as a demigod, in the battle which was fought at Marathon against the Medes, many of the soldiers believed they saw an apparition of Theseus in arms, rushing on at the head of them against the barbarians. And after the Median war, Phædo being archon of Athens, the Athenians, consulting the oracle at Delphi, were commanded to gather together the bones of Theseus, and, laying them in some honorable place, keep them as sacred in the city. But it was very difficult to recover these relics, or so much as to find out the place where they lay, on account of the inhospitable and savage temper of the barbarous people that inhabited the island. Nevertheless, afterwards, when Cimon took the island (as is related in his life), and had a great ambition to find out the place where Theseus was buried, he, by chance, spied an eagle upon a rising ground pecking with her beak and tearing up the earth with her talons, when on the sudden it came into his mind, as it were by some divine inspiration, to dig there, and search for the bones of Theseus. There were found in that place a coffin of a man of more than ordinary size, and a brazen spear-head, and a sword lying by it, all which he took aboard his galley and brought with him to Athens. Upon which the Athenians, greatly delighted, went out to meet and receive the relics with splendid processions and with sacrifices, as if it were Theseus himself returning alive to the city. He lies interred in the middle of the city, near the present gymnasium. His tomb is a sanctuary and refuge for slaves, and all those of mean condition that fly from the persecution of men in power, in memory that The seus while he lived was an assister and protector of the distressed, and never refused the petitions of the afflicted that fled to him. The chief and most solemn sacrifice which they celebrate to him is kept on the eighth day of Pyanepsion, on which he returned with the Athenian young men from Crete. Besides which, they sacrifice to him on the eighth day of every month, either because he returned from Trœzen the eighth day of Hecatombæon, as Diodorus the geographer writes, or else thinking that number to be proper to him, because he was reputed to be born of Neptune, because they sacrifice to Neptune on the eighth day of every month. The number eight being the first cube of an even number, and the double of the first square, seemed to be an emblem of the steadfast and immovable power of this god, who from thence has the names of Asphalius and Gæiochus, that is, the establisher and stayer of the earth.

ROMULUS.

From whom, and for what reason, the city of Rome, a name so great in glory, and famous in the mouths of all men, was so first called, authors do not agree.

But the story which is most believed and has the greatest number of vouchers in general outline runs thus: the kings of Alba reigned in lineal descent from Æneas, and the succession devolved at length upon two brothers, Numitor and Amulius. Amulius proposed to divide things into two equal shares, and set as equivalent to the kingdom the treasure and gold that were brought from Troy. Numitor chose the kingdom; but Amulius, having the money, and being able to do more with that than Numitor, took his kingdom from him with great ease, and, fearing lest his daughter might have children who would supplant him, made her a Vestal, bound in that condition forever to live a single and maiden life. This lady some call Ilia, others Rhea, and others Silvia; however, not long after, contrary to the established laws of the Vestals, she had two sons of more than human size and beauty, whom Amulius, becoming yet more alarmed, commanded a servant to take and cast away; this man some call Faustulus, others say Faustulus was the man who brought them up. He put the children, however, in a small trough, and went towards the river with a design to cast them in; but, seeing the waters much swollen and coming violently down, was afraid to go nearer, and, dropping the children near the bank, went away. The river overflowing, the flood at last bore up the trough, and, gently wafting it, landed them on a smooth piece of ground, which they now call Cermanus, formerly Germanus, perhaps from *Germani*, which signifies brothers.

While the infants lay here, history tells us, a she-wolf nursed them, and a woodpecker constantly fed and watched them. These creatures are esteemed holy to the god Mars; the woodpecker the Latins still especially worship and honor. Which things, as much as any, gave credit to what the mother of the children said, that their father was the god Mars.

Meantime Faustulus, Amulius's swineherd, brought up the children without any man's knowledge; or, as those say who wish to keep closer to probabilities, with the knowledge and secret assistance of Numitor; for it is said, they went to school at Gabii, and were well instructed in letters, and other accomplishments befitting their birth. And they were called Romulus and Remus (from *ruma*, the dug), because they were found sucking the wolf. In their very infancy, the size and beauty of their bodies intimated their natural superiority; and when they grew up, they both proved brave and manly, attempting all enterprises that seemed hazardous, and showing in them a courage altogether undaunted. But Romulus seemed rather to act by counsel, and to show the sagacity of a statesman, and in all his dealings with their neighbors, whether relating to feeding of flocks or to hunting, gave the idea of being born rather to rule than to obey. To their comrades and inferiors they were therefore dear; but the king's servants, his bailiffs and overseers, as being in nothing better men than themselves, they despised and slighted, nor were the least concerned at their commands and menaces. They used honest pastimes and liberal studies, not esteeming sloth and idleness honest and liberal, but rather such exercises as hunting and running, repelling robbers, taking of thieves, and delivering the wronged and oppressed from injury. For doing such things they became famous.

A quarrel occurring betwixt Numitor's and Amulius's cowherds, the latter, not enduring the driving away of their cattle by the others, fell upon them and put them to flight, and rescued the greatest part of the prey. At which Numitor being highly incensed, they little regarded it, but collected and took into their company a number of needy men and runaway slaves,—acts which looked like the first stages of rebellion. It so happened, that when Romulus was attending a sacrifice, being fond of sacred rites and divination, Numitor's herdsmen, meeting with Remus on a journey with few companions, fell upon him, and, after some fighting, took him prisoner, carried him before Numitor, and there accused him. Numitor would not punish him himself, fearing his brother's anger, but went to Amulius and desired justice, as he was Amulius's brother and was affronted by Amulius's servants. The men of Alba likewise resenting the thing, and thinking he had been dishonorably used, Amulius was induced to deliver Remus up into Numitor's hands, to use him as he thought fit. He therefore took and carried him home, and, being struck with admiration of the youth's person, in stature and strength of body exceeding all men, and perceiving in his very countenance the courage and force of his mind, which stood unsubdued and unmoved by his present circumstances, and hearing further that all the enterprises and actions of his life were answerable to what he saw of him, but chiefly, as it seemed, a divine influence aiding and directing the first steps that were to lead to great results, out of the mere thought of his mind, and casually, as it were, he put his hand upon the fact, and, in gentle terms and with a kind aspect, to inspire him with confidence and hope, asked him who he was, and whence he was derived. He, taking heart, spoke thus: "I will hide nothing from you, for you seem to be of a more princely temper than Amulius, in that you give a hearing and examine before you punish, while he condemns before the cause is heard. Formerly, then, we (for we are twins) thought ourselves the sons of Faustulus and Larentia, the king's servants; but since we have been accused and aspersed with calumnies, and brought in peril of our lives here before you, we hear great things of ourselves, the truth of which my present danger is likely to bring to the test. Our birth is said to have been secret, our fostering and nurture in our infancy still more strange; by birds and beasts, to whom we were cast out, we were fed—by the milk of a wolf, and the morsels of a woodpecker, as we lay in a little trough by the side of the river. The trough is still in being, and is preserved, with brass plates round it, and an inscription in letters almost effaced, which may prove hereafter unavailing tokens to our parents when we are dead and gone." Numitor, upon these words, and computing the dates by the young man's looks, slighted not the hope that flattered him, but considered how to come at his daughter privately (for she was still kept under restraint), to talk with her concerning these matters.

Faustulus, hearing Remus was taken and delivered up, called on Romulus to assist in his rescue, informing him then plainly of the particulars of his birth—not but he had before given hints of it—and told as much as an attentive man might make no small conclusions from; he himself, full of concern and fear of not coming in time, took the trough, and ran instantly to Numitor; but giving a suspicion to some of the king's sentry at his gate, and being gazed upon by them and perplexed with their questions, he let it be seen that he was hiding the trough under his cloak. By chance there was one among them who was at the exposing of the children, and was one employed in the office; he, seeing the trough and knowing it by its make and inscription, guessed at the business, and, without further delay, telling the king of it, brought in the man to be examined. Faustulus, hard beset, did not show himself altogether proof against terror; nor yet was he wholly forced out of all: confessed indeed the children were alive, but lived, he said, as shepherds, a great way from Alba; he himself was going to carry the trough to Ilia, who had often greatly desired to see and handle it, for a confirmation of her hopes of her children. As men generally do who are troubled in mind and act either in fear or passion, it so fell out Amulius now did; for he sent in haste as a messenger, a man, otherwise honest and friendly to Numitor, with commands to learn from Numitor whether any tidings were come to him of the children's being alive. He, coming and seeing how little Remus wanted of being received into the arms and embraces of Numitor, both gave him surer confidence in his hope, and advised them, with all expedition, to proceed to action; himself too joining and assisting them, and indeed, had they wished it, the time would not have let them demur. For Romulus was now come very near, and many of the citizens, out of fear and hatred of Amulius, were running out to join him; besides, he brought great forces with him, divided into companies, each of an hundred men, every captain carrying a small bundle of grass and shrubs tied to a pole. The Latins call such bundles *manipuli*, and from hence it is that in their armies still they call their captains *manipulares*. Remus rousing the citizens within to revolt, and Romulus making attacks from without, the tyrant, not knowing either what to do, or what expedient to think of for his security, in this perplexity and confusion was taken and put to death. This narrative, for the most part given by Fabius and Diocles of Peparethos, who seem to be the earliest historians of the foundation of Rome, is suspected by some because of its dramatic and fictitious appearance; but it would not wholly be disbelieved, if men would remember what a poet Fortune sometimes shows herself, and consider that the Roman power would hardly have reached so high a pitch without a divinely ordered origin, attended with great and extraordinary circumstances.

Amulius now being dead and matters quietly disposed, the two brothers would neither dwell in Alba without governing there, nor take the government into their own hands during the life of their grandfather. Having therefore delivered the dominion up into his hands, and paid their mother befitting honor, they resolved to live by themselves, and build a city in the same place where they were in their infancy brought up.

This seems the most honorable reason for their departure; though perhaps it was necessary, having such a body of slaves and fugitives collected about them, either to come to nothing by dispersing them, or if not so, then to live with them elsewhere. For that the inhabitants of Alba did not think fugitives worthy of being received and incorporated as citizens among them plainly appears from the matter of the women, an attempt made not wantonly but of necessity, because they could not get wives by good-will. For they certainly paid unusual respect and honor to those whom they thus forcibly seized.

Not long after the first foundation of the city, they opened a sanctuary of refuge for all fugitives, which they called the temple of the god Asylæus, where they received and protected all, delivering none back, neither the servant to his master, the debtor to his creditor, nor the murderer into the hands of the magistrate, saying it was a privileged place, and they could so maintain it by an order of the holy oracle; insomuch that the city grew presently very populous, for, they say, it consisted at first of no more than a thousand houses. But of that hereafter.

Their minds being fully bent upon building, there arose presently a difference about the place where. Romulus chose what was called Roma Quadrata, or the Square Rome, and would have the city there. Remus laid out a piece of ground on the Aventine Mount, well fortified by nature, which was from him called Remonium, but now Rignarium. Concluding at last to decide the contest by a divination from a flight of birds, and placing themselves apart at some distance, Remus, they say, saw six vultures, and Romulus double the number; others say Remus did truly see his number, and that Romulus feigned his, but, when Remus came to him, that then he did, indeed, see twelve. Hence it is that the Romans, in their divinations from birds, chiefly regard the vulture, though Herodorus Ponticus relates that Hercules was always very joyful when a vulture appeared to him upon any occasion. For it is a creature the least hurtful of any, pernicious neither to corn, fruit-tree, nor cattle; it preys only upon carrion, and never kills or hurts any living thing; and as for birds, it touches not them, though they are dead, as being of its own species, whereas eagles, owls, and hawks mangle and kill their own fellow-creatures; yet, as Æschylus says,—

> What bird is clean that preys on fellow bird?

Besides, all other birds are, so to say, never out of our eyes; they let themselves be seen of us continually; but a vulture is a very rare sight, and you can seldom meet with a man that has seen their young; their rarity and infrequency has raised a strange opinion in some, that they come to us from some other world; as soothsayers ascribe a divine origination to all things not produced either of nature or of themselves.

When Remus knew the cheat, he was much displeased; and as Romulus was casting up a ditch, where he designed the foundation of the city wall, he turned some pieces of the work to ridicule, and obstructed others: at last, as he was in contempt leaping over it, some say Romulus himself struck him, others Celer, one of his companions; he fell, however, and in the scuffle Faustulus also was slain, and Plistinus, who, being Faustulus's brother, story tells us, helped to bring up Romulus. Celer upon this fled instantly into Tuscany, and from him the Romans call all men that are swift of foot Celeres; and because Quintus Metellus, at his father's funeral, in a few days' time gave the people a show of gladiators, admiring his expedition in getting it ready, they gave him the name of Celer.

Romulus, having buried his brother Remus, together with his two foster-fathers, on the mount Remonia, set to building his city; and sent for men out of Tuscany, who directed him by sacred usages and written rules in all the ceremonies to be observed, as in a religious rite. First, they dug a round trench about that which is now the Comitium, or Court of Assembly and into it solemnly threw the first-fruits of all things either good by custom or necessary by nature; lastly, every man taking a small piece of earth of the country from whence he came, they all threw them in promiscuously together. This trench they call, as they do the heavens, Mundus; making which their centre, they described the city in a circle round it. Then the founder fitted to a plough a bronze ploughshare, and, yoking together a bull and a cow, drove himself a deep line or furrow round the bounds; while the business of those that followed after was to see that whatever earth was thrown up should be turned all inwards towards the city, and not to let any clod lie outside. With this line they described the wall, and called it, by a contraction, Pomœrium, that is, *post murum*, after or beside the wall; and where they designed to make a gate, there they took out the share, carried the plough over, and left a space; for which reason they consider the whole wall as holy, except where the gates are; for had they adjudged them also sacred, they could not, without offence to religion, have given free ingress and egress for the necessaries of human life, some of which are in themselves unclean.

As for the day they began to build the city, it is universally agreed to have been the twenty-first of April, and that day the Romans annually keep holy, calling it their country's birthday. At first, they say, they sacrificed no living creature on this day, thinking it fit to preserve the feast of their country's birthday pure and without stain of blood. Yet before ever the city was built, there was a feast of herdsmen and shepherds kept on this day, which went by the name of Palilia. The Roman and Greek months have now little or no agreement; they say, however, the day on which Romulus began to build was quite certainly the thirtieth of the month, at which time there was an eclipse of the sun which they conceive to be that seen by Antimachus, the Teian poet, in the third year of the sixth Olympiad. In the times of Varro the philosopher, a man deeply read in Roman history, lived one Tarrutius, his familiar acquaintance, a good philosopher and mathematician, and one, too, that out of curiosity had studied the way of drawing schemes and tables, and was thought to be a proficient in the art; to him Varro propounded to cast Romulus's nativity, even to the first day and hour, making his deductions from the several events of the man's life which he should be informed of, exactly as in working back a geometrical problem; for it belonged, he said, to the same science both to foretell a man's life by knowing the time of his birth, and also to find out his birth by the knowledge of his life. This task Tarrutius undertook, and first looking into the actions and casualties of the man, together with the time of his life and manner of his death, and then comparing all these remarks together, he very confidently and positively pronounced that Romulus was born the twenty-first day of the month Thoth, about sun-rising; and that the first stone of Rome was laid by him the ninth day of the month Pharmuthi, between the second and third hour. For the fortunes of cities as well as of men, they think, have their certain periods of time prefixed, which may be collected and foreknown from the position of the stars at their first foundation. But these and the like relations may perhaps not so much take and delight the reader with their novelty and curiosity as offend him by their extravagance.

The city now being built, Romulus enlisted all that were of age to bear arms into military companies, each company consisting of three thousand footmen and three hundred horse. These companies were called legions, because they were the choicest and most select of the people for fighting men. The rest of the multitude he called the people; an hundred of the most eminent he chose for counsellors; these he styled patricians, and their assembly the senate, which signifies a council of elders.

In the fourth month after the city was built, as Fabius writes, the adventure of stealing the women was attempted. It would seem that, observing his city to be filled by a confluence of foreigners, few of whom had wives, and that the multitude in general, consisting of a mixture of mean and obscure men, fell under contempt, and seemed to be of no long continuance together, and hoping farther, after the women were appeased, to make this injury in some measure an occasion of confederacy and mutual commerce with the Sabines, Romulus took in hand this exploit after this manner. First, he gave it out that he had found an altar of a certain god hid under ground, perhaps the equestrian Neptune, for the altar is kept covered in the Circus Maximus at all other times, and only at horse-races is exposed to public view. Upon discovery of this altar, Romulus, by proclamation, appointed a day for a splendid sacrifice, and for public games and shows, to entertain all sorts of people; many flocked thither, and he himself sat in front, amidst his nobles, clad in purple. Now the signal for their falling on was to be whenever he rose and gathered up his robe and threw it over his body; his men stood all ready armed, with their eyes intent upon him, and when the sign was given, drawing their swords and falling on with a great shout, they stole away the daughters of the Sabines, the men themselves flying without any let or hindrance. Some say there were but thirty taken, and from them the Curiæ or Fraternities were named; but Valerius Antias says five hundred and twenty-seven, Juba, six hundred and eighty-three.

It continues a custom at this very day for the bride not of herself to pass her husband's threshold, but to be lifted over, in memory that the Sabine virgins were carried in by violence, and did not go in of their own will. Some say, too, the custom of parting the bride's hair with the head of a spear was in token their marriages began at first by war and acts of hostility.

The Sabines were a numerous and martial people, but lived in small, unfortified villages, as it befitted, they thought, a colony of the Lacedæmonians to be bold and fearless; nevertheless, seeing themselves bound by such hostages to their good behavior, and being solicitous for their daughters, they sent ambassadors to Romulus with fair and equitable requests, that he would return their young women and recall that act of violence, and afterwards, by persuasion and lawful means, seek friendly correspondence between both nations. Romulus would not part with the young women, yet proposed to the Sabines to enter into an alliance with them; upon which point some consulted and demurred long, but Acron, king of the Ceninenses, a man of high spirit and a good warrior, who had all along a jealousy of Romulus's bold attempts, and considering particularly from this exploit upon the women that he was growing formidable to all people, and indeed insufferable, were he not chastised, first rose up in arms, and with a powerful army advanced against him. Romulus likewise prepared to receive him; but when they came within sight and viewed each other, they made a challenge to fight a single duel, the armies standing by under arms, without participation. And Romulus, making a vow to Jupiter, if he should conquer, to carry, himself, and dedicate his adversary's armor to his honor, overcame him in combat, and, a battle ensuing, routed his army also, and then took his city; but did those he found in it no injury, only commanded them to demolish the place and attend him to Rome, there to be admitted to all the privileges of citizens. And indeed there was nothing did more advance the greatness of Rome, than that she did always unite and incorporate those whom she conquered into herself. Romulus, that he might perform his vow in the most acceptable manner to Jupiter, and withal make the pomp of it delightful to the eye of the city, cut down a tall oak which he saw growing in the camp, which he trimmed to the shape of a trophy, and fastened on it Acron's whole suit of armor disposed in proper form; then he himself, girding his clothes about him, and crowning his head with a laurel-garland, his hair gracefully flowing, carried the trophy resting erect upon his right shoulder, and so marched on, singing songs of triumph, and his whole army following after, the citizens all receiving him with acclamations of joy and wonder. The procession of this day was the origin and model of all after triumphs. But the statues of Romulus in triumph are, as may be seen in Rome, all on foot.

After the overthrow of the Ceninensians, the other Sabines still protracting the time in preparations, the people of Fidenæ, Crustumerium, and Antemna, joined their forces against the Romans; they in like manner were defeated in battle, and surrendered up to Romulus their cities to be seized, their lands and territories to be divided, and themselves to be transplanted to Rome. All the lands which Romulus acquired he distributed among the citizens, except only what the parents of the stolen virgins had; these he suffered to possess their own. The rest of the Sabines, enraged thereat, choosing Tatius their captain, marched straight against Rome. The city was almost inaccessible, having for its fortress that which is now the Capitol, where a strong guard was placed, and Tarpeius their captain. But Tarpeia, daughter to the captain, coveting the golden bracelets she saw them wear, betrayed the fort into the Sabines' hands, and asked, in reward of her treachery, the things they wore on their left arms. Tatius conditioning thus with her, in the night she opened one of the gates and received the Sabines in. And truly Antigonus, it would seem, was not solitary in saying he loved betrayers, but hated those who had betrayed; nor Cæsar, who told Rhymitalces the Thracian that he loved the treason, but hated the traitor; but it is the general feeling of all who have occasion for wicked men's service, as people have for the poison of venomous beasts; they are glad of them while they are of use, and abhor their baseness when it is over. And so then did Tatius behave towards Tarpeia, for he commanded the Sabines, in regard to their contract, not to refuse her the least part of what they wore on their left arms; and he himself first took his bracelet off his arm, and threw that, together with his buckler, at her; and all the rest following, she, being borne down and quite buried with the multitude of gold and their shields, died under the weight and pressure of them; Tarpeius also himself, being prosecuted by Romulus, was found guilty of treason, and that part of the Capitol they still call the Tarpeian Rock, from which they used to cast down malefactors.

The Sabines being possessed of the hill, Romulus, in great fury, bade them battle, and Tatius was confident to accept it. There were many brief conflicts, we may suppose, but the most memorable was the last, in which Romulus having received a wound on his head by a stone, and being almost felled to the ground by it, and disabled, the Romans gave way, and, being driven out of the level ground, fled towards the Palatium. Romulus, by this time recovering from his wound a little, turned about to renew the battle, and, facing the fliers, with a loud voice encouraged them to stand and fight. But being overborne with numbers, and nobody daring to face about, stretching out his hands to heaven, he prayed to Jupiter to stop the army, and not to neglect but maintain the Roman cause, now in extreme danger. The prayer was no sooner made than shame and respect for their king checked many; the fears of the fugitives changed suddenly into confidence. The place they first stood at was where now is the temple of Jupiter Stator (which may be translated the Stayer); there they rallied again into ranks, and repulsed the Sabines to the place called now Regia, and to the temple of Vesta; where both parties, preparing to begin a second battle, were prevented by a spectacle, strange to behold, and defying description. For the daughters of the Sabines, who had been carried off, came running, in great confusion, some on this side, some on that, with miserable cries and lamentations, like creatures possessed, in the midst of the army, and among the dead bodies, to come at their husbands and their fathers; some with their young babes in their arms, others their hair loose about their ears, but all calling, now upon the Sabines, now upon the Romans, in the most tender and endearing words.

Hereupon both melted into compassion, and fell back, to make room for them betwixt the armies. The sight of the women carried sorrow and commiseration upon both sides into the hearts of all, but still more their words, which began with expostulation and upbraiding, and ended with entreaty and supplication.

"Wherein," say they, "have we injured or offended you, as to deserve such sufferings, past and present? We were ravished away unjustly and violently by those whose now we are; that being done, we were so long neglected by our fathers, our brothers, and countrymen, that time, having now by the strictest bonds united us to those we once mortally hated, has made it impossible for us not to tremble at the danger and weep at the death of the very men who once used violence to us. You did not come to vindicate our honor, while we were virgins, against our assailants; but do come now to force away wives from their husbands and mothers from their children, a succor more grievous to its wretched objects than the former betrayal and neglect of them. Which shall we call the worst, their love-making or your compassion? If you were making war upon any other occasion, for our sakes you ought to withhold your hands from those to whom we have made you fathers-in-law and grandsires. If it be for our own cause, then take us, and with us your sons-in-law and grandchildren. Restore to us our parents and kindred, but do not rob us of our children and husbands. Make us not, we entreat you, twice captives." Having spoken many such words as these, and earnestly praying, a truce was made, and the chief officers came to a parley; the women, in the meantime, brought and presented their husbands and children to their fathers and brothers; gave those that wanted, meat and drink, and carried the wounded home to be cured, and showed also how much they governed within doors, and how indulgent their husbands were to them, in demeaning themselves towards them with all kindness and respect imaginable. Upon this, conditions were agreed upon, that what women pleased might stay where they were, exempt from all drudgery and labor but spinning; that the Romans and Sabines should inhabit the city together; that the city should be called Rome, from Romulus; but the Romans, Quirites, from the country of Tatius; and that they both should govern and command in common. The place of the ratification is still called Comitium, from *coire*, to meet.

The city being thus doubled in number, an hundred of the Sabines were elected senators, and the legions were increased to six thousand foot and six hundred horse; then they divided the people into three tribes: the first, from Romulus, named Ramnenses; the second, from Tatius, Tatienses; the third, Luceres, from the *lucus*, or grove, where the Asylum stood, whither many fled for sanctuary, and were received into the city. And that they were just three, the very name of *tribe* and *tribune* seems to show. They then constituted many things in honor to the women, such as to give them the way wherever they met them; to speak no ill word in their presence; that their children should wear an ornament about their necks called the *bulla* (because it was like a bubble), and the *prætexta*, a gown edged with purple.

The princes did not immediately join in council together, but at first each met with his own hundred; afterwards all assembled together. Tatius dwelt where now the temple of Moneta stands, and Romulus, close by the steps, as they call them, of the Fair Shore, near the descent from the Mount Palatine to the Circus Maximus. There, they say, grew the holy cornel tree, of which they report that Romulus once, to try his strength, threw a dart from the Aventine Mount, the staff of which was made of cornel, which struck so deep into the ground that no one of many that tried could pluck it up; and the soil, being fertile, gave nourishment to the wood, which sent forth branches, and produced a cornel-stock of considerable bigness. This did posterity preserve and worship as one of the most sacred things; and, therefore, walled it about; and if to any one it appeared not green nor flourishing, but inclining to pine and wither, he immediately made outcry to all he met, and they, like people hearing of a house on fire, with one accord would cry for water, and run from all parts with bucketfuls to the place. But when Gaius Cæsar, they say, was repairing the steps about it, some of the laborers digging too close, the roots were destroyed, and the tree withered.

The Sabines adopted the Roman months, of which whatever is remarkable is mentioned in the Life of Numa. Romulus, on the other hand, adopted their long shields, and changed his own armor and that of all the Romans, who before wore round targets of the Argive pattern. Feasts and sacrifices they partook of in common, not abolishing any which either nation observed before, and instituting several new ones. This, too, is observable as a singular thing in Romulus, that he appointed no punishment for real parricide, but called all murder so, thinking the one an accursed thing, but the other a thing impossible; and, for a long time, his judgment seemed to have been right; for in almost six hundred years together, nobody committed the like in Rome; Lucius Hostius, after the wars of Hannibal, is recorded to have been the first parricide. Let thus much suffice concerning these matters.

In the fifth year of the reign of Tatius, some of his friends and kinsmen, meeting ambassadors coming from Laurentum to Rome, attempted on the road to take away their money by force, and, upon their resistance, killed them. So great a villany having been committed, Romulus thought the malefactors ought at once to be punished, but Tatius shuffled off and deferred the execution of it; and this one thing was the beginning of open quarrel betwixt them; in all other respects they were very careful of their conduct, and administered affairs together with great unanimity. The relations of the slain, being debarred of lawful satisfaction by reason of Tatius, fell upon him as he was sacrificing with Romulus at Lavinium, and slew him; but escorted Romulus home, commending and extolling him for a just prince. Romulus took the body of Tatius, and buried it very splendidly in the Aventine Mount.

The Roman cause daily gathering strength, their weaker neighbors shrunk away, and were thankful to be left untouched; but the stronger, out of fear or envy, thought they ought not to give way to Romulus, but to curb and put a stop to his growing greatness. The first were the Veientes, a people of Tuscany, who had large possessions, and dwelt in a spacious city; they took occasion to commence a war, by claiming Fidenæ as belonging to them. But being scornfully retorted upon by Romulus in his answers, they divided themselves into two bodies; with one they attacked the garrison of Fidenæ, the other marched against Romulus; that which went against Fidenæ got the victory, and slew two thousand Romans; the other was worsted by Romulus, with the loss of eight thousand men. A fresh battle was fought near Fidenæ, and here all men acknowledge the day's success to have been chiefly the work of Romulus himself, who showed the highest skill as well as courage, and seemed to manifest a strength and swiftness more than human. But what some write, that, of fourteen thousand that fell that day, above half were slain by Romulus's own hand, verges too near to fable, and is, indeed, simply incredible: since even the Messenians are thought to go too far in saying that Aristomenes three times offered sacrifices for the death of a hundred enemies, Lacedæmonians, slain by himself. The army being thus routed, Romulus, suffering those that were left to make their escape, led his forces against the city; they, having suffered such great losses, did not venture to oppose, but, humbly suing to him, made a league and friendship for an hundred years; surrendering also a large district of land called Septempagium, that is, the seven parts, as also their salt-works upon the river, and fifty noblemen for hostages. He made his triumph for this on the Ides of October, leading, among the rest of his many captives, the general of the Veientes, an elderly man, but who had not, it seemed, acted with the prudence of age ; whence even now, in sacrifices for victories, they lead an old man through the market-place to the Capitol, apparelled in purple, with a *bulla*, or child's toy, tied to it, and the crier cries, *Sardians to be sold;* for the Tuscans are said to be a colony of the Sardians, and the Veientes are a city of Tuscany.

This was the last battle Romulus ever fought ; afterwards he, as most, nay all men, very few excepted, do, who are raised by great and miraculous good-haps of fortune to power and greatness, so, I say, did he : relying upon his own great actions, and growing of an haughtier mind, he forsook his popular behavior for kingly arrogance, odious to the people ; to whom in particular the state which he assumed was hateful. For he dressed in scarlet, with the purple-bordered robe over it ; he gave audience on a couch of state, having always about him some young men called *Celeres*, from their swiftness in doing commissions. He suddenly disappeared on the Nones of July, as they now call the month which was then Quintilis, leaving nothing of certainty to be related of his death ; the senators suffered the people not to search, or busy themselves about the matter, but commanded them to honor and worship Romulus as one taken up to the gods, and about to be to them, in the place of a good prince, now a propitious god. The multitude, hearing this, went away believing and rejoicing in hopes of good things from him ; but there were some, who, canvassing the matter in a hostile temper, accused the patricians, as men that persuaded the people to believe ridiculous tales, when they themselves were the murderers of the king.

Things being in this disorder, one, they say, of the patricians, of noble family and approved good character, and a faithful and familiar friend of Romulus himself, having come with him from Alba, Julius Proculus by name, presented him self in the forum; and, taking a most sacred oath, protested before them all, that, as he was travelling on the road, he had seen Romulus coming to meet him, looking taller and comelier than ever, dressed in shining and flaming armor; and he, being affrighted at the apparition, said, "Why, O king, or for what purpose, have you abandoned us to unjust and wicked surmises, and the whole city to bereavement and endless sorrow?" and that he made answer, "It pleased the gods, O Proculus, that we, who came from them, should remain so long a time amongst men as we did; and, having built a city to be the greatest in the world for empire and glory, should again return to heaven. But farewell; and tell the Romans, that, by the exercise of temperance and fortitude, they shall attain the height of human power; we will be to you the propitious god Quirinus." This seemed credible to the Romans, upon the honesty and oath of the relator, and laying aside all jealousies and detractions, they prayed to Quirinus and saluted him as a god.

This is like some of the Greek fables of Aristeas the Proconnesian, and Cleomedes the Astypalæan; for they say Aristeas died in a fuller's workshop, and his friends, coming to look for him, found his body vanished; and that some presently after, coming from abroad, said they met him travelling towards Croton. And that Cleomedes, being an extraordinarily strong and gigantic man, but also wild and mad, committed many desperate freaks; and at last, in a schoolhouse, striking a pillar that sustained the roof with his fist, broke it in the middle, so that the house fell and destroyed the children in it; and being pursued, he fled into a great chest, and, shutting to the lid, held it so fast that many men, with their united strength, could not force it open; afterwards, breaking the chest to pieces, they found no man in it alive or dead.

And many such improbabilities do your fabulous writers relate, deifying creatures naturally mortal; for though altogether to disown a divine nature in human virtue were impious and base, so again to mix heaven with earth is ridiculous. Let us believe with Pindar, that

> All human bodies yield to Death's decree:
> The soul survives to all eternity.

For that alone is derived from the gods, thence comes, and thither returns.

It was in the fifty-fourth year of his age and the thirty-eighth of his reign that Romulus, they tell us, left the world.

COMPARISON OF THESEUS AND ROMULUS.

BOTH Theseus and Romulus were by nature meant for governors; yet neither lived up to the true character of a king, but fell off, and ran, the one into popularity, the other into tyranny, falling both into the same fault out of different passions. For a ruler's first end is to maintain his office, which is done no less by avoiding what is unfit than by observing what is suitable. Whoever is either too remiss or too strict is no more a king or a governor, but either a demagogue or a despot, and so becomes either odious or contemptible to his subjects. Though certainly the one seems to be the fault of easiness and good-nature, the other of pride and severity.

But Romulus has, first of all, one great plea, that his performances proceeded from very small beginnings; for both the brothers, being thought servants and the sons of swineherds, before becoming freemen themselves gave liberty to almost all the Latins, obtaining at once all the most honorable titles, as, destroyers of their country's enemies, preservers of their friends and kindred, princes of the people, founders of cities; not removers, like Theseus, who raised and compiled only one house out of many, demolishing many cities bearing the names of ancient kings and heroes. Romulus, indeed, did the same afterwards, forcing his enemies to deface and ruin their own dwellings, and to sojourn with their conquerors; but at first, not by removal, or increase of an existing city, but by foundation of a new one, he obtained himself lands, a country, a kingdom, wives, children, and relations. And, in so doing, he killed or destroyed nobody, but benefited those that wanted houses and homes, and were willing to be of a society and become citizens. Robbers and malefactors he slew not; but he subdued nations, he overthrew cities, he triumphed over kings and commanders. As to Remus, it is doubtful by whose hand he fell; it is generally imputed to others. His mother he clearly retrieved from death, and placed his grandfather, who was brought under base and dishonorable vassalage, on the ancient throne of Æneas, to whom he did voluntarily many good offices, but never did him harm even inadvertently. But Theseus, in his forgetfulness and neglect of the command concerning the flag, can scarcely, methinks, by any excuses, or before the most indulgent judges, avoid the imputation of parricide. And, indeed, one of the Attic writers, perceiving it to be very hard to make an excuse for this, feigns that Ægeus, at the approach of the ship, running hastily to the Acropolis to see what news there was, slipped and fell down; as if he had no servants, or none would attend him on his way to the shore.

LYCURGUS.

Those authors who are most worthy of credit deduce the genealogy of Lycurgus, the lawgiver of Sparta, as follows:

| Polydectes by his first wife. | Lycurgus by Dionassa his second |

Soüs certainly was the most renowned of all his ancestors, under whose conduct the Spartans made slaves of the Helots, and added to their dominions, by conquest, a good part of Arcadia. There goes a story of this king Soüs, that, being besieged by the Clitorians in a dry and stony place so that he could come at no water, he was at last constrained to agree with them upon these terms, that he would restore to them all his conquests, provided that himself and all his men should drink of the nearest spring. After the usual oaths and ratifications, he called his soldiers together, and offered to him that would forbear drinking, his kingdom for a reward; and when not a man of them was able to forbear, in short, when they had all drunk their fill, at last comes king Soüs himself to the spring, and, having sprinkled his face only, without swallowing one drop, marches off in the face of his enemies, refusing to yield up his conquests, because himself and all his men had not, according to the articles, drunk of their water.

Although he was justly had in admiration on this account, yet his family was not surnamed from him, but from his son Eurypon (of whom they were called Eurypontids); the reason of which was that Eurypon relaxed the rigor of the monarchy, seeking favor and popularity with the many. They, after this first step, grew bolder; and the succeeding kings partly incurred hatred with their people by trying to use force, or, for popularity's sake and through weakness, gave way; and anarchy and confusion long prevailed in Sparta, causing, moreover, the death of the father of Lycurgus. For as he was endeavoring to quell a riot, he was stabbed with a butcher's knife, and left the title of king to his eldest son Polydectes.

He, too, dying soon after, the right of succession (as every one thought) rested in Lycurgus; and reign he did for a time, but declared that the kingdom belonged to the child of his sister-in-law the queen, and that he himself should exercise the regal jurisdiction only as his guardian; the Spartan name for which office is *prodicus*. Soon after, an overture was made to him by the queen, that she would herself in some way destroy the infant, upon condition that he would marry her when he came to the crown. Abhorring the woman's wickedness, he nevertheless did not reject her proposal, but, making show of closing with her, despatched the messenger with thanks and expressions of joy, with orders that they should bring the boy baby to him, wheresoever he were, and whatsoever doing. It so fell out that when he was at supper with the principal magistrates, the queen's child was presented to him, and he, taking him into his arms, said to those about him, "Men of Sparta, here is a king born unto us;" this said, he laid him down in the king's place, and named him Charilaus, that is, the joy of the people; because that all were transported with joy and with wonder at his noble and just spirit. His reign had lasted only eight months, but he was honored on other accounts by the citizens, and there were more who obeyed him because of his eminent virtues, than because he was regent to the king and had the royal power in his hands. Some, however, envied and sought to impede his growing influence while he was still young; chiefly the kindred and friends of the queen-mother, who pretended to have been dealt with injuriously. Her brother Leonidas, in a warm debate which fell out betwixt him and Lycurgus, went so far as to tell him to his face that he was well assured that ere long he should see him king; suggesting suspicions and preparing the way for an accusation of him, as though he had made away with his nephew, if the child should chance to fail, though by a natural death. Words of the like import were designedly cast abroad by the queen-mother and her adherents.

Troubled at this, and not knowing what it might come to, he thought it his wisest course to avoid their envy by a voluntary exile, and to travel from place to place until his nephew came to marriageable years, and, by having a son, had secured the succession. Setting sail, therefore, with this resolution, he first arrived at Crete, where, having considered their several forms of government, and got an acquaintance with the principal men amongst them, some of their laws he very much approved of, and resolved to make use of them in his own country; a good part he rejected as useless. Amongst the persons there the most renowned for their learning and their wisdom in state matters was one Thales, whom Lycurgus, by importunities and assurances of friendship, persuaded to go over to Lacedæmon; where, though by his outward appearance and his own profession he seemed to be no other than a lyric poet, in reality he performed the part of one of the ablest lawgivers in the world. The very songs which he composed were exhortations to obedience and concord, and the very measure and cadence of the verse, conveying impressions of order and tranquillity, had so great an influence on the minds of the listeners that they were insensibly softened and civilized, insomuch that they renounced their private feuds and animosities, and were reunited in a common admiration of virtue. So that it may truly be said that Thales prepared the way for the discipline introduced by Lycurgus.

From Crete he sailed to Asia, with design, as is said, to examine the difference betwixt the manners and rules of life of the Cretans, which were very sober and temperate, and those of the Ionians, a people of sumptuous and delicate habits, and so to form a judgment; just as physicians do by comparing healthy and diseased bodies. Here he had the first sight of Homer's works, in the hands, we may suppose, of the posterity of Creophylus; and, having observed that the few loose expressions and actions of ill example which are to be found in his poems were much outweighed by serious lessons of state and rules of morality, he set himself eagerly to transcribe and digest them into order, as thinking they would be of good use in his own country. They had, indeed, already obtained some slight repute amongst the Greeks, and scattered portions, as chance conveyed them, were in the hands of individuals; but Lycurgus first made them really known.

The Egyptians say that he took a voyage into Egypt, and that, being much taken with their way of separating the soldiery from the rest of the nation, he transferred it from them to Sparta; a removal from contact with those employed in low and mechanical occupations giving high refinement and beauty to the state. Some Greek writers also record this. But as for his voyages into Spain, Africa, and the Indies, and his conferences there with the Gymnosophists, the whole relation, as far as I can find, rests on the single credit of the Spartan Aristocrates, the son of Hipparchus.

Lycurgus was much missed at Sparta, and often sent for, "For kings indeed we have," they said, "who wear the marks and assume the titles of royalty, but as for the qualities of their minds, they have nothing by which they are to be distinguished from their subjects;" adding that in him alone was the true foundation of sovereignty to be seen, a nature made to rule, and a genius to gain obedience. Nor were the kings themselves averse to see him back, for they looked upon his presence as a bulwark against the insolencies of the people.

Things being in this posture at his return, he applied himself, without loss of time, to a thorough reformation, and resolved to change the whole face of the commonwealth; for what could a few particular laws and a partial alteration avail? He must act as wise physicians do, in the case of one who labors under a complication of diseases,—by force of medicines reduce and exhaust him, change his whole temperament, and then set him upon a totally new regimen of diet. Having thus projected things, away he goes to Delphi to consult Apollo there; which having done, and offered his sacrifice, he returned with that renowned oracle, in which he is called beloved of God, and rather God than man: that his prayers were heard, that his laws should be the best, and the commonwealth which observed them the most famous in the world. Encouraged by these things, he set himself to bring over to his side the leading men of Sparta, exhorting them to give him a helping hand in his great undertaking: he broke it first to his particular friends, and then by degrees gained others, and animated them all to put his design in execution. When things were ripe for action, he gave order to thirty of the principal men of Sparta to be ready armed at the market-place at break of day, to the end that he might strike a terror into the opposite party. Hermippus hath set down the names of twenty of the most eminent of them: but the name of him whom Lycurgus most confided in, and who was of most use to him both in making his laws and putting them in execution, was Arthmiadas. Things growing to a tumult, king Charilaus, apprehending that it was a conspiracy against his person, took sanctuary in the temple of Athena of the Brazen House; but, being soon after undeceived, and having taken an oath of them that they had no designs against him, he quitted his refuge, and himself also entered into the confederacy with them; of so gentle and flexible a disposition he was, to which Archelaus, his brother-king, alluded, when, hearing him extolled for his goodness, he said: "Who can say he is anything but good? he is so even to the bad."

Amongst the many changes and alterations which Lycurgus made, the first and of greatest importance was the establishment of the senate, which, having a power equal to the kings' in matters of great consequence, and, as Plato expresses it, allaying and qualifying the fiery genius of the royal office, gave steadiness and safety to the commonwealth. For the state, which before had no firm basis to stand upon, but leaned one while towards an absolute monarchy, when the kings had the upper hand, and another while towards a pure democracy, when the people had the better, found in this establishment of the senate a central weight, like ballast in a ship, which always kept things in a just equilibrium; the twenty-eight always adhering to the kings so far as to resist democracy, and, on the other hand, supporting the people against the establishment of absolute monarchy. As for the determinate number of twenty-eight, Aristotle states that it so fell out because two of the original associates, for want of courage, fell off from the enterprise; but Sphærus assures us that there were but twenty-eight of the confederates at first; perhaps there is some mystery in the number, which consists of seven multiplied by four, and is the first of perfect numbers after six, being, as that is, equal to all its parts.* For my part, I believe Lycurgus fixed upon the number of twenty-eight, that, the two kings being reckoned amongst them, they might be thirty in all. So eagerly set was he upon this establishment, that he took the trouble to obtain an oracle about it from Delphi; and the Rhetra (or sacred ordinance) runs thus: "After that you have built a temple to Jupiter Hellanius, and to Minerva Hellania,

---

* 14, 2, 7, 4, 1, make by addition 28; as 3, 2, 1, make 6.

and after that you have *phyle'd* the people into *phyles*, and *obe'd* them into *obes*, you shall establish a council of thirty elders, the leaders included, and shall, from time to time, assemble the people betwixt Babyca and Cnacion, there propound and put to the vote. The commons have the final voice and decision." By *phyles* and *obes* are meant the divisions of the people; by the *leaders*, the two kings; Aristotle says Cnacion is a river, and Babyca a bridge. Betwixt this Babyca and Cnacion, their assemblies were held, for they had no council-house or building to meet in. Lycurgus was of opinion that ornaments were so far from advantaging them in their councils, that they were rather an hinderance, by diverting their attention from the business before them to statues and pictures, and roofs curiously fretted, the usual embellishments of such places amongst the other Greeks. The people then being thus assembled in the open air, it was not allowed to any one of their order to give his advice, but only either to ratify or reject what should be propounded to them by the king or senate.

After the creation of the thirty senators, his next task, and, indeed, the most hazardous he ever undertook, was the making of a new division of their lands. For there was an extreme inequality amongst them, and their state was overloaded with a multitude of indigent and necessitous persons, while its whole wealth had centred upon a very few. To the end, therefore, that he might expel from the state arrogance and envy, luxury and crime, and those yet more inveterate diseases of want and superfluity, he obtained of them to renounce their properties, and to consent to a new division of the land, and that they should live all together on an equal footing; merit to be their only road to eminence, and the disgrace of evil, and credit of worthy acts, their one measure of difference between man and man.

Upon their consent to these proposals, proceeding at once to put them into execution, he divided the country of Laconia in general into thirty thousand equal shares, and the part attached to the city of Sparta into nine thousand; these he distributed among the Spartans, as he did the others to the country citizens. A lot was so much as to yield, one year with another, about seventy bushels of grain for the master of the family, and twelve for his wife, with a suitable proportion of oil and wine. And this he thought sufficient to keep their bodies in good health and strength; superfluities they were better without. It is reported, that, as he returned from a journey shortly after the division of the lands, in harvest time, the ground being newly reaped, seeing the stacks all standing equal and alike, he smiled, and said to those about him, "Methinks all Laconia looks like one family estate just divided among a number of brothers."

Not contented with this, he resolved to make a division of their movables too, that there might be no odious distinction or inequality left amongst them; but finding that it would be very dangerous to go about it openly, he took another course, and defeated their avarice by the following stratagem: he commanded that all gold and silver coin should be called in, and that only a sort of money made of iron should be current, a great weight and quantity of which was worth but very little; so that to lay up a hundred or two dollars there was required a pretty large closet, and, to remove it, nothing less than a yoke of oxen. With the diffusion of this money, at once a number of vices were banished from Lacedæmon; for who would rob another of such a coin? Who would unjustly detain or take by force, or accept as a bribe, a thing which it was not easy to hide, nor a credit to have, nor indeed of any use to cut in pieces? For when it was just red-hot, they quenched it in vinegar, and by that means spoilt it, and made it almost incapable of being worked.

In the next place, he declared an outlawry of all needless and superfluous arts; but here he might almost have spared his proclamation; for they of themselves would have gone with the gold and silver, the money which remained being not so proper payment for curious work; for, being of iron, it was scarcely portable, neither, if they should take the pains to export it, would it pass amongst the other Greeks, who ridiculed it. So there was now no more means of purchasing foreign goods and small wares; merchants sent no shiploads into Laconian ports; no rhetoric-master, no itinerant fortune-teller, or gold or silversmith, engraver, or jeweler, set foot in a country which had no money; so that luxury, deprived little by little of that which fed and fomented it, wasted to nothing, and died away of itself. For the rich had no advantage here over the poor, as their wealth and abundance had no road to come abroad by, but were shut up at home doing nothing. And in this way they became excellent artists in common necessary things; bedsteads, chairs, and tables, and such like staple utensils in a family, were admirably well made there; their cup, particularly, was very much in fashion, and eagerly sought for by soldiers, as Critias reports; for its color was such as to prevent water, drunk upon necessity and disagreeable to look at, from being noticed; and the shape of it was such that the mud stuck to the sides, so that only the purer part came to the drinker's mouth. For this, also, they had to thank their lawgiver, who, by relieving the artisans of the trouble of making useless things, set them to show their skill in giving beauty to those of daily and indispensable use.

The third and most masterly stroke of this great lawgiver, by which he struck a yet more effectual blow against luxury and the desire of riches, was the ordinance he made that they should all eat in common, of the same bread and same meat, and of kinds that were specified, and should not spend their lives at home, laid on costly couches at splendid tables, delivering themselves up into the hands of their tradesmen and cooks, to fatten them in corners, like greedy brutes, and to ruin not their minds only but their very bodies, which, enfeebled by indulgence and excess, would stand in need of long sleep, warm bathing, freedom from work, and, in a word, of as much care and attendance as if they were continually sick. It was certainly an extraordinary thing to have brought about such a result as this, but a greater yet to have taken away from wealth, as Theophrastus observes, not merely the property of being coveted, but its very nature of being wealth. For the rich, being obliged to go to the same table with the poor, could not make use of or enjoy their abundance, nor so much as please their vanity by looking at or displaying it. So that the common proverb, that Plutus, the god of riches, is blind, was nowhere in all the world literally verified but in Sparta. There, indeed, he was not only blind, but, like a picture, without either life or motion. Nor were they allowed to take food at home first, and then attend the public tables, for every one had an eye upon those who did not eat and drink like the rest, and reproached them with being dainty and effeminate.

This last ordinance in particular exasperated the wealthier men. They collected in a body against Lycurgus, and from ill words came to throwing stones, so that at length he was forced to run out of the market-place, and make to sanctuary to save his life; by good-hap he outran all excepting one Alcander, a young man otherwise not ill accomplished, but hasty and violent, who came up so close to him, that, when he turned to see who was near him, he struck him upon the face with his stick, and put out one of his eyes. Lycurgus, so far from being daunted and discouraged by this accident, stopped short and showed his disfigured face and eye beat out to his countrymen; they, dismayed and ashamed at the sight, delivered Alcander into his hands to be punished, and escorted him home, with expressions of great concern for his ill usage. Lycurgus, having thanked them for their care of his person, dismissed them all, excepting only Alcander; and, taking him with him into his house, neither did nor said anything severe to him, but dismissing those whose place it was, bade Alcander to wait upon him at table. The young man, who was of an ingenuous temper, did without murmuring as he was commanded;

and, being thus admitted to live with Lycurgus, he had an opportunity to observe in him, beside his gentleness and calmness of temper, an extraordinary sobriety and an indefatigable industry, and so, from an enemy, became one of his most zealous admirers, and told his friends and relations that Lycurgus was not that morose and ill-natured man they had formerly taken him for, but the one mild and gentle character of the world. And thus did Lycurgus, for chastisement of his fault, make of a wild and passionate young man one of the discreetest citizens of Sparta.

In memory of this accident, Lycurgus built a temple to Minerva. Some authors, however, say that he was wounded, indeed, but did not lose his eye from the blow; and that he built the temple in gratitude for the cure. Be this as it will, certain it is, that, after this misadventure, the Lacedæmonians made it a rule never to carry so much as a staff into their public assemblies.

But to return to their public repasts. They met by companies of fifteen, more or less, and each of them stood bound to bring in monthly a bushel of meal, eight gallons of wine, five pounds of cheese, two pounds and a half of figs, and some very small sum of money to buy flesh or fish with. Besides this, when any of them made sacrifice to the gods, they always sent a dole to the common hall; and, likewise, when any of them had been a-hunting, he sent thither a part of the venison he had killed; for these two occasions were the only excuses allowed for supping at home. The custom of eating together was observed strictly for a great while afterwards; insomuch that king Agis himself, after having vanquished the Athenians, sending for his commons at his return home, because he desired to eat privately with his queen, was refused them by the polemarchs; and when he resented this refusal so much as to omit next day the sacrifice due for a war happily ended, they made him pay a fine.

They used to send their children to these tables as to schools of temperance; here they were instructed in state affairs by listening to experienced statesmen; here they learnt to converse with pleasantry, to make jests without scurrility, and take them without ill humor. In this point of good breeding, the Lacedæmonians excelled particularly, but if any man were uneasy under it, upon the least hint given there was no more to be said to him. It was customary also for the eldest man in the company to say to each of them, as they came in, "Through this" (pointing to the door), "no words go out." When any one had a desire to be admitted into any of these little societies, he was to go through the following probation: each man in the company took a little ball of soft bread, which they were to throw into a deep basin, that a waiter carried round upon his head; those that liked the person to be chosen dropped their ball into the basin without altering its figure, and those who disliked him pressed it betwixt their fingers, and made it flat; and this signified as much as a negative voice. And if there were but one of these flattened pieces in the basin, the suitor was rejected, so desirous were they that all the members of the company should be agreeable to each other. The basin was called *caddichus*, and the rejected candidate had a name thence derived. Their most famous dish was the black broth, which was so much valued that the elderly men fed only upon that, leaving what flesh there was to the younger.

They say that a certain king of Pontus, having heard much of this black broth of theirs, sent for a Lacedæmonian cook on purpose to make him some, but had no sooner tasted it than he found it extremely bad, which the cook observing, told him, "Sir, to make this broth relish, you should have bathed yourself first in the river Eurotas."

After drinking moderately, every man went to his home without lights, for the use of them was, on all occasions, forbid, to the end that they might accustom themselves to march boldly in the dark. Such was the common fashion of their meals.

Lycurgus would never reduce his laws into writing; nay, there is a Rhetra expressly to forbid it. For he thought that the most material points, and such as most directly tended to the public welfare, being imprinted on the hearts of their youth by a good discipline, would be sure to remain, and would find a stronger security, than any compulsion would be, in the principles of action formed in them by their best lawgiver, education.

One, then, of the Rhetras was, that their laws should not be written; another is particularly leveled against luxury and expensiveness, for by it it was ordained that the ceilings of their houses should only be wrought by the axe, and their gates and doors smoothed only by the saw. Epaminondas's famous dictum about his own table, that "Treason and a dinner like this do not keep company together," may be said to have been anticipated by Lycurgus. Luxury and a house of this kind could not well be companions. For, a man must have a less than ordinary share of sense that would furnish such plain and common rooms with silver-footed couches and purple coverlets and gold and silver plate. Doubtless he had good reason to think that they would proportion their beds to their houses, and their coverlets to their beds, and the rest of their goods and furniture to these. It is reported that King Leotychides, the first of that name, was so little used to the sight of any other kind of work, that, being entertained at Corinth in a stately room, he was much surprised to see the timber and ceilings so finely carved and paneled, and asked his host whether the trees grew so in his country.

A third ordinance or Rhetra was that they should not make war often, or long, with the same enemy, lest they should train and instruct them in war, by habituating them to defend themselves. And this is what Agesilaus was much blamed for a long time after; it being thought that, by his continual incursions into Bœotia, he made the Thebans a match for the Lacedæmonians; and therefore Antalcidas, seeing him wounded one day, said to him that he was very well paid for taking such pains to make the Thebans good soldiers, whether they would or no. These laws were called the Rhetras, to intimate that they were divine sanctions and revelations.

In order to the good education of their youth (which, as I said before, he thought the most important and noblest work of a lawgiver), he took in their case all the care that was possible; he ordered the maidens to exercise themselves with wrestling, running, throwing the quoit, and casting the dart, to the end that they might have strong and healthy bodies.

It was not in the power of the father to dispose of his child as he thought fit; he was obliged to carry it before certain "triers" at a place called Lesche; these were some of the elders of the tribe to which the child belonged; their business it was carefully to view the infant, and, if they found it stout and well made, they gave order for its rearing, and allotted to it one of the nine thousand shares of land above mentioned for

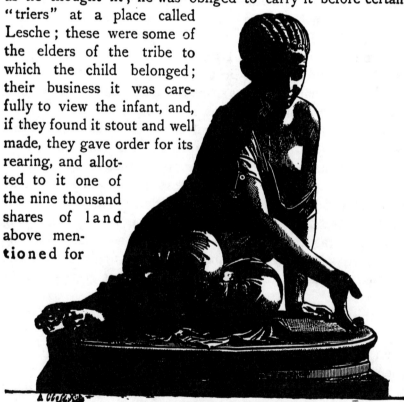

GIRL PLAYING AT DICE.

its maintenance; but if they found it puny and ill-shaped, ordered it to be taken to what was called the Apothetæ, a sort of chasm under Taygetus; as thinking it neither for the good of the child itself, nor for the public interest, that it should be brought up, if it did not, from the very outset, appear made to be healthy and vigorous. Upon the same account, the women did not bathe the new-born children with water, as is the custom in all other countries, but with wine, to prove the temper and complexion of their bodies; from a notion they had that epileptic and weakly children faint and waste away upon their being thus bathed, while, on the contrary, those of a strong and vigorous habit acquire firmness and get a temper by it like steel. There was much care and art, too, used by the nurses; they had no swaddling bands; the children grew up free and unconstrained in limb and form, and not dainty and fanciful about their food; nor afraid in the dark, or of being left alone; without any peevishness or ill humor or crying. Upon this account, Spartan nurses were often bought up, or hired by people of other countries.

Lycurgus was of another mind; he would not have masters bought out of the market for his young Spartans, nor such as should sell their pains; nor was it lawful, indeed, for the

GIRL OF TANAGRA WEARING THE CHITON.

father himself to raise his children after his own fancy; but as soon as they were seven years old they were to be enrolled in certain companies and classes, where they all lived under the same order and discipline, doing their exercises and taking their play together. Of these he who showed the most conduct and courage was made captain; they had their eyes always upon him, obeyed his orders, and underwent patiently whatsoever punishment he inflicted; so that the whole course of their education was one continued exercise of a ready and perfect obedience. The old men, too, were spectators of their performances, and often raised quarrels and disputes among them, to have a good opportunity of finding out their different characters, and of seeing which would be valiant, which a coward, when they should come to more dangerous encounters. Reading and writing they gave them, just enough to serve their turn; their chief care was to make them good subjects, and to teach them to endure pain and conquer in battle. To this end, as they grew in years, their discipline was proportionally increased; their heads were close-clipped; they were accustomed to go barefoot, and for the most part to play naked.

After they were twelve years old they were no longer allowed

YOUTH WITH CHLAMYS AND HAT.

to wear any under-garment; they had one coat to serve them a year;* their bodies were hard and dry, with but little acquaintance of baths and unguents; these human indulgences they were allowed only on some few particular days in the year. They lodged together in little bands upon beds made of the rushes which grew by the banks of the river Eurotas, which they were to break off with their hands without a knife; if it were winter, they mingled some thistledown with their rushes, which it was thought had the property of giving warmth.

Besides all this, there was always one of the best and most honest men in the city appointed to undertake the charge and governance of them; he again arranged them into their several bands, and set over each of them for their captain the most temperate and bold of those they called Irens, who were usually twenty years old, two years out of boyhood; and the eldest of the boys, again, were Mell-Irens, as much as to say, "who would shortly be men." This young man, therefore,

YOUTH WITH CHLAMYS AND HAT.

---

* The *chitōn* and the *himation*, one inside and one out, constituted the ordinary Greek dress; corresponding in use to the Roman tunic and toga. The chlamys, a short garment of Thessalian origin, thrown over the left shoulder and fastened upon the right with a brooch, was the ordinary dress of youths, the chitōn of boys.

was their captain when they fought, and their master at home, using them for the offices of his house; sending the oldest of them to fetch wood, and the weaker and less able, to gather salads and herbs, and these they must either go without or steal; which they did by creeping into the gardens, or conveying themselves cunningly and closely into the eating-houses; if they were taken in the act, they were whipped without mercy, for thieving so ill and awkwardly. They stole, too, all other meat they could lay their hands on, looking out and watching all opportunities, when people were asleep or more careless than usual. If they were caught, they were not only punished with whipping, but hunger, too, being reduced to their ordinary allowance, which was but very slender, and so contrived on purpose, that they might set about to help themselves, and be forced to exercise their energy and address.

So seriously did the Lacedæmonian children go about their stealing, that a youth, having stolen a young fox and hid it under his coat, suffered it to tear out his very bowels with its teeth and claws, and died upon the place, rather than let it be seen. What is practised to this very day in Lacedæmon is 'enough to gain credit to this story, for I myself have seen several of the youths endure whipping to death at the foot of the altar of Diana surnamed Orthia.

The Iren, or under-master, used to stay a little with them after supper, and one of them he bade to sing a song, to another he put a question which required an advised and deliberate answer; for example, Who was the best man in the city? What he thought of such an action of such a man? They accustomed them thus early to pass a right judgment upon persons and things, and to inform themselves of the abilities or defects of their countrymen. If they had not an answer ready to the question, Who was a good or who an ill-reputed citizen? they were looked upon as of a dull and careless disposition, and to have little or no sense of virtue and honor; besides this, they were to give a good reason for what they said, and in as few words and as comprehensive as might be; he that failed of this, or answered not to the purpose, had his thumb bit by his master.

They taught them, also, to speak with a natural and graceful raillery, and to comprehend much matter of thought in few words. For Lycurgus, who ordered, as we saw, that a great piece of money should be but of an inconsiderable value, on the contrary would allow no discourse to be current which did not contain in few words a great deal of useful and curious sense; children in Sparta, by a habit of long silence, came to give just and sententious answers; for, indeed, loose talkers seldom originate many sensible words. King Agis, when some Athenian laughed at their short swords, and said that the jugglers on the stage swallowed them with ease, answered him, "We find them long enough to reach our enemies with;" and as their swords were short and sharp, so, it seems to me, were their sayings. They reach the point and arrest the attention of the hearers better than any others. Lycurgus himself seems to have been short and sententious, if we may trust the anecdotes of him; as appears by his answer to one who by all means would set up democracy in Lacedæmon. "Begin, friend," said he, "and set it up in your family." Another asked him why he allowed of such mean and trivial sacrifices to the gods. He replied, "That we may always have something to offer to them." Being asked what sort of martial exercises or combats he approved of, he answered, "All sorts, except that in which you stretch out your hands." *

Of their dislike to talkativeness, the following apophthegms are evidence. King Leonidas said to one who held him in discourse upon some useful matter, but not in due time and place, "Much to the purpose, sir, elsewhere." King Charilaus, the nephew of Lycurgus, being asked why his uncle had made so few laws, answered, "Men of few words require but

---

* The form of crying quarter among the ancients.

few laws." When one blamed Hecatæus the sophist because that, being invited to the public table, he had not spoken one word all supper-time, Archidamidas answered in his vindication, "He who knows how to speak, knows also when."

The sharp, and yet not ungraceful, retorts which I mentioned may be instanced as follows. Demaratus, being asked in a troublesome manner by an importunate fellow, Who was the best man in Lacedæmon? answered at last, "He, sir, that is the least like you." Some, in company where Agis was, much extolled the Eleans for their just and honorable management of the Olympic games; "Indeed," said Agis, "they are highly to be commended if they can do justice one day in five years."

We may see their character, too, in their very jests. For they did not throw them out at random, but the very wit of them was grounded upon something or other worth thinking about. For instance, one, being asked to go hear a man who exactly counterfeited the voice of a nightingale, answered, "Sir, I have heard the nightingale itself." Another, having read the following inscription upon a tomb,—

> Seeking to quench a cruel tyranny,
> They, at Selinus, did in battle die,

said, it served them right; for instead of trying to quench the tyranny they should have let it burn out. A lad, being offered some game-cocks that would die upon the spot, said he cared not for cocks that would die, but for such as would live and kill others. In short, their answers were so sententious and pertinent, that one said well that intellectual, much more truly than athletic, exercise was the Spartan characteristic.

Nor was their instruction in music and verse less carefully attended to than their habits of grace and good breeding in conversation. And their very songs had a life and spirit in them that inflamed and possessed men's minds with an enthusiasm and ardor for action; the style of them was plain and without affectation; the subject always serious and moral; most usually it was in praise of such men as had died in defence of their country, or in derision of those that had been cowards; the former they declared happy and glorified; the life of the latter they described as most miserable and abject. There were also vaunts of what they would do, and boasts of what they had done, varying with the various ages, as, for example, they had three choirs in their solemn festivals, the first of the old men, the second of the young men, and the last of the children; the old men began thus:

> We once were young, and brave and strong;

the young men answered them, singing,

> And we're so now, come on and try;

the children came last and said,

> But we'll be strongest by and by.

Before they engaged in battle, the Lacedæmonians abated a little the severity of their manners in favor of their young men, suffering them to curl and adorn their hair, and to have costly arms, and fine clothes; and were well pleased to see them, like proud horses, neighing and pressing to the course. And therefore, as soon as they came to be well grown, they took a great deal of care of their hair, to have it parted and trimmed, especially against a day of battle, pursuant to a saying recorded of their lawgiver, that a large head of hair added beauty to a good face, and terror to an ugly one.

The senate, as I said before, consisted of those who were Lycurgus's chief aiders and assistants in his plan. The vacancies he ordered to be supplied out of the best and most deserving men past sixty years old. The manner of their election was as follows: the people being called together, some selected persons were locked up in a room near the place of election, so contrived that they could neither see nor be seen, but could only hear the noise of the assembly without; for they decided this, as most other affairs of moment, by the shouts of the people. This done, the competitors were not brought in and presented all together, but one after another by lot, and passed in order through the assembly without speaking a word. Those who were locked up had writing-tables with them, in which they recorded and marked each shout by its loudness, without knowing in favor of which candidate each of them was made, but merely that they came first, second, third, and so forth. He who was found to have the most and loudest acclamations was declared senator duly elected.

When he perceived that his more important institutions had taken root in the minds of his countrymen, that custom had rendered them familiar and easy, that his commonwealth was now grown up and able to go alone, then, as Plato somewhere tells us the Maker of the world, when first he saw it existing and beginning its motion, felt joy, even so Lycurgus, viewing with joy and satisfaction the greatness and beauty of his political structure, now fairly at work and in motion, conceived the thought to make it immortal too, and as far as human forecast could reach, to deliver it down unchangeable to posterity. He called an extraordinary assembly of all the people, and told them that he now thought everything reasonably well established, both for the happiness and the virtue of the state; but that there was one thing still behind, of the greatest importance, which he thought not fit to impart until he had consulted the oracle; in the meantime, his desire was that they would observe the laws without even the least alteration until his return, and then he would do as the god should direct him. They all consented readily, and bade him hasten his journey; but, before he departed, he administered an oath to the two kings, the senate, and the whole commons, to abide by and maintain the established form of polity until Lycurgus should come back. This done, he set out for Delphi, and, having sacrificed to

Apollo, asked him whether the laws he had established were good and sufficient for a people's happiness and virtue. The oracle answered that the laws were excellent, and that the people, while it observed them, should live in the height of renown. Lycurgus took the oracle in writing, and sent it over to Sparta, and, having sacrificed a second time to Apollo, and taken leave of his friends and his son, he resolved that the Spartans should not be released from the oath they had taken, and that he would, of his own act, close his life where he was. He was now about that age in which life was still tolerable, and yet might be quitted without regret. Everything, moreover, about him was in a sufficiently prosperous condition. He, therefore, made an end of himself by a total abstinence from food; thinking it a statesman's duty to make his very death, if possible, an act of service to the state, and even in the end of his life to give some example of virtue and effect some useful purpose. Nor was he deceived in his expectations, for the city of Lacedæmon continued the chief city of all Greece for the space of five hundred years, in strict observance of Lycurgus's laws; in all which time there was no manner of alteration made, during the reign of fourteen kings, down to the time of Agis, the son of Archidamus.

King Theopompus, when one said that Sparta held up so long because their kings could command so well, replied, "Nay, rather because the people know so well how to obey." For people do not obey, unless rulers know how to command; obedience is a lesson taught by commanders. A true leader himself creates the obedience of his own followers; as it is the greatest attainment in the art of riding to make a horse gentle and tractable, so is it of the science of government to inspire men with a willingness to obey.

It is reported that when his bones were brought home to Sparta his tomb was struck with lightning, an accident which befell no eminent person but himself and Euripides. But Aristocrates, the son of Hipparchus, says that he died in Crete, and that his Cretan friends, in accordance with his own request, when they had burned his body, scattered the ashes into the sea, for fear lest, if his relics should be transported to Lacedæmon, the people might pretend to be released from their oaths, and make innovations in the government.

SOLON.

Solon, as Hermippus writes, when his father had ruined his estate in doing benefits and kindnesses to other men, though he had friends enough that were willing to contribute to his relief, yet was ashamed to be beholden to others, since he was descended from a family who were accustomed to do kindnesses rather than receive them; and therefore applied himself to merchandise in his youth; though others assure us that he traveled rather to get learning and experience than to make money. It is certain that he was a lover of knowledge, for when he was old he would say that he

> Each day grew older, and learnt something new.

But that he accounted himself rather poor than rich is evident from the lines,

> Some wicked men are rich, some good are poor,
> We will not change our virtue for their store;
> Virtue's a thing that none can take away,
> But money changes owners all the day.

It is stated that Anacharsis and Solon and Thales were familiarly acquainted, and some have quoted parts of their discourse; for, they say, Anacharsis, coming to Athens, knocked at Solon's door, and told him that he, being a stranger, was come to be his guest, and contract a friendship with him; and Solon replying, "It is better to make friends at home," Anacharsis replied, "Then you that are at home make friendship with me." Solon, somewhat surprised at the readiness of the repartee, received him kindly, and kept him some time with him, being already engaged in public business and the compilation of his laws; which when Anacharsis understood, he laughed at him for imagining the dishonesty and covetousness of his countrymen could be restrained by written laws, which were like spiders' webs, and would catch, it is true, the weak and poor, but easily be broken by the mighty and rich. To this Solon rejoined that men keep their promises when neither side can get anything by the breaking of them; and he would so fit his laws to the citizens, that all should understand it was more eligible to be just than to break the laws. But the event rather agreed with the conjecture of Anacharsis than Solon's hope. Anacharsis, being once at the assembly, expressed his wonder that in Greece wise men spoke and fools decided.

Now, when the Athenians were tired with a tedious and difficult war that they conducted against the Megarians for the island Salamis, and made a law that it should be death for any man, by writing or speaking, to assert that the city ought to endeavor to recover it, Solon, vexed at the disgrace, and perceiving thousands of the youth wished for somebody to begin, but did not dare to stir first for fear of the law, counterfeited a distraction, and by his own family it was spread about the city that he was mad. He then secretly composed some elegiac verses, and getting them by heart, that it might seem extempore, ran out into the market-place with a cap upon his head, and, the people gathering about him, got upon the herald's stand, and sang that elegy which begins thus:—

> I am a herald come from Salamis the fair,
> My news from thence my verses shall declare.

The poem is called "Salamis"; it contains a hundred verses, very elegantly written. When it had been sung, his friends commended it, and especially Pisistratus exhorted the citizens to obey his directions; insomuch that they recalled the law, and renewed the war under Solon's conduct. The popular tale is, that with Pisistratus he sailed to Colias, and, finding the

THE GULF OF SALAMIS.

women, according to the custom of the country there, sacrificing to Ceres, he sent a trusty friend to Salamis, who should pretend himself a renegade, and advise them, if they desired to seize the chief Athenian women, to come with him at once to Colias; the Megarians presently sent off men in the vessel with him, and Solon, seeing it put off from the island, commanded the women to be gone, and some beardless youths, dressed in their clothes, their shoes, and caps, and privately armed with daggers, to dance and play near the shore till the enemies had landed and the vessel was in their power. Things being thus ordered, the Megarians were allured with the appearance, and, coming to the shore, jumped out, eager who should first seize a prize, so that not one of them escaped; and the Athenians set sail for the island and took it.

For this Solon grew famed and powerful; but his advice in favor of defending the oracle at Delphi, to give aid, and not to suffer the Cirrhæans to profane it, but to maintain the honor of the god, got him most repute among the Greeks: for upon his persuasion the Amphictyons undertook the war.

Now the Cylonian pollution had a long time disturbed the commonwealth, ever since the time when Megacles the archon persuaded the conspirators with Cylon that took sanctuary in Athena's temple to come down and stand to a fair trial. And they, tying a thread to the image, and holding one end of it, went down to the tribunal; but when they came to the temple of the Furies, the thread broke of its own accord, upon which, as if the goddess had refused them protection, they were seized by Megacles and the other magistrates; as many as were without the temples were stoned, those that fled for sanctuary were butchered at the altar, and only those escaped who made supplication to the wives of the magistrates.

The Athenians, now the Cylonian sedition was over and the polluted gone into banishment, fell into their old quarrels about the government, there being as many different parties as there were diversities in the country. The Hill quarter favored democracy; the Plain, oligarchy; and those that lived by the Sea-side stood for a mixed sort of government, and so hindered either of the parties from prevailing. And the disparity of fortune between the rich and the poor at that time also reached its height; so that the city seemed to be in a truly dangerous condition, and no other means for freeing it from disturbances and settling it to be possible but a despotic power.

Then the wisest of the Athenians, perceiving Solon was of all men the only one not implicated in the troubles, that he had not joined in the exactions of the rich, and was not involved in the necessities of the poor, pressed him to succor the commonwealth and compose the differences. Solon, reluctantly at first, engaged in state affairs, being afraid of the pride of one party and the greediness of the other; he was chosen archon, however, after Philombrotus, and empowered to be an arbitrator and lawgiver; the rich consenting because he was wealthy, the poor because he was honest. There was a saying of his current before the election, that when things are *even* there never can be war, and this pleased both parties, the wealthy and the poor; the one conceiving him to mean, when all have their fair proportion; the other, when all are absolutely equal. Thus, there being great hopes on both sides, the chief men pressed Solon to take the government into his own hands, and, when he was once settled, manage the business freely and according to his pleasure; and many of the commons, perceiving it would be a difficult change to be effected by law and reason, were willing to have one wise and just man set over the affairs; and some say that Solon had this oracle from Apollo:

> Take the mid-seat, and be the vessel's guide;
> Many in Athens are upon your side.

From which it is manifest that he was a man of great reputation before he gave his laws. The several mocks that were put upon him for refusing the power, he records in these words:

> Solon surely was a dreamer, and a man of simple mind;
> When the gods would give him fortune, he of his own will declined;
> When the net was full of fishes, over-heavy thinking it,
> He declined to haul it up, through want of heart and want of wit.
> Had but I that chance of riches and of kingship for one day,
> I would give my skin for flaying, and my house to die away.

Thus he makes the many and the low people speak of him. Yet, though he refused the government, he did not show himself mean and submissive to the powerful, nor make his laws to pleasure those that chose him. For the first thing which he settled was, that what debts remained should be forgiven, and no man, for the future, should engage the body of his debtor for security. Though some, as Androtion, affirm that the debts were not canceled, but the interest only lessened, which sufficiently pleased the people; so that they named this benefit the Seisacthea, together with the enlarging of their measures, and raising the value of their money; for he made a pound, which before passed for seventy-three drachmas, go for a hundred; so that, though the number of pieces in the payment was equal, the value was less; which proved a considerable benefit to those that were to discharge great debts, and no loss to the creditors.

While he was designing this, a most vexatious thing happened; for when he had resolved to take off the debts, and was considering the proper form and fit beginning for it, he told some of his friends, Conon, Clinias, and Hipponicus, in whom he had a great deal of confidence, that he would not meddle with the lands, but only free the people from their debts; upon which, they, using their advantage, made haste and borrowed some considerable sums of money, and purchased some large farms; and when the law was enacted, they kept the possessions, and would not return the money; which brought Solon into great suspicion and dislike, as if he himself had not been abused, but was concerned in the contrivance. But he presently stopped this suspicion, by releasing his own debtors of five talents (for he had lent so much), according to the law; others, as Polyzelus the Rhodian, say fifteen.

Soon becoming sensible of the good that was done, the people laid by their grudges, made a public sacrifice, and chose Solon to new-model and make laws for the commonwealth, giving him the entire power over everything, their magistracies, their assemblies, courts, and councils; that he should appoint the number, times of meeting, and what estate they must have that could be capable of these, and dissolve or continue any of the present constitutions, according to his pleasure.

First, then, he repealed all Draco's laws, except those concerning homicide, because they were too severe and the punishments too great; for death was appointed for almost all offences, insomuch that those that were convicted of idleness were to die, and those that stole a cabbage or an apple to suffer even as villains that committed sacrilege or murder. So that Demades, in after time, was thought to have said very happily, that Draco's laws were written not with ink, but blood; and he himself, being once asked why he made death the punishment of most offences, replied: "Small ones deserve that, and I have no higher for the greater crimes."

Next, Solon, being willing to continue the magistracies in the hands of the rich men, and yet receive the people into the other part of the government, took an account of the citizens' estates, and those that were worth five hundred measures of fruits, dry and liquid, he placed in the first rank; those that could keep a horse, or were worth three hundred measures, were made the second class; those that had two hundred measures, were in the third; and all the other were called Thetes, who were not admitted to any office, but could come to the assembly, and act as jurors; which at first seemed nothing, but afterward was found an enormous privilege, as almost every matter of dispute came before them in this latter capacity. Besides, it is said that he was obscure and ambiguous in the wording of his laws, on purpose to increase the honor of his courts; for since their differences could not be adjusted by the letter, they would have to bring all their causes to the judges, who thus were in a manner masters of the laws. Of this equalization he himself makes mention in this manner:

> Such power I gave the people as might do,
> Abridged not what they had, nor lavished new.
> Those that were great in wealth and high in place,
> My counsel likewise kept from all disgrace.
> Before them both I held my shield of might,
> And let not either touch the other's right.

When he had constituted the Areopagus of those who had been yearly archons, of which he himself was a member therefore, observing that the people, now free from their debts, were unsettled and imperious, he formed another council of four hundred, a hundred out of each of the four tribes, which was to inspect all matters before they were propounded to the people, and to take care that nothing but what had been first examined should be brought before the general assembly. The upper council, or Areopagus, he made inspectors and keepers of the laws, conceiving that the commonwealth, held by these two councils like anchors, would be less liable to be tossed by tumults, and the people be more at quiet. Such is the general statement that Solon instituted the Areopagus.

Amongst his other laws, one is very peculiar and surprising, which disfranchises all who stand neuter in a sedition; for it seems he would not have any one remain insensible and regardless of the public good, but at once join with the good party and those that have the right upon their side, assist and venture with them, rather than keep out of harm's way and watch who would get the better.

Another commendable law of Solon's is that which forbids men to speak evil of the dead.

Since the country has but few rivers, lakes, or large springs, and many used wells which they had dug, there was a law made, that, where there was a public well within a *hippicon*, that is, four furlongs, all should draw at that; but when it was farther off, they should try and procure a well of their own; and, if they had dug ten fathoms deep and could find no water, they had liberty to fetch a pitcherful of four gallons and a half in a day from their neighbors'; for he thought it prudent to make provision against want, but not to supply laziness. He showed skill in his orders about planting, for any one that would plant another tree was not to set it within five feet of his neighbor's field; but if a fig or an olive, not within nine, for their roots spread farther, nor can they be planted near all sorts of trees without damage, for they draw away the nourishment, and in some cases are noxious by their effluvia. He that would dig a pit or a ditch was to dig it at the distance of its own depth from his neighbor's ground; and he that would raise stocks of bees was not to place them within three hundred feet of those which another had already raised.

He permitted only oil to be exported, and those that exported any other fruit, the archon was solemnly to curse, or else pay an hundred drachmas* himself; and this law was written in his first table, and, therefore, let none think it incredible, as some affirm, that the exportation of figs was once unlawful. He made a law also, concerning hurts and injuries from beasts, in which he commands the master of any dog that bit a man to deliver him up with a log about his neck four and a half feet long—a happy device for men's security.

All his laws he established for an hundred years, and wrote them on wooden tables or rollers, named axones, which might be turned round in oblong cases; some of their relics were in my time still to be seen in the Prytaneum, or common hall, at Athens. These, as Aristotle states, were called cyrbes, and there is a passage of Cratinus the comedian,

> By Solon, and by Draco, if you please,
> Whose Cyrbes make the fires that parch our peas.

---

* A drachma was about twenty cents.

But some say those are properly cyrbes, which contain laws concerning sacrifices and the rites of religion, and all the other axones. The council all jointly swore to confirm the laws, and every one of the Thesmothetæ vowed for himself at the stone in the market-place, that, if he broke any of the statutes, he would dedicate a golden statue, as big as himself, at Delphi.

Now when these laws were enacted, and some came to Solon every day, to commend or dispraise them, and to advise, if possible, to leave out, or put in something, and many criticised, and desired him to explain, and tell the meaning of such and such a passage, he, to escape all displeasure, it being a hard thing, as he himself says,

> In great affairs to satisfy all sides,

as an excuse for traveling, bought a trading vessel, and, having obtained leave for ten years' absence, departed, hoping that by that time his laws would have become familiar.

His first voyage was for Egypt, and he lived, as he himself says,

> Near Nilus' mouth, by fair Canopus' shore,

and spent some time in study with Psenophis of Heliopolis, and Sonchis the Saite, the most learned of all the priests; from whom, as Plato says, getting knowledge of the Atlantic story, he put it into a poem, and proposed to bring it to the knowledge of the Greeks. From thence he sailed to Cyprus, where he was made much of by Philocyprus, one of the kings there, who had a small city built by Demophon, Theseus's son, near the river Clarius, in a strong situation, but incommodious and uneasy of access. Solon persuaded him, since there lay a fair plain below, to remove, and build there a pleasanter and more spacious city. And he stayed himself, and assisted in gathering inhabitants, and in fitting it both for defence and convenience of living; insomuch that many flocked to Philocyprus, and the other kings imitated the design; and, therefore, to honor Solon, he called the city Soli.

That Solon should discourse with Crœsus, some think not agreeable with chronology; but I cannot reject so famous and well-attested a narrative, and, what is more, so agreeable to Solon's temper, and so worthy his wisdom and greatness of mind, because, forsooth, it does not agree with some chronological canons, which thousands have endeavored to regulate, and yet, to this day, could never bring their differing opinions to any agreement. They say, therefore, that Solon, coming to Crœsus at his request, was in the same condition as an inland man when first he goes to see the sea; for as he fancies every river he meets with to be the ocean, so Solon, as he passed through the court, and saw a great many nobles richly dressed, and proudly attended with a multitude of guards and footboys, thought every one to be the king, till he was brought to Crœsus, who was decked with every possible rarity and curiosity, in ornaments of jewels, purple, and gold, that could make a grand and gorgeous spectacle of him. Now when Solon came before him, and seemed not at all surprised, nor gave Crœsus those compliments he expected, but showed himself to all discerning eyes to be a man that despised the gaudiness and petty ostentation of it, he commanded them to open all his treasure houses, and carry him to see his sumptuous furniture and luxuries, though Solon did not wish it; he could judge of him well enough by the first sight of him; and, when he returned from viewing all, Crœsus asked him if ever he had known a happier man than he. And when Solon answered that he had known one Tellus, a fellow-citizen of his own, and told him that this Tellus had been an honest man, had had good children, a competent estate, and died bravely in battle for his country, Crœsus took him for an ill-bred fellow and a fool, for not measuring happiness by the abundance of gold and silver, and preferring the life and death of a private and mean man before so much power and empire. He asked him, however, again, if, besides Tellus, he knew any other man more happy. And Solon replying, Yes, Cleobis and Biton, who were loving brothers, and extremely dutiful sons to their mother, and, when the oxen delayed her, harnessed themselves to the wagon, and drew her to Juno's temple, her neighbors all calling her happy, and she herself rejoicing; then, after sacrificing and feasting, they went to rest, and never rose again, but died in the midst of their honor a painless and tranquil death. "What," said Crœsus, angrily, "and dost not thou reckon us amongst the happy men at all?" Solon, unwilling either to flatter or exasperate him more, replied, "The gods, O king, have given the Greeks all other gifts in moderate degree; and so our wisdom, too, is a cheerful and a homely, not a noble and kingly, wisdom; and this, observing the numerous misfortunes that attend all conditions, forbids us to grow insolent upon our present enjoyments, or to admire any man's happiness that may yet, in course of time, suffer change. For the uncertain future has yet to come, with every possible variety of fortune; and him only to whom the divinity has continued happiness unto the end, we call happy; to salute as happy one that is still in the midst of life and hazard, we think as little safe and conclusive as to crown and proclaim as victorious the wrestler that is yet in the ring." After this, he was dismissed, having given Crœsus some pain, but no instruction.

Æsop, who wrote the fables, being then at Sardis upon Crœsus's invitation, and very much esteemed, was concerned that Solon was so ill-received, and gave him this advice: "Solon, let your converse with kings be either short or seasonable." "Nay, rather," replied Solon, "either short or reasonable." So at this time Crœsus despised Solon; but when he was overcome by Cyrus, had lost his city, was taken alive, condemned to be burnt, and laid bound upon the pile before all the Persians and Cyrus himself, he cried out as loud as he possibly could three times, "O Solon!" and Cyrus being surprised, and sending some to inquire what man or god this Solon was, whom alone he invoked in this extremity, Crœsus told him the whole story, saying, "He was one of the wise men of Greece, whom I sent for, not to be instructed, or to learn anything that I wanted, but that he should see and be a witness of my happiness; the loss of which was, it seems, to be a greater evil than the enjoyment was a good; for when I had them they were goods only in opinion, but now the loss of them has brought upon me intolerable and real evils. And he, conjecturing from what then was, this that now is, bade me look to the end of my life, and not rely and grow proud upon uncertainties." When this was told Cyrus, who was a wiser man than Crœsus, and saw in the present example Solon's maxim confirmed, he not only freed Crœsus from punishment, but honored him as long as he lived; and Solon had the glory, by the same saying, to save one king and instruct another.

When Solon was gone, the citizens began to quarrel; Lycurgus headed the Plain; Megacles, the son of Alcmæon, those of the Sea-side; and Pisistratus the Hill-party, in which were the poorest people, the Thetes, and greatest enemies to the rich; insomuch that, though the city still used the new laws, yet all looked for and desired a change of government, hoping severally that the change would be better for them, and put them above the contrary faction. Affairs standing thus, Solon returned, and was reverenced by all, and honored; but his old age would not permit him to be as active, and to speak in public, as formerly; yet, by privately conferring with the heads of the factions, he endeavored to compose the differences, Pisistratus appearing the most tractable; for he was extremely smooth and engaging in his language, a great friend to the poor, and moderate in his resentments; and what nature had not given him, he had the skill to imitate; so that he was trusted more than the others, being accounted a prudent and orderly man, one that loved equality, and would be an enemy to any that moved against the present settlement. Thus he deceived the majority of people; but Solon quickly discovered his character, and found out his design before any one else;

yet did not hate him upon this, but endeavored to humble him, and bring him off from his ambition, and often told him and others, that if any one could banish the passion for pre-eminence from his mind, and cure him of his desire of absolute power, none would make a more virtuous man or a more excellent citizen. Thespis, at this time, beginning to act tragedies, and the thing, because it was new, taking very much with the multitude, though it was not yet made a matter of competition, Solon, being by nature fond of hearing and learning something new, and now, in his old age, living idly, and enjoying himself, indeed, with music and with wine, went to see Thespis himself, as the ancient custom was, act; and after the play was done, he addressed him, and asked him if he was not ashamed to tell so many lies before such a number of people; and Thespis replying that it was no harm to say or do so in play, Solon vehemently struck his staff against the ground: "Ay," said he, "if we honor and commend such play as this, we shall find it some day in our business."

Now when Pisistratus, having wounded himself, was brought into the market-place in a chariot, and stirred up the people, as if he had been thus treated by his opponents because of his political conduct, and a great many were enraged and cried out, Solon, coming close to him, said, "This, O son of Hippocrates, is a bad copy of Homer's Ulysses; you do, to trick your countrymen, what he did to deceive his enemies." After this, the people were eager to protect Pisistratus, and met in an assembly, where one Ariston made a motion that they should allow Pisistratus fifty clubmen for a guard to his person. Now, the people, having passed the law, were not nice with Pisistratus about the number of his clubmen, but took no notice of it, though he enlisted and kept as many as he would, until he seized the Acropolis. When that was done, and the city in an uproar, Megacles, with all his family, at once fled; but Solon, though he was now very old, and had none to back him, yet came into the market-place and made a speech to the citizens, partly blaming their inadvertency and meanness of spirit, and in part urging and exhorting them not thus tamely to lose their liberty; and likewise then spoke that memorable saying, that, before, it was an easier task to stop the rising tyranny, but now the greater and more glorious action to destroy it, when it was begun already, and had gathered strength. But all being afraid to side with him, he returned home, and, taking his arms, he brought them out and laid them in the porch before his door, with these words: "I have done my part to maintain my country and my laws," and then he busied himself no more.

But Pisistratus, having got the command, so extremely courted Solon, so honored him, obliged him, and sent to see him, that Solon gave him his advice, and approved many of his actions; for he retained most of Solon's laws, observed them himself, and compelled his friends to obey. And he added other laws, one of which is that the maimed in the wars should be maintained at the public charge, following Solon's example in this, who had decreed it in the case of one Thersippus, that was maimed.

Solon lived after Pisistratus seized the government a long time. But the story that his ashes were scattered about the island Salamis is too strange to be easily believed, or be thought anything but a mere fable; and yet it is given, among other good authors, by Aristotle the philosopher.

THEMISTOCLES.

THE birth of Themistocles was somewhat too obscure to do him honor. His father, Neocles, was not of the distinguished people of Athens, but of the township of Phrearrhi; and by his mother's side, as it is reported, he was low-born.

> "I am not of the noble Grecian race,
> I'm poor Abrotonon, and born in Thrace:
> Let the Greek women scorn me, if they please,
> I was the mother of Themistocles."

From his youth he was of a vehement and impetuous nature, of a quick apprehension, and a strong and aspiring bent for action and great affairs. The holidays and intervals in his studies he did not spend in play or idleness, as other children, but would be always inventing or arranging some oration or declamation to himself, the subject of which was generally the excusing or accusing of his companions, so that his master would often say to him, "You, my boy, will be nothing small, but great one way or other, for good or else for bad." He received reluctantly and carelessly instructions given him to improve his manners and behavior, or to teach him any pleasing or graceful accomplishment, but whatever was said to improve him in sagacity, or in management of affairs, he would give attention to beyond one of his years, from confidence in his natural capacities for such things.

In the first essays of his youth he was not regular nor happily balanced; he allowed himself to follow mere natural character, which, without the control of reason and instruction, is apt to hurry, upon either side, into sudden and violent courses.

and very often to break away and determine upon the worst; as he afterwards owned himself, saying, that the wildest colts make the best horses, if they only get properly trained and broken in.

Yet it is evident that his mind was early imbued with the keenest interest in public affairs, and the most passionate ambition for distinction. It is said that Themistocles was so transported with the thoughts of glory, and so inflamed with the passion for great actions, that, though he was still young when the battle of Marathon was fought against the Persians, upon the skilful conduct of the general, Miltiades, being everywhere talked about, he was observed to be thoughtful and reserved; he passed the nights w i t h o u t sleep, and avoided all his usual places of recreation, and to those who wondered at the change, and inquired the reason of it, he gave the answer that "the trophy of Miltiades would not let him sleep." And when others were of opinion that the battle of Marathon would be an end to the war, Themistocles thought that it was but the beginning of far greater conflicts, and for these, to the benefit of all Greece, he kept himself in continual readiness, and his city also in proper training, foreseeing from far before what would happen.

MILTIADES.

And, first of all, the Athenians being accustomed to divide amongst themselves the revenue proceeding from the silver mines at Laurium, he was the only man that durst propose to the people that this distribution should cease, and that with the money, ships should be built to make war against the Æginetans, who were the most flourishing people in all Greece, and by the number of their ships held the sovereignty of the sea; and Themistocles thus, little by little, turned and drew the city down towards the sea, in the belief that, whereas by land they were not a match for their next neighbors, with their ships they might be able to repel the Persians and command Greece: thus, as Plato says, from steady soldiers he turned them into mariners and seamen tossed about the sea, and gave occasion for the reproach against him, that he took away from the Athenians the spear and the shield, and bound them to the bench and the oar. He was well liked by the common people, would salute every particular citizen by his own name, and always showed himself a just judge in questions of business between private men; he said to Simonides, the poet of Ceos, who desired something of him when he was commander of the army that was not reasonable, "Simonides, you would be no good poet if you wrote false measure, nor should I be a good magistrate if for favor I made false law."

Gradually growing to be great, and winning the favor of the people, he at last gained the day with his faction over that of Aristides, and procured his banishment by ostracism. When the king of Persia was now advancing against Greece, and sent messengers into Greece, with an interpreter, to demand earth and water, as an acknowledgment of subjection, Themistocles, by the consent of the people, seized upon the interpreter, and put him to death, for presuming to publish the barbarian orders and decrees in the Greek language; and having taken upon himself the command of the Athenian forces, he immediately endeavored to persuade the citizens to leave the city, and to embark upon their galleys, and meet with the Persians at a great distance from Greece.

When the contingents met at the straits of Artemisium, the

Greeks would have the Lacedæmonians to command, and Eurybiades to be their admiral; but the Athenians, who surpassed all the rest together in number of vessels, would not submit to come after any other, till Themistocles, perceiving the danger of this contest, yielded his own command to Eurybiades, and got the Athenians to submit, persuading them that if in this war they behaved themselves like men, he would answer for it after that, that the Greeks, of their own will, would submit to their command.

Though the fights between the Greeks and Persians in the straits of Eubœa were not so important as to make any final decision of the war, yet the experience which the Greeks obtained in them was of great advantage; for thus, by actual trial and in real danger, they found out, that neither number of ships, nor riches and ornaments, nor boasting shouts, nor barbarous songs of victory, were any way terrible to men that knew how to fight, and were resolved to come hand to hand with their enemies. This, Pindar appears to have seen, and says justly enough of the fight at Artemisium, that

> There the sons of Athens set
> The stone that freedom stands on yet.

For the first step towards victory undoubtedly is to gain courage. Artemisium is in Eubœa, beyond the city of Histiæa, a sea-beach open to the north; there is a small temple there, dedicated to Diana, surnamed of the Dawn, and trees about it, around which again stand pillars of white marble; and if you rub them with your hand, they send forth both the smell and color of saffron.

But when news came from Thermopylæ to Artemisium, informing them that king Leonidas was slain, and that Xerxes had made himself master of all the passages by land, they returned back to the interior of Greece. Xerxes had already passed through Doris and invaded the country of Phocis, and was burning and destroying the cities of the Phocians, yet the Greeks sent them no relief; and, though the Athenians earnestly desired them to meet the Persians in Bœotia, before they could come into Attica, as they themselves had come forward by sea at Artemisium, they gave no ear to their request, being wholly intent upon Peloponnesus, and resolved to gather all their forces together within the Isthmus, and to build a wall from sea to sea in that narrow neck of land; so that the Athenians were enraged to see themselves betrayed, and at the same time afflicted and dejected at their own destitution. For to fight alone against such a numerous army was to no purpose, and the only expedient now left them was to leave their city and cling to their ships; which the people were very unwilling to submit to, imagining that it would signify little now to gain a victory, and not understanding how there could be deliverance any longer after they had once forsaken the temples of their gods and exposed the tombs and monuments of their ancestors to the fury of their enemies.

Themistocles, being at a loss, and not able to draw the people over to his opinion by any human reason, set his machines to work, as in a theatre, and employed prodigies and oracles. The serpent of Athena, kept in the inner part of her temple, disappeared; the priests gave it out to the people that the offerings which were set for it were found untouched, and declared, by the suggestion of Themistocles, that the goddess had left the city, and taken her flight before them towards the sea. And he often urged them with the oracle which bade them "trust to walls of wood," showing them that walls of wood could signify nothing else but ships; and that the island of Salamis was termed in it not miserable or unhappy, but had the epithet of divine, for that it should one day be associated with a great good fortune of the Greeks. At length his opinion prevailed, and he obtained a decree that the city should be committed to the protection of Athena, "queen of Athens"; that they who were of age to bear arms should embark, and that each should see to sending away his children, women, and slaves where he could. This decree being confirmed, most of the Athenians removed their parents, wives, and children to Trœzen, where they were received with eager good-will by the Trœzenians, who passed a vote that they should be maintained at the public charge.

Among the great actions of Themistocles at this crisis, the recall of Aristides was not the least, for, before the war, he had been ostracized by the party which Themistocles headed, and was in banishment; but now, perceiving that the people regretted his absence, and were fearful that he might go over to the Persians to revenge himself, and thereby ruin the affairs of Greece, Themistocles proposed a decree that those who were banished for a time might return again, to give assistance by word and deed to the cause of Greece with the rest of their fellow citizens.

Eurybiades, by reason of the greatness of Sparta, was admiral of the Greek fleet, but yet was faint-hearted in time of danger, and willing to weigh anchor and set sail for the Isthmus of Corinth, near which the land army lay encamped; which Themistocles resisted; and this was the occasion of the well-known words, when Eurybiades, to check his impatience, told him that at the Olympic games they that start up before the rest are lashed. "And they," replied Themistocles, "that are left behind are not crowned." Some say that while Themistocles was thus speaking things upon the deck, an owl was seen flying to the right hand of the fleet, which came and sat upon the top of the mast; and this happy omen so far disposed the Greeks to follow his advice, that they presently prepared to fight. Yet, when the enemy's fleet was arrived at the haven of Phalerum, upon the coast of Attica, and with the number of their ships concealed all the shore, and when they saw the king himself in person come down with his land army to the sea-side, with all his forces united, then the good counsel of Themistocles was soon forgotten, and the Peloponnesians cast their eyes again towards the Isthmus, and took it very ill if any one spoke against their returning home; and, **resolving to depart that night**, the pilots had order what course to steer.

Themistocles, in great distress that the Greeks should retire, and lose the advantage of the narrow seas and strait passage, and slip home every one to his own city, considered with himself, and contrived that stratagem which was carried out by Sicinnus. This Sicinnus was a Persian captive, but a great lover of Themistocles, and the attendant of his children. Upon this occasion he sent him privately to Xerxes, commanding him to tell the king that Themistocles, the admiral of the Athenians, having espoused his interest, wished to be the first to inform him that the Greeks were ready to make their escape, and that he counselled him to hinder their flight, to set upon them while they were in this confusion and at a distance from their land army, and thereby destroy all their forces by sea. Xerxes was very joyful at this message, and received it as from one who wished him all that was good, and immediately issued instructions to the commanders of his ships that they should instantly set out with two hundred galleys to encompass all the islands, and inclose all the straits and pas-

THEMISTOCLES.

sages, that none of the Greeks might escape, and that they should afterwards follow with the rest of their fleet at leisure. This being done, Aristides, the son of Lysimachus, was the first man that perceived it, and went to the tent of Themistocles, not out of any friendship, for he had been formerly banished by his means, as has been related, but to inform him how they were encompassed by their enemies. Themistocles, knowing the generosity of Aristides, and much struck by his visit at that time, imparted to him all that he had transacted by Sicinnus, and entreated him that, as he would be more readily believed among the Greeks, he would make use of his credit to help to induce them to stay and fight their enemies in the narrow seas. Aristides applauded Themistocles, and went to the other commanders and captains of the galleys and encouraged them to engage; yet they did not perfectly assent to him till a galley of Tenos, which deserted from the Persians, of which Panætius was commander, came in, while they were still doubting, and confirmed the news that all the straits and passages were beset; and then their rage and fury, as well as their necessity, provoked them all to fight.

As soon as it was day, Xerxes placed himself high up, to view his fleet, as Acestodorus writes, in the confines of Megara, upon those hills which are called the Horns, where he sat in a chair of gold, with many secretaries about him to write down all that was done in the fight.

The number of the enemy's ships the poet Æschylus gives in his tragedy called the Persians, as on his certain knowledge, in the following words:

> Xerxes, I know, did into battle lead
> One thousand ships; of more than usual speed
> Seven and two hundred. So is it agreed.

The Athenians had a hundred and eighty; in every ship eighteen men fought upon the deck, four of whom were archers and the rest men-at-arms.

As Themistocles had fixed upon the most advantageous place, so, with no less sagacity, he chose the best time of fighting; for he would not run the prows of his galleys against the Persians, nor begin the fight till the time of day was come when there regularly blows in a fresh breeze from the open sea, and brings in with it a strong swell into the channel; this was no inconvenience to the Greek ships, which were low-built, and little above the water, but did much hurt to the Persians, which had high sterns and lofty decks, and were heavy and cumbrous in their movements, as it presented them broadside to the quick charges of the Greeks, who kept their eyes upon the motions of Themistocles, as their best example, and more particularly because, opposed to his ship, Ariamenes, admiral to Xerxes, a brave man, and by far the best and worthiest of the king's brothers, was seen throwing darts and shooting arrows from his huge galley, as from the walls of a castle. Aminias the Decelean and Sosicles the Pedian, who sailed in the same vessel, upon the ships meeting stem to stem, and transfixing each the other with their brazen prows, so that they were fastened together, when Ariamenes attempted to board theirs, ran at him with their pikes, and thrust him into the sea; his body, as it floated amongst other shipwrecks, was discovered by Artemisia, and carried to Xerxes.

The first man that took a ship was Lycomedes the Athenian, captain of a galley, who cut down its ensign, and dedicated it to Apollo the Laurel-crowned. And as the Persians fought in a narrow arm of the sea, and could bring but part of their fleet to fight, and fell foul of one another, the Greeks thus equaled them in strength, and fought with them till the evening, forced them back, and obtained, as says Simonides, that noble and famous victory, than which neither amongst the Greeks nor barbarians was ever known more glorious exploit on the seas; by the joint valor, indeed, and zeal of all who fought, but most by the wisdom and sagacity of Themistocles.

After this sea-fight, Xerxes, enraged at his ill-fortune, attempted, by casting great heaps of earth and stones into the sea, to stop up the channel and to make a dam, upon which he might lead his land forces over into the island of Salamis.

Themistocles, being desirous to try the opinion of Aristides, told him that he proposed to set sail for the Hellespont, to break the bridge of ships, so as to shut up, he said, Asia a prisoner within Europe; but Aristides, disliking the design, said: "We have hitherto fought with an enemy who has regarded little else but his pleasure and luxury; but if we shut him up within Greece, and drive him to necessity, he that is master of such great forces will no longer sit quietly with an umbrella of gold over his head, looking upon the fight for his pleasure; but he will be resolute, and attempt all things. Therefore, it is noways our interest, Themistocles," he said, "to take away the bridge that is already made, but rather to build another, if it were possible, that he might make his retreat with the more expedition." To which Themistocles answered: "If this be requisite, we must immediately use all diligence, art, and industry, to rid ourselves of him as soon as may be;" and to this purpose he found out among the captives one named Arnaces, whom he sent to the king, to inform him that the Greeks, being now victorious by sea, had decreed to sail to the Hellespont, where the boats were fastened together, and destroy the bridge; but that Themistocles, being concerned for the king, revealed this to him, that he might hasten toward the Asiatic seas, and pass over into his own dominions; and in the meantime would cause delays, and hinder the confederates from pursuing him. Xerxes no sooner heard this than, being very much terrified, he proceeded to retreat out of Greece with all speed. The prudence of Themistocles and Aristides in this was afterward more fully understood at the battle of Platæa, where Mardonius, with a very small fraction of the forces of Xerxes put the Greeks in danger of losing all.

Herodotus writes that, of all the cities of Greece, Ægina

was held to have performed the best service in the war; while all single men yielded to Themistocles, though, out of envy unwillingly; and when they returned to the entrance of Peloponnesus, where the several commanders delivered their suffrages at the altar, to determine who was most worthy, every one gave the first vote for himself and the second for Themistocles. The Lacedæmonians carried him with them to Sparta, where, giving the rewards of valor to Eurybiades, and of wis-

THEMISTOCLES RECEIVING THE TROPHY OF VICTORY.

dom and conduct to Themistocles, they crowned him with olive, presented him with the best chariot in the city, and sent three hundred young men to accompany him to the confines of their country. And at the next Olympic games, when Themistocles entered the course, the spectators took no further notice of those who were competing for the prizes, but spent the whole day in looking upon him, showing him to the strangers, admiring him, and applauding him by clapping their hands, and other expressions of joy, so that he himself, much gratified, confessed to his friends that he then reaped the fruit of all his labors for the Greeks.

He was, indeed, by nature, a great lover of honor, as is evident from the anecdotes recorded of him. When chosen admiral by the Athenians, he would not quite conclude any single matter of business, either public or private, but deferred all till the day they were to set sail, that, by dispatching a great quantity of business all at once, and having to meet a great variety of people, he might make an appearance of greatness and power. Viewing the dead bodies cast up by the sea, he perceived bracelets and necklaces of gold about them, yet passed on, only showing them to a friend that followed him, saying, "Take you these things, for you are not Themistocles." He said to Antiphates, a handsome young man, who had formerly avoided, but now in his glory, courted him, "Time, young man, has taught us both a lesson." He said that the Athenians did not honor him or admire him, but made, as it were, a sort of plane-tree of him; sheltered themselves under him in bad weather, and, as soon as it was fine, plucked his leaves and cut his branches. When a Seriphian told him that he had not obtained this honor by himself, but by the greatness of his city, he replied: "You speak truth; I should never have been famous if I had been of Seriphus; nor you, had you been of Athens." Laughing at his own son, who got his mother, and, by his mother's means, his father also, to indulge him, he told him that he had the most power of any one in Greece: "For the Athenians command the rest of Greece, I command the Athenians, your mother commands me, and you command your mother." Of the two who made love to his daughter, he preferred the man of worth to the one who was rich, saying he desired a man without riches, rather than riches without a man.

When the citizens of Athens began to listen willingly to those who traduced and reproached him, he was forced, with somewhat obnoxious frequency, to put them in mind of the great services he had performed. And he yet more provoked the people by building a temple to Diana with the epithet of Aristobule, or Diana of Best Counsel; intimating thereby that he had given the best counsel, not only to the Athenians, but to all Greece. At length the Athenians banished him, making use of the ostracism to humble his eminence and authority, as they ordinarily did with all whom they thought too powerful,

EXILE OF THEMISTOCLES.

or, by their greatness, disproportionate to the equality thought requisite in a popular government. For the ostracism was instituted, not so much to punish the offender as to mitigate and pacify the violence of the envious, who delighted to humble eminent men, and who, by fixing this disgrace upon them, might vent some part of their rancor.

Themistocles being banished from Athens, while he stayed at Argos the detection of Pausanias happened. And after

Pausanias was put to death, letters and writings were found which rendered Themistocles suspected, and his enemies among the Athenians accused him. In answer to the malicious detractions of his enemies, he merely wrote to the citizens urging that he who was always ambitious to govern, and not of a character or a disposition to serve, would never sell himself and his country into slavery to a barbarous and hostile nation.

Notwithstanding this, the people, being persuaded by his accusers, sent officers to take him and bring him away to be tried before a council of the Greeks; but, having timely notice of it, he passed over into the island of Corcyra, where the state was under obligations to him; for, being chosen as arbitrator in a difference between them and the Corinthians, he decided the controversy by ordering the Corinthians to pay down twenty talents, and declaring the town and island of Leucas a joint colony from both cities. From thence he fled into Epirus, and, the Athenians and Lacedæmonians still pursuing him, he threw himself upon chances of safety that seemed all but desperate. For he fled for refuge to Admetus, king of the Molossians, who had formerly made some request to the Athenians when Themistocles was in the height of his authority, and had been disdainfully used and insulted by him, and had let it appear plain enough that could he lay hold of him he would take his revenge. Yet in this misfortune, Themistocles, fearing the recent hatred of his neighbors and fellow-citizens more than the old displeasure of the king, put himself at his mercy, and became an humble suppliant to Admetus, after a peculiar manner, different from the custom of other countries. For taking the king's son, who was then a child, in his arms, he laid himself down at his hearth, this being the most sacred and only manner of supplication, among the Molossians, which was not to be refused.

Thucydides says, that, passing over land to the Ægean Sea, he took ship at Pydna in the bay of Thermæ, not being known to any one in the ship, till, being terrified to see the vessel driven by the winds near to Naxos, which was then besieged by the Athenians, he made himself known to the master and pilot, and, partly entreating them, partly threatening, he compelled them to bear off and stand out to sea, and sail forward toward the coast of Asia.

When he arrived at Cyme, and understood that all along the coast many laid in wait for him (the king of Persia having offered by public proclamation two hundred talents to him that should take him), he fled to Ægæ, a small city of the Æolians, where no one knew him but only his host Nicogenes, who was the richest man in Æolia, and well known to the great men of Inner Asia. There Themistocles, going to bed, dreamed that he saw a snake coil itself up upon his belly, and so creep to his neck; then, as soon as it touched his face, it turned into an eagle, which spread its wings over him, and took him up and flew away with him a great distance; then there appeared a herald's golden wand, and upon this at last it set him down securely, after infinite terror and disturbance.

His departure was effected by Nicogenes by the following artifice: the barbarous nations, and among them the Persians especially, are extremely jealous, severe, and suspicious about their wives, whom they keep so strictly that no one ever sees them abroad; they spend their lives shut up within doors, and, when they take a journey, are carried in close tents, curtained in on all sides, and set upon a wagon. Such a traveling carriage being prepared for Themistocles, they hid him in it, and carried him on his journey, and told those whom they met or spoke with upon the road that they were conveying a young Greek woman out of Ionia to a nobleman at court.

When he was introduced to the king, and had paid his reverence to him, he stood silent, till the king commanding the interpreter to ask him who he was, he replied: "O king, I am Themistocles the Athenian, driven into banishment by the Greeks. The evils that I have done to the Persians are numerous; but my benefits to them yet greater, in withholding the

Greeks from pursuit, so soon as the deliverance of my own country allowed me to show kindness also to you. I come with a mind suited to my present calamities; prepared alike for favors and for anger; to welcome your gracious reconciliation, and to deprecate your wrath. Take my own countrymen for witnesses of the services I have done for Persia, and make use of this occasion to show the world your virtue, rather than to satisfy your indignation. If you save me, you will save your suppliant; if otherwise, you will destroy an enemy of the Greeks."

In the morning, calling together the chief of his court, he had Themistocles brought before him, who expected no good of it. Yet, when he came into the presence, and again fell down, the king saluted him, and spake to him kindly, telling him he was now indebted to him two hundred talents; for it was just and reasonable that he should receive the reward which was proposed to whosoever should bring Thèmistocles; and promising much more, and encouraging him, he commanded him to speak freely what he would concerning the affairs of Greece. Themistocles replied, that a man's discourse was like to a rich Persian carpet, the beautiful figures and patterns of which can only be shown by spreading and extending it out; when it is contracted and folded up, they are obscured and lost; and, therefore, he desired time. The king being pleased with the comparison, and bidding him take what time he would, he desired a year; in which time, having learnt the Persian language sufficiently, he spoke with the king by himself without the help of an interpreter; the king invited him to partake of his own pastimes and recreations both at home and abroad, carrying him with him a-hunting, and made him his intimate so far that he permitted him to see the queen-mother, and converse frequently with her. By the king's command, he also was made acquainted with the Magian learning.

They relate, also, how Themistocles, when he was in great prosperity, and courted by many, seeing himself splendidly served at his table, turned to his children and said: "Children, we had been undone if we had not been undone." Most writers say that he had three cities given him—Magnesia, Myus and Lampsacus—to maintain him in bread, meat and wine; and some add two more, the city of Palæscepsis, to provide him with clothes, and Percote, with bedding and furniture for his house.

He lived quietly in his own house in Magnesia, where for a long time he passed his days in great security, being courted by all, and enjoying rich presents, and honored equally with the greatest persons in the Persian empire; the king, at that time, not minding his concerns with Greece, being taken up with the affairs of Inner Asia.

But when Egypt revolted, being assisted by the Athenians, and the Greek galleys roved about as far as Cyprus and Cilicia, and Cimon had made himself master of the seas, the king turned his thoughts thither, and, bending his mind chiefly to resist the Greeks, and to check the growth of their power against him, began to raise forces, and send out commanders, and to dispatch messengers to Themistocles at Magnesia, to put him in mind of his promise, and to summon him to act against the Greeks. Yet this did not increase his hatred nor exasperate him against the Athenians, but, being ashamed to sully the glory of his former great actions, and of his many victories and trophies, he determined to put a conclusion to his life, agreeable to its previous course. He sacrificed to the gods, and invited his friends; and, having entertained them and shaken hands with them, drank bull's blood, as is the usual story; as others state, a poison, producing instant death; and ended his days in the city of Magnesia, having lived sixty-five years, most of which he had spent in politics and in the wars, in government and command. The king, being informed of the cause and manner of his death, admired him more than ever, and continued to show kindness to his friends and relations.

The Magnesians possess a splendid sepulchre of Themistocles, placed in the middle of their market-place. And various honors and privileges were granted to the kindred of Themistocles at Magnesia, which were observed down to our times, and were enjoyed by another Themistocles of Athens, with whom I had an intimate acquaintance and friendship in the house of Ammonius the philosopher.

CAMILLUS

Among the many remarkable things that are related of Furius Camillus, it seems singular that he, who continually was in the highest commands, and obtained the greatest successes, was five times chosen dictator, triumphed four times, and was styled a second founder of Rome, yet never was so much as once consul. The reason of which was the state and temper of the commonwealth at that time; for the people, being at dissension with the senate, refused to return consuls, but they instead elected other magistrates, called military tribunes, who acted, indeed, with full consular power, but were thought to exercise a less obnoxious amount of authority, because it was divided among a larger number.

The house of the Furii was not, at that time, of any considerable distinction; he, by his own acts, first raised himself to honor, serving under Postumius Tubertus, dictator, in the great battle against the Æquians and Volscians. For, riding out from the rest of the army, and in the charge receiving a wound in his thigh, he for all that did not quit the fight, but, letting the dart drag in the wound, and engaging with the bravest of the enemy, put them to flight; for which action, among other rewards bestowed on him, he was created censor, an office in those days of great repute and authority. During his censorship one very good act of his is recorded, that, whereas the wars had made many widows, he obliged such as had no wives, some by fair persuasion, others by threatening to set fines on their heads, to take them in marriage; another necessary one, in causing orphans to be rated, who before were exempted from taxes, the frequent wars requiring more than ordinary expenses to maintain them. What, however, pressed them most was the siege of Veii. Some call this people Veientani. This was the head city of Tuscany, not inferior to Rome either in number of arms or multitude of soldiers, insomuch that, presuming on her wealth and luxury, and priding herself upon her refinement and sumptuousness, she engaged in many honorable contests with the Romans for glory and empire. But now they had abandoned their former ambitious hopes, having been weakened by great defeats, so that, having fortified themselves with high and strong walls, and furnished the city with all sorts of weapons offensive and defensive, as likewise with corn and all manner of provisions, they cheerfully endured a siege, which, though tedious to them, was no less troublesome and distressing to the besiegers. For the Romans, having never been accustomed to stay away from home except in summer, and for no great length of time, and constantly to winter at home, were then first compelled by the tribunes to build forts in the enemy's country, and, raising strong works about their camp, to join winter and summer together. And now, the seventh year of the war drawing to an end, the commanders began to be suspected as too slow and remiss in driving on the siege, insomuch that they were discharged and others chosen for the war, among whom was Camillus, then second time tribune. But at present he had no hand in the siege, the duties that fell by lot to him being to make war upon the Faliscans and Capenates, who, taking advantage of the Romans being occupied on all hands, had carried ravages into their country, and, through all the Tuscan war, given them much annoyance, but were now reduced by Camillus, and with great loss shut up within their walls.

And now, in the very heat of the war, a strange phenomenon in the Alban lake, which, in the absence of any known cause and explanation by natural reasons, seemed as great a prodigy as the most incredible that are reported, occasioned great alarm. It was the beginning of autumn, and the summer now ending had, to all observation, been neither rainy nor much troubled with southern winds; and of the many lakes, brooks, and springs of all sorts with which Italy abounds, some were wholly dried up, others had very little water in them; all the rivers, as is usual in summer, ran in a very low and hollow channel. But the Alban lake, which is fed by no other waters but its own, and is on all sides encircled with fruitful mountains, without any cause, unless it were divine, began visibly to rise and swell, increasing to the feet of the mountains, and by degrees reaching the level of the very tops of some of them, and all this without any waves or agitation. At first it was the wonder of shepherds and herdsmen; but when the earth, which, like a great dam, held up the lake from falling into the lower grounds, through the quantity and weight of water was broken down, and in a violent stream it ran through the ploughed fields and plantations to discharge itself in the sea, it not only struck terror into the Romans, but was thought by all the inhabitants of Italy to portend some extraordinary event. But the greatest talk of it was in the camp that besieged Veii, so that in the town itself, also, the occurrence became known.

As in long sieges it commonly happens that parties on both sides meet often and converse with one another, so it chanced that a Roman had gained much confidence and familiarity with one of the besieged, a man versed in ancient prophecies, and of repute for more than ordinary skill in divination. The Roman, observing him to be overjoyed at the story of the lake, and to mock at the siege, told him that this was not the only prodigy that of late had happened to the Romans; others more wonderful yet than this had befallen them, which he was willing to communicate to him, that he might the better provide for his private interests in these public distempers. The man greedily embraced the proposal, expecting to hear some wonderful secrets; but when, little by little, he had led him on in conversation, and insensibly drawn him a good way from the gates of the city, he snatched him up by the middle, being stronger than he, and, by the assistance of others who came running from the camp, seized and delivered him to the commanders. The man, reduced to this necessity, and sensible now that destiny was not to be avoided, discovered to them the secret oracle of Veii, that it was not possible the city should be taken until the Alban lake, which now broke forth and had found out new passages, was drawn back from that course, and so diverted that it could not mingle with the sea. The senate, having heard and satisfied themselves about the matter, decreed to send to Delphi, to ask counsel of the god. The messengers returned with the answer that the Alban water, if possible, they should keep from the sea, and shut it up in its ancient bounds; but if that was not to be done, then they should carry it off by ditches and trenches into the lower grounds, and so dry it up; which message being delivered, the priests performed what related to the sacrifices, and the people went to work and turned the water.

And now the senate, in the tenth year of the war, taking away all other commands, created Camillus dictator, who chose Cornelius Scipio for his general of horse, and, having made vows, marched into the country of the Faliscans, and in a great battle overthrew them and the Capenates, their confederates; afterwards he turned to the siege of Veii, and finding that to take it by assault would prove a difficult and hazardous attempt, proceeded to cut mines under ground, the earth about the city being easy to break up, and allowing such depth for the works as would prevent their being discovered by the enemy. This design going on in a hopeful way, he openly gave assaults to the enemy, to keep them to the walls, until they that worked underground in the mines might, without being perceived, arrive within the citadel, close to the temple of Juno, which was the greatest and most honored in all the city. It is said that the prince of the Tuscans was at that very time at sacrifice, and that the priest, after he had looked into the entrails of the beast, cried out with a loud voice that the gods would give the victory to those that should complete those offerings; and that the Romans who were in the mines, hearing the words, immediately pulled down the floor, and, ascending with noise and clashing of weapons, frightened away the enemy, and, snatching up the entrails, carried them to Camillus. But this may look like a fable. The city, however, being taken by storm, and the soldiers busied in pillaging and gathering an infinite quantity of riches and spoil, Camillus, from the high tower viewing what was done, at first wept for pity; and when the bystanders congratulated him upon his success, he lifted up his hands to heaven, and broke out into this prayer: "O most mighty Jupiter, and ye gods that are judges of good and evil actions, ye know that not without just cause, but constrained by necessity, we have been forced to revenge ourselves on the city of our unrighteous and wicked enemies. But if, in the vicissitude of things, there be any calamity due, to counterbalance this great felicity, I beg that it may be diverted from the city and army of the Romans, and fall, with as little hurt as may be, upon my own head." Having said these words, and just turning about (as the custom of the Romans is to turn to the right after adoration or prayer), he stumbled and fell, to the astonishment of all that were present. But, recovering himself presently from the fall, he told them that he had received what he had prayed for, a small mischance, in compensation for the greatest good fortune.

Camillus, however, whether puffed up with the greatness of his achievement in conquering a city that was the rival of Rome, and held out a ten years' siege, or exalted with the felicitations of those that were about him, assumed to himself more than became a civil and legal magistrate; among other things, in the pride and haughtiness of his triumph, driving through Rome in a chariot drawn with four white horses, which no general either before or since ever did; for the Romans consider such a mode of conveyance to be sacred, and specially set apart to the king and father of the gods. This alienated the hearts of his fellow-citizens, who were not accustomed to such pomp and display.

The second pique they had against him was his opposing the law by which the city was to be divided; for the tribunes of the people brought forward a motion that the people and senate should be divided into two parts, one of which should remain at home, the other, as the lot should decide, remove to the new-taken city. By which means they should not only have much more room, but, by the advantage of two great and magnificent cities, be better able to maintain their territories and their fortunes in general. The people, therefore, who were numerous and indigent, greedily embraced it, and crowded continually to the forum, with tumultuous demands to have it put to the vote. But the senate and the noblest citizens, judging the proceedings of the tribunes to tend rather to a destruction than a division of Rome, greatly averse to it, went to Camillus for assistance, who, fearing the result if it came to a direct contest, contrived to occupy the people with other business, and so staved it off. He thus became unpopular.

And now the tribunes of the people again resuming their motion for the division of the city, the war against the Faliscans luckily broke out, giving liberty to the chief citizens to choose what magistrates they pleased, and to appoint Camillus military tribune, with five colleagues; affairs then requiring a commander of authority and reputation, as well as experience. And when the people had ratified the election, he marched with his forces into the territories of the Faliscans, and laid siege to Falerii, a well-fortified city, and plentifully stored with all necessaries of war. And although he perceived it would be no small work to take it, and no little time would be required for it, yet he was willing to exercise the citizens and keep them abroad, that they might have no leisure, idling at home, to follow the tribunes in factions and seditions: a very common remedy, indeed, with the Romans, who thus carried off, like good physicians, the ill humors of their commonwealth. The Falerians,* trusting in the strength of their city, which was well fortified on all sides, made so little account of the siege, that all, with the exception of those that guarded the walls, as in times of peace, walked about the streets in their common dress; the boys went to school, and were led by their master to play and exercise about the town walls; for the Falerians, like the Greeks, used to have a single teacher for many pupils, wishing their children to live and be brought up from the beginning in each other's company.

This schoolmaster, designing to betray the Falerians by their children, led them out every day under the town wall, at first but a little way, and, when they had exercised, brought them home again. Afterwards by degrees he drew them farther and farther, till by practice he had made them bold and fearless, as if no danger was about them; and at last, having got them all together, he brought them to the outposts of the Romans, and delivered them up, demanding to be led to Camillus. Where being come, and standing in the middle, he said that he was the master and teacher of these children, but, preferring his favor before all other obligations, he had come to deliver up his charge to him, and, in that, the whole city. When Camillus had heard him out, he was astounded at the treachery of the act, and, turning to the standers-by, observed that "War, indeed, is of necessity attended with much injustice and violence! Certain laws, however, all good men observe even in war itself, nor is victory so great an object as to induce us to incur for its sake obligations for base and impious acts. A great general should rely on his own virtue, and not on other men's vices." Which said, he commanded the officers to tear off the man's clothes, and bind his hands behind him, and give the boys rods and scourges, to punish the traitor and drive him back to the city. By this time the Falerians had discovered the treachery

---

* The Falerians, in this narrative, are the people of the town; the Faliscans, the nation in general.

of the schoolmaster, and the city, as was likely, was full of lamentations and cries for their calamity, men and women of worth running in distraction about the walls and gates; when, behold, the boys came whipping their master on, naked and bound, calling Camillus their preserver and god and father; so that it struck not only the parents, but the rest of the citizens, with such admiration and love of Camillus's justice, that, immediately meeting in assembly, they sent ambassadors to him, to resign whatever they had to his disposal. Camillus sent them to Rome, where, being brought into the senate, they spoke to this purpose: that the Romans, preferring justice before victory, had taught them rather to embrace submission than liberty; they did not so much confess themselves to be inferior in strength as they must acknowledge them to be superior in virtue. The senate remitted the whole matter to Camillus, to judge and order as he thought fit; who, taking a sum of money of the Falerians, and making a peace with the whole nation of the Faliscans, returned home.

But the soldiers, who had expected to have the pillage of the city, when they came to Rome empty-handed railed against Camillus among their fellow-citizens, as a hater of the people, and one that grudged all advantage to the poor. The people were exasperated against him, and it was plain they would take hold of any occasion to condemn him. Gathering, therefore, together his friends and fellow-soldiers, and such as had borne command with him, a considerable number in all, he besought them that they would not suffer him to be unjustly overborne by shameful accusations, and left the mock and scorn of his enemies. His friends, having advised and consulted among themselves, made answer, that, as to the sentence, they did not see how they could help him, but that they would contribute to whatsoever fine should be set upon him. Not able to endure so great an indignity, he resolved in his anger to leave the city and go into exile; and so, having taken leave of his wife and son, he went silently to the gate of the city, and, there stopping and turning round, stretched out his hands to the Capitol, and prayed to the gods, that if, without any fault of his own, but merely through the malice and violence of the people, he was driven out into banishment, the Romans might quickly repent of it; and that all mankind might witness their need for the assistance, and desire for the return, of Camillus.

And there is not a Roman but believes that immediately upon the prayers of Camillus a sudden judgment followed, and that he received a revenge for the injustice done unto him, which was very remarkable, and noised over the whole world: such a punishment visited the city of Rome, an era of such loss and danger and disgrace so quickly succeeded; whether it thus fell out by fortune, or it be the office of some god not to see injured virtue go unavenged.

The first token that seemed to threaten some mischief to ensue was the death of the censor Julius; for the Romans have a religious reverence for the office of a censor, and esteem it sacred. The second was, that, just before Camillus went into exile, Marcus Cædicius, a person of no great distinction, nor of the rank of senator, but esteemed a good and respectable man, reported to the military tribunes a thing worthy their consideration: that, going along the night before in the street called the New Way, and being called by somebody in a loud voice, he turned about, but could see no one, but heard a voice greater than human, which said these words, "Go, Marcus Cædicius, and early in the morning tell the military tribunes that they are shortly to expect the Gauls." But the tribunes made a mock and sport with the story, and a little after came Camillus's banishment.

The Gauls are of the Celtic race, and are reported to have been compelled by their numbers to leave their country, which was insufficient to sustain them all, and to have gone in search of other homes. And being, many thousands of them, young men and able to bear arms, and carrying with them a still greater number of women and young children, some of them passing the Riphæan mountains, fell upon the Northern Ocean, and possessed themselves of the farthest parts of Europe; others, seating themselves between the Pyrenean mountains and the Alps, lived there a considerable time, near to the Senones and Celtorii; but, afterwards tasting wine, which was then first brought them out of Italy, they were all so much taken with the liquor, and transported with the hitherto unknown delight, that, snatching up their arms and taking their families along with them, they marched directly to the Alps, to find out the country which yielded such fruit, pronouncing all others barren and useless. He that first brought wine among them and was the chief instigator of their coming into Italy is said to have been one Aruns, a Tuscan, a man of noble extraction.

At their first coming they at once possessed themselves of all that country which anciently the Tuscans inhabited, reaching from the Alps to both the seas, as the names themselves testify; for the North or Adriatic Sea is named from the Tuscan city Adria, and that to the south the Tuscan Sea simply. The whole country is rich in fruit trees, has excellent pasture, and is well watered with rivers. It had eighteen large and beautiful cities, well provided with all the means for industry and wealth, and all the enjoyments and pleasures of life. The Gauls cast out the Tuscans, and seated themselves in them.

The Gauls at this time were besieging Clusium, a Tuscan city. The Clusinians sent to the Romans for succor, desiring them to interpose with the barbarians by letters and ambassadors. The Romans, perceiving that Brennus, the leader of the Gauls, was not to be treated with, went into Clusium and encouraged the inhabitants to make a sally with them upon the barbarians, which they did either to try their strength or to show their own. The sally being made, and the fight growing hot about the walls, one of the Fabii, Quintus Ambustus, who had come as an ambassador, being well mounted, and setting spurs to his horse, made full against a Gaul, a man of huge bulk and stature, whom he saw riding out at a distance from the rest. At the first he was not recognized, through the quickness of the conflict and the glittering of his armor, that precluded any view of him; but when he had overthrown the Gaul, and was going to gather the spoils, Brennus knew him; and, invoking the gods to be witnesses that, contrary to the known and common law of nations, which is holily observed by all mankind, he who had come as an ambassador had now engaged in hostility against him, he drew off his men, and, bidding Clusium farewell, led his army directly against Rome.

Whilst the barbarians were hastening with all speed, the millitary tribunes brought the Romans into the field to be ready to engage them, being not inferior to the Gauls in number (for they were no less than forty thousand foot), but most of them raw soldiers, and such as had never handled a weapon before. Besides, they had wholly neglected all religious usages, had not obtained favorable sacrifices, nor made inquiries of the prophets, natural in danger and before battle. No less did the multitude of commanders distract and confound their proceedings; frequently before, upon less occasions, they had chosen a single leader, with the title of dictator, being sensible of what great importance it is in critical times to have the soldiers united under one general with the entire and absolute control placed in his hands. Add to all, the remembrance of Camillus's treatment, which made it now seem a dangerous thing for officers to command without humoring their soldiers. In this condition they left the city, and encamped by the river Allia, about ten miles from Rome, and not far from the place where it falls into the Tiber; and here the Gauls came upon them, and, after a disgraceful resistance, devoid of order and discipline, they were miserably defeated. The left wing was immediately driven into the river, and there destroyed; the right had less damage by declining the shock, and from the low grounds getting to the tops of the hills, from whence most of them afterwards dropped into the city; the rest, as many as escaped, the enemy being weary of the slaughter, stole by night to Veii, giving up Rome and all that was in it for lost.

This battle was fought about the summer solstice, the moon being at full, the very same day in which the sad disaster of the Fabii had happened, when three hundred of that name were at one time cut off by the Tuscans.

And now, after the battle, had the Gauls immediately pursued those that fled, there had been no remedy but Rome must have wholly been ruined, and all those who remained in it utterly destroyed; such was the terror that those who escaped the battle brought with them into the city, and with such distraction and confusion were they themselves in turn infected. But the Gauls, not imagining their victory to be so considerable, and overtaken with the present joy, fell to feasting and dividing the spoil, by which means they gave leisure to those who were for leaving the city to make their escape, and to those that remained, to anticipate and prepare for their coming.

On the third day after the battle, Brennus appeared with his army at the city, and, finding the gates wide open and no guards upon the walls, first began to suspect it was some design or stratagem, never dreaming that the Romans were in so desperate a condition. But when he found it to be so indeed, he entered at the Colline gate, and took Rome, in the three hundred and sixtieth year, or a little more, after it was built.

Brennus having taken possession of Rome, set a strong guard about the Capitol, and, going himself down into the forum, was there struck with amazement at the sight of so many men sitting in such order and silence, observing that they neither rose at his coming, nor so much as changed color or countenance, but remained without fear or concern, leaning upon their staves, and sitting quietly, looking at each other. The Gauls, for a great while, stood wondering at the strangeness of the sight, not daring to approach or touch them, taking them for an assembly of superior beings. But when one, bolder than the rest, drew near to Marcus Papirius, and, putting forth his hand, gently touched his chin and stroked his long beard, Papirius with his staff struck him a severe blow on the head; upon which the barbarian drew his sword and slew him. This was the introduction to the slaughter; for the rest, following his example, set upon them all and killed them, and dispatched all others that came in their way; and so went on to the sacking and pillaging of the houses, which they continued for many days ensuing.

Camillus then sojourned in the city of Ardea, having, ever since his leaving Rome, sequestered himself from all business, and taken to a private life; but now he began to rouse up himself, and consider not how to avoid or escape the enemy, but to find out an opportunity to be revenged upon them. And perceiving that the Ardeatians wanted not men, but rather enterprise, through the inexperience and timidity of their officers, he began to speak with the young men, first to the effect that they ought not to ascribe the misfortune of the Romans to the courage of their enemy, nor attribute the losses they sustained by rash counsel to the conduct of men who had no title to victory: the event had been only an evidence of the power of fortune. When he found the young men embraced the thing, he went to the magistrates and council of the city, and, having persuaded them also, he mustered all that could bear arms, and drew them up within the walls, that they might not be perceived by the enemy, who was near; who, having scoured the country, and now returned heavy laden with booty, lay encamped in the plains in a careless and negligent posture, so that, with the night ensuing upon debauch and drunkenness, silence prevailed through all the camp. When Camillus learned this from his scouts, he drew out the Ardeatians, and in the dead of the night, passing in silence over the ground that lay between, came up to their works, and, commanding his trumpets to sound and his men to shout and halloo, he struck terror into them from all quarters; while drunkenness impeded and sleep retarded their movements. A few whom fear had sobered, getting into some order, for awhile resisted; and so died with their weapons in their hands. But the greatest part of them, buried in wine and sleep, were surprised without their arms, and dispatched; and as many of them as by the advantage of the night got out of the camp were the next day found scattered abroad and wandering in the fields, and were picked up by the horse that pursued them.

The fame of this action soon flew through the neighboring cities, and stirred up the young men from various quarters to come and join themselves with him. But none were so much concerned as those Romans who escaped in the battle of Allia, and were now at Veii, thus lamenting with themselves, "O heavens, what a commander has Providence bereaved Rome of, to honor Ardea with his actions! And that city, which brought forth and nursed so great a man, is lost and gone, and we, destitute of a leader and shut up within strange walls, sit idle, and see Italy ruined before our eyes. Come, let us send to the Ardeatians to have back our general, or else, with weapons in our hands, let us go thither to him." To this they all agreed, and sent to Camillus to desire him to take the command; but he answered that he would not until they that were in the Capitol should legally appoint him. When this answer was returned, they admired the modesty and temper of Camillus; but they could not tell how to find a messenger to carry the intelligence to the Capitol, or rather, indeed, it seemed altogether impossible for any one to get to the citadel whilst the enemy was in full possession of the city. But among the young men there was one Pontius Cominius, of ordinary birth, but ambitious of honor, who proffered himself to run the hazard, and took no letters with him to those in the Capitol, lest, if he were intercepted, the enemy might learn the intentions of Camillus; but, putting on a poor dress and carrying corks under it, he boldly traveled the greatest part of the way by day, and came to the city when it was dark; the bridge he could not pass, as it was guarded by the barbarians; so that taking his clothes, which were neither many nor heavy, and binding them about his head, he laid his body upon the corks, and, swimming with them, got over to the city. And avoiding those quarters where he perceived the enemy was awake, which he guessed at by the lights and noise, he went to the Carmental gate, where there was greatest silence, and where the hill of the Capitol is steepest, and rises with craggy and broken rock. By this way he got up, though with much difficulty, by the hollow of the cliff, and presented himself to the guards, saluting them, and telling them his name; he was taken in, and carried to the commanders. And a senate being immediately called, he related to them in order the victory of Camillus, which they had not heard of before, and the proceedings of the soldiers, urging them to confirm Camillus in the command, as on him alone all their fellow-countrymen outside the city would rely. Having heard and consulted of the matter, the senate declared Camillus dictator, and sent back Pontius the same way that he came, who, with the same success as before, got through the enemy without being discovered, and delivered to the Romans outside the decision of the senate, who joyfully received it. Camillus, on his arrival, found twenty thousand of them ready in arms; with which forces, and those confederates he brought along with him, he prepared to set upon the enemy.

But at Rome some of the barbarians passing by chance near the place at which Pontius by night had got into the Capitol, spied in several places marks of feet and hands, where he had laid hold and clambered, and places where the plants that grew to the rock had been rubbed off, and the earth had slipped, and went accordingly and reported it to the king, who, coming in person, and viewing it, for the present said nothing, but in the evening, picking out such of the Gauls as were nimblest of body, and by living in the mountains were accustomed to climb, he said to them, "The enemy themselves have shown us a way how to come at them; where it was easy for one man to get up, it will not be hard for many, one after another; nay, when many shall undertake it, they will be aid and strength to each other. Rewards and honors shall be bestowed on every man as he shall acquit himself."

When the king had thus spoken, the Gauls cheerfully undertook to perform it, and in the dead of night a good party of them together, with great silence, began to climb the rock. clinging to the precipitous and difficult ascent, which yet upon trial offered a way to them, and proved less difficult than they had expected. So that the foremost of them having gained the top of all, and put themselves into order, they all but surprised the outworks, and mastered the watch, who were fast asleep; for neither man nor dog perceived their coming. But there were sacred geese kept near the temple of Juno, which at other times were plentifully fed, but now, by reason that corn and all other provisions were grown scarce for all, were in but a poor condition. The creature is by nature of quick sense, and apprehensive of the least noise, so that these, being moreover watchful through hunger, and restless, immediately discovered the coming of the Gauls, and, running up and down with their noise and cackling, they raised the whole camp; while the barbarians, on the other side, perceiving themselves discovered, no longer endeavored to conceal their attempt, but with shouting and violence advanced to the assault. The Romans, every one in haste snatching up the first weapon that came to hand, did what they could on the sudden occasion. Manlius, a man of consular dignity, of strong body and great spirit, was the first that made head against them, and, engaging with two of the enemy at once, with his sword cut off the right arm of one just as he was lifting up his blade to strike, and, running his target full in the face of the other, tumbled him headlong down the steep rock; then mounting the rampart, and there standing with others that came running to his assistance, drove down the rest of them, who, indeed, to begin with, had not been many, and did nothing worthy of so bold an attempt. The Romans, having thus escaped this danger, early in the morning took the captain of the watch and flung him down the rock upon the heads of their enemies, and to Manlius for his victory voted a reward, intended more for honor than advantage, bringing him, each man of them, as much as he received for his daily allowance, which was half a pound of bread and one eighth of a pint of wine.

Henceforward, the affairs of the Gauls were daily in a worse and worse condition; they wanted provisions, being withheld from foraging through fear of Camillus, and sickness also was amongst them, occasioned by the number of carcasses that lay in heaps unburied. Neither, indeed, were things on that account any better with the besieged, for famine increased upon them, and despondency with not hearing anything of Camillus, it being impossible to send any one to him, the city was so guarded by the barbarians. Things being in this sad condition on both sides, a motion of treaty was made at first by some of the outposts, as they happened to speak with one another; which being embraced by the leading men, Sulpicius, tribune of the Romans, came to a parley with Brennus, in which it was agreed that the Romans laying down a thousand weight of gold, the Gauls upon the receipt of it should immediately quit the city and territories. The agreement being confirmed by oath on both sides, and the gold brought forth, the Gauls used false dealing in the weights, secretly at first, but afterwards openly pulled back and disturbed the balance; at which the Romans indignantly complaining, Brennus in a scoffing and insulting manner pulled off his sword and belt, and threw them both into the scales; and when Sulpicius asked what that meant, "What should it mean," says he, "but woe to the conquered?" which afterwards became a proverbial saying.

Whilst this difference remained still unsettled, both amongst themselves and with the Gauls, Camillus was at the gates with his army; and, having learned what was going on, commanded the main body of his forces to follow slowly after him in good order, and himself with the choicest of his men hastening on, went at once to the Romans; where all giving way to him, and receiving him as their sole magistrate, with profound silence and order, he took the gold out of the scales, and delivered it to his officers, and commanded the Gauls to take their weights and scales and depart; saying that it was customary with the Romans to deliver their country with iron, not with gold. And when Brennus began to rage, and say that he was unjustly dealt with in such a breach of contract, Camillus answered that it was never legally made, and the agreement of no force or obligation; for that himself being declared dictator, and there being no other magistrate by law, the engagement had been made with men who had no power to enter into it; but now they might say anything they had to urge, for he had come with full power by law to grant pardon to such as should ask it, or inflict punishment on the guilty, if they did not repent. At this, Brennus broke into violent anger, and an immediate quarrel ensued; both sides drew their swords and attacked, but in confusion, as could not otherwise be amongst houses, and in narrow lanes and places where it was impossible to form in any order. But Brennus, presently recollecting himself, called off his men, and, with the loss of a few only, brought them to their camp; and, rising in the night with all his forces, left the city, and, advancing about eight miles, encamped upon the way to Gabii. As soon as day appeared, Camillus came up with him, splendidly armed himself, and his soldiers full of courage and confidence; and there engaging with him in a sharp conflict, which lasted a long while, overthrew his army with great slaughter, and took their camp. Of those that fled, some were presently cut off by the pursuers; others, and these were the greatest number, dispersed hither and thither, and were despatched by the people that came sallying out from the neighboring towns and villages.

Thus Rome was strangely taken, and more strangely recovered, having been seven whole months in the possession of the barbarians, who entered her a little after the Ides of July, and were driven out about the Ides of February following. Camillus triumphed, as he deserved, having saved his country that was lost, and brought the city, so to say, back again to itself. For those that had fled abroad, together with their wives and children, accompanied him as he rode in; and those who had been shut up in the Capitol, and were reduced almost to the point of perishing with hunger, went out to meet him, embracing each other as they met, and weeping for joy, and, through the excess of the present pleasure, scarcely believing in its truth.

It was a hard task, amidst so much rubbish, to discover and re-determine the consecrated places; but by the zeal of Camillus, and the incessant labor of the priests, it was at last accomplished. But when it came also to rebuilding the city, which was wholly demolished, despondency seized the multitude, and a backwardness to engage in a work for which they had no materials. The senate, therefore, fearing a sedition, would not suffer Camillus, though desirous, to lay down his authority within the year, though no other dictator had ever held it above six months.

Camillus thought good to refer the matter of rebuilding to general deliberation, and himself spoke largely and earnestly in behalf of his country, as also many others. At last, calling to Lucius Lucretius, whose place it was to speak first, he commanded him to give his sentence, and the rest as they followed, in order. Silence being made, and Lucretius just about to begin, by chance a centurion, passing by outside with his company of the day-guard, called out with a loud voice to the ensign-bearer to halt and fix his standard, for this was the best place to stay in. This voice, coming in that moment of time, and at that crisis of uncertainty and anxiety for the future, was taken as a direction what was to be done; so that Lucretius, assuming an attitude of devotion, gave sentence in concurrence with the gods, as he said, as likewise did all that followed. Even among the common people it created a wonderful change of feeling: every one now cheered and encouraged his neighbor, and set himself to the work, proceeding in it, however, not by any regular lines or divisions, but every one pitching upon that plot of ground which came next to hand, or best pleased his fancy; by which haste and hurry in building they constructed their city in narrow and ill-designed lanes, and with houses huddled together one upon another; for it is said that within the compass of the year the whole city was raised up anew, both in its public walls and private buildings.

And now they had scarcely got a breathing time from their trouble when a new war came upon them; and the Æquians, Volscians, and Latins all at once invaded their territories, and the Tuscans besieged Sutrium, their confederate city. Camillus, being the third time chosen dictator, armed not only those under, but also those over, the age of service; and taking a large circuit around the mountain Mæcius, undiscovered by the enemy, lodged his army on their rear, and then by many fires gave notice of his arrival. The besieged, encouraged by this, prepared to sally forth and join battle; but the Latins and Volscians, fearing this exposure to an enemy on both sides, drew themselves within their works, and fortified their camp with a strong palisade of trees on every side, resolving to wait for more supplies from home, and expecting, also, the assistance of the Tuscans, their confederates. Camillus, detecting their object, and fearing to be reduced to the same position to which he had brought them, namely, to be besieged himself, resolved to lose no time; and finding their rampart was all of timber, and observing that a strong wind constantly at sun-rising blew off from the mountains, after having prepared a quantity of combustibles, about break of day he drew forth his forces, commanding a part with their missiles to assault the enemy with noise and shouting on the other quarter, whilst he, with those that were to fling in the fire, went to that side of the enemy's camp to which the wind usually blew, and there waited his opportunity. When the skirmish was begun, and the sun risen, and a strong wind set in from the mountains, he gave the signal of onset; and, heaping in an immense quantity of fiery matter, filled all their rampart with it, so that the flame being fed by the close timber and wooden palisades, went on and spread into all quarters. The Latins, having nothing ready to keep it off or extinguish it, when the camp was now almost full of fire, were driven back within a very small compass, and at last forced by necessity to come into their enemy's hands, who stood before the works ready armed and prepared to receive them; of these very few escaped, while those that stayed in the camp were all a prey to the fire, until the Romans, to gain the pillage, extinguished it.

These things performed, Camillus, leaving his son Lucius in the camp to guard the prisoners and secure the booty, passed into the enemy's country, where, having taken the city of the Æquians and reduced the Volscians to obedience, he then immediately led his army to Sutrium, not having heard what had befallen the Sutrians, but making haste to assist them, as if they were still in danger and besieged by the Tuscans. They, however, had already surrendered their city to their enemies, and destitute of all things, with nothing left but their clothes, met Camillus on the way, leading their wives and children, and bewailing their misfortune. Camillus himself was struck with compassion, and perceiving the soldiers weeping, and commiserating their case, while the Sutrians hung about and clung to them, resolved not to defer revenge, but that very day to lead his army to Sutrium; conjecturing that the enemy, having just taken a rich and plentiful city, without an enemy left within it, nor any from without to be expected, would be found abandoned to enjoyment, and unguarded. Neither did his opinion fail him: he not only passed through their country without discovery, but came up to their very gates and possessed himself of the walls, not a man being left to guard them, but their whole army scattered about in the houses, drinking and making merry. Nay, when at last they did perceive that the enemy had seized the city, they were so overloaded with meat and wine that few were able so much as to endeavor to escape, but either waited shamefully for their death within doors, or surrendered themselves to the conqueror. Thus the city of the Sutrians was twice taken in one day; and they who were in possession lost it, and they who had lost regained it, alike by the means of Camillus. For all which actions he received a triumph which brought him no less honor and reputation than the two former ones; for those citizens who before most regarded him with an evil eye, and ascribed his successes to a certain luck rather than real merit, were compelled by these last acts of his to allow the whole honor to his great abilities and energy.

Of all the adversaries and enviers of his glory, Marcus Manlius was the most distinguished, he who first drove back the Gauls when they made their night attack upon the Capitol, and who for that reason had been named Capitolinus. This man, affecting the first place in the commonwealth, and not able by noble ways to outdo Camillus's reputation, took that ordinary course toward usurpation of absolute power, namely, to gain the multitude, those of them especially that were in debt; defending some by pleading their causes against their creditors, rescuing others by force, and not suffering the law to proceed against them; insomuch that in a short time he got great numbers of indigent people about him, whose tumults and uproars in the forum struck terror into the principal citizens. After that Quintius Capitolinus, who was made dictator to suppress these disorders, had committed Manlius to prison, the people immediately changed their apparel, a thing never done but in great and public calamities, and the senate, fearing some tumult, ordered him to be released. He, however, when set at liberty, changed not his course, but was rather the more insolent in his proceedings, filling the whole city with faction and sedition. They chose, therefore, Camillus again military tribune; and a day being appointed for Manlius to answer to his charge, the prospect from the place where his trial was held proved a great impediment to his accusers; for the very spot where Manlius by night fought with the Gauls overlooked the forum from the Capitol, so that, stretching forth his hands that way, and weeping, he called to their remembrance his past actions, raising compassion in all that beheld him. Insomuch that the judges were at a loss what to do, and several times adjourned the trial, unwilling to acquit him of the crime, which was sufficiently proved, and yet unable to execute the law while his noble action remained, as it were, before their eyes. Camillus, considering this, transferred the court outside the gates to the Peteline Grove, from whence there is no prospect of the Capitol. Here his accuser went on with his charge, and his judges were capable of remembering and duly resenting his guilty deeds. He was convicted, carried to the Capitol, and flung headlong from the rock; so that one and the same spot was thus the witness of his greatest glory, and monument of his most unfortunate end. The Romans, besides, razed his house, and built there a temple to the goddess they call Moneta, ordaining for the future that none of the patrician order should ever dwell on the Capitoline.

And now Camillus, being called to his sixth tribuneship, desired to be excused, as being aged, and perhaps not unfearful of the malice of fortune, and those reverses which seem to ensue upon great prosperity. But the most apparent pretence was the weakness of his body, for he happened at that time to be sick; the people, however, would admit of no excuses, but, crying that they wanted not his strength for horse or for foot service, but only his counsel and conduct, constrained him to undertake the command, and with one of his fellow-tribunes to lead the army immediately against the enemy. These were the Prænestines and Volscians, who, with large forces, were laying waste the territory of the Roman confederates. Having marched out with his army, he sat down and encamped near the enemy, meaning himself to protract the war, or if there should come any necessity or occasion of fighting, in the meantime to regain his strength. But Lucius Furius, his colleague, carried away with the desire of glory, was not to be held in, but, impatient to give battle, inflamed the inferior officers of the army with the same eagerness; so that Camillus, fearing he might seem out of envy to be wishing to rob the young man of the glory of a noble exploit, consented, though unwillingly, that he should draw out the forces, whilst himself, by reason of weakness, stayed behind with a few in the camp. Lucius, engaging rashly, was discomfited, when Camillus, perceiving the Romans to give ground and fly, could not contain himself, but, leaping from his bed, with those he had about him ran to meet them at the gates of the camp, making his way through the flyers to oppose the pursuers; so that those who had got within the camp turned back at once and followed him, and those that came flying from without made head again and gathered about him, exhorting one another not to forsake their general. Thus the enemy, for that time, was stopped in his pursuit. The next day Camillus, drawing out his forces and joining battle with them, overthrew them by main force, and, following close upon them, entered pell-mell with them into their camp, and took it, slaying the greatest part of them. Afterwards, having heard that the city of Satricum was taken by the Tuscans, and the inhabitants, all Romans, put to the sword, he sent home to Rome the main body of his forces and heaviest-armed, and, taking with him the lightest and most vigorous soldiers, set suddenly upon the Tuscans, who were in the possession of the city, and mastered them, slaying some and expelling the rest; and so, returning to Rome with great spoils, gave signal evidence of their superior wisdom, who, not mistrusting the weakness and age of a commander endowed with courage and conduct, had rather chosen him who was sickly and desirous to be excused, than younger men who were forward and ambitious to command.

When, therefore, the revolt of the Tusculans was reported, they gave Camillus the charge of reducing them, choosing one of his five colleagues to go with him. And when every one was eager for the place, contrary to the expectation of all, he passed by the rest and chose Lucius Furius, the very same man who lately, against the judgment of Camillus, had rashly hazarded and nearly lost a battle; willing, as it should seem, to dissemble that miscarriage, and free him from the shame of it. The Tusculans, hearing of Camillus's coming against them, made a cunning attempt at revoking their act of revolt; their fields, as in times of highest peace, were full of ploughmen and shepherds; their gates stood wide open, and their children were being taught in the schools; of the people, such as were tradesmen, he found in their workshops, busied about their several employments, and the better sort of citizens walking in the public places in their ordinary dress; the magistrates hurried about to provide quarters for the Romans, as if they stood in fear of no danger and were conscious of no fault. Which arts, though they could not dispossess Camillus of the conviction he had of their treason, yet induced some compassion for their repentance; he commanded them to go to the senate and deprecate their anger, and joined himself as an intercessor in their behalf, so that their city was acquitted of all guilt and admitted to Roman citizenship. These were the most memorable actions of his sixth tribuneship.

After these things, Licinius Stolo raised a great sedition in the city, and brought the people to dissension with the senate, contending, that of two consuls one should be chosen out of the commons, and not both out of the patricians. Tribunes of the people were chosen, but the election of consuls was interrupted and prevented by the people. And as this absence of any supreme magistrate was leading to yet further confusion, Camillus was the fourth time created dictator by the senate, sorely against the people's will, and not altogether in accordance with his own; he had little desire for a conflict with men whose past services entitled them to tell him that he had achieved far greater actions in war along with them than in politics with the patricians, who, indeed, had only put him forward now out of envy; that, if successful, he might crush the people, or, failing, be crushed himself. However, to provide as good a remedy as he could for the present, knowing the day on which the tribunes of the people intended to prefer the law, he appointed it by proclamation for a general muster, and called the people from the forum into the Campus, threatening to set heavy fines upon such as should not obey. On the other side, the tribunes of the people met his threats by solemnly protesting they would fine him in fifty thousand drachmas of silver, if he persisted in obstructing the people from giving their suffrages for the law. Whether it were, then, that he feared another banishment or condemnation, which would ill become his age and past great actions, or found himself unable to stem the current of the multitude, which ran strong and violent, he betook himself, for the present, to his house, and afterwards, for some days together, professing sickness, finally laid down his dictatorship. The senate created another dictator; who, choosing Stolo, leader of the sedition, to be his general of horse, suffered that law to be enacted and ratified, which was most grievous to the patricians, namely, that no person whatsoever should possess above five hundred acres of land. Stolo was much distinguished by the victory he had gained; but, not long after was found himself to possess more than he had allowed to others, and suffered the penalties of his own law.

And now the contention about election of consuls coming on (which was the main point and original cause of the dissension, and had throughout furnished most matter of division between the senate and the people), certain intelligence arrived, that the Gauls again, proceeding from the Adriatic Sea, were marching in vast numbers upon Rome. On the very heels of the report followed manifest acts also of hostility; the country through which they marched was all wasted, and such as by flight could not make their escape to Rome were dispersing and scattering among the mountains. The terror of this war quieted the sedition; nobles and commons, senate and people together, unanimously chose Camillus the fifth time dictator; who, though very aged, not wanting much of fourscore years, yet, considering the danger and necessity of his country, did not, as before, pretend sickness, or depreciate his own capacity, but at once undertook the charge, and enrolled soldiers. And, knowing that the great force of the barbarians lay chiefly in their swords, with which they laid about them in a rude and inartificial manner, hacking and hewing the head and shoulders, he caused head-pieces entire of iron to be made for most of his men, smoothing and polishing the outside, that the enemy's swords, lighting upon them, might either slide off or be broken; and fitted also their shields with a little rim of brass, the wood itself not being sufficient to bear off the blows. Besides, he taught his soldiers to use their long javelins in close encounter, and, by bringing them under their enemy's swords, to receive their strokes upon them.

When the Gauls drew near, about the river Anio, dragging a heavy camp after them, and loaded with infinite spoil, Camillus drew forth his forces, and planted himself upon a hill of easy ascent, and which had many dips in it, with the object that the greatest part of his army might lie concealed, and those who appeared might be thought to have betaken themselves, through fear, to those upper grounds. And the more to increase this opinion in them, he suffered them, without any disturbance, to spoil and pillage even to his very trenches, keeping himself quiet within his works, which were well fortified ; till, at last, perceiving that part of the enemy were scattered about the country foraging, and that those that were in the camp did nothing day and night but drink and revel, in the night time he drew up his lightest-armed men, and sent them out before to impede the enemy while forming into order, and to harass them when they should first issue out of their camp ; and early in the morning brought down his main body, and set them in battle array in the lower grounds, a numerous and courageous army, not, as the barbarians had supposed, an inconsiderable and fearful division. The first thing that shook the courage of the Gauls was, that their enemies had, contrary to their expectation, the honor of being aggressors. In the next place, the light-armed men, falling upon them before they could get into their usual order or range themselves in their proper squadrons, so disturbed and pressed upon them, that they were obliged to fight at random, without any order at all. But at last, when Camillus brought on his heavy-armed legions, the barbarians, with their swords drawn, went vigorously to engage them; the Romans, however, opposing their javelins, and receiving the force of their blows on those parts of their defences which were well guarded with steel, turned the edge of their weapons, being made of a soft and ill-tempered metal, so that their swords bent and doubled up in their hands; and their shields were pierced through and through, and grew heavy with the javelins that stuck upon them. And thus forced to quit their own weapons, they endeavored to take advantage of those of their enemies, laid hold of the javelins with their hands, and tried to pluck them away. But the Romans, perceiving them now naked and defenceless, betook themselves to their swords, which they so well used, that in a little time great slaughter was made in the foremost ranks, while the rest fled over all parts of the level country ; the hills and upper grounds Camillus had secured beforehand, and their camp they knew it would not be difficult for the enemy to take, as, through confidence of victory, they had left it unguarded. This fight, it is stated, was thirteen years after the sacking of Rome; and from henceforward the Romans took courage, and surmounted the apprehensions they had hitherto entertained of the barbarians, whose previous defeat they had attributed rather to pestilence and a concurrence of mischances than to their own superior valor. And, indeed, this fear had been formerly so great, that they made a law, that priests should be excused from service in war, unless in an invasion from the Gauls.

This was the last military action that Camillus ever performed; for the voluntary surrender of the city of the Velitrani was but a mere accessory to it. But the greatest of all civil contests, and the hardest to be managed, was still to be fought out against the people; who, returning home full of victory and success, insisted, contrary to established law, to have one of the consuls chosen out of their own body. The senate strongly opposed it, and would not suffer Camillus to lay down his dictatorship, thinking, that, under the shelter of his great name and authority, they should be better able to contend for the power of the aristocracy. But when Camillus was sitting upon the tribunal, dispatching public affairs, an officer, sent by the tribunes of the people, commanded him to rise and follow him, laying his hand upon him, as ready to seize and carry him away; upon which, such a noise and tumult as was never heard before, filled the whole forum; some that were about Camillus thrusting the officer from the bench, and the multitude below calling out to him to bring Camillus down. Being at a loss what to do in these difficulties, he yet laid not down his authority, but, taking the senators along with him, he went to the senate-house; but before he entered, besought the gods that they would bring these troubles to a happy conclusion, solemnly vowing, when the tumult was ended, to build a temple to Concord. A great conflict of opposite opinions arose in the senate; but, at last, the most moderate and most acceptable to the people prevailed, and consent was given, that of two consuls, one should be chosen from the commonalty. When the dictator proclaimed this determination of the senate to the people, at the moment pleased and reconciled with the senate, as they could not well otherwise be, they accompanied Camillus home with all expressions and acclamations of joy; and the next day, assembling together, they voted a temple of Concord to be built, according to Camillus's vow, facing the assembly and the forum; and to the feasts, called the Latin holidays, they added one day more, making four in all; and ordained that, on the present occasion the whole people of Rome should sacrifice with garlands on their heads.

In the election of consuls held by Camillus, Marcus Æmilius was chosen of the patricians, and Lucius Sextius the first of the commonalty; and this was the last of all Camillus's actions. In the year following, a pestilential sickness infected Rome, which, besides an infinite number of the common people, swept away most of the magistrates, among whom was Camillus; whose death cannot be called premature, if we consider his great age, or greater actions, yet was he more lamented than all the rest put together that then died of that distemper.

PERICLES.

WE are inspired by acts of virtue with an emulation and eagerness that may lead on to imitation. In other things there does not immediately follow upon the admiration and

RESTORATION OF THE WEST END OF THE ACROPOLIS.

liking of the thing done, any strong desire of doing the like. Nay, many times, on the very contrary, when we are pleased with the work, we slight and set little by the workman or artist himself, as, for instance, in perfumes and purple dyes, we are taken

ATHENS FROM MOUNT HYMETTUS.

with the things themselves well enough, but do not think dyers and perfumers otherwise than low and sordid people. It was not said amiss by Antisthenes, when people told him that one Ismenias was an excellent piper, "It may be so, but he is but a wretched human being, otherwise he would not have been an excellent piper." And King Philip, to the same purpose, told his son Alexander, who once at a merry meeting played a piece of music charmingly and skillfully, "Are you not ashamed, my son, to play so well?" For it is enough for a king or prince to find leisure sometimes to hear others sing, and he does the muses quite honor enough when he pleases to be but present, while others engage in such exercises and trials of skill.

He who busies himself in mean occupations produces, in the very pains he takes about things of little or no use, an evidence against himself of his negligence and indisposition to what is really good. Nor did any generous and ingenuous young man, at the sight of the statue of Jupiter at Pisa, ever desire to be a Phidias, or, on seeing that of Juno at Argos, long to be a Polycletus, or feel induced by his pleasure in their poems to wish to be an Anacreon or Philetas or Archilochus. But virtue, by the bare statement of its actions, can so affect men's minds as to create at once both admiration of the things done and desire to imitate the doers of them. The goods of fortune we would possess and would enjoy; those of virtue we long to practice and exercise; we are content to receive the former from others the latter we wish others to experience from us.

And so we have thought fit to spend our time and pains in writing of the lives of famous persons; and have composed this tenth book upon that subject, containing the life of Pericles, and that of Fabius Maximus, who carried on the war against Hannibal, men alike, as in their other virtues and good parts, so especially in their mild and upright temper and demeanor, and in that capacity to bear the cross-grained humors of their fellow-citizens and colleagues in office which made them both most useful and serviceable to the interests of their countries. Whether we take a right aim at our intended purpose, it is left to the reader to judge by what he shall here find.

Pericles was of the tribe Acamantis, and the township Cholargus, of the noblest birth both on his father's and mother's side. Xanthippus, his father, who defeated the king of Persia's generals in the battle at Mycale, took to wife Agariste, the grandchild of Clisthenes, who drove out the sons of Pisistratus, and nobly put an end to their tyrannical usurpation, and moreover made a body of laws, and settled a model of government admirably tempered and suited for the harmony and safety of the people.

Pericles in other respects was perfectly formed physically, only his head was somewhat longish and out of proportion. For which reason almost all the images and statues that were made of him have the head covered with a helmet, the workmen apparently being willing not to expose him. The poets of Athens called him *Schinocephalos*, or squill-head, from *schinos*, a squill, or sea-onion.

Pericles was a hearer of Zeno, the Eleatic, who treated of natural philosophy in the same manner as Parmenides did, but had also perfected himself in an art of his own for refuting and silencing opponents in argument; as Timon of Phlius describes it,—

> Also the two-edged tongue of mighty Zeno, who,
> Say what one would, could argue it untrue.

But he that saw most of Pericles, and furnished him most especially with a weight and grandeur of sense, superior to all arts of popularity, and in general gave him his elevation and sublimity of purpose and of character, was Anaxagoras of Clazomenæ; whom the men of those times called by the name of Nous, that is mind, or intelligence, whether in admiration of the great and extraordinary gift he displayed for the science of nature, or because he was the first of the philosophers who did not refer the first ordering of the world to fortune or chance, nor to necessity or compulsion, but to a pure, unadulterated intelligence, which in all other existing mixed and compound things acts as a principle of discrimination, and of combination of like with like.

For this man, Pericles entertained an extraordinary esteem and admiration, and, filling himself with this lofty and, as they call it, up-in-the-air sort of thought, derived hence not merely, as was natural, elevation of purpose and dignity of language, raised far above the base and dishonest buffooneries of mob-eloquence, but, besides this, a composure of countenance, and a serenity and calmness in all his movements, which no occurrence whilst he was speaking could disturb, a sustained and even tone of voice, and various other advantages of a similar kind, which produced the greatest effect on his hearers. Once, after being reviled and ill-spoken of all day long in his own hearing by some abandoned fellow in the open market-place where he was engaged in the despatch of some urgent affair, he continued his business in perfect silence, and in the evening returned home composedly, the man still dogging him at the heels, and pelting him all the way with abuse and foul language; and stepping into his house, it being by this time dark, he ordered one of his servants to take a light and to go along with the man and see him safe home.

Nor were these the only advantages which Pericles derived from Anaxagoras's acquaintance; he seems also to have become, by his instructions, superior to that superstition with which an ignorant wonder at appearances, for example, in the heavens, possesses the minds of people unacquainted with their causes, eager for the supernatural, and excitable through an inexperience which the knowledge of natural causes removes, replacing wild and timid superstition by the good hope and assurance of an intelligent piety.

There is a story that once Pericles had brought to him from

a country farm of his, a ram's head with one horn, and that Lampon, the diviner, upon seeing the horn grow strong and solid out of the midst of the forehead, gave it as his judgment that, there being at that time two potent factions, parties, or interests in the city, the one of Thucydides and the other of Pericles, the government would come about to that one of them in whose ground or estate this token or indication of fate had shown itself. But that Anaxagoras, cleaving the skull in sunder, showed to the bystanders that the brain had not filled up its natural place, but being oblong, like an egg, had collected from all parts of the vessel which contained it, in a point to that place from whence the root of the horn took its rise. And that, for that time, Anaxagoras was much admired for his explanation by those that were present; and Lampon no less a little while after, when Thucydides was overpowered, and the whole affairs of the state and government came into the hands of Pericles.

Pericles, while yet but a young man, stood in considerable apprehension of the people, as he was thought in face and figure to be very like the tyrant Pisistratus, and those of great age remarked upon the sweetness of his voice, and his volubility and rapidity in speaking, and were struck with amazement at the resemblance. But when Aristides was now dead, and Themistocles driven out, and Cimon was for the most part kept abroad by the expeditions he made in parts out of Greece, Pericles, seeing things in this posture, now advanced and took his side, not with the rich and few, but with the many and poor, contrary to his natural bent, which was far from democratical; but, most likely, fearing he might fall under suspicion of aiming at arbitrary power, and seeing Cimon on the side of the aristocracy, and much beloved by the better and more distinguished people, he joined the party of the people, with a view at once both to secure himself and procure means against Cimon.

He immediately entered, also, on quite a new course of life

and management of his time. For he was never seen to walk in any street but that which led to the market-place and the council-hall, and he avoided invitations of friends to supper, and all friendly visits and intercourse whatever; in all the time he had to do with the public, which was not a little, he was never known to have gone to any of his friends to a supper, except that once when his near kinsman Euryptolemus married, he remained present till the ceremony of the drink-offering,* and then immediately rose from table and went his way. For these friendly meetings are very quick to defeat any assumed superiority, and in intimate familiarity an exterior of gravity is hard to maintain. Real excellence, indeed, is best recognized when most openly looked into; and in really good men, nothing which meets the eyes of external observers so truly deserves their admiration, as their daily common life does that of their nearer friends. Pericles, however, to avoid any feeling of commonness, or any satiety on the part of the people, presented himself at intervals only, not speaking on every business, nor at all times coming into the assembly, but, as Critolaus says, reserving himself, like the Salaminian galley,† for great occasions, while matters of lesser importance were despatched by friends or other speakers under his direction. And of this number we are told Ephialtes made one, who broke the power of the council of Areopagus, giving the people, according to Plato's expression, so copious and so strong a draught of liberty, that, growing wild and unruly, like an unmanageable horse, it, as the comic poets say,—

"——got beyond all keeping in,
Champing at Euboea, and among the islands leaping in."

The style of speaking most consonant to his form of life

---

* The *spondai*, or libations, like the modern grace, which concluded the meal, and were followed by the dessert.

† The Salaminia and the Paralus were the two sacred state-galleys of Athens, used only on special missions.

and the dignity of his views he found, so to say, in the tones of that instrument with which Anaxagoras had furnished him; of his teaching he continually availed himself, and deepened the colors of rhetoric with the dye of natural science.

A saying of Thucydides, the son of Melesias, stands on record, spoken by him by way of pleasantry upon Pericles's dexterity. Thucydides was one of the noble and distinguished citizens, and had been his greatest opponent; and, when Archidamus, the king of the Lacedæmonians, asked him whether he or Pericles were the better wrestler, he made this answer: "When I," said he, "have thrown him and given him a fair fall, he by persisting that he had no fall, gets the better of me, and makes the bystanders, in spite of their own eyes, believe him."

The rule of Pericles has been described as an aristocratical government, that went by the name of a democracy, but was, indeed, the supremacy of a single great man ; while many say, that by him the common people were first encouraged and led on to such evils as appropriations of subject territory, allowances for attending theatres, payments for performing public duties, and by these bad habits were, under the influence of his public measures, changed from a sober, thrifty people, that maintained themselves by their own labors, to lovers of expense, intemperance, and license.

At the first, as has been said, when he set himself against Cimon's great authority, he did caress the people. Finding himself come short of his competitor in wealth and money, by which advantages the other was enabled to take care of the poor, inviting every day some one or other of the citizens that was in want to supper, and bestowing clothes on the aged people, and breaking down he hedges and enclosures of his grounds, that all that would might freely gather what fruit they pleased, Pericles, thus outdone in popular arts, turned to the distribution of the public moneys ; and in a short time having bought the people over, what with moneys allowed for shows and for service on juries, and what with other forms of pay and largess, he made use of them against the council of Areopagus, and directed the exertions of his party against this council with such success, that most of those causes and matters which had been formerly tried there, were removed from its cognizance; Cimon, also, was banished by ostracism as a favorer of the Lacedæmonians and a hater of the people, though in wealth and noble birth he was among the first, and had won several most glorious victories over the barbarians, and had filled the city with money and spoils of war. So vast an authority had Pericles obtained among the people.

The ostracism was limited by law to ten years; but the Lacedæmonians, in the meantime, entering with a great army into the territory of Tanagra, and the Athenians going out against them, Cimon, coming from his banishment before his time was out, put himself in arms and array with those of his fellow-citizens that were of his own tribe, and desired by his deeds to wipe off the suspicion of his favoring the Lacedæmonians, by venturing his own person along with his countrymen. But Pericles's friends, gathering in a body, forced him to retire as a banished man. For which cause also Pericles seems to have exerted himself more than in any other battle, and to have been conspicuous above all for his exposure of himself to danger. All Cimon's friends, also, to a man, fell together side by side, whom Pericles had accused with him of taking part with the Lacedæmonians. Defeated in this battle on their own frontiers, and expecting a new and perilous attack with return of spring, the Athenians now felt regret and sorrow for the loss of Cimon, and repentance for their expulsion of him. Pericles, being sensible of their feelings, did not hesitate or delay to gratify it, and himself made the motion for recalling him home. He, upon his return, concluded a peace betwixt the two cities; for the Lacedæmonians entertained as kindly feelings towards him as they did the reverse towards Pericles and the other popular leaders.

Cimon, while he was admiral, ended his days in the Isle of

Cyprus. And the aristocratical party, seeing that Pericles was already before this grown to be the greatest and foremost man of all the city, but nevertheless wishing there should be somebody set up against him, to blunt and turn the edge of his power, that it might not altogether prove a monarchy, put forward Thucydides of Alopece, a discreet person, and a near kinsman of Cimon's, to conduct the opposition against him. And so Pericles, at that time more than at any other, let loose the reins to the people, and made his policy subservient to their pleasure, contriving continually to have some great public show or solemnity, some banquet, or some procession or other in the town to please them, coaxing his countrymen like children, with such delights and pleasures as were not, however, unedifying. Besides that, every year he sent out threescore galleys, on board of which there went numbers of the citizens, who were in pay eight months, at the same time learning and practicing the art of seamanship.

He sent, moreover, a thousand of them into the Chersonese as planters, to share the land among them by lot, and five hundred more into the isle of Naxos, and half that number to Andros, a thousand into Thrace to dwell among the Bisaltæ, and others into Italy, when the city Sybaris, which now was called Thurii, was to be repeopled. And this he did to ease and discharge the city of an idle, and, by reason of their idleness, a busy, meddling crowd of people; and at the same time to meet the necessities and restore the fortunes of the poor townsmen, and to intimidate, also, and check their allies from attempting any change, by posting such garrisons, as it were, in the midst of them.

That which gave most pleasure and ornament to the city of Athens, and the greatest admiration and even astonishment to all strangers, and that which now is Greece's only evidence that the power she boasts of and her ancient wealth are no romance or idle story, was his construction of the public and sacred buildings.

ATHENS FROM THE ROAD TO ELEUSIS.

The materials were stone, brass, ivory, gold, ebony, and cypress-wood; the artisans that wrought and fashioned them were smiths and carpenters, moulders, founders and braziers, stone-cutters, dyers, goldsmiths, ivory-workers, painters, embroiderers, turners; those again that conveyed them to the town for use, merchants and mariners and ship-masters by sea; and by land, cartwrights, cattle-breeders, wagoners, rope-makers, flax-workers, shoe-makers and leather-dressers, road-makers, miners. And every trade in the same nature, as a captain in an army has his particular company of soldiers under him, had its own hired company of journeymen and laborers belonging to it banded together as in array, to be as it were the instrument and body for the performance of the service. Thus, to say all in a word, the occasions and services of these public works distributed plenty through every age and condition.

As then grew the works up, no less stately in size than exquisite in form, the workmen striving to outvie the material and the design with the beauty of their workmanship, yet the most wonderful thing of all was the rapidity of their execution. Undertakings, any one of which singly might have required, they thought, for their completion, several successions and ages of men, were every one of them accomplished in the height and prime of one man's political service. Although they say, too, that Zeuxis once, having heard Agatharchus, the painter, boast of despatching his work with speed and ease, replied, "I take a long time." For ease and speed in doing a thing do not give the work lasting solidity or exactness of beauty; the expenditure of time allowed to a man's pains beforehand for the production of a thing is repaid by way of interest with a vital force for its preservation when once produced. For which reason Pericles's works are especially admired, as having been made quickly, to last long. For every particular piece of his work was immediately, even at that time, for its beauty and elegance, antique; and yet in its vigor and freshness looks to this day as if it were just executed. There is a sort of bloom of newness upon those works of his, preserving them from the touch of time, as if they had some perennial spirit and undying vitality mingled in the composition of them.

Phidias had the oversight of all the works, and was surveyor-general, though upon the various portions other great masters and workmen were employed. For Callicrates and Ictinus built the Parthenon; the chapel at Eleusis, where the mysteries were celebrated, was begun by Corœbus, who erected the pillars that stand upon the floor or pavement, and joined them to the architraves; and after his death Metagenes of Xypete added the frieze and the upper line of columns; Xenocles of Cholargus roofed or arched the lantern on the top of the temple of Castor and Pollux; and the long wall, which Socrates says he himself heard Pericles propose to the people, was undertaken by Callicrates.

The Odeum, or music-room, which in its interior was full of seats and ranges of pillars, and outside had its roof made to slope and descend from one single point at the top, was constructed, we are told, in imitation of the king of Persia's Pavilion; this likewise by Pericles's order; which Cratinus again, in his comedy called The Thracian Women, made an occasion of raillery,—

> So, we see here,
> Jupiter Long-pate Pericles appear,
> Since ostracism time he's laid aside his head,
> And wears the new Odeum in its stead.

Pericles, also, eager for distinction, then first obtained the decree for a contest in musical skill to be held yearly at the Panathenæa, and he himself, being chosen judge, arranged the order and method in which the competitors should sing and play on the flute and on the harp. And both at that time, and at other times also, they sat in this music-room to see and hear all such trials of skill

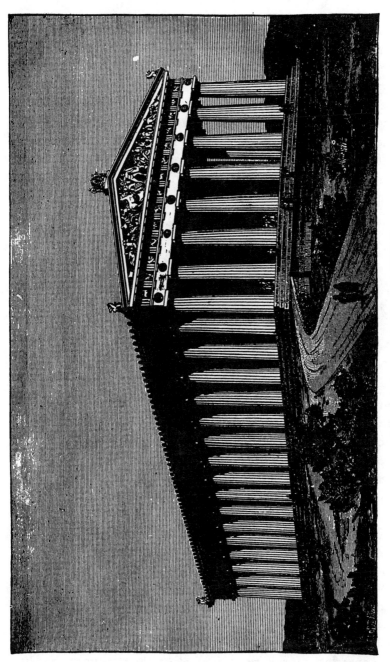

THE PARTHENON IN THE TIME OF PERICLES.

The propylæa, or entrances to the Acropolis, were finished in five years' time, Mnesicles being the principal architect. A strange accident happened in the course of building, which showed that the goddess was not averse to the work, but was aiding and co-operating to bring it to perfection. One of the artificers, the quickest and the handiest workman among them all, with a slip of his foot fell down from a great height, and lay in a miserable condition, the physicians having no hopes of his recovery. When Pericles was in distress about this, Athena

TEMPLE OF HERCULES.

appeared to him at night in a dream, and ordered a course of treatment which he applied, and in a short time, and with great ease, cured the man. And upon this occasion it was that he set up a brass statue of Athena, surnamed Health, in the citadel near the altar, which they say was there before. But it was Phidias who wrought the goddess's image in gold, and he has his name inscribed on the pedestal as the workman of it; and indeed the whole work in a manner was under his charge, and he had, as we have said already, the oversight over all the artists and workmen, through Pericles's friendship for him.

When the orators, who sided with Thucydides and his party, were at one time crying out, as their custom was, against Pericles, as one who squandered away the public money and made havoc of the state revenues, he rose in the open assembly and put the question to the people, whether they thought that he had laid out much; and they saying, "Too much, a great deal,"

"Then," said he, "since it is so, let the cost not go to your account, but to mine; and let the inscription upon the buildings stand in my name." When they heard him say thus, whether it were out of a surprise to see the greatness of his spirit, or out of emulation of the glory of the works, they cried aloud, bidding him to spend on, and lay out what he thought fit from the public purse, and to spare no cost, till all were finished.

At length, coming to a final contest with Thucydides, which of the two should ostracize the other out of the country, and, having gone through this peril, he threw his antagonist out, and broke up the confederacy that had been organized against him. So that now all schism and division being at an end, and the city brought to evenness and unity, he got all Athens and all affairs that pertained to the Athenians into his own hands, their tributes, their armies and their galleys, the islands, the sea, and their wide-extended power, partly over other Greeks and partly over barbarians, and all that empire which they possessed, founded and fortified upon subject nations and royal friendships and alliances.

After this he was no longer the same man he had been before, nor as tame and gentle and familiar as formerly with the populace, so as readily to yield to their pleasures and to comply with the desires of the multitude, as a steersman shifts with the winds. Quitting that loose, remiss, and, in some cases, licentious court of the popular will, he turned those soft and flowery modulations to the austerity of aristocratical and regal rule; but, employing this uprightly and undeviatingly for the country's best interests, he was able generally to lead the people along, with their own will and consent, by persuading and showing them what was to be done.

The source of this predominance was not barely his power of language, but, as Thucydides the historian assures us, the reputation of his life, and the confidence felt in his character; his manifest freedom from every kind of corruption, and superiority to all considerations of money. Notwithstanding he had made the city of Athens, which was great of itself, as great and rich as can be imagined, and though he were himself in power and interest more than equal to many kings and absolute rulers, who some of them also bequeathed by will their power to their children, he for his part, did not make the patrimony his father left him greater than it was by one drachma.

Teleclides says the Athenians had surrendered to him—

> The tribute of the cities, and, with them, the cities too, to do with them as he pleases, and undo;
> To build up, if he likes, stone walls around a town; and again, if so he likes, to pull them down;
> Their treaties and alliances, power, empire, peace, and war, their wealth and their success forevermore.

Nor was all this the luck of some happy occasion; nor was it the mere bloom and grace of a policy that flourished for a season; but having for fifty-five years together maintained the first place among statesmen, in the exercise of one continuous unintermitted command in the office, to which he was annually reëlected, of General, he preserved his integrity unspotted; though otherwise he was not altogether idle or careless in looking after his pecuniary advantage; his paternal estate, which of right belonged to him, he so ordered that it might neither through negligence be wasted or lessened, nor yet, being so full of business as he was, cost him any great trouble or time with taking care of it; and put it into such a way of management as he thought to be the most easy for himself, and the most exact. All his yearly products and profits he sold together in a lump, and supplied his household needs afterward by buying everything that he or his family wanted out of the market. Upon which account, his children, when they grew to age, were not well pleased with his management; since there was not there, as is usual in a great family and a plentiful estate, any thing to spare, or over and above; but all that went out or came in, all disbursements and all receipts, proceeded as it were by number and measure. His manager in all this was a single servant, Evangelus by name, a man either naturally gifted or instructed by Pericles so as to excel every one in this art of domestic economy.

The Lacedæmonians beginning to show themselves troubled at the growth of the Athenian power, Pericles, on the other hand, to elevate the people's spirit yet more, and to raise them to the thought of great actions, proposed a decree to summon all the Greeks in what part soever, whether of Europe or Asia, every city, little as well as great, to send their deputies to Athens to a general assembly or convention, there to consult and advise concerning the Greek temples which the barbarians had burnt down; and also concerning the navigation of the sea, that they might henceforward all of them pass to and fro and trade securely, and be at peace among themselves.

Nothing was effected, nor did the cities meet by their deputies, as was desired; the Lacedæmonians, as it is said, crossing the design underhand, and the attempt being disappointed and baffled first in Peloponnesus. I thought fit, however, to introduce the mention of it, to show the spirit of the man and the greatness of his thoughts.

In his military conduct he gained a great reputation for wariness; he would not by his good-will engage in any fight which had much uncertainty or hazard; he did not envy the glory of generals whose rash adventures fortune favored with brilliant success, however they were admired by others; nor did he think them worthy his imitation, but always used to say to his citizens that, so far as lay in his power, they should continue immortal, and live forever. Seeing Tolmides, the son of Tolmæus, upon the confidence of his former successes, and flushed with the honor his military actions had procured him, making preparation to attack the Bœotians in their own country, when there was no likely opportunity, and that he had prevailed with the bravest and most enterprising of the youth to enlist themselves as volunteers in the service, who besides his other force made up a thousand, he endeavored to withhold him, and advised him against it in the public assembly, telling him in a memorable saying of his which still goes about, that, if he would not take Pericles's advice, yet he would not do amiss to wait and be ruled by time, the wisest counselor of all. This saying, at that time, was but slightly commended; but, within a few days after, when news was brought that Tolmides himself had been defeated and slain in battle near Coronea, and that many brave citizens had fallen with him, it gained him great repute as well as good-will among the people, for wisdom and for love of his countrymen.

But of all his expeditions, that to the Chersonese gave most satisfaction and pleasure, having proved the safety of the Greeks who inhabited there. For not only by carrying along with him a thousand fresh citizens of Athens he gave new strength and vigor to the cities, but also by belting the neck of land, which joins the peninsula to the continent, with bulwarks and forts from sea to sea, he put a stop to the inroads of the Thracians, who lay all about the Chersonese, and closed the door against a continual and grievous war, with which that country had been long harassed, lying exposed to the encroachments and influx of barbarous neighbors, and groaning under the evils of a predatory population both upon and within its borders.

Entering also the Euxine Sea with a large and finely equipped fleet, he obtained for the Greek cities any new arrangements they wanted, and entered into friendly relations with them; and to the barbarous nations, and kings and chiefs round about them, displayed the greatness of the power of the Athenians, their perfect ability and confidence to sail wherever they had a mind, and to bring the whole sea under their control. He left the Sinopians thirteen ships of war, with soldiers under the command of Lamachus, to assist them against Timesileus the tyrant; and, when he and his accomplices had been thrown out, obtained a decree that six hundred of the Athenians that were willing should sail to Sinope and plant themselves there with the Sinopians, sharing among them the houses and land which the tyrant and his party had previously held.

But in other things he did not comply with the giddy impulses of the citizens, nor quit his own resolutions to follow their fancies, when, carried away with the thought of their strength and great success, they were eager to interfere again in Egypt, and to disturb the king of Persia's maritime dominions. Nay, there were a good many who were, even then, possessed with that unblest and unauspicious passion for Sicily, which afterward the orators of Alcibiades's party blew up into a flame. There were some also who dreamt of Tuscany and of Carthage, and not without plausible reason in their present large dominion and the prosperous course of their affairs.

But Pericles curbed this passion for foreign conquest, and unsparingly pruned and cut down their ever-busy fancies for a multitude of undertakings, and directed their power for the most part to securing and consolidating what they had already got, supposing it would be quite enough for them to do, if they could keep the Lacedæmonians in check; to whom he entertained all along a sense of opposition; which, as upon many other occasions, he particularly showed by what he did in the time of the holy war. The Lacedæmonians, having gone with an army to Delphi, restored Apollo's temple, which the Phocians had got into their possession, to the Delphians; immediately after their departure, Pericles, with another army, came and restored it to the Phocians. And the Lacedæmonians having engraven the record of their privilege of consulting the oracle before others, which the Delphians gave them, upon the forehead of the brazen wolf which stands there, he, also, having received from the Phocians the like privilege for the Athenians, had it cut upon the same wolf of brass, on his right side.

When Pericles, in giving up his accounts, stated a disbursement of ten talents, as laid out upon fit occasion, the people, without any question, nor troubling themselves to investigate the mystery, freely allowed it. And some historians, in which number is Theophrastus the philosopher, have given it as a truth that Pericles every year used to send privately the sum of ten talents to Sparta, with which he complimented those in office, to keep off the war; not to purchase peace either, but time, that he might prepare at leisure, and be the better able to carry on war hereafter.

After this, having made a truce between the Athenians and Lacedæmonians for thirty years, he ordered, by public decree, the expedition against the Isle of Samos, on the ground, that, when they were bid to leave off their war with the Milesians, they had not complied. For the two states were at war for the possession of Priene; and the Samians, getting the better, refused to lay down their arms and to have the controversy betwixt them decided by arbitration before the Athenians. Pericles, therefore, fitting out a fleet, went and broke up the oligarchical government at Samos, and, taking fifty of the principal men of the town as hostages, and as many of their children, sent them to the isle of Lemnos, there to be kept, though he had offers, as some relate, of a talent apiece for himself from each one of the hostages, and of many other presents from those who were anxious not to have a democracy. Moreover, Pissuthnes the Persian, one of the king's lieutenants, bearing some good-will to the Samians, sent him ten thousand pieces of gold to excuse the city. Pericles, however, would receive none of all this; but after he had taken that course with the Samians which he thought fit, and set up a democracy among them, sailed back to Athens.

But they, however, immediately revolted, Pissuthnes having privily got away their hostages for them, and provided them with means for the war. Whereupon Pericles came out with a fleet a second time against them, and found them not idle nor slinking away, but manfully resolved to try for the dominion of the sea. The issue was, that, after a sharp sea-fight about the island called Tragia, Pericles obtained a decisive victory, having with forty-four ships routed seventy of the enemy's, twenty of which were carrying soldiers.

Together with his victory and pursuit, having made himself master of the port, he laid siege to the Samians, and blocked them up, who yet, one way or other, still ventured to make sallies, and fight under the city walls. But after another greater fleet from Athens had arrived, and the Samians were now shut up with a close leaguer on every side, Pericles, taking with him sixty galleys, sailed out into the main sea, with the intention, as most authors give the account, to meet a squadron of Phœnician ships that were coming for the Samians' relief, and to fight them at as great a distance as could be from the island; but, as Stesimbrotus says, with a design of putting over to Cyprus; which does not seem to be probable. But whichever of the two was his intent, it seems to have been a miscalculation. For on his departure, Melissus, the son of Ithagenes, a philosopher, being at that time general in Samos, despising either the small number of the ships that were left or the inexperience of the commanders, prevailed with the citizens to attack the Athenians. And the Samians having won the battle and taken several of the men prisoners, and disabled several of the ships, were masters of the sea, and brought into port all necessaries they wanted for the war, which they had not before. Aristotle says, too, that Pericles himself had been once before this worsted by this Melissus in a sea-fight.

The Samians, that they might requite an affront which had before been put upon them, branded the Athenians whom they took prisoners, in their foreheads, with the figure of an owl. For so the Athenians had marked them before with a Samæna, which is a sort of ship, low and flat in the prow, so as to look snub-nosed, but wide and large and well-spread in the hold, by which it both carries a large cargo and sails well.

And it was so called, because the first of that kind was seen at Samos, having been built by order of Polycrates the tyrant. These brands upon the Samians' foreheads, they say, are the allusion in the passage of Aristophanes, where he says,—

> For, oh, the Samians are a lettered people.

Pericles, as soon as news was brought him of the disaster that had befallen his army, made all the haste he could to come in to their relief, and having defeated Melissus, who bore up against him, and put the enemy to flight, he immediately proceeded to hem them in with a wall, resolving to master them and take the town, rather with some cost and time than with the wounds and hazards of his citizens. But as it was a hard matter to keep back the Athenians, who were vexed at the delay, and were eagerly bent to fight, he divided the whole multitude into eight parts, and arranged by lot that that part which had the white bean should have leave to feast and take their ease, while the other seven were fighting. And this is the reason, they say, that people, when at any time they have been merry, and enjoyed themselves, call it white day, in allusion to this white bean.

Ephorus, the historian, tells us besides, that Pericles made use of engines of battery in this siege, being much taken with the curiousness of the invention, with the aid and presence of Artemon himself, the engineer, who, being lame, used to be carried about in a litter, where the works required his attendance, and for that reason was called Periphoretus. But Heraclides Ponticus disproves this out of Anacreon's poems, where mention is made of this Artemon Periphoretus several ages before the Samian war, or any of these occurrences. And he says that Artemon, being a man who loved his ease, and had a great apprehension of danger, for the most part kept close within doors, having two of his servants to hold a brazen shield over his head, that nothing might fall upon him from above; and if he were at any time forced upon necessity to go abroad, that he was carried about in a little hanging-bed, close to the very ground, and that for this reason he was called Periphoretus.

In the ninth month, the Samians surrendering themselves and delivering up the town, Pericles pulled down their walls, and seized their shipping, and set a fine of a large sum upon them, part of which they paid down at once, and they agreed to bring in the rest by a certain time, and gave hostages for security. Pericles, however, after the reduction of Samos, returning back to Athens, took care that those who died in the war should be honorably buried, and made a funeral harangue, as the custom is, in their commendation at their graves, for which he gained great admiration. As he came down from the stage on which he spoke, all the women except Elpinice, the aged sister of Cimon, came and complimented him, taking him by the hand, and crowning him with garlands and ribbons, like a victorious athlete in the games.

After this was over, the Peloponnesian war beginning to break out in full tide, he advised the people to send help to the Corcyræans, who were attacked by the Corinthians, and to secure to themselves an island possessed of great naval resources, since the Peloponnesians were already all but in actual hostilities against them. Archidamus, the king of the Lacedæmonians, endeavoring to bring the greater part of the complaints and matters in dispute to a fair determination, and to pacify and allay the heats of the allies, it is very likely that the war would not upon any other grounds of quarrel have fallen upon the Athenians, could they have been prevailed upon to be reconciled with the inhabitants of Megara.

The true occasion of the quarrel is not easy to find out. The worst motive of all, which is confirmed by most witnesses, is to the following effect. Phidias the Moulder had, as has before been said, undertaken to make the statue of Athena. Now he, being admitted to friendship with Pericles, and a great favorite of his, had many enemies upon this account, who envied and maligned him; and they, to make trial in a case of his what kind of judges the commons would prove, should there be occasion to bring Pericles himself before them, having tampered with Menon, one who had been a workman with Phidias, stationed him in the market-place, with a petition desiring public security upon his discovery and impeachment of Phidias. The people admitting the man to tell his story, and the prosecution proceeding in the assembly, there was nothing of theft or cheat proved against him; for Phidias, from the very first beginning, by the advice of Pericles, had so wrought and wrapt the gold that was used in the work about the statue, that they might take it all off and make out the just weight of it, which Pericles at that time bade the accusers do. But the reputation of his works was what brought envy upon Phidias, especially that where he represents the fight of the Amazons upon the goddesses' shield, he had introduced a likeness of himself as a bald old man holding up a great stone with both hands, and had put in a very fine representation of Pericles fighting with an Amazon. And the position of the hand, which holds out the spear in front of the face, was ingeniously contrived to conceal in some degree the likeness, which, meantime, showed itself on either side.

Phidias then was carried away to prison, and there died of a disease; but, as some say, of poison administered by the enemies of Pericles, to raise a slander, or a suspicion at least, as though he had procured it. The informer Menon, upon Glycon's proposal, the people made free from payment of taxes and customs, and ordered the generals to take care that nobody should do him any hurt. And Pericles, finding that in Phidias's case he had miscarried with the people, being afraid of impeachment, kindled the war, which hitherto had lingered and smothered, and blew it up into a flame; hoping, by that means, to disperse and scatter these complaints and charges, and to allay their jealousy; the city usually throwing herself upon him alone, and trusting to his sole conduct, upon the urgency of great affairs and public dangers, by reason of his authority and the sway he bore.

These are given out to have been the reasons which induced Pericles not to suffer the people of Athens to yield to the proposals of the Lacedæmonians; but their truth is uncertain.

The Lacedæmonians, therefore, and their allies, with a great army, invaded the Athenian territories, under the conduct of king Archidamus, and laying waste the country, marched on as far as Acharnæ, and there pitched their camp, presuming that the Athenians would never endure that, but would come out and fight them for their country's and their honor's sake. But Pericles looked upon it as dangerous to engage in battle, to the risk of the city itself, against sixty thousand men-at-arms of Peloponnesians and Bœotians; for so many they were in number that made the inroad at first; and he endeavored to appease those who were desirous to fight, and were grieved and discontented to see how things went, and gave them good words, saying, that "trees, when they are lopped and cut, grow up again in a short time, but men, being once lost, cannot easily be recovered." He did not convene the people into an assembly, for fear lest they should force him to act against his judgment; and many of his enemies threatened and accused him for doing as he did, and many made songs and lampoons upon him, which were sung about the town to his disgrace, reproaching him with the cowardly exercise of his office of general, and the tame abandonment of everything to the enemy's hands.

Cleon, also, already was among his assailants, making use of the feeling against him as a step to the leadership of the people, as appears in the anapæstic verses of Hermippus.

> Satyr-king, instead of swords,
> Will you always handle words?
> Very brave indeed we find them,
> But a Teles* lurks behind them.

---

* Apparently some notorious coward.

> Yet to gnash your teeth you're seen
> When the little dagger keen,
> Whetted every day anew,
> Of sharp Cleon touches you.

Pericles, however, was not at all moved by any attacks, but took all patiently, and submitted in silence to the disgrace they threw upon him and the ill-will they bore him; and, sending out a fleet of a hundred galleys to Peloponnesus, he did not go along with it in person, but stayed behind, that he might watch at home and keep the city under his own control, till the Peloponnesians broke up their camp and were gone. Yet to soothe the common people, jaded and distressed with the war, he relieved them with distributions of public moneys, and ordained new divisions of subject land. For having turned out all the people of Ægina, he parted the island among the Athenians, according to lot. Some comfort, also, and ease in their miseries, they might receive from what their enemies endured. For the fleet sailing round the Peloponnesus, ravaged a great deal of the country, and pillaged and plundered the towns and smaller cities; and by land he himself entered with an army the Megarian country, and made havoc of it all. Whence it is clear that the Peloponnesians, though they did the Athenians much mischief by land, yet suffering as much themselves from them by sea, would not have protracted the war to such a length, but would quickly have given it over, as Pericles at first foretold they would, had not some divine power crossed human purposes.

In the first place, the pestilential disease, or plague, seized upon the city, and ate up all the flower and prime of their youth and strength. Upon occasion of which, the people, distempered and afflicted in their souls, as well as in their bodies, were utterly enraged like madmen against Pericles, and, like patients grown delirious, sought to lay violent hands on their physician, or, as it were, their father.

Finding the Athenians ill affected and highly displeased with

TEMPLE OF MINERVA IN ÆGINA.
Formerly called Jupiter Panhellenius.

him, he tried and endeavored what he could to appease and re-encourage them. But he could not pacify or allay their anger, nor persuade or prevail with them any way, till they freely passed their votes upon him, resumed their power, took away his command from him, and fined him in a sum of money.

After this, public troubles were soon to leave him unmolested; the people, so to say, discharged their passion in their stroke, and lost their stings in the wound. But his domestic concerns were in an unhappy condition, many of his friends and acquaintance having died in the plague time, and those of his family having long since been in disorder and in a kind of mutiny against him. For the eldest of his sons, Xanthippus by name, being naturally prodigal, and marrying a young and expensive wife, was highly offended at his father's economy in making him but a scanty allowance, by little and little at a time. He sent, therefore, to a friend one day, and borrowed some money of him in his father Pericles's name, pretending it was by his order. The man coming afterward to demand the debt, Pericles was so far from yielding to pay it, that he entered an action against him. Upon which the young man, Xanthippus, thought himself so ill used and disobliged, that he openly reviled his father; telling first, by way of ridicule, stories about his conversations at home, and the discourses he had with the sophists and scholars that came to his house. As for instance, how one who was a practiser of the five games of skill,* having with a dart or javelin unawares against his will struck and killed Epitimus the Pharsalian, his father spent a whole day with Protagoras in a serious dispute, whether the javelin, or the man that threw it, or the masters of the games who appointed these sports, were, according to the strictest and best reason, to be accounted the cause of this mischance. And in general this difference of the young man's with his

---

* These are recorded in a pentameter verse by Simonides.
Halma, podokeïēn, discon, aconta, palēn.
Leaping, and swiftness of foot, wrestling, the discus, the dart.

father, and the breach betwixt them, continued never to be healed or made up till his death. For Xanthippus died in the plague time of the sickness. At which time Pericles also lost his sister, and the greatest part of his relations and friends, and those who had been most useful and serviceable to him in managing the affairs of state. However, he did not shrink or give in upon these occasions, nor betray or lower his high spirit and the greatness of his mind under all his misfortunes; he was not even so much as seen to weep or to mourn, or even attend the burial of any of his friends or relations, till at last he lost his only remaining son. Subdued by this blow, and yet striving still, as far as he could, to maintain his principle, and to preserve and keep up the greatness of his soul, when he came, however, to perform the ceremony of putting a garland of flowers upon the head of the corpse, he was vanquished by his passion at the sight, so that he burst into exclamations, and shed copious tears, having never done any such thing in all his life before.

The city having made trial of other generals for the conduct of war, and orators for business of state, when they found there was no one who was of weight enough for such a charge, or of authority sufficient to be trusted with so great a command, regretted the loss of him, and invited him again to address and advise them, and to resume the office of general. He, however, lay at home in dejection and mourning; but was persuaded by Alcibiades and others of his friends to come abroad and show himself to the people; who having, upon his appearance, made their acknowledgments, and apologized for their untowardly treatment of him, he undertook the public affairs once more.

About this time, it seems, the plague seized Pericles, not with sharp and violent fits, as it did others that had it, but with a dull and lingering distemper, attended with various changes and alterations, leisurely, by little and little, wasting the strength of his body, and undermining the noble faculties of his soul.

When he was now near his end, the best of the citizens and those of his friends who were left alive, sitting about him, were speaking of the greatness of his merit, and his power, and reckoning up his famous actions and the number of his victories; for there were no less than nine trophies, which, as their chief commander and conqueror of their enemies, he had set up, for the honor of the city. They talked thus together among themselves, as though he were unable to understand or mind what they said, but had now lost his consciousness. He had listened, however, all the while, and attended to all, and speaking out among them, said, that he wondered they should commend and take notice of things which were as much owing to fortune as to anything else, and had happened to many other commanders, and, at the same time, should not speak or make mention of that which was the most excellent and greatest thing of all. "For," said he, "no Athenian, through my means, ever wore mourning."

He was indeed a character deserving our high admiration, not only for his equable and mild temper, which all along in the many affairs of his life, and the great animosities which he incurred, he constantly maintained; but also for the high spirit and feeling which made him regard it the noblest of all his honors that, in the exercise of such immense power, he never had gratified his envy or his passion, nor ever had treated any enemy as irreconcilably opposed to him. And to me it appears that this one thing gives that otherwise childish and arrogant title a fitting and becoming significance; so dispassionate a temper, a life so pure and unblemished, in the height of power and place, might well be called "Olympian," in accordance with our conceptions of the divine beings, to whom, as the natural authors of all good and of nothing evil, we ascribe the rule and government of the world.

The course of public affairs after his death produced a quick and speedy sense of the loss of Pericles. Those who, while he lived, resented his great authority, as that which eclipsed themselves, presently after his quitting the stage, making trial of other orators and demagogues, readily acknowleged that there never had been in nature such a disposition as his was, more moderate and reasonable in the height of that state he took upon him, or more grave and impressive in the mildness which he used.

RUINS OF THE PARTHENON.

DEMOSTHENES.

WHOEVER it was, Sosius, that wrote the poem in honor of Alcibiades, upon his winning the chariot-race at the Olympian Games, whether it was Euripides, as is most commonly thought, or some other person he tells us, that to a man's being happy it is pre-eminently requisite that he should be born in "some famous city."

But if anybody undertakes to write a history, that has to be collected from materials gathered by observation and the reading of works not easy to be got in all places, nor written always in his own language, but many of them foreign and dispersed in other hands, for him, undoubtedly, it is above all things most necessary, to reside in some city of good note, devoted to liberal arts, and populous; where he may have plenty of all sorts of books, and upon inquiry may hear and inform himself of such particulars as, having escaped the pens of writers, are more faithfully preserved in the memories of men.

But for me, I live in a little town, where I am willing to continue, lest it should grow less; and having had no leisure, while I was in Rome and other parts of Italy, to practice myself in the Roman language, on account of public business and of those who came to be instructed by me in philosophy, it was very late, and in the decline of my age, before I applied myself to the reading of Latin authors. But to appreciate the graceful and ready pronunciation of the Roman tongue, to understand the various figures and connection of words, and such other ornaments, in which the beauty of speaking consists, is,

I doubt not, an admirable and delightful accomplishment; but it requires a degree of practice and study which is not easy, and will better suit those who have more leisure, and time enough yet before them for the occupation.

And so in this book of my Parallel Lives, in giving an account of Demosthenes and Cicero, my comparison of their natural dispositions and their characters will be formed upon their actions and their lives as statesmen, and I shall not pretend to criticise their orations one against the other, to show which of the two was the more charming or the more powerful speaker. For there, as Ion says,

> We are but like a fish upon dry land.

The divine power seems originally to have designed Demosthenes and Cicero upon the same plan, giving them many similarities in their natural characters, as their passion for distinction and their love of liberty in civil life, and their want of courage in dangers and war, and at the same time also to have added many accidental resemblances. I think there can hardly be found two other orators, who, from small and obscure beginnings, became so great and mighty; who both contested with kings and tyrants; both lost their daughters, were driven out of their country, and returned with honor; who, flying from thence again, were both seized upon by their enemies, and at last ended their lives with the liberty of their countrymen. So that if we were to suppose that there had been a trial of skill between nature and fortune, as there is sometimes between artists, it would be hard to judge, whether that succeeded best in making them alike in their dispositions and manners, or this, in the coincidences of their lives. We will speak of the eldest first.

Demosthenes, the father of Demosthenes, was a citizen of good rank and quality, as Theopompus informs us, surnamed the Sword-maker, because he had a large workhouse, and kept servants skilful in that art at work. Demosthenes, when only seven years old, was left by his father in affluent circumstances, the whole value of his estate being little short of fifteen talents, but was wronged by his guardians, part of his fortune being embezzled by them, and the rest neglected; insomuch that even his teachers were defrauded of their salaries. This was the reason that he did not obtain the liberal education that he should have had; besides that on account of weakness and delicate health, his mother would not let him exert himself, and his teachers forebore to urge him. He was meagre and sickly from the first, and hence had the nickname of Batalus, given him, it is said, by the boys, in derision of his appearance; Batalus being a certain enervated flute-player, in ridicule of whom Antiphanes wrote a play.

The first occasion of his eager inclination to oratory, they say, was this. Callistratus, the orator, was to plead in open court for Oropus, and the expectation of the issue of

DEMOSTHENES.

that cause was very great, as well for the ability of the orator, who was then at the height of his reputation, as also for the fame of the action itself. Therefore, Demosthenes, having heard the tutors and schoolmasters agreeing among themselves to be present at this trial, with much importunity pursuades his tutor to take him along with him to the hearing; who, having some acquaintance with the doorkeepers, procured a place where the boy might sit unseen, and hear what was said. Callistratus having got the day, and being much admired, the boy began to look upon his glory with emulation, observing how he was courted on all hands, and attended on his way by the multitude; but his wonder was more than all excited by the power of his eloquence, which seemed able to subdue and win over any thing. From this time, therefore, bidding farewell to other sorts of learning and study, he now began to exercise himself, and to take pains in declaiming, as one that meant to be himself also an orator. He made use of Isæus as his guide to the art of speaking, though Isocrates at that time was giving lessons; whether, as some say, because he was an orphan, and was not able to pay Isocrates his appointed fee of ten minæ, or because he preferred Isæus's speaking, as being more business-like and effective in actual use.

As soon, therefore, as he was grown up to man's estate, he began to go to law with his guardians, and to write orations against them; who, in the meantime, had recourse to various subterfuges and pleas for new trials, and Demosthenes, though he was thus, as Thucydides says, taught his business in dangers, and by his own exertions was successful in his suit, was yet unable for all this to recover so much as a small fraction of his patrimony. He only attained some degree of confidence in speaking, and some competent experience in it. And having got a taste of the honor and power which are acquired by pleadings, he now ventured to come forth, and to undertake public business. And, as it is said of Laomedon, the Orchomenian, that by advice of his physician, he used to run long distances to keep off some disease of his spleen, and by that means having, through labor and exercise, framed the habit of his body, he betook himself to the great garland games,* and became one of the best runners at the long race; so it happened to Demosthenes, who, first venturing upon oratory for the recovery of his own private property, by this acquired ability in speaking, and at length, in public business, as it were in the great games, came to have the pre-eminence of all competitors in the assembly. But when he first addressed himself to the people, he met with great discouragements, and was derided for his strange and uncouth style, which was cumbered with long sentences and tortured with formal arguments to a most harsh and disagreeable excess. Besides, he had, it seems, a weakness in his voice, a perplexed and indistinct utterance and a shortness of breath, which, by breaking and disjointing his sentences, much obscured the sense and meaning of what he spoke. So that in the end, being quite disheartened, he foresook the assembly; and as he was walking carelessly and sauntering about the Piræus, Eunomus, the Thriasian, then a very old man, seeing him, upbraided him, saying that his diction was very much like that of Pericles, and that he was wanting to himself through cowardice and meanness of spirit, neither bearing up with courage against popular outcry, nor fitting his body for action, but suffering it to languish through mere sloth and negligence.

Another time, when the assembly had refused to hear him, and he was going home with his head muffled up, taking it very heavily, they relate that Satyrus, the actor followed him, and being his familiar acquaintance, entered into conversation with him. To whom Demosthenes bemoaned, that although he had been the most industrious of all the plead-

---

* The Olympic, Pythian, Isthmian and Nemean Games, where the victors were crowned with garlands.

ers, and had spent almost the whole strength and vigor of his body in that employment, he could not yet find any acceptance with the people, while drunken sots, mariners, and illiterate fellows were heard, and had the hustings for their own. "You say true, Demosthenes," replied Satyrus, "but I will quickly remedy the cause of all this, if you will repeat to me some passage out of Euripides or Sophocles." When Demosthenes had pronounced one, Satyrus presently taking it up after him, gave the same passage, in his rendering of it, such a new form, by accompanying it with the proper mien and gesture, that to Demosthenes it seemed quite another thing. By this being convinced how much grace and ornament language acquires from action, he began to esteem it a small matter, and as good as nothing for a man to exercise himself in declaiming, if he neglected enunciation and delivery. Hereupon he built himself a place under ground to study in (which was still remaining in our time), and hither he would come constantly every day to form his action, and to exercise his voice; and here he would continue, oftentimes without intermission, two or three months together, shaving one half of his head, so that for shame he might not go abroad, though he desired it never so much.

Nor was this all, but he also made his conversation with people abroad, his common speech, and his business, subservient to his studies, taking from hence occasions and arguments as matter to work upon. For as soon as he was parted from his company, down he would go at once into his study, and run over everything in order that had passed, and the reasons that might be alleged for and against it. Any speeches, also, that he was present at, he would go over again with himself, and reduce into periods; and whatever others spoke to him, or he to them, he would correct, transform, and vary in several ways. Hence it was, that he was looked upon as a person of no great natural genius, but one who owed all the power and ability he had in speaking to labor and industry. He was very rarely heard to speak off-hand, but though he were by name frequently called upon by the people, as he sat in the assembly, yet he would not rise unless he had previously considered the subject, and come prepared for it. So that many of the popular pleaders used to make it a jest against him; and Pytheas once, scoffing at him, said that his arguments smelt of the lamp. To which Demosthenes gave the sharp answer, "It is true, indeed, Pytheas, that your lamp and mine are not conscious of the same things." To others, however, he would not deny it, but would admit frankly enough, that he neither entirely wrote his speeches beforehand, nor yet spoke wholly extempore. And he would affirm, that it was the more truly popular act to use premeditation, such preparation being a kind of respect to the people.

How then, some may say, was it, that Æschines speaks of him as a person much to be wondered at for his boldness in speaking? And, when Lamachus, the Myrinæan, had written a panegyric upon king Philip and Alexander, in which he uttered many things in reproach of the Thebans and Olynthians, and at the Olympic Games recited it publicly, Demosthenes, then rising up, and recounting historically and demonstratively what benefits and advantages all Greece had received from the Thebans and Chalcidians, and on the contrary, what mischiefs the flatterers of the Macedonians had brought upon it, so turned the minds of all that were present that the sophist, in alarm at the outcry against him, secretly made his way out of the assembly. But Demosthenes, it would seem, regarded the reserve and sustained manner of Pericles, and his forbearing to speak on the sudden, or upon every occasion, as being the things to which he principally owed his greatness, and this he followed, and endeavored to imitate, neither wholly neglecting the glory which present occasion offered, nor yet willing too often to expose his faculty to the mercy of chance. For, in fact, the orations which were spoken by him had much more of boldness and confidence in them than those that he wrote. Eratos thenes says that often in his speaking he would be transported into a kind of ecstasy, and Demetrius, that he uttered the famous metrical adjuration to the people,

>By the earth, the springs, the rivers, and the streams,

as a man inspired, and beside himself. One of the comedians calls him a *rhopoperperethras*—a loud declaimer about petty matters; from *rhopos*, small wares, and *perperos*, a loud talker; and another scoffs at him for the use of antithesis:—

>And what he took, took back; a phrase to please
>The very fancy of Demosthenes.

Unless, indeed, this also is meant by Antiphanes for a jest upon the speech on Halonesus, which Demosthenes advised the Athenians not to *take* at Philip's hands, but to *take back*.*

All, however, used to consider Demades, in the mere use of his natural gifts, an orator impossible to surpass, and that in what he spoke on the sudden, he excelled all the study and preparation of Demosthenes. And Ariston, the Chian, has recorded a judgment which Theophrastus passed upon the orators; for being asked what kind of orator he accounted Demosthenes, he answered, "Worthy of the city of Athens;" and then, what he thought of Demades, he answered, "Above it." And the same philosopher reports, that Polyeuctus, the Sphettian, one of the Athenian politicians about that time, was wont to say that Demosthenes was the greatest orator, but Phocion the ablest, as he expressed the most sense in the fewest words. And, indeed, it is related, that Demosthenes himself, as often as Phocion stood up to plead against him, would say to his acquaintance, "Here comes the knife to my speech." Yet it does not appear whether he had this feeling

---

* Halonesus had belonged to Athens, but had been seized by pirates, from whom Philip took it. He was willing to make a present of it to the Athenians, but Demosthenes warned them not on any account to *take* it, unless it were expressly understood that they *took* it *back:* Philip had no right to give what it was his duty to give back.

for his powers of speaking, or for his life and character, and meant to say that one word or nod from a man who was really trusted, would go further than a thousand lengthy periods from others.

Demetrius, the Phalerian, tells us, that he was informed by Demosthenes himself, when old, that the ways he made use of to remedy his natural bodily infirmities and defects were such as these: his inarticulate and stammering pronunciation he overcame and rendered more distinct by speaking with pebbles in his mouth; his voice he disciplined by declaiming and reciting speeches or verses when he was out of breath, while running or going up steep places; and that in his house he had a large looking-glass, before which he would stand and go through his exercises. It is told that some one once came to request his assistance as a pleader, and related how he had been assaulted and beaten. "I am sure," said Demosthenes, "nothing of the kind can have happened to you." Upon which the other, raising his voice, exclaimed loudly, "What, Demosthenes, nothing has been done to me?" "Ah," replied Demosthenes, "now I hear the voice of one that has been injured and beaten." Of so great consequence towards the gaining of belief did he esteem the tone and action of the speaker. When a thief, who had the nickname of the Brazen, was attempting to upbraid him for sitting up late, and writing by candlelight, "I know very well," said he, "that you had rather have all lights out; and wonder not, O ye men of Athens, at the many robberies which are committed, since we have thieves of brass and walls of clay."

His first entering into public business was about the time of the Phocian war. But the object which he chose for himself in the commonwealth was noble and just, the defence of the Greek against Philip; and in this he behaved himself so worthily that he soon grew famous, and excited attention everywhere for his eloquence and courage in speaking. He was admired through all Greece, the king of Persia courted him, and by

Philip himself he was more esteemed than all the other orators. His very enemies were forced to confess that they had to do with a man of mark; for such a character even Æschines and Hyperides give him, where they accuse and speak against him.

Demosthenes would never turn aside or prevaricate, either in word or deed. Panætius, the philosopher, said, that most of his orations were written, as if they were to prove this one conclusion: that only what is honest and virtuous is to be chosen; as that of the Crown, that against Aristocrates, that for the Immunities, and the Philippics; in all which he persuades his fellow-citizens to pursue not that which seems most pleasant, easy, or profitable; but declares over and over again, that they ought in the first place to prefer that which is just and honorable, before their own safety and preservation.

Excepting only Phocion, he far surpassed, even in his life and manners, the other orators of his time. None of them addressed the people so boldly; he attacked the faults, and opposed himself to the unreasonable desires of the multitude, as may be seen in his orations. Theopompus writes, that the Athenians having by name selected Demosthenes, and called upon him to accuse a certain person, he refused to do it; upon which the assembly being all in an uproar, he rose up and said, "Your counsellor, whether you will or no, O ye men of Athens, you shall always have me; but a sycophant or false accuser, I shall never be." And his conduct in the case of Antiphon was perfectly aristocratical; whom, after he had been acquitted in the assembly, he took and brought before the court of Areopagus, and, setting at naught the displeasure of the people, convicted him there of having promised Philip to burn the arsenal; whereupon the man was condemned by that court, and suffered for it. He accused, also, Theoris, the priestess, among other misdemeanors, of having instructed and taught the slaves to deceive and cheat their masters, for which the sentence of death was passed upon her, and she was executed.

It was evident, even in time of peace, what course Demosthenes would steer in the commonwealth; for whatever was done by the Macedonian, he criticised and found fault with, and upon all occasions was stirring up the people of Athens, and inflaming them against him. Therefore, in the court of Philip, no man was so much talked of, or of so great account as he; and when he came thither, as one of the ten ambassadors who was sent into Macedonia, his speech was answered with most care and exactness. But in other respects, Philip entertained him not so honorably as the rest, neither did he show him the same kindness and civility with which he applied himself to the party of Æschines and Philocrates. So that, when the others commended Philip for his able speaking, his beautiful person, nay, and also for his good companionship in drinking, Demosthenes could not refrain from cavilling at these praises; the first, he said, was a quality which might well enough become a rhetorician, the second a woman, and the last was only the property of a sponge; no one of them was the proper commendation of a prince.

Not long after, he undertook an embassy through the States of Greece, which he solicited and so far incensed against hilip, that a few only excepted, he brought them all into a general league. So that, besides the forces composed of the citizens themselves, there was an army consisting of fifteen thousand foot and two thousand horse, and the money to pay these strangers was levied and brought in with great cheerfulness. On which occasion it was, says Theophrastus, on the allies requesting that their contributions for the war might be ascertained and stated, Crobylus, the orator, made use of the saying, "War can't be fed at so much a day." Now was all Greece up in arms, and in great expectation what would be the event. The Eubœans, the Achæans, the Corinthians, the Megarians, the Leucadians, and Corcyræans, their people and their cities were all joined together in a league. But the hardest task was yet behind, left for Demosthenes, to draw the Thebans into this confederacy with the rest. Their country bordered next upon Attica, they had great forces for the war, and at that time they were accounted the best soldiers of all Greece, but it was no easy matter to make them break with Philip, who, by many good offices, had so lately obliged them in the Phocian war; especially considering how the subjects of dispute and variance between the two cities were continually renewed and exasperated by petty quarrels, arising out of the proximity of their frontiers.

But after Philip, puffed up with his good success at Amphissa, on a sudden surprised Elatea and possessed himself of Phocis, the Athenians were in a great consternation, none durst venture to rise up to speak, all were at a loss, and the whole assembly was in silence and perplexity. In this extremity of affairs, Demosthenes was the only man who appeared, his counsel to them being alliance with the Thebans. And having in other ways encouraged the people, and, as his manner was, raised their spirits up with hopes, he, with some others was sent ambassador to Thebes. To oppose him, as Marsyas says, Philip also sent thither his envoys. Now the Thebans, in their consultations, were well enough aware what suited best with their own interest, but every one had before his eye the terrors of war, and their losses in the Phocian troubles were still recent: but such was the force and power of the orator, fanning up their courage, and firing their emulation, that, casting away every thought of prudence, fear, or obligation, in a sort of divine possession, they chose the path of honor, to which his words invited them. And this success, thus accomplished by an orator, was thought to be so glorious and of such consequence, that Philip immediately sent heralds to treat and petition for a peace: all Greece was aroused, and up in arms to help. And the commanders-in-chief, not only of Attica, but of Bœotia, applied themselves to Demosthenes, and observed his directions. He managed all the assemblies of the Thebans, no less than those of the Athenians; he was beloved both by the one and by the other, and exercised the same supreme authority with both; and that not by unfair means, or without just cause, but it was no more than was due to his merit.

But there was, it should seem, some divinely-ordered fortune, commissioned, in the revolution of things, to put a period at this time to the liberty of Greece, which opposed and thwarted all their actions, and by many signs foretold what should happen. Such were the sad predictions uttered by the Pythian priestess, and this old oracle cited out of the Sibyl's verses:

> The battle on Thermodon that shall be
> Safe at a distance I desire to see,
> Far, like an eagle, watching in the air.
> Conquered shall weep, and conqueror perish there.

This Thermodon, they say, is a little rivulet here in our country in Chæronea, running into the Cephisus. But we know of none that is so called at the present time; and can only conjecture that the streamlet which is now called Hæmon, and runs by the Temple of Hercules, where the Greeks were encamped, might perhaps in those days be called Thermodon.

But of Demosthenes it is said, that he had such great confidence in the Greek forces, and was so excited by the sight of the courage and resolution of so many brave men ready to engage the enemy, that he would by no means endure they should give any heed to oracles, or hearken to prophecies, but gave out that he suspected even the prophetess herself, as if she had been tampered with to speak in favor of Philip. He put the Thebans in mind of Epaminondas, the Athenians of Pericles, who always took their own measures and governed their actions by reason, looking upon things of this kind as mere pretexts for cowardice. Thus far, therefore, Demosthenes acquitted himself like a brave man. But in the fight he did nothing honorable, nor was his performance answerable to his speeches. For he fled, deserting his place disgracefully, and throwing away his arms, not ashamed, as Pytheas observed, to belie the inscription written on his shield, in letters of gold, "With good fortune."

In the meantime Philip, in the first moment of victory, was so transported with joy, that he grew extravagant, and going out, after he had drunk largely, to visit the dead bodies, he chanted the first words of the decree that had been passed on the motion of Demosthenes,

<blockquote>The motion of Demosthenes, Demosthenes's son,</blockquote>

dividing it metrically into feet, and marking the beats.

But when he came to himself, and had well considered the danger he was lately under, he could not forbear from shuddering at the wonderful ability and power of an orator who had made him hazard his life and empire on the issue of a few brief hours. The fame of it also reached even to the court of Persia, and the king sent letters to his lieutenants, commanding them to supply Demosthenes with money, and to pay every attention to him, as the only man of all the Greeks who was able to give Philip occupation and find employment for his forces near home, in the troubles of Greece.

At this time, however, upon the ill success which now happened to the Greeks, those of the contrary faction in the commonwealth turned upon Demosthenes, and took the opportunity to frame several informations and indictments against him. But the people not only acquitted him of these accusations, but continued towards him their former respect, and when the bones of those who had been slain at Chæronea were brought home to be solemnly interred, Demosthenes was the man they chose to make the funeral oration. The speech, therefore, was spoken by Demosthenes. But the subsequent decrees he would not allow to be passed in his own name, but made use of those of his friends, one after another, looking upon his own as unfortunate and inauspicious; till at length he took courage again after the death of Philip, who did not long outlive his victory at Chæronea. And this, it seems, was that which was foretold in the last verse of the oracle,

> Conquered shall weep, and conqueror perish there.

Demosthenes had secret intelligence of the death of Philip, and laying hold of this opportunity to prepossess the people with courage and better hopes for the future, he came into the assembly with a cheerful countenance, pretending to have had a dream that presaged some great good fortune for Athens; and, not long after, arrived the messengers who brought the news of Philip's death. No sooner had the people received it, but immediately they offered sacrifice to the gods, and decreed that Pausanias should be presented with a crown. Demosthenes appeared publicly in a rich dress, with a chaplet on his head, though it were but the seventh day since the death of his daughter, as is said by Æschines, who upbraids him upon this account, and rails at him as one void of natural affection towards his children. Whereas, Æschines rather betrays himself to be of a poor spirit, if he really means to make wailings and lamentation the only signs of a gentle and affectionate nature. I must commend the behavior of Demosthenes, who, leaving tears and lamentations and domestic sorrows to the women, made it his business to attend to the interests of the commonwealth.

But now to return to my narrative. The cities of Greece were inspirited once more by the efforts of Demosthenes to form a league together. The Thebans, whom he had provided with arms, set upon their garrison, and slew many of them; the Athenians made preparations to join their forces with them; Demosthenes ruled supreme in the popular assembly, and wrote letters to the Persian officers who commanded under the king in Asia, inciting them to make war upon the Macedonian, calling him child and simpleton. But as soon as Alexander had settled matters in his own country, and come in person with his army into Bœotia, down fell the courage of the Athenians, and Demosthenes was hushed; the Thebans, deserted by them, fought by themselves, and lost their city. After which, the people of Athens, all in distress and great perplexity, resolved to send ambassadors to Alexander, and amongst others, made choice of Demosthenes for one; but his heart failing him for fear of the king's anger, he returned back from Cithæron, and left the embassy. In the mean time, Alexander sent to Athens, requiring eight of the orators to be delivered up to him,—Demosthenes, Polyeuctus, Ephialtes, Lycurgus, Mœrocles, Demon, Callisthenes, and Charidemus. It was upon this occasion that Demosthenes related to them the fable in which the sheep are said to deliver up their dogs to the wolves; himself and those who with him contended for the people's safety, being, in his comparison, the dogs that defended the flock, and Alexander "the Macedonian arch wolf." He further told them, "As we see corn-dealers sell their whole stock by a few grains of wheat which they carry about with them in a dish, as a sample of the rest, so you, by delivering up us, who are but a few, do at the same time unawares surrender up yourselves all together with us." The Athenians were deliberating, and at a loss what to do, when Demades, having agreed with the persons whom Alexander had demanded, for five talents, undertook to go ambassador, and to intercede with the king for them; and, whether it was that he relied on his friendship and kindness, or that he hoped to find him satiated, as a lion glutted with slaughter, he certainly went, and prevailed with him both to pardon the men, and to be reconciled to the city.

So he and his friends, when Alexander went away, were great men, and Demosthenes was quite put aside. Yet when Agis, the Spartan, made his insurrection, he also for a short time attempted a movement in his favor; but he soon shrunk back again, as the Athenians would not take any part in it, and, Agis being slain, the Lacedæmonians were vanquished. During this time it was that the indictment against Ctesiphon concerning the Crown, was brought to trial. The action was commenced a little before the battle in Chæronea, when Chærondas was archon, but it was not proceeded with till about ten years after, Aristophon being then archon. Never was any public cause more celebrated than this, alike for the fame of the orators, and for the generous courage of the judges, who, though at that time the accusers of Demosthenes, were in the height of power, and supported by all the favor of the Macedonians, yet would not give judgment against him, but acquitted him so honorably, that Æschines did not obtain the fifth part of their suffrages on his side, so that, immediately after, he left the city, and spent the rest of his life in teaching rhetoric about the island of Rhodes, and upon the continent in Ionia.

It was not long after that Harpalus fled from Alexander, and came to Athens out of Asia; knowing himself guilty of many misdeeds into which his love of luxury had led him, and fearing the king, who was now grown terrible even to his best friends. Yet this man had no sooner addressed himself to the people, and delivered up his goods, his ships, and himself to their disposal, but the other orators of the town had their eyes quickly fixed upon his money, and came in to his assistance, persuading the Athenians to receive and protect their suppliant. Demosthenes at first gave advice to chase him out of the country, and to beware lest they involved their city in a war upon an unnecessary and unjust occasion. But some few days after, as they were taking an account of the treasure, Harpalus, perceiving how much he was pleased with a cup of Persian manufacture, and how curiously he surveyed the sculpture and fashion of it, desired him to poise it in his hand, and consider the weight of the gold. Demosthenes, being amazed to feel how heavy it was asked him what weight it *came to*. "To you," said Harpalus, smiling, " it shall *come with* twenty talents." And presently after, when night drew on, he sent him the cup with so many talents. Harpalus, it seems, was a person of singular skill to discern a man's covetousness by the air of his countenance, and the look and movement of his eyes. For Demosthenes could not resist the temptation, but admitting the present, like an armed garrison, into the citadel of his house, he surrendered himself up to the interest of Harpalus. The next day he came into the assembly with his neck swathed about with wool and rollers, and when they called on him to rise up and speak, he made signs as if he had lost his voice. But the wits, turning the matter to ridicule, said that certainly the orator had been seized that night with no other than a silver quinsy. And soon after, the people, becoming aware of the bribery, grew angry, and would not suffer him to speak, or make any apology for himself, but ran him down with noise; and one man stood up and cried out, "What, ye men of Athens, will you not hear the cup-bearer?" So at length they banished Harpalus out of the city; and fearing lest they should be called to account for the treasures which the orators had purloined, they made a strict inquiry, going from house to house.

Demosthenes resisted the inquisition, and proposed a decree to refer the business to the court of Areopagus, and to punish those whom that court should find guilty. But being himself one of the first whom the court condemned, when he came to the bar, he was fined fifty talents, and committed to prison; where, out of shame of the crime for which he was condemned, and through the weakness of his body, growing incapable of supporting the confinement, he made his escape, by the carelessness of some and by the connivance of others of the citizens. He did not show much fortitude in his banishment, spending his time for the most part in Ægina and Trœzen, and, with tears in his eyes, looking towards the country of Attica. The young men that came to visit and converse with him, he deterred from meddling with state affairs, telling them, that if at first two ways had been proposed to him, the one leading to the speaker's stand and the assembly, the other going direct to destruction, and he could have foreseen the many evils which attend those who deal in public business, such as fears, envies, calumnies, and contentions, he would certainly have taken that which led straight on to his death.

But now happened the death of Alexander, while Demosthenes was in this banishment which we have been speaking of. And the Greeks were once again up in arms, encouraged by the brave attempts of Leosthenes, who was then drawing a circumvallation about Antipater, whom he held close besieged in Lamia. Pytheas, therefore, the orator, and Callimedon, called the Crab, fled from Athens, and taking sides with Antipater, went about with his friends and ambassadors to keep the Greeks from revolting and taking part with the Athenians. But, on the other side, Demosthenes, associating himself with the ambassadors that came from Athens, used his utmost endeavors and gave them his best assistance in persuading the cities to fall unanimously upon the Macedonians, and to drive them out of Greece. With this conduct the people of Athens were so well pleased, that they decreed the recall of Demosthenes from banishment. The decree was brought in by Demon the Pæanian, cousin to Demosthenes. So they sent him a ship to Ægina, and he landed at the port of Piræus, where he was met and joyfully received by all the citizens, not so much as an Archon or a priest staying behind. And Demetrius, the Magnesian, says, that he lifted up his hands towards heaven, and blessed this day of his happy return, as far more honorable than that of Alcibiades; since he was recalled by his countrymen, not through any force or constraint put upon them, but by their own good-will and free inclinations. There remained only his pecuniary fine, which, according to law, could not be remitted by the people. But they found out a way to elude the law. It was a custom with them to allow a certain quantity of silver to those who were to furnish and adorn the altar for the sacrifice of Jupiter Soter. This office, for that turn, they bestowed on Demosthenes, and for the performance of it ordered him fifty talents, the very sum in which he was condemned.

Yet it was no long time that he enjoyed his country after his return, the attempts of the Greeks being soon all utterly defeated. And in the month of Pyanepsion following Demosthenes died after this manner.

Upon the report that Antipater was coming to Athens, Demosthenes with his party took their opportunity to escape privily out of the city; but sentence of death was, upon the motion of Demades, passed upon them by the people. They dispersed themselves, flying some to one place, some to another; and Antipater sent about his soldiers into all quarters to apprehend them. Archias, formerly an actor, was their captain, and was thence called the exile-hunter. This Archias finding Hyperides the orator, Aristonicus and Himeræus in Ægina, took them by force out of the temple of Æacus, whither they had fled for safety, and sent them to Antipater, and put them all to death; and Hyperides, they say, had his tongue cut out.

Demosthenes, he heard, had taken sanctuary at the temple of Neptune at Calauria, and, crossing over thither in some light vessels, as soon as he had landed himself, and the Thracian spear-men that came with him, he endeavored to persuade Demosthenes to accompany him to Antipater, as if he should meet with no hard usage from him. But Demosthenes, in his sleep the night before, had a strange dream. It seemed to him that he was acting a tragedy, and contended with Archias for the victory; and though he acquitted himself well, and gave good satisfaction to the spectators, yet for want of better furniture and provision for the stage, he lost the day. And so, while Archias was discoursing to him with many expressions of kindness, he sat still in the same posture, and looking up steadfastly upon him, said: "O Archias, I am as little affected by your promises now as I used formerly to be by your acting." Archias at this beginning to grow angry and to threaten him, "Now," said Demosthenes, "you speak like the genuine Macedonian oracle; before you were but acting a part. Therefore forebear only a little, while I write a word or two home to my family." Having thus spoken, he withdrew into the temple, and taking a scroll, as if he meant to write, he put the reed into his mouth, and biting it, as he was wont to do when he was thoughtful or writing, he held it there for some time. Then he bowed down his head and covered it. The soldiers that stood at the door, supposing all this to proceed from want of courage and fear of death, in derision called him effeminate, and faint-hearted, and coward. And Archias, drawing near, desired him to rise up, and repeating the same kind things he had spoken before, he once more promised him to make his peace with Antipater. But Demosthenes, perceiving that now the poison had pierced and seized his vitals, uncovered his head, and fixing his eyes upon Archias, "Now," said he, "as soon as you please you may commence the part of Creon in the tragedy, and cast out this body of mine unburied. But, O gracious Neptune, I, for my part, while I am yet alive, arise up and depart out of this sacred place; though Antipater and the Macedonians have not left so much as thy temple unpolluted." After he had thus spoken and desired to be held up, because already he began to tremble and stagger, as he was going forward, and passing by the altar, he fell down, and with a groan gave up the ghost.

Ariston says that he took the poison out of a reed, as we have shown before. And Eratosthenes also says that he kept the poison in a hollow ring, which he wore about his arm. There are various other statements made by the many authors who have related the story, but there is no need to enter into their discrepancies; yet I must not omit what is said by Demochares, the relation of Demosthenes, who is of opinion, it was not by the help of poison that he met with so sudden and so easy a death, but that by the singular favor and providence of the gods he was thus rescued from the cruelty of the

Macedonians. He died on the sixteenth of Pyanepsion, the most sad and solemn day of the Thesmophoria, which the women observe by fasting in the temple of the goddess.

Soon after his death, the people of Athens bestowed on him such honors as he had deserved. They erected his statue of brass; they decreed that the eldest of his family should be maintained in the Prytaneum; and on the base of his statue was engraven the famous inscription,—

> Had you for Greece been strong, as wise you were,
> The Macedonian had not conquered her.

A little before we went to Athens, the following incident was said to have happened. A soldier, being summoned to appear before his superior officer, and answer to an accusation brought against him, put a little gold which he had into the hands of Demosthenes's statue. The fingers of this statue were folded one within another, and near it grew a small plane-tree, from which many leaves, either accidentally blown thither by the wind, or placed so on purpose by the man himself, falling together, and lying round about the gold, concealed it for a long time. In the end, the soldier returned, and found his treasure entire, and the fame of this incident was spread abroad. And many ingenious persons of the city competed with each other, on this occasion, to vindicate the integrity of Demosthenes, in several epigrams which they made on the subject.

As for Demades, he did not long enjoy the new honors he now came in for, divine vengeance for the death of Demosthenes pursuing him into Macedonia, where he was justly put to death by those whom he had basely flattered.

CICERO.

It is generally said that Helvia, the mother of Cicero, was well born; but of his father nothing is reported but in extremes. For whilst some would have him the son of a fuller, and educated in that trade, others carry back the origin of his family to Tullus Attius, an illustrious king of the Volscians, who waged war not without honor against the Romans. However, he who first of that house was surnamed Cicero seems to have been a person worthy to be remembered; since those who succeeded him not only did not reject, but were fond of that name, though vulgarly made a matter of reproach. For the Latins call a vetch *Cicer*, and a nick or dent at the tip of his nose, which resembled the opening in a vetch, gave him the surname of *Cicero*.

Cicero, whose story I am writing, is said to have replied with spirit to some of his friends, who recommended him to lay aside or change the name when he first stood for office and engaged in politics, that he would make it his endeavor to render the name of Cicero more glorious than that of the Scauri and Catuli. And when he was quæstor in Sicily, and was making an offering of silver plate to the gods, and had inscribed his two names, Marcus and Tullius, instead of the third, he jestingly told the artificer to engrave the figure of a vetch by them.

Cicero was born on the third of January, the same day on which now the magistrates of Rome pray and sacrifice for the emperor. As soon as he was of an age to begin to have lessons, he became so distinguished for his talent, and got such a name and reputation amongst the boys, that their fathers would often visit the school, that they might see young Cicero, and might be able to say that they themselves had witnessed the quickness and readiness in learning for which he was renowned. And the more rude among them used to be angry with their children, to see them, as they walked together, receiving Cicero with respect into the middle place. And being, as Plato would have the scholar-like and philosophical temper, eager for every kind of learning, and indisposed to no description of knowledge or instruction, he showed, however, a more peculiar propensity to poetry; and there is a poem now extant, made by him when a boy, in tetrameter verse, called Pontius Glaucus. And afterwards, when he applied himself more curiously to these accomplishments, he had the name of being not only the best orator, but also the best poet of Rome. And the glory of his rhetoric still remains, notwithstanding the many new modes in speaking since his time; but his verses are forgotten and out of all repute, so many ingenious poets have followed him.

Leaving his juvenile studies, he became an auditor of Philo the Academic, whom the Romans, above all the other scholars of Clitomachus, admired for his eloquence and loved for his character. He also sought the company of the Mucii, who were eminent statesmen and leaders in the senate, and acquired from them a knowledge of the laws. For some short time he served in arms under Sylla, in the Marsian war. But perceiving the commonwealth running into factions, and from faction all things tending to an absolute monarchy, he betook himself to a retired and contemplative life, and conversing with the learned Greeks, devoted himself to study, till Sylla had obtained the government.

At this time, Chrysogonus, Sylla's emancipated slave, having laid an information about an estate belonging to one who was said to have been put to death by proscription, had bought it himself for two thousand drachmas. And when Roscius, the son and heir of the dead, complained, and demonstrated the estate to be worth two hundred and fifty talents, Sylla took it angrily to have his actions questioned, and preferred a process against Roscius for the murder of his father, Chrysogonus managing the evidence. None of the advocates durst assist him, but fearing the cruelty of Sylla, avoided the cause. The young man, being thus deserted, came for refuge to Cicero. Cicero's friends encouraged him, saying he was not likely ever to have a fairer and more honorable introduction to public life; he therefore undertook the defence, carried the cause, and got much renown for it.

But fearing Sylla, he travelled into Greece, and gave it out that he did so for the benefit of his health. And indeed he was lean and meagre, and had such a weakness in his stomach that he could take nothing but a spare and thin diet, and that not till late in the evening. His voice was loud and good, but so harsh and ill-managed that in vehemence and heat of speaking he always raised it to so high a tone, that there seemed to be reason to fear for his health.

At Athens, he became a hearer of Antiochus of Ascalon, with whose fluency and elegance of diction he was much taken, although he did not approve of his innovations in doctrine. And Cicero made up his mind that if he should be disappointed of any employment in the commonwealth, to retire from pleading and politics, and pass his life quietly in the study of philosophy.

But after he had received the news of Sylla's death, and his body, strengthened again by exercise, had grown vigorous, and his voice was rendered sweet and full to the ear, his friends at Rome earnestly solicited him by letters to return to public affairs. He, therefore, again prepared for use his orator's instrument of rhetoric, and summoned into action his political faculties, diligently exercising himself in declamations, and attending the most celebrated rhetoricians of the time. He sailed from Athens for Asia and Rhodes. Among the Asian masters, he conversed with Xenocles of Adramyttium, Dionysius of Magnesia, and Menippus of Caria; at Rhodes, he studied oratory with Apollonius, the son of Molon, and philosophy with Posidonius. Apollonius, we are told, not understanding Latin, requested Cicero to declaim in Greek. He complied willingly, thinking that his faults would thus be better pointed out to him. After he finished, all his other hearers were astonished, and vied with each other in praising him, but Apollonius showed no signs of excitement while he was hearing him, and now, when he had finished, sat musing for some time, without any remark. And when Cicero was discomposed at this, he said, "You have my praise and admiration, Cicero, and Greece my pity and commiseration, since those arts and that eloquence which are the only glories that remain to her, will now be transferred by you to Rome."

And now when Cicero, full of expectation, was again bent upon political affairs, a certain oracle blunted the edge of his inclination; for consulting the god of Delphi how he should attain most glory, the Pythoness answered, "By making your own genius and not the opinion of the people the guide of your life;" and therefore at first he passed his time in Rome cautiously, and was very backward in pretending to public offices, so that he was at that time in little esteem, and had got the names, so readily given by low and ignorant people in Rome, of Greek and Scholar. But when his own desire of fame and the eagerness of his father and relations had made him take in earnest to pleading, he made no slow or gentle advance to the first place, but shone out in full lustre at once, and far surpassed all the advocates at the bar. At first, it is said, he, as well as Demosthenes, was defective in his delivery, and on that account paid much attention to the instructions, sometimes of Roscius, the comedian, and sometimes of Æsop, the tragedian. They tell of this Æsop, that while representing in the theatre Atreus deliberating the revenge of Thyestes, he was so transported beyond himself in the heat of action, that he struck with his sceptre one of the servants, who was running across the stage, so violently, that he laid him dead upon the place. And such afterwards was Cicero's delivery, that it did not a little contribute to render his eloquence persuasive. He used to ridicule loud speakers, saying that they shouted because they could not speak, like lame men who get on horseback because they cannot walk. And his readiness and address in wit and sarcasm were thought to suit a pleader well.

He was appointed quæstor in a great scarcity of corn, and had Sicily for his province, where, at first, he displeased many, by compelling them to send in their provisions to Rome, yet after they had had experience of his care, justice, and clemency, they honored him more than ever they did any of their governors before. It happened, also, that some young Romans of good and noble families, charged with neglect of discipline and misconduct in military service, were brought before the prætor in Sicily. Cicero undertook their defence, which he conducted admirably, and got them acquitted. So returning to Rome with a great opinion of himself for these things, a ludicrous incident befell him, as he tells us himself. Meeting an eminent citizen in Campania, whom he accounted his friend, he asked him what the Romans said and thought of his actions, as if the whole city had been filled with the glory of what he had done. His friend asked him in reply, "Where is it you have been, Cicero?" Utterly mortified and cast down, he perceived that the report of his actions had sunk into the city of Rome as into an immense ocean, without any visible effect or result in reputation.

On beginning to apply himself more resolutely to public business, he remarked it as unreasonable that artificers, using vessels and instruments inanimate, should know the name, place, and use of every one of them, and yet the statesman, whose instruments for carrying out public measures are men, should be negligent and careless in the knowledge of persons. And so he not only acquainted himself with the names, but also knew the very place where every one of the more eminent citizens dwelt, what lands he possessed, his friends and his neighbors, and when he travelled on any road in Italy, he could readily name and show the estates and seats of his acquaintances. Having a small competency for his own expenses, it was much wondered at that he took neither fees nor gifts from his clients, and especially, that he did not do so when he undertook the prosecution of Verres. This Verres, who had been prætor of Sicily, and stood charged by the Sicilians with many evil practices during his government there, Cicero succeeded in getting condemned, not by speaking, but, as it were, by holding his tongue. For the prætors, favoring Verres, had deferred the trial by several adjournments to the last day, in which it was evident there could not be sufficient time for the advocates to be heard, and the cause brought to an issue. Cicero, therefore, came forward, and said there was no need of speeches; and after producing and examining witnesses, he required the judges to proceed to sentence. Many witty sayings are on record, as having been used by Cicero on the occasion. When a man named Cæcilius, one of the freed slaves, who was said to be given to Jewish practices, would have put by the Sicilians, and undertaken the prosecution of Verres himself, Cicero asked, "What has a Jew to do with swine?" *verres* being the Roman word for a boar. And when Verres began to reproach Cicero with effeminate living, "You ought," replied he, "to use this language at home, to your sons;" Verres having a son who had fallen into disgraceful courses. Hortensius, the orator, not daring directly to undertake the defence of Verres, was yet persuaded to appear for him at the laying on of the fine, and received an ivory sphinx for his reward; and when Cicero, in some passage of his speech, obliquely reflected on him, and Hortensius told him he was not skilful in solving riddles, "No," said Cicero, "and yet you have the Sphinx in your house!"

Verres was thus convicted; though Cicero, who set the fine

at seventy-five myriads,* lay under the suspicion of being corrupted by bribery to lessen the sum. But the Sicilians, in testimony of their gratitude, came and brought him all sorts of presents from the island, when he was ædile; of which he made no private profit himself, but used their generosity only to reduce the public price of provisions.

He had a very pleasant seat at Arpi,† he had also a farm near Naples, and another near Pompeii, but none were of any great value. The portion of his wife, Terentia, amounted to ten myriads, and he had a bequest valued at nine myriads of denarii: upon these he lived in a liberal but temperate style, with the learned Greeks and Romans that were his familiars. He rarely, if at any time, sat down to meat till sunset, and that not so much on account of business as for his health and the weakness of his stomach. He was otherwise in the care of his body nice and delicate, appointing himself, for example, a set number of walks and rubbings. And after this manner managing the habit of his body, he brought it in time to be healthful, and capable of supporting many great fatigues and trials. His father's house he made over to his brother, living himself near the Palatine Hill, that he might not give the trouble of long journeys to those that made suit to him. And, indeed, there were not fewer daily appearing at his door, to do their court to him, than there were that came to Crassus for his riches, or to Pompey for his power among the soldiers, these being at that time the two men of the greatest repute and influence in Rome. Nay, even Pompey himself used to pay court to Cicero, and Cicero's public actions did much to establish Pompey's authority and reputation in the state.

Numerous distinguished competitors stood with him for the

---

* Seventy-five ten thousands, *i.e.*, 750,000 drachmas, about $125,000; Plutarch counting the drachma as equivalent to the denarius. But the sum does not agree with the figures given in Cicero's own orations, and must be regarded as quite uncertain.

† Plutarch calls this Arpi, which is far from Rome, in Apulia; but it is, of course, Arpinum, Cicero's native place.

prætor's office; but he was chosen before them all, and managed the decision of causes with justice and integrity. It is related that Licinius Macer, a man himself of great power in the city, and supported also by the assistance of Crassus, was accused before him of extortion, and that, in confidence on his own interest and the diligence of his friends, whilst the judges were debating about the sentence, he went to his house, where hastily trimming his hair and putting on a clean gown, as already acquitted, he was setting off again to go to the Forum; but at his hall door meeting Crassus, who told him that he was condemned by all the votes, he went in again, threw himself upon his bed, and died immediately. This verdict was considered very creditable to Cicero, as showing his careful management of the courts of justice.

Yet he was preferred to the consulship no less by the nobles than the common people for the good of the city; and both parties jointly assisted his promotion, for the following reasons. The change of government made by Sylla, which at first seemed a senseless one, by time and usage had now come to be considered by the people no unsatisfactory settlement. But there were some that endeavored to alter and subvert the whole present state of affairs, not from any good motives, but for their own private gain; and Pompey being at this time employed in the wars with the kings of Pontus and Armenia, there was no sufficient force at Rome to suppress any attempts at a revolution. These people had for their head a man of bold, daring, and restless character, Lucius Catiline, who was accused, besides other great offences, of killing his own brother; and fearing to be prosecuted at law, he persuaded Sylla to set his brother down, as though he were yet alive, amongst those that were to be put to death by proscription. This man the profligate citizens choosing for their captain, gave faith to one another, amongst other pledges, by sacrificing a man and eating of his flesh; and a great part of the young men of the city were corrupted by him, he providing for every one pleasures and drink, and profusely supplying the expense of their debauches. Etruria, moreover, had all been excited to revolt, as well as a great part of Gaul within the Alps. But Rome itself was in the most dangerous inclination to change on account of the unequal distribution of wealth and property, those of highest rank and greatest spirit having impoverished themselves by shows, entertainments, running for office, and sumptuous buildings, and the riches of the city had thus fallen into the hands of mean and low-born persons. So that it required but a slight impetus to set all in motion, it being in the power of any daring man to overturn a sickly commonwealth.

Catiline, however, being desirous of procuring a strong position to carry out his designs, stood for the consulship, and had great hopes of success, thinking he should be appointed, with Caius Antonius as his colleague, who was a man fit to lead neither in a good cause nor in a bad one, but might be a valuable accession to another's power. The greater part of the good and honest citizens apprehending these things, put Cicero upon standing for the consulship; whom the people readily receiving, Catiline was put by, so that he and Caius Antonius were chosen, although amongst the competitors he was the only man descended from the father of the equestrian, and not of the senatorial, order.

Though the designs of Catiline were not yet publicly known, yet considerable trouble immediately followed Cicero's entrance upon the consulship. For, on the one side, those who were disqualified by the laws of Sylla from holding any public offices, being neither inconsiderable in power nor in number, came forward as candidates and entreated the people; on the other hand, the tribunes of the people proposed laws to the same purpose, constituting a commission of ten persons, with unlimited powers, in whom as supreme governors should be vested the right of selling the public lands of all Italy and Syria and Pompey's new conquests, of judging and banishing whom they pleased, of planting colonies, of taking money out of the treasury, and of levying and paying what soldiers should be thought needful. And several of the nobility favored this law, but especially Caius Antonius, Cicero's colleague, in hopes of being one of the ten. But what gave the greatest fear to the nobles was, that he was thought privy to the conspiracy of Catiline, and not to dislike it because of his great debts.

Cicero, endeavoring in the first place to provide a remedy against this danger, procured a decree assigning to Antonius the province of Macedonia, he himself declining that of Gaul, which was offered to him. And this piece of favor so completely won over Antonius, that he was ready to second, like a hired player, whatever Cicero said for the good of the country. And now, having made his colleague tame and tractable, he could with greater courage attack the conspirators. Therefore, in the senate, making an oration against the law of the ten commissioners, he so confounded those who proposed it, that they had nothing to reply.

For Cicero, it may be said, was the one man, above all others, who made the Romans feel how great a charm eloquence lends to what is good, and how invincible justice is if it be well presented. An incident occurred in the theatre, during his consulship, which showed what his speaking could do, Formerly the knights of Rome were mingled in the theatre with the common people, and took their places amongst them just as it happened; but when Marcus Otho became prætor he distinguished them from the other citizens, and appointed them special seats, which they still enjoy as their place in the theatre. This the common people took as an indignity done to them, and, therefore, when Otho appeared in the theatre they hissed him; the knights, on the contrary, received him with loud clapping. The people repeated and increased their hissing; the knights continued their clapping. Upon this, turning upon one another, they broke out into insulting words, so that the theatre was in great disorder. Cicero, being informed of it, came himself to the theatre, and summoning the people into the temple of Bellona, he so effectually chid and chastised them for it, that, again returning into the theatre, they received Otho with loud applause, contending with the knights as to who should give him the greatest demonstrations of honor and respect.

The conspirators with Catiline, at first cowed and disheartened, began presently to take courage again. And assembling together, they exhorted one another boldly to undertake the design before Pompey's return. But the old soldiers of Sylla were Catiline's chief stimulus to action. They had been disbanded all about Italy, but the greatest number and the fiercest of them lay scattered among the cities of Etruria entertaining themselves with dreams of new plunder and rapine among the hoarded riches of Italy. These, having for their leader Manlius, who had served with distinction in the wars under Sylla, joined themselves to Catiline, and came to Rome to assist him with their suffrages at the election. For he again aspired for the consulship, having resolved to kill Cicero in a tumult at the elections. The divine powers seemed to give intimation of the coming troubles, by earthquakes, thunderbolts and strange appearances. Nor was human evidence wanting, certain enough in itself, though not sufficient to convict the noble and powerful Catiline. Therefore Cicero, deferring the day of election, summoned Catiline into the senate, and questioned him as to the charges made against him. Catiline, believing there were many in the senate desirous of change, and to give a specimen of himself to the conspirators present, returned an audacious answer. "What harm," said he, "when I see two bodies, the one lean and consumptive with a head, the other one great and strong without one, if I put a head to that body which wants one?" This covert representation of the senate and the people excited yet greater apprehensions in Cicero. He put on armor, and was attended from his house by the noble citizens in a body; and a number of the young men went with him into the Plain. Here, designedly letting his tunic slip partly off from his shoulders, he showed his armor underneath, and discovered his danger to the spectators, who, being much moved at it, gathered around about him for his defence. At length, Catiline was by general suffrage again put by, and Silanus and Murena chosen consuls.

Not long after this, Catiline's soldiers got together in a body in Etruria, and began to form themselves into companies, the day appointed for the design being near at hand. About midnight, some of the principal and most powerful citizens of Rome, Marcus Crassus, Marcus Marcellus, and Scipio Metellus went to Cicero's house, where, knocking at the gate, and calling up the porter, they commanded him to awake Cicero, and tell him they were there. The business was this: Crassus's porter after supper had delivered to him letters brought by an unknown person. Some of them were directed to others, but one to Crassus, without a name; this only Crassus read, which informed him that there was a great slaughter intended by Catiline, and advised him to leave the city. The others he did not open, but went with them immediately to Cicero, being affrighted at the danger, and to free himself of the suspicion he lay under for his familiarity with Catiline. Cicero, considering the matter, summoned the senate at break of day. The letters he brought with him, and delivered them to those to whom they were directed, commanding them to read them publicly; they all alike contained an account of the conspiracy. And when Quintus Arrius, a man of prætorian dignity, recounted to them, how soldiers were collecting in companies in Etruria, and Manlius was stated to be in motion with a large force, hovering about those cities, in expectation of intelligence from Rome, the senate made a decree to place all in the hands of the consuls, who should undertake the conduct of everything, and do their best to save the state. This was not a common thing, but only done by the senate in cases of imminent danger.

After Cicero had received this power, he committed all affairs outside to Quintus Metellus; but the management of the city he kept in his own hands. Such a numerous attendance guarded him every day when he went abroad that the greater part of the forum was filled with his train when he entered it. Catiline, impatient of further delay, resolved himself to break forth and go to Manlius; but he commanded Marcius and Cethegus to take their swords and go early in the morning to Cicero's gates, as if only intending to salute him, and then to fall upon him and slay him. A noble lady, Fulvia, coming by night, discovered this to Cicero, bidding him beware of Cethegus and Marcius. They came by break of day, and being denied entrance, made an outcry and disturbance at the gates, which excited all the more suspicion. But Cicero, going forth, summoned the senate into the temple of Jupiter Stator, which stands at the end of the Sacred Street, going up to the Palatine. And when Catiline with others of his party also came, as though intending to make his defence, none of the senators would sit by him, but all of them left the bench where he had placed himself. And when he began to speak, they interrupted him with outcries. At length, Cicero, standing up, commanded him to leave the city; for, since one governed the commonwealth with words, the other with arms, it was necessary that there should be a wall betwixt them. Catiline, therefore, immediately left the town, with three hundred armed men; and assuming, like a magistrate, the rods, axes, and military ensigns, he went to Manlius, and having got together a body of near twenty thousand men, with these he marched to the several cities, endeavoring to persuade or force them to revolt. It being now come to open war, Antonius was sent forth to fight him.

The remainder of those in the city whom he had corrupted, Cornelius Lentulus kept together and encouraged. He had the surname Sura, and was a man of a noble family, but a dissolute liver, who for his debauchery was formerly turned out of the senate, and was now holding the office of prætor for the second time, as the custom is with those who desire to regain the dignity of senator. It is said that he got the surname Sura upon this occasion; being quæstor in the time of Sylla, he had lavished away and consumed a great quantity of the public moneys, at which Sylla, being provoked, called him to give an account in the senate. He appeared with great coolness and contempt, and said he had no account to give, but they might take this, holding up the calf of his leg, as boys do at ball, when they have missed. Upon which he was surnamed *Sura*, *sura* being the Roman word for the calf of the leg. Being at another time prosecuted at law, and having bribed some of the judges, he escaped by only two votes, and complained of the needless expense he had gone to in paying for a second, as one would have sufficed to acquit him. This man, such in his own nature, and now inflamed by Catiline, false prophets and fortune-tellers had also corrupted with vain hopes, quoting to him fictitious verses and oracles, and proving from the Sibylline prophecies that there were three of the name Cornelius designed by fate to be monarchs of Rome; two of whom, Cinna and Sylla, had already fulfilled the decree, and that divine fortune was now advancing with the gift of monarchy for the remaining third Cornelius; and that therefore he ought by all means to accept it, and not lose opportunity by delay, as Catiline had done.

Lentulus, therefore, designed no mean or trivial matter, for he had resolved to kill the whole senate, and as many other citizens as he could, to fire the city, and spare nobody, except Pompey's children, intending to seize and keep them as pledges of his reconciliation with Pompey. For there was then a common report that Pompey was on his way homeward from his great expedition. The night appointed for the design was one of the Saturnalia; swords, flax, and sulphur they carried and hid in the house of Cethegus; and providing one hundred men, and dividing the city into as many parts, they had allotted to every one singly his proper place, so that in a moment, many kindling the fire, the city might be in a flame all together. Others were appointed to stop up the aqueducts, and to kill those who should endeavor to carry water to put it out. While these plans were preparing, it happened that there were two embassadors from the Allobroges staying in Rome; a nation at that time in a distressed condition, and very uneasy under the Roman government. These Lentulus and his party, judging useful instruments to move Gaul to revolt, admitted into the conspiracy, and they gave them letters to their own magistrates, and letters to Catiline; in those they promised liberty, in these they exhorted Catiline to set all slaves free, and to bring them along with him to Rome. They sent also to accompany them to Catiline, one Titus, a native of Croton, who was to carry those letters to him.

These counsels of inconsidering men, who conversed together over their wine, Cicero watched with sober industry and forethought, and with most admirable sagacity, having several emissaries abroad, who observed and traced with him all that was done, and keeping also a secret correspondence with many who pretended to join in the conspiracy. He thus knew all the discourse which passed between them and the strangers; and lying in wait for them by night, he took the Crotonian with his letters, the ambassadors of the Allobroges acting secretly in concert with him.

By break of day, he summoned the senate into the temple of Concord, where he read the letters and examined the informers. Junius Silanus further stated that several persons had heard Cethegus say that three consuls and four prætors were to be slain; Piso, also, a person of consular dignity, testified other matters of like nature; and Caius Sulpicius, one of the prætors, being sent to Cethegus's house, found there a quantity of darts and of armor, and a still greater number of swords and daggers, all recently whetted. At length, the senate, decreeing indemnity to the Crotonian upon his confession of the whole matter, Lentulus was convicted, abjured his office (for he was then prætor), and put off his robe edged with purple in the senate, changing it for another garment more agreeable to his present circumstances. He, thereupon, with the rest of his confederates present, was committed to the charge of the prætors in free custody.

It being evening, and the common people in crowds expecting without, Cicero went forth to them, and told them what was done, and then, attended by them, went to the house of a friend and near neighbor; for his own was taken up by the women, who were celebrating with secret rites the feast of the goddess whom the Romans call the Good, and the Greeks, the Women's goddess. For a sacrifice is annually performed to her in the consul's house, either by his wife or mother, in the presence of the vestal virgins. And having got into his friend's house privately, a few only being present, he began to deliberate how he should treat these men. The severest and the only punishment fit for such heinous crimes, he was somewhat shy and fearful of inflicting, as well from the clemency of his nature, as also lest he should be thought to exercise his authority too insolently, and to treat too harshly men of the noblest birth and most powerful friendships in the city; and yet, if he should use them more mildly, he had a dreadful prospect of danger from them. For there was no likelihood that, if they suffered less than death, they would be reconciled, but, rather, adding new rage to their former wickedness, they would rush into every kind of audacity, while he himself, whose character for courage already did not stand very high with the multitude, would be thought guilty of the greatest cowardice and want of manliness.

While Cicero was in doubt what course to take, a portent happened to the women in their sacrificing. For on the altar, where the fire seemed wholly extinguished, a great and bright flame issued forth from the ashes of the burnt wood; at which others were affrighted, but the holy virgins called to Terentia, Cicero's wife, and bade her hasten to her husband, and command him to execute what he had resolved for the good of his country, for the goddess had sent a great light to the increase of his safety and glory. Terentia, therefore, as she was otherwise in her own nature neither tender-hearted nor timorous, but a woman eager for distinction (who, as Cicero himself says, would rather thrust herself into his public affairs than communicate her domestic matters to him), told him these things, and excited him against the conspirators. So also did Quintus his brother, and Publius Nigidius, one of his philosophical friends, whom he often made use of in his most weighty affairs of state.

The next day, a debate arising in the senate about the punishment of the men, Silanus, being the first who was asked his opinion, said, it was fit that they should be all sent to prison, and there suffer the utmost penalty. With him all agreed in order till it came to Caius Cæsar, who was afterwards dictator. He was then but a young man, and only at the outset of his career, but had already directed his hopes and policy to that course by which he afterwards changed the Roman state into a monarchy.

When it came Cæsar's turn to give his opinion, he stood up and proposed that the conspirators should not be put to death, but their estates confiscated, and their persons confined in such cities in Italy as Cicero should approve, there to be kept in custody till Catiline was conquered. To this sentence, as it was the most moderate, and he that delivered it a most powerful speaker, Cicero himself gave no small weight, for he stood up and, turning the scale on either side, spoke in favour partly of the former, partly of Cæsar's sentence. And all Cicero's friends, judging Cæsar's sentence most expedient for Cicero, because he would incur the less blame if the conspirators were not put to death, chose rather the latter; so that Silanus, also, changing his mind, retracted his opinion, and said he had not declared for capital, but only the utmost punishment, which to a Roman senator is imprisonment. The first man who spoke against Cæsar's motion was Catulus Lutatius. Cato followed, and so vehemently urged in his speech the strong suspicion about Cæsar himself, and so filled the senate with anger and resolution, that a decree was passed for the execution of the conspirators. But Cæsar opposed the confiscation of their goods, not thinking it fair that those who had rejected the mildest part of his sentence should avail themselves of the severest. And when many insisted upon it, he appealed to the tribunes, but they would do nothing; till Cicero himself yielding, remitted that part of the sentence.

After this, Cicero went out with the senate to the conspirators; they were not all together in one place, but the several prætors had them, some one, some another, in custody. And first he took Lentulus from the Palatine, and brought him by the Sacred Street, through the middle of the market-place, a circle of the most eminent citizens encompassing and protecting him. The people, affrighted at what was doing, passed along in silence, especially the young men; as if, with fear and trembling, they were undergoing a rite of initiation into some ancient, sacred mysteries of aristocratic power. Thus passing from the market-place, and coming to the gaol, he delivered Lentulus to the officer, and commanded him to execute him; and after him Cethegus, and so all the rest in order, he brought and delivered up to execution. And when he saw many of the conspirators in the market-place, still standing together in companies, ignorant of what was done, and waiting for the night, supposing the men were still alive and in a possibility of being rescued, he called out in a loud voice, and said, "*They did live*"; for so the Romans, to avoid inauspicious language, name those that are dead.

It was now evening, when he returned from the market-place to his own house, the citizens no longer attending him with silence, nor in order, but receiving him, as he passed with acclamations and applauses, and saluting him as the savior and founder of his country. A bright light shone through the streets from the lamps and torches set up at the doors, and the women showed lights from the tops of the houses, to honor Cicero, and to behold him returning home with a splendid train of the principal citizens; amongst whom were many who had conducted great wars, celebrated triumphs, and added to the possessions of the Roman empire, both by sea and land. These, as they passed along with him, acknowledged to one another, that though the Roman people were indebted to several officers and commanders of that age for riches, spoils, and power, yet to Cicero alone they owed the safety and security of all these, for delivering them from so great and imminent a danger. For though it might seem no wonderful thing to prevent the design, and punish the conspirators, yet to defeat the greatest of all conspiracies with so little disturbance, trouble, and commotion, was very extraordinary. For the greater part of those who had flocked in to Catiline, as soon as they heard of the fate of Lentulus and Cethegus, forsook him, and he himself, with his remaining forces, joining battle with Antonius, was destroyed with his army.

And yet there were some who were very ready both to speak ill of Cicero, and to do him hurt for these actions; and they had for their leaders some of the magistrates of the ensuing year, as Cæsar, who was one of the prætors, and Metellus and Bestia, the tribunes. These, entering upon their office some few days before Cicero's consulate expired, would not permit him to make any address to the people, but, throwing the benches before the Rostra, hindered his speaking, telling him he might, if he pleased, make the oath of withdrawal from office, and then come down again. Cicero, accordingly, accepting the conditions, came forward to make his withdrawal; and silence being made, he recited his oath, not in the usual, but in a new and peculiar form, namely, that he had saved his country, and preserved the empire; the truth of which oath all the people confirmed with theirs. Cæsar and the tribunes, all the more exasperated by this, endeavored to create him further trouble, and for this purpose proposed a law for calling Pompey home with his army, to put an end to Cicero's usurpation. But it was a very great advantage for Cicero and the whole commonwealth that Cato was at that time one of the tribunes. For he, being of equal power with the rest, and of greater reputation, could oppose their designs. He easily defeated their other projects, and, in an oration to the people, so highly extolled Cicero's consulate, that the greatest honors were decreed him, and he was publicly declared the Father of his Country, which title he seems to have obtained, the first man who did so, when Cato applied it to him in this address to the people.

At this time, therefore, his authority was very great in the city; but he created himself much envy, and offended very many, not by any evil action, but because he was always lauding and magnifying himself. For neither senate, nor assembly of the people, nor court of judicature could meet, in which he was not heard to talk of Catiline and Lentulus. Indeed, he filled his books and writings with his own praises, to such an excess as to render a style, in itself most pleasant and delightful, nauseous and irksome to his hearers. This ungrateful humor, like a disease, always clove to him. Still, though fond of his own glory, he was very free from envying others, but was, on the contrary, most liberally profuse in commending both the ancients and his contemporaries, as any one may see in his writings. He called Aristotle a river of flowing gold, and said of Plato's Dialogues, that if Jupiter were to speak, it would be in language like theirs. He used to call Theophrastus his special luxury. And being asked which of Demosthenes's orations he liked best, he answered, "The longest." And as for the eminent men of his own time, either in eloquence or philosophy, there was not one of them whom he did not, by writing or speaking favorably of him, render more illustrious.

An example of his love of praise is the way in which sometimes, to make his orations more striking, he neglected decorum and dignity. When Munatius, who had escaped conviction by his advocacy, immediately prosecuted his friend Sabinus, he said in the warmth of his resentment, "Do you suppose you were acquitted for your own merits, Munatius, or was it not that I so darkened the case, that the court could not see your guilt?" When from the Rostra he had made a eulogy on Marcus Crassus, with much applause, and within a few days after again as publicly reproached him, Crassus called to him, and said, " Did not you yourself two days ago, in this same place, commend me?" "Yes," said Cicero, "I exercised my eloquence in declaiming upon a bad subject." At another time, Crassus had said that no one of his family had ever lived beyond sixty years of age, and afterwards denied it, and asked, "What should put it into my head to say so?" "It was to gain the people's favor," answered Cicero; "you knew how glad they would be to hear it." When Vatinius, who had swellings in his neck, was pleading a cause, he called him the *tumid* orator; and having been told by some one that Vatinius was dead, on hearing soon after that he was alive, he said, "may the rascal perish, for his news not being true."

Upon Cæsar's bringing forward a law for the division of the lands in Campania amongst the soldiers, many in the senate opposed it; amongst the rest, Lucius Gellius, one of the oldest men in the house, said it should never pass whilst he lived. "Let us postpone it," said Cicero, "Gellius does not ask us to wait long." There was a man of the name of Octavius, suspected to be of African descent. He once said, when Cicero was pleading, that he could not hear him; "Yet there are holes," said Cicero, "in your ears." * When Metellus Nepos told him that he had ruined more as a witness than he had

---

* The marks of the ears having been bored for ear-rings would be considered proof of his being of barbarian origin.

saved as an advocate, "I admit," said Cicero, "that I have more truth than eloquence." To a young man who was suspected of having given a poisoned cake to his father, and who talked largely of the invectives he meant to deliver against Cicero, "Better these," replied he, "than your cakes." Publius Sextius, having amongst others retained Cicero as his advocate in a certain cause, was yet desirous to say all for himself, and would not allow anybody to speak for him; when he was about to receive his acquittal from the judges, and the ballots were passing, Cicero called to him, "make haste, Sextius, and use your time; to-morrow you will be nobody." He cited Publius Cotta to bear testimony in a certain cause, one who affected to be thought a lawyer, though ignorant and unlearned; but when Cotta had said, "I know nothing at all about the matter," Cicero answered: "You think, perhaps, we are asking you about a point of law." When Marcus Appius, in the opening of some speech in a court of justice, said that his friend had desired him to employ industry, eloquence, and fidelity in that cause, Cicero asked, "And how have you had the heart not to accede to any one of his requests?"

One Clodius, whom Cicero had vehemently opposed in an important trial, having got himself chosen one of the tribunes, immediately attacked Cicero, endeavoring to incite everybody against him. The common people he gained over with popular laws; to each of the consuls he decreed large provinces, to Piso, Macedonia, and to Gabinius, Syria. Of the three men then in greatest power, Crassus was Cicero's open enemy, Pompey indifferently made advances to both, and Cæsar was going with an army into Gaul. To him, though not his friend, Cicero applied, requesting an appointment as one of his lieutenants in the province. Cæsar accepted him, and Clodius, perceiving that Cicero would thus escape his tribunician authority, professed to be inclinable to a reconciliation, made always a favorable mention of him, and addressed him with kind expressions, as one who felt no hatred or ill-will, but who merely wished to urge his complaints in a moderate and friendly way. By these artifices, he so freed Cicero of all his fears, that he resigned his appointment to Cæsar, and betook himself again to political affairs. At which Cæsar being exasperated, joined the party of Clodius against him, and wholly alienated Pompey from him; he also himself declared in a public assembly of the people, that he did not think Lentulus and Cethegus, with their accomplices, were fairly and legally put to death without being brought to trial. And this, indeed, was the crime charged upon Cicero, and this impeachment he was summoned to answer. And so, as an accused man, and in danger for the result, he changed his dress, and went round with his hair untrimmed, in the attire of a suppliant, to beg the people's grace. But Clodius met him in every corner, having a band of abusive and daring fellows about him, who derided Cicero for his change of dress and his humiliation, and often, by throwing dirt and stones at him, interrupted his supplication to the people.

However, first of all, almost the whole equestrian order changed their dress with him, and no less than twenty thousand young gentlemen followed him with their hair untrimmed, and supplicating with him to the people. And then the senate met, to pass a decree that the people should change their dress as in time of public sorrow. But the consuls opposing it, and Clodius with armed men besetting the senate-house, many of the senators ran out, crying aloud and tearing their clothes. But this sight moved neither shame nor pity; Cicero must either fly or determine it by the sword with Clodius. He entreated Pompey to aid him, who on purpose had gone out of the way, and was staying at his country-house in the Alban hills; and first he sent his son-in-law Piso to intercede with him, and afterwards set out to go himself. But Pompey being informed, would not stay to see him, being ashamed at the remembrance of the many conflicts in the commonwealth which

Cicero had undergone in his behalf, and how much of his policy he had directed for his advantage. But being now Cæsar's son-in-law, at his instance he had set aside all former kindness, and, slipping out at another door, avoided the interview. Thus being forsaken by Pompey, and left alone to himself, he fled to the consuls. Gabinius was rough with him, as usual, but Piso spoke more courteously, desiring him to yield for a while to the fury of Clodius, and to await a change of times, and to be now, as before, his country's savior from the peril of these troubles and commotions which Clodius was exciting.

Cicero, receiving this answer, consulted with his friends. Lucullus advised him to stay, as being sure to prevail at last; others to fly, because the people would soon desire him again, when they should have enough of the rage and madness of Clodius. This last Cicero approved. But first he took a statue of Minerva, which had been long set up and greatly honored in his house, and carrying it to the capitol, there dedicated it, with the inscription, "To Minerva, Patroness of Rome." And receiving an escort from his friends, about the middle of the night he left the city, and went by land through Lucania, intending to reach Sicily.

But as soon as it was publicly known that he was fled, Clodius proposed to the people a decree of exile, and by his own order interdicted him fire and water, prohibiting any within five hundred miles in Italy to receive him into their houses. Most people, out of respect for Cicero, paid no regard to this edict, offering him every attention, and escorting him on his way. But at Hipponium, a city of Lucania, now called Vibo, one Vibius, a Sicilian by birth, who, amongst many other instances of Cicero's friendship, had been made head of the state engineers when he was consul, would not receive him into his house, sending him word that he would appoint a place in the country for his reception. Caius Vergilius, the prætor of Sicily, who had been on the most intimate terms with him, wrote to him to forbear coming into Sicily. Cicero, thoroughly disheartened at these things, went to Brundusium, whence he put forth with a prosperous wind, but a contrary gale blowing from the sea carried him back to Italy the next day. He put again to sea, and having reached Dyrrachium, on his coming to shore there, it is reported that an earthquake and a convulsion in the sea happened at the same time, signs which the diviners said intimated that his exile would not be long, for these were prognostics of change. Although many visited him with respect, and the cities of Greece contended with each other in honoring him, he yet continued disconsolate, like an unfortunate lover, often casting his looks back upon Italy; and, indeed, he had become more humiliated and dejected by his misfortunes than any one could have expected in a man who had devoted so much of his life to study and learning. And yet he often desired his friends not to call him orator, but philosopher, because he had made philosophy his business, and had only used rhetoric as an instrument for attaining his objects in public life.

Clodius, having thus driven away Cicero, fell to burning his farm-buildings and villas, and afterwards his city house, and built on the site of it a temple to Liberty. The rest of his property he exposed for sale by daily proclamation, but nobody came to buy. By this course he became formidable to the noble citizens, and, being followed by the commonalty, whom he had filled with insolence and licentiousness, he began at last to try his strength against Pompey, some of whose arrangements in the countries he conquered, he attacked. The disgrace of this made Pompey begin to reproach himself for his cowardice in deserting Cicero, and, changing his mind, he now wholly set himself with his friends to contrive his return. And when Clodius opposed it, the senate made a vote that no public measure should be ratified or passed by them till Cicero was recalled. But when Lentulus was consul, the commotions grew so high upon this matter, that the tribunes were wounded in the Forum, and Quintus, Cicero's brother, was left as dead, lying unobserved amongst the slain. The people began to change in their feelings; and Annius Milo, one of their tribunes, was the first who had the courage to summon Clodius to trial for acts of violence. Many of the common people in Rome and the neighboring cities formed a party with Pompey, who headed them in person, drove Clodius out of the Forum, and summoned the people to pass their vote. And, it is said, the people never passed any suffrage more unanimously than this. The senate, also, striving to outdo the people, sent letters of thanks to those cities which had received Cicero with respect in his exile, and decreed that his house and his country-places, which Clodius had destroyed, should be rebuilt at the public charge.

Thus Cicero returned sixteen months after his exile, and the cities were so glad, and the people so zealous to meet him, that his boast, that Italy had brought him on her shoulders home to Rome, was rather less than the truth. And Crassus himself, who had been his enemy before his exile, went voluntarily to meet him, and was reconciled, as he said, to please his son Publius, who was Cicero's affectionate admirer.

Cicero had not been long at Rome, when, taking the opportunity of Clodius's absence, he went, with a great company, to the capitol, and there tore and defaced the tribunician tables, in which were recorded the acts done in the time of Clodius. And on Clodius calling him in question for this, he answered, that he, being of the patrician order, had obtained the office of tribune against the law, and, therefore, nothing done by him was valid. Cato was displeased at this, and opposed Cicero, not that he commended Clodius, but rather disapproved of his whole administration; yet, he contended, that it was an irregular and violent course for the senate to vote the illegality of so many decrees and acts, including those of Cato's own government in Cyprus and at Byzantium. This occasioned a **breach** between Cato and Cicero, which, though it did not come to open enmity, made a more reserved friendship between them.

After this, Milo killed Clodius, and, being arraigned for the murder, he procured Cicero for his advocate. The senate, fearing lest the questioning of so eminent and high-spirited a citizen as Milo might disturb the peace of the city, committed the superintendence of this and of the other trials to Pompey, who should undertake to maintain the security alike of the city and of the courts of justice. Pompey, therefore, went in the night, and occupying the high grounds about it, surrounded the Forum with soldiers. Milo, fearing lest Cicero, being disturbed by such an unusual sight, should conduct his cause the less successfully, persuaded him to come in a litter into the Forum, and there rest till the judges had taken their seats, and the court was filled. For Cicero, it seems, not only wanted courage in arms, but, in his speaking also, began with timidity, and in many cases scarcely left off trembling and shaking when he had got thoroughly into the current and the substance of his speech. Once when he had to defend Licinius Murena against the prosecution of Cato, being eager to outdo Hortensius, who had made his plea with great applause, he took so little rest the night before, and was so disordered with thought and over-watching, that he spoke much worse than usual. And so now, on quitting his litter to commence the cause of Milo, at the sight of Pompey, encamped, as it were, with his troops, and seeing arms shining round about the Forum, he was so confounded that he could hardly begin his speech, for the trembling of his body and hesitancy of his tongue; whereas Milo, meantime, was so bold and intrepid in his demeanor, that he disdained either to let his hair grow, or to put on the mourning habit. And this, indeed, seems to have been the principal cause of his condemnation. And Cicero was thought not so much to have shown timidity for himself, as anxiety about his friend.

When the outbreak between Cæsar and Pompey came,

THE CAPITOL.

Cicero wavered painfully between both, for he writes in his epistles, "To which side should I turn? Pompey has the fair and honorable plea for war; and Cæsar, on the other hand, has managed his affairs better, and is more able to secure himself and his friends. So that I know whom I should fly from, not whom I should fly to." But when Trebatius, one of Cæsar's friends, by letter signified to him that Cæsar thought it was his most desirable course to join his side, but if he considered himself too old a man for this, he would do better to retire into Greece, and stay quietly there, out of the way of either party, Cicero, wondering that Cæsar had not written himself, replied angrily that he should do nothing unbecoming his past life.

But as soon as Cæsar had marched into Spain, he immediately sailed away to join Pompey. And he was welcomed by all but Cato; who, taking him privately aside, chid him for coming to Pompey. As for himself, he said, it would have been indecent to forsake that part in the commonwealth which he had chosen from the beginning; but Cicero might have been more useful to his country and friends, if, remaining neutral, he had attended and used his influence to moderate the result, instead of coming hither to make himself, without reason or necessity, an enemy to Cæsar, and a partner in such great dangers. By this language, Cicero's feelings were altered, and partly, also, because Pompey made no great use of him. Although he was himself really the cause of it, by his not denying that he was sorry he had come, by his deprecating Pompey's resources, finding fault underhand with his counsels, and continually indulging in jests and sarcastic remarks on his fellow-soldiers.

After the battle of Pharsalia was over, at which he was not present for want of health, and Pompey had fled, Cato, having considerable forces and a great fleet at Dyrrachium, would have had Cicero commander-in-chief, according to law, and the precedence of his consular dignity. But on his refusing the command, and wholly declining to take part in their plans for continuing the war, he was in the greatest danger of being killed, young Pompey and his friends calling him traitor, and drawing their swords upon him; only that Cato interposed, and with difficulty rescued and brought him out of the camp.

Afterwards, arriving at Brundusium, he tarried there some time in expectation of Cæsar, who was delayed by his affairs in Asia and Egypt. And when it was told him that he had arrived at Tarentum, and was coming thence by land to Brundusium, he hastened towards him, not altogether without hope, and yet in some fear of making experiment of the temper of an enemy and conqueror in the presence of many witnesses. But there was no necessity for him either to speak or do anything unworthy of himself; for Cæsar, as soon as he saw him coming a good way before the rest of the company, went forward to meet him, saluted him, and, leading the way, conversed with him alone for some furlongs. And from that time on he continued to treat him with honor and respect, so that, when Cicero wrote an oration in praise of Cato, Cæsar, in writing an answer to it, took occasion to commend Cicero's own life and eloquence, comparing him to Pericles and Theramenes. Cicero's oration was called "Cato"; Cæsar's, "Anti-Cato."

So also, it is related that when Quintus Ligarius was prosecuted for having been in arms against Cæsar, and Cicero had undertaken his defence, Cæsar said to his friends, "Ligarius, without question, is a wicked man and an enemy. But why might we not as well once more hear a speech from Cicero?" Yet when Cicero began to speak, he wonderfully moved him, and proceeded in his speech with such varied pathos, and such a charm of language, that the color of Cæsar's countenance often changed, and it was evident that all the passions of his soul were in commotion. And when at length, the orator touched upon the Pharsalian battle, he was so affected that his whole frame trembled, and some of the papers he held dropped out of his hands. And thus he was overpowered, and acquitted Ligarius.

Henceforth, the commonwealth being changed into a monarchy, Cicero withdrew himself from public affairs, and employed his leisure in instructing those young men that wished, in philosophy; and by the near intercourse he thus had with some of the noblest and highest in rank, he again began to possess great influence in the city. The work which he set himself to do was to compose and translate philosophical dialogues and to render logical and physical terms into the Roman idiom. For he it was, as it is said, who first or principally gave Latin names to technical Greek terms, which, either by metaphors or other means of accommodation, he succeeded in making intelligible to the Romans. For his recreation, he exercised his dexterity in poetry, and when he was set to it, would make five hundred verses in a night. He spent the greatest part of his time at his country-house near Tusculum.

He had a design, it is said, of writing the history of his country, combining with it much of that of Greece, and incorporating in it all the stories and legends of the past that he had collected. But his purposes were interfered with by various public and various private unhappy occurrences and misfortunes; for most of which he was himself in fault. For first of all, he put away his wife, Terentia, by whom he had been neglected in the time of the war, and sent away destitute of necessaries for his journey; neither did he find her kind when he returned into Italy, for she did not join him at Brundusium, where he staid a long time, and would not allow her young daughter, who undertook so long a journey, decent attendance, or the requisite expenses; besides, she left him a naked and empty house, and yet had involved him in many and great debts. These were alleged as the fairest reasons for the divorce. But Terentia, who denied them all, had the most unmistakable defence furnished her by her husband himself who not long after married a young maiden for the love of her beauty, as Terentia upbraided him; or as Tiro, his emancipated slave, has written, for her riches, to discharge his debts. For the young woman was very rich, and Cicero had the custody of her estate, being left guardian in trust; and being in debt many myriads of money, he was persuaded by his friends and relations to marry her, notwithstanding their disparity of age, and to use her money to satisfy his creditors. Antony, who mentions this marriage in his answer to the Philippics, reproaches him for putting away a wife with whom he had lived to old age; adding some happy strokes of sarcasm on Cicero's domestic, inactive, unsoldier-like habits. Not long after this marriage, his daughter died at Lentulus's house, to whom she had been married after the death of Piso, her former husband. The philosophers from all parts came to comfort Cicero; for his grief was so excessive, that he put away his newly-married wife, because she seemed to be pleased at the death of Tullia.

He had no concern in the design that was now forming to kill Cæsar, although, in general, he was Brutus's confidant.

But as soon as the act was committed by Brutus and Cassius, and the friends of Cæsar had assembled, so that there was danger of another civil war, Antony, being consul, convened the senate, and made a short address recommending concord. And Cicero, following with various remarks such as the occasion called for, persuaded the senate to imitate the Athenians, and decree an amnesty for what had been done in Cæsar's case, and to bestow provinces on Brutus and Cassius. But neither of these things took effect. For as soon as the common people, who were naturally inclined to pity, saw the dead body of Cæsar borne through the market-place, and Antony showing his clothes stained with blood, and pierced through in every part with swords, they were enraged to such a degree of frenzy, that they made a search for the murderers, and with firebrands in their hands ran to their houses to burn them.

Antony at this was in exultation, and every one was alarmed

at the prospect that he would make himself sole ruler, and Cicero more than any one else. For Antony, seeing his influence reviving in the commonwealth, and knowing how closely he was connected with Brutus, was ill-pleased to have him in the city. Besides, there had been some former jealousy between them, occasioned by the difference of their manners. Cicero, fearing the event, was inclined to go as lieutenant with Dolabella into Syria. But Hirtius and Pansa, consuls-elect as successors of Antony, good men and lovers of Cicero, entreated him not to leave them, undertaking to put down Antony if he would stay in Rome. And he, neither distrusting wholly, nor trusting them, let Dolabella go without him, promising Hirtius that he would go and spend his summer at Athens, and return again when he entered upon his office. So he set out on his journey; but some delay occurring in his passage, new intelligence, as often happens, came suddenly from Rome, that Antony had made an astonishing change, and was managing the public affairs in harmony with the will of the senate, and that there wanted nothing but his presence to bring things to a happy settlement. Therefore, blaming himself for his cowardice, he returned to Rome, and was not deceived in his hopes at the beginning. For such multitudes flocked out to meet him, that the compliments and civilities which were paid him at the gates, and at his entrance into the city, took up almost a whole day's time.

On the morrow, Antony convened the senate, and summoned Cicero thither. But he kept his bed, pretending to be ill from his journey; but the true reason seemed to be the fear of some design against him, upon a suspicion and intimation given him on his way to Rome. Antony, however, showed great offence at the affront, and sent soldiers, commanding them to bring him or burn his house; but many interceding and supplicating for him, he was contented to accept sureties. Ever after, when they met, they passed one another in silence, and continued on their guard, till the younger Cæsar (Augustus), coming from Apollonia, entered on the first Cæsar's inheritance, and was engaged in a dispute with Antony about two thousand five hundred myriads of money, which Antony detained from the estate.

Upon this, Philippus, who married the mother, and Marcellus, who married the sister of young Cæsar, came with the young man to Cicero, and agreed with him that Cicero should give them the aid of his eloquence and political influence with the senate and people, and Cæsar give Cicero the defence of his riches and arms. For the young man had already a great party of the soldiers of Cæsar about him. And Cicero's readiness to join him was founded, it is said, on some yet stronger motives; for it seems, while Pompey and Cæsar were yet alive, Cicero, in his sleep, had fancied himself engaged in calling some of the sons of the senators into the capitol, Jupiter, according to the dream, being about to declare one of them the chief ruler of Rome. The citizens, running up with curiosity, stood about the temple, and the youths, sitting in their purple-bordered robes, kept silence. On a sudden the doors opened, and the youths, arising one by one in order, passed round the god, who reviewed them all, and, to their sorrow, dismissed them; but when this one was passing by, the god stretched forth his right hand and said, "O ye Romans, this young man, when he shall be lord of Rome, shall put an end to all your civil wars." It is said that Cicero formed from his dream a distinct image of the youth, and retained it afterwards perfectly, but did not know who it was. The next day, going down into the Campus Martius, he met the boys returning from their gymnastic exercises, and the first was he, just as he had appeared to him in his dream. Being astonished at it, he asked him who were his parents. And it proved to be this young Cæsar, whose father was a man of no great eminence, Octavius, and his mother, Attia, Cæsar's sister's daughter; for which reason, Cæsar, who had no children, made him by will the heir of his house and property. From that time, it is said that Cicero studiously noticed the youth whenever he met him, and he as kindly received the civility; and by fortune he happened to be born when Cicero was consul.

These were the reasons spoken of; but it was principally Cicero's hatred of Antony, and a temper unable to resist honor, which fastened him to Cæsar, with the purpose of getting the support of Cæsar's power for his own public designs. For the young man went so far in his court to him, that he called him Father; at which Brutus was so highly displeased, that, in his epistles to Atticus he reflected on Cicero saying, it was manifest, by his courting Cæsar for fear of Antony, he did not intend liberty to his country, but an indulgent master to himself. Notwithstanding, Brutus took Cicero's son, then studying philosophy at Athens, gave him a command, and employed him in various ways, with a good result. Cicero's own power at this time was at the greatest height in the city, and he did whatsoever he pleased; he completely overpowered and drove out Antony, and sent the two consuls, Hirtius and Pansa, with an army, to reduce him; and, on the other hand, persuaded the senate to allow Cæsar the lictors and ensigns of a prætor, as though he were his country's defender. But after Antony was defeated in battle, and the two consuls slain, the armies united, and ranged themselves with Cæsar. And the senate, fearing the young man, and his extraordinary fortune, endeavored by honors and gifts, to call off the soldiers from him, and to lessen his power; professing there was no further need of arms, now Antony was put to flight.

This gave Cæsar a fright, and he privately sent friends to entreat Cicero to procure the consular dignity for them both together; saying that he should manage the affair as he pleased, should have the supreme power, and govern the young man who was only desirous of name and glory.

And now, more than at any other time, Cicero let himself be carried away and deceived, though an old man, by the persuasions of a boy. He joined him in soliciting votes, and procured the good-will of the senate, not without blame at the time on the part of his friends; and he, too, soon enough after, saw that he had ruined himself, and betrayed the liberty of his country. For the young man, once established, and possessed of the office of consul, bade Cicero farewell; and reconciling himself with Antony and Lepidus, joined his power with theirs, and divided the government, like a piece of property, with them. Thus united, they made a schedule of above two hundred persons who were to be put to death. But the greatest contention in all their debates was on the question of Cicero's case. Antony would come to no conditions, unless he should be the first man to be killed. Lepidus held with Antony, and Cæsar opposed them both. They met secretly and by themselves, for three days together, near the town of Bononia. The spot was not far from the camp, with a river surrounding it. Cæsar, it is said, contended earnestly for Cicero the first two days; but on the third day he yielded, and gave him up. The terms of their mutual concessions were these; that Cæsar should desert Cicero, Lepidus his brother Paulus, and Antony, Lucius Cæsar, his uncle by his mother's side. Thus they let their anger and fury take from them the sense of humanity, and demonstrated that no beast is more savage than man, when possessed with power proportioned to his rage.

While these things were contriving, Cicero was with his brother at his country-house near Tusculum; whence, hearing of the proscriptions, they determined to pass to Astura, a villa of Cicero's near the sea, and to take shipping from there for Macedonia to Brutus, of whose strength in that province news had already been heard. They travelled together in their separate litters, overwhelmed with sorrow; and often stopping on the way till their litters came together, condoled with one another. But Quintus was the more disheartened, when he reflected on his want of means for his journey; for, as he said, he had brought nothing with him from home. And even

Cicero himself had but a slender provision. It was judged, therefore most expedient that Cicero should make what haste he could to fly, and Quintus return home to provide necessaries, and thus resolved, they mutually embraced, and parted with many tears.

Quintus, within a few days after, was betrayed by his servants to those who came to search for him, and slain, together with his young son. But Cicero was carried to Astura, where, finding a vessel, he immediately went on board of her, and sailed as far as Circæum with a prosperous gale; but when the pilots resolved immediately to set sail from there, whether he feared the sea, or did not wholly lose faith in Cæsar, he went on shore, and passed by land a hundred furlongs, as if he was going to Rome. But losing resolution and changing his mind, he again returned to the sea, and there spent the night in fear and perplexity. Sometimes he resolved to go into Cæsar's house privately, and there kill himself upon the altar of his household gods, to bring divine vengeance upon him; but the fear of torture restrained him. And after passing through a variety of confused and uncertain counsels, at last he let his servants carry him by sea to Capitæ,* where he had a house, an agreeable place to retire to in the heat of summer, when the Etesian winds are so pleasant.

There was at that place a chapel of Apollo, not far from the sea-side, from which a flight of crows rose with a great noise, and made towards Cicero's vessel as it rowed to land, and lighting on both sides of the yard, some croaked, others pecked the ends of the ropes. This was looked upon by all as an evil omen; and, therefore, Cicero went again ashore, and entering his house, lay down upon his bed to compose himself to rest. Many of the crows settled about the window, making a dismal cawing; but one of them alighted upon the bed where Cicero lay covered up, and with its bill, little by little pecked off the

---

*This as we find from other authority, means Caieta, the present Gaeta.

clothes from his face. His servants, seeing this, blamed themselves that they should stay to be spectators of their master's murder, and do nothing in his defence, while the brute creatures came to assist and take care of him in his undeserved affliction; and, therefore, partly by entreaty, partly by force they took him up, and carried him in his litter toward the seaside.

But in the meantime the assassins had come with a band of soldiers—Herennius, a centurion, and Popillius, a tribune, whom Cicero had formerly defended when prosecuted for the murder of his father. Finding the door shut, they broke them open, and when Cicero did not appear and those within said they did not know where he was, it is stated that a youth, who had been educated by Cicero in the liberal arts and sciences, an emancipated slave of his brother Quintus, Philologus by name, informed the tribune that the litter was on its way to the sea through the close and shady walks. The tribune, taking a few with him, ran to the place where he was to come out. And Cicero, perceiving Herennius running in the walks, commanded his servants to set down the litter; and stroking his chin, as he used to do, with his left hand, he looked steadfastly upon his murderers, his person covered with dust, his beard and hair untrimmed, and his face worn with his troubles. So that the greatest part of those that stood by covered their faces whilst Herennius slew him. And thus was he murdered, stretching forth his neck out of the litter, being now in his sixty-fourth year. Herennius cut off his head, and, by Antony's command, his hands also, by which his Philippics were written; for so Cicero styled those orations he wrote against Antony, and so they are called to this day.

When these members of Cicero were brought to Rome, Antony was holding an assembly for the choice of public officers; and when he heard it, and saw them, he cried out, "Now let there be an end of our proscriptions." He commanded his head and hands to be fastened up over the Rostra, where the orators spoke; a sight which the Roman people shuddered to behold, and they believed they saw there not the face of Cicero, but the image of Antony's own soul.

A long time after, Augustus, when visiting one of his daughter's sons, found him with a book of Cicero's in his hand. The boy for fear endeavored to hide it under his gown; but Cæsar took it from him, and turning over a great part of the book standing, gave it to him again, and said, "My child, this was a learned man, and a lover of his country." And immediately after he had vanquished Antony, being then consul, he made Cicero's son his colleague in the office; and, under that consulship, the senate took down all the statues of Antony, and abolished all the other honors that had been given him, and decreed that none of that family should thereafter bear the name of Marcus; and thus the final acts of the punishment of Antony were, by the divine powers, devolved upon the family of Cicero.

WRITING IMPLEMENTS.

COMPARISON OF DEMOSTHENES AND CICERO.

These are the most memorable circumstances recorded in history of Demosthenes and Cicero which have come to our knowledge. But, omitting an exact comparison of their respective faculties in speaking, yet this seems fit to be said: That Demosthenes, to make himself a master in rhetoric, applied all the faculties he had, natural or acquired, wholly that way; that he far surpassed in force and strength of eloquence in political and judicial speaking all his contemporaries, in grandeur and majesty all the panegyrical orators, and in accuracy and science all the logicians and rhetoricians of his day; that Cicero was highly educated, and by his diligent study became a most accomplished general scholar in all these branches, having left behind him numerous philosophical treatises of his own on Academic principles; as, indeed, even in his written speeches, both political and judicial, we see him continually trying to show his learning by the way. And one may discover the different temper of each of them in their speeches. For Demosthenes's oratory was, without all embellishment and jesting, wholly composed for real effect and seriousness; not smelling of the lamp, as Pytheas scoffingly said, but of the temperance, thoughtfulness, austerity, and grave earnestness of his temper. Whereas, Cicero's love of mockery often ran him into scurrility; and in his love of laughing away serious arguments in judicial cases by jests and facetious remarks, with a view to the advantage of his clients, he paid too little regard to what was decent. We are told that Cicero, being consul, undertook the defence of Murena against Cato's prosecution; and, by way of bantering Cato, made a long series of jokes upon the absurd *paradoxes*, as they are called, of the Stoic sect. When loud laughter passed from the crowd to the judges, Cato, with a quiet smile, said to those that sat next to him, "My friends, what an amusing consul we have."

And, indeed, Cicero was by natural temper very much disposed to mirth and pleasantry, and always appeared with a smiling and serene countenance. But Demosthenes had constant care and thoughtfulness in his look, and a serious anxiety which he seldom, if ever, laid aside; and, therefore, was accounted by his enemies, as he himself confessed, morose and ill-mannered.

Also, it is very evident, out of their several writings, that Demosthenes never touched upon his own praises but decently and without offence when there was need of it, and for some weightier end. But Cicero's immeasurable boasting of himself in his orations argues him guilty of an uncontrollable appetite for distinction, his cry being evermore that "Arms should give place to the gown, and the soldier's laurel to the tongue."* And at last we find him extolling not only his deeds and actions, but his orations, as well those that were only spoken, as those that were published.

It is necessary for a political leader to be an able speaker; but it is an ignoble thing for any man to admire the glory of his own eloquence. And, in this matter, Demosthenes had a more than ordinary gravity and magnificence of mind, for he considered his talent in speaking nothing more than a mere accomplishment and matter of practice, the success of which must depend greatly on the good-will and candor of his hearers, and regarded those who pride themselves on such accounts to be men of a low and petty disposition.

The power of persuading and governing the people did, indeed, equally belong to both, so that those who had armies and camps at command stood in need of their assistance; as Chares, Diopithes, and Leosthenes did that of Demosthenes, and Pompey and young Cæsar of Cicero's, as the latter

---
* Translating Cicero's famous verse upon himself—
Cedant arma togæ, concedat laurea linguæ.

himself admits in his Memoirs addressed to Agrippa and
Mæcenas. But what are thought and commonly said most to
demonstrate and try the tempers of men, namely, authority
and place, by moving every passion, and discovering every
frailty, these are things which Demosthenes never received;
nor was he ever in a position to give such proof of himself,
having never obtained any eminent office, nor led any of those
armies into the field against Philip which he raised by his eloquence. Cicero, on the other hand, was sent quæstor into
Sicily, and proconsul into Cilicia and Cappadocia, at a time
when avarice was at the height, and the commanders and governors who were employed abroad, as though they thought it
a mean thing to steal, set themselves to seize by open force;
so that it seemed no heinous matter to take bribes, but he that
did it most moderately was in good esteem. And yet he, at
this time, gave the most abundant proofs alike of his contempt
of riches and of his humanity and good-nature. And at Rome,
when he was created consul in name, but indeed received
sovereign and dictatorial authority against Catiline and his
conspirators, he attested the truth of Plato's prediction, that
then only would the miseries of states be at an end, when by a
happy fortune supreme power, wisdom, and justice should be
united in one.*

It is said, to the reproach of Demosthenes, that his eloquence was mercenary; that he privately made orations for
Phormion and Apollodorus, though adversaries in the same
cause; that he was charged with moneys received from the
king of Persia, and condemned for bribes from Harpalus.
And should we grant that all those (and they are not few)
who have made these statements against him have spoken
what is untrue, yet we cannot assert that Demosthenes was not
the character to look without desire on the presents offered
him out of respect and gratitude by royal persons. But that
Cicero refused, from the Sicilians when he was quæstor, from

---

* Or, as the dictum is in his Republic, "When the philosopher should be king."

the king of Cappadocia when he was proconsul, and from his friends at Rome when he was in exile, many presents, though urged to receive them, has been said already.

Moreover, Demosthenes's banishment was infamous, upon conviction for bribery; Cicero's very honorable, for ridding his country of a set of villains. Therefore, when Demosthenes fled from his country, no man regarded it; for Cicero's sake the senate changed their habit, and put on mourning, and would not be persuaded to make any act before Cicero's return was decreed. Cicero, however, passed his exile idly in Macedonia. But the very exile of Demosthenes made up a great part of the services he did for his country; for he went through the cities of Greece, and everywhere, as we have said, joined in the conflict on behalf of the Greeks, driving out the Macedonian ambassadors, and approving himself a much better citizen than Themistocles and Alcibiades did in a similar fortune. And, after his return, he again devoted himself to the same public service, and continued firm in his opposition to Antipater and the Macedonians. Whereas Lælius reproached Cicero in the senate for sitting silent when Cæsar, a beardless youth, asked leave to come forward, contrary to the law, as a candidate for the consulship; and Brutus, in his epistles, charges him with nursing and rearing a greater and more heavy tyranny than that they had removed.

Finally, Cicero's death excites our pity; for an old man to be miserably carried up and down by his servants, flying and hiding himself from that death which was, in the course of nature, so near at hand; and yet at last to be murdered. Demosthenes, though he seemed to supplicate a little at first, yet, by his preparing and keeping the poison by him, demands our admiration; and still more admirable was his using it. When the temple of the god no longer afforded him a sanctuary, he took refuge, as it were, at a mightier altar, freeing himself from arms and soldiers, and laughing to scorn the cruelty of Antipater.

ALCIBIADES.

ALCIBIADES, it is supposed, was descended from Ajax, by his father's side; and by his mother's side from Alcmæon. Dinomache, his mother, was the daughter of Megacles. His father (Clinias) having fitted out a galley at his own expense, gained great honor in the seafight at Artemisium, and was afterwards slain in the battle of Coronea, fighting against the Bœotians. The friendship which Socrates felt for him has much contributed to his fame; and though we have no account from any writer concerning the mother of Nicias or Demosthenes, of Lamachus or Phormion, of Thrasybulus or Theramenes, notwithstanding these were all illustrious men of the same period, yet we know even the nurse of Alcibiades, that her country was Lacedæmon, and her name Amycla; and

ALCIBIADES.

that Zopyrus was his teacher and attendant; the one being recorded by Antisthenes, and the other by Plato.

It is not, perhaps, material to say anything of the beauty of

Alcibiades, only that it bloomed with him in all the ages of his life, in his infancy, in his youth, and in his manhood; and, in the peculiar character becoming to each of these periods, gave him, in every one of them a grace and a charm. What Euripides says, that

> "Of all fair things the autumn, too, is fair,"

is by no means universally true. But it happened so with Alcibiades, amongst few others, by reason of his happy constitution and natural vigor of body. It is said that his lisping, when he spoke, became him well, and gave a grace and persuasiveness to his rapid speech. Aristophanes takes notice of it in the verses in which he jests at Theorus: "How like a *colax* he is," says Alcibiades, meaning a *corax;** on which it is remarked,

> "How very happily he lisped the truth."

His conduct displayed many inconsistencies, not unnaturally, in accordance with the many wonderful vicissitudes of his fortunes; but, among the many strong passions of his real character, the most powerful of all was his ambition for superiority, which appears in several anecdotes told of him while he was a child. Once being hard pressed in wrestling, and fearing to be thrown, he got the hand of his antagonist to his mouth, and bit it with all his force; and when the other loosed his hold presently, and said, "You bite, Alcibiades, like a woman." "No," replied he, "like a lion." Another time, when playing at dice in the street, being then only a child, a loaded cart came that way, just as it was his turn to throw; at first he called to the driver to stop, because he was about to throw in the way over which the cart would pass; but when the man paid him no attention, and was driving on, the rest of the boys divided and sprang away; but Alcibiades threw him-

---

* This fashionable Attic lisp, or careless articulation, turned the sound *r* into *l*. *Colax*, a flatterer; *Corax*, a crow.

self on his face before the cart, and, stretching himself out, bade the carter pass on now if he would. The man was so startled that he put back his horses, while all that saw it were terrified, and, crying out, ran to assist Alcibiades. When he began to study, he obeyed all his other masters fairly well, but refused to learn upon the flute, as a thing unbecoming a free citizen; saying that to play on the lute or the harp does not in any way disfigure a man's body or face, but one is hardly to be known by his most intimate friends, when playing on the flute. Besides, one who plays on the harp may speak or sing at the same time; but the use of the flute stops the mouth, intercepts the voice, and prevents all articulation. "Therefore," said he, "let the Theban youths pipe, who do not know how to speak, but we Athenians, as our ancestors have told us, have Athena for our patroness, and Apollo for our protector, one of whom threw away the flute, and the other stripped the Flute-player of his skin." Thus, between raillery and good earnest, Alcibiades kept not only himself but others from learning, as it presently became the talk of the young boys, how Alcibiades despised playing on the flute, and ridiculed those who studied it. In consequence of which, it ceased to be reckoned amongst the liberal accomplishments, and became generally neglected.

It was manifest that the many well-born persons who were continually seeking his company, and making court to him, were attracted and captivated by his extraordinary beauty only. But the affection which Socrates entertained for him is a great evidence of the natural noble qualities and good disposition of the boy, which Socrates, detected under his personal beauty; and, fearing that his wealth and station, and the great number both of strangers and Athenians who flattered and caressed him, might at last corrupt him, resolved, if possible, to interpose, and preserve so hopeful a plant from perishing in the flower, before its fruit came to perfection. For never did fortune surround a man with so many of those things which we vulgarly call goods, or so protect him from every weapon of philosophy, and fence him from every access of free and searching words, as she did Alcibiades; who, from the beginning, was exposed to the flatteries of those who sought merely his gratification, such as might well unnerve him, and indispose him to listen to any real adviser or instructor. Yet such was the happiness of his genius, that he selected Socrates from the rest, and admitted him, while he drove away the wealthy and the noble who made court to him. In a little time, they grew intimate, and Alcibiades, listening now to language entirely free from every thought of unmanly fondness and silly displays of affection, found himself with one who sought to lay open to him the deficiencies of his mind and repress his vain and foolish arrogance, and

"Dropped like the craven cock his conquered wing."

He esteemed these endeavors of Socrates as most truly a means which the gods made use of for the care and preservation of youth, and it was a matter of general wonder, when people saw him joining Socrates in his meals and his exercises, living with him in the same tent, while he was reserved and rough to all others who made their addresses to him.

He behaved in the same manner to all others who courted him, except one stranger, who, as the story is told, having but a small estate, sold it all for about a hundred staters, which he presented to Alcibiades, and besought him to accept. Alcibiades, smiling and well pleased at the thing, invited him to supper, and, after a very kind entertainment, gave him his gold again, requiring him, moroever, not to fail to be present the next day, when the public revenue was offered to farm, and to outbid all others. The man would have excused himself, because the contract was so large, and would cost many talents; but Alcibiades, who had at that time a private pique against the existing farmers of the revenue, threatened to have him beaten if he refused. The next morning, the stranger, coming to the market-place, offered a talent more than the existing rate; upon which the farmers, enraged and consulting together, called upon him to name his sureties, concluding that he could find none. The poor man, being startled at the proposal, began to retire; but Alcibiades, standing at a distance, cried out to the magistrates, "Set my name down, he is a friend of mine; I will be security for him." When the other bidders heard this, they perceived that all their contrivance was defeated; for their way was, with the profits of the second year to pay the rent for the year preceding; so that, not seeing any other way to extricate themselves out of the difficulty, they began to treat with the stranger, and offered him a sum of money. Alcibiades would not suffer him to accept of less than a talent; but when that was paid down, he commanded him to relinquish the bargain, having by this device relieved his necessity.

Though Socrates had many powerful rivals, yet the natural good qualities of Alcibiades gave his affection the mastery His words overcame him so much, as to draw tears from his eyes, and to disturb his very soul. Yet sometimes he would abandon himself to flatteries, when they proposed to him varieties of pleasure, and would desert Socrates; who, then, would pursue him, as if he had been a fugitive slave. He despised every one else, and had no reverence or awe for any but him. But as iron which is softened by the fire grows hard with the cold, and all its parts are closed again; so, as often as Socrates observed Alcibiades to be misled by luxury or pride he reduced and corrected him by his addresses, and made him humble and modest, by showing him in how many things he was deficient, and how very far from perfection in virtue.

When he was past his childhood, he went once to a grammar-school, and asked the master for one of Homer's books and when he made answer that he had nothing of Homer's, Alcibiades gave him a blow with his fist, and went away. Another schoolmaster telling him that he had a copy of Homer corrected by himself; "Why?" said Alcibiades, "do you employ your time in teaching children to read? You, who are able to amend Homer, may well undertake to instruct men."

When he was very young, he was a soldier in the expedition against Potidæa, where Socrates lodged in the same tent with him, and stood next to him in battle. Once there happened a sharp skirmish, in which they both behaved with signal bravery; but Alcibiades receiving a wound, Socrates threw himself before him to defend him, and beyond any question saved him and his arms from the enemy, and so in all justice might have challenged the prize of valor. But the generals appearing eager to adjudge the honor to Alcibiades, because of his rank, Socrates, who desired to increase his thirst after glory of a noble kind, was the first to give evidence for him, and pressed them to crown him, and to decree to him the complete suit of armor. Afterwards, in the battle of Delium, when the Athenians were routed and Socrates with a few others was retreating on foot, Alcibiades, who was on horseback, observed it, and would not pass on, but stayed to shelter him from the danger, and brought him safely off, though the enemy pressed hard upon them, and cut off many.

He gave a box on the ear to Hipponicus, the father of Callias, whose birth and wealth made him a person of great influence and repute. And this he did unprovoked by any passion or quarrel between them, but only because, in a frolic, he had agreed with his companions to do it. People were justly offended at this insolence, when it became known through the city; but early the next morning, Alcibiades went to his house and knocked at the door, and, being admitted to him, took off his outer garment, and, presenting his naked body, desired him to scourge and chastise him as he pleased. Upon this Hipponicus forgot all his resentment, and not only pardoned him, but soon after gave him his daughter Hipparete in marriage.

Alcibiades had a dog which cost him seventy minas, and was very large and handsome. His tail, which was his principal ornament, he caused to be cut off, and an acquaintance exclaiming at him for it, and telling him that all Athens was sorry for the dog, and cried out against him for this action, he laughed, and said, "Just what I wanted has happened, then. I wished the Athenians to talk about this, that they might not say something worse of me."

It is said that the first time he came into the assembly was upon occasion of a largess of money which he made to the people. This was not done by design, but as he passed along he heard a shout, and inquired the cause; and having learned that there was a gift-making to the people, he went in among them and gave money also. The multitude thereupon applauding him, and shouting, he was so transported at it, that he forgot a quail which he had under his robe, and the bird, being frightened at the noise, flew off; upon which the people made louder acclamations than before, and many of them started up to pursue the bird; and Antiochus, a pilot, caught it and restored it to him, for which he was ever after a favorite with Alcibiades.

He had great advantages for entering public life; his noble birth, his riches, the personal courage he had shown in divers battles, and the multitude of his friends and dependents, threw open, so to say, folding doors for his admittance. But he did not consent to let his power with the people rest on any thing, rather than on his own gift of eloquence. That he was a master in the art of speaking, the comic poets bear him witness; and the most eloquent of public speakers, in his oration against Midias, allows that Alcibiades, among other perfections, was a most accomplished orator.

His expenses in horses kept for the public games, and in the number of his chariots, were matters of great observation; never did any one but he, either private person or king, send seven chariots to the Olympic games. And to have carried away at once the first, the second, and the fourth prize, as Thucydides says, or the third, as Euripides relates it, outdoes every distinction that was ever thought of in that kind.

The emulation displayed by the deputations of various states, in the presents which they made to him, rendered this success yet more illustrious. The Ephesians erected a tent for him, adorned magnificently; the city of Chios furnished him with provender for his horses and with great numbers of beasts for sacrifice; and the Lesbians sent him wine and other provisions for the many entertainments which he made.

As soon as he began to intermeddle in the government, which was when he was very young, he quickly lessened the credit of all who aspired to the confidence of the people, except Phæax and Nicias, who alone could contest with him. Nicias was arrived at a mature age, and was esteemed their first general. Phæax was but a rising statesman like Alcibiades; he was descended from noble ancestors, but was his inferior in many other things, but principally in eloquence.

Alcibiades was not less disturbed at the distinctions which Nicias gained among the enemies of Athens, than at the honors which the Athenians themselves paid to him. It was commonly said in Greece, that the war in the Peloponnesus was begun by Pericles, and that Nicias made an end of it, and the peace was generally called the peace of Nicias. Alcibiades was extremely annoyed at this, and, being full of envy, set himself to break the league. First, therefore, observing that the Argives as well out of fear as hatred to the Lacedæmonians, sought for protection against them, he gave them a secret assurance of alliance with Athens. He exclaimed fiercely against Nicias, and accused him of many things, which seemed probable enough: as that, when he was general, he made no attempt himself to capture their enemies that were shut up in the isle of Sphacteria, but, when they were afterwards made prisoners by others, he procured their release and sent them back to the Lacedæmonians, only to get favor with them.

It happened, at the very time when Nicias was by these arts brought into disgrace with the people, that ambassadors arrived from Lacedæmon, who, at their first coming, said what seemed very satisfactory, declaring that they had full powers to arrange all matters in dispute upon fair and equal terms. The council received their propositions, and the people was to

SPHACTERIA AND PYLOS FROM NAVARINO.

assemble on the morrow to give them audience. Alcibiades grew very apprehensive of this, and contrived to gain a secret conference with the ambassadors. When they were met, he said: "What is it you intend, you men of Sparta? If you expect to obtain equal terms from the Athenians, and would not have things extorted from you contrary to your inclinations, begin to treat with the people upon some reasonable articles, not avowing yourselves plenipotentiaries; and I will be ready to assist you, out of good-will to the Lacedæmonians." When he had said this, he gave them his oath for the performance of what he promised, and by this way drew them from Nicias to rely entirely upon himself, and left them full of admiration of the discernment and sagacity they had seen in him. The next day, when the people were assembled and the ambassadors introduced, Alcibiades, with great apparent courtesy, demanded of them: With what powers they had come? They made answer that they had not come as plenipotentiaries.

Instantly upon that, Alcibiades, with a loud voice, as though he had received and not done the wrong, began to call them dishonest prevaricators, and to urge that such men could not possibly come with a purpose to say or do anything that was sincere. The council was incensed, the people were in a rage, and Nicias, who knew nothing of the deceit and the imposture, was in the greatest confusion, equally surprised and ashamed at such a change in the men. So thus the Lacedæmonian ambassadors were utterly rejected, and Alcibiades was declared general, who presently united the Argives, the Eleans, and the people of Mantinea, into a confederacy with the Athenians.

No man commended the method by which Alcibiades effected all this, yet it was a great political feat thus to divide and shake almost all Peloponnesus, and to combine so many men in arms against the Lacedæmonians in one day before Mantinea; and, moreover, to remove the war and the danger so far from the frontier of the Athenians, that even success would profit the enemy but little, should they be conquerors, whereas, if they were defeated, Sparta itself was hardly safe.

But with all these words and deeds, and with all this sagacity and eloquence, he intermingled exorbitant luxury and wantonness in his eating and drinking and dissolute living; wore long purple robes like a woman, which dragged after him as he went through the market-place; caused the planks of his galley to be cut away, that so he might lie the softer, his bed not being placed on the boards, but hanging upon girths. His shield, again, which was richly gilded, had not the usual ensigns of the Athenians, but a Cupid, holding a thunderbolt in his hand, was painted upon it. The sight of all this made the people of good repute in the city feel disgust and abhorrence, and apprehension also, at his free-living, and his contempt of law, as things monstrous in themselves, and indicating designs of usurpation. Aristophanes has well expressed the people's feeling towards him :—

"They love, and hate, and cannot do without him."

And still more strongly, under a figurative expression,

"Best rear no lion in your state, 't is true ;
But treat him like a lion if you do."

The truth is, his liberalities, his public shows, and other munificence to the people, which were such as nothing could exceed, the glory of his ancestors, the force of his eloquence, the grace of his person, his strength of body, joined with his great courage and knowledge in military affairs, prevailed upon the Athenians to endure patiently his excesses, to indulge him in many things, and, according to their habit, to give the softest names to his faults, attributing them to youth and good nature. As, for example, he kept Agatharcus, the painter, a prisoner till he had painted his whole house, but then dismissed him with a reward. He publicly struck Taureas, who exhibited certain shows in opposition to him, and contended with him for the prize. When Aristophon, the artist, had drawn Nemea sitting and holding Alcibiades in her arms, the multitude seemed pleased with the piece, and thronged to see it, but elder people did not relish it, but looked on these things as enormities, and moyements toward tyranny. So that it was not said amiss by Archestratus, that Greece could not support a second Alcibiades. Once, when Alcibiades succeeded well in an oration which he made, and the whole assembly attended upon him to do him honor, Timon, the misanthrope, did not pass slightly by him, nor avoid him, as he did others, but purposely met him, and, taking him by the hand, said, "Go on boldly, my son, and increase in credit with the people, for thou wilt one day bring them calamities enough." Some that were present laughed at the saying, and some reviled Timon; but there were others upon whom it made a deep impression.

The Athenians, even in the lifetime of Pericles, had already cast a longing eye upon Sicily; but did not attempt any thing till after his death. Then, under pretence of aiding their confederates, they sent succor upon all occasions to those who were oppressed by the Syracusans, preparing the way for sending over a greater force. But Alcibiades was the person who inflamed this desire of theirs to the height, and prevailed with them no longer to proceed secretly, and little by little, in their design, but to sail out with a great fleet, and undertake at once to make themselves masters of the island. He possessed the people with great hopes, and he himself entertained yet greater; and the conquest of Sicily, which was the utmost bound of their ambition, was but the mere outset of his expectation. Nicias endeavored to divert the people from the expedition, by representing to them that the taking of Syracuse would be a work of great difficulty; but Alcibiades dreamed of nothing less than the conquest of Carthage and Libya, and by the accession of these conceiving himself at once made master of Italy and of Peloponnesus, seemed to look upon Sicily as little more than a magazine for the war. The young men were soon elevated with these hopes, and listened gladly to those of riper years, who talked wonders of the countries they were going to; so that you might see great numbers sitting in the wrestling grounds and public places, drawing on the ground the figure of the island and the situation of Libya and Carthage.

Together with Alcibiades, Nicias, much against his will, was appointed general: and he endeavored to avoid the command, not the less on account of his colleague. But the Athenians thought the war would proceed more prosperously, if they did not send Alcibiades free from all restraint, but tempered his heat with the caution of Nicias. This they chose the rather to do, because Lamachus, the third general, though he was of mature years, yet in several battles had appeared no less hot and rash than Alcibiades himself.

When all things were fitted for the voyage, many unlucky omens appeared. The mutilation of the images of Mercury, most of which, in one night, had their faces all disfigured, terrified many persons who were wont to despise most things of that nature. Alike enraged and terrified at the thing, looking upon it to proceed from a conspiracy of persons who designed some commotions in the state, the council, as well as the assembly of the people, which was held frequently in a few days' space, examined diligently every thing that might administer ground for suspicion. During this examination, Androcles, one of the demagogues, produced slaves and strangers before them, who accused Alcibiades and some of his friends of defacing other images in the same manner, and of having profanely acted the sacred mysteries at a drunken meeting. The people were highly exasperated and incensed against Alcibiades upon this accusation. But when they perceived that all the seamen designed for Sicily were for him, and the soldiers declared that they had undertaken this distant maritime expedition for the sake of Alcibiades, and that, if he was ill-used, they would all go home, they let him set sail at once, and decided that when the war should be at an end, he might then in person make his defence according to the laws.

Alcibiades perceived the malice of this postponement, and, appearing in the assembly, represented that it was monstrous for him to be sent with the command of so large an army, when he lay under such accusations and calumnies. But he could not prevail with the people, who commanded him to sail immediately. So he departed, together with the other generals, having with them near 140 galleys, 5,100 men at arms, and about 1,300 archers, slingers, and light-armed men, and all the other provisions corresponding.

Arriving on the coast of Italy, he landed at Rhegium, and there stated his views of the manner in which they ought to conduct the war. He was opposed by Nicias; but Lamachus being of his opinion, they sailed for Sicily forthwith, and took Catana. This was all that was done while he was there, for he was soon after recalled by the Athenians to abide his trial. At first, as we before said, there were only some slight suspicions advanced against Alcibiades. But afterwards, in his absence, his enemies attacked him more violently, and confounded together the breaking the images with the profanation of the mysteries, as though both had been committed in pursuance of the same conspiracy for changing the government. The truth is, his accusers alleged nothing against him which could be positively proved. One of them, being asked how he knew the men who defaced the images, replied, that he saw them by the light of the moon, making a palpable misstatement, for it was just new moon when the act was committed. This made all men of understanding cry out upon the thing; but the people were as eager as ever to receive further accusations. And, in conclusion, they sent the galley named the Salaminian, to recall Alcibiades. But they expressly commanded those that were sent, to use no violence, nor seize upon his person, but address themselves to him in the mildest terms, requiring him to follow them to Athens in order to abide his trial, and clear himself before the people. For they feared mutiny and sedition in the army in an enemy's country, which indeed it would have been easy for Alcibiades to effect, if he had wished it. For the soldiers were dispirited upon his departure, expecting for the future tedious delays, and that the war would be drawn out into a lazy length by Nicias, when Alcibiades, who was the spur to action, was taken away. For though Lamachus was a soldier, and a man of courage poverty deprived him of authority and respect in the army

Alcibiades, just upon his departure, prevented Messena from falling into the hands of the Athenians. There were some in that city who were upon the point of delivering it up, but he, knowing the persons, gave information to some friends of the Syracusans, and so defeated the whole contrivance. When he arrived at Thurii, he went on shore, and, concealing himself there, escaped those who searched after him. But to one who knew him, and asked him if he durst not trust his own native country, he made answer, "In every thing else, yes; but in a matter that touches my life, I would not even my own mother, lest she might by mistake throw in the black ball instead of the white." When, afterwards, he was told that the assembly had pronounced judgment of death against him, all he said was "I will make them feel that I am alive."

The information against him was framed in this form:—

"Thessalus lays information that Alcibiades has committed a crime against the goddesses Ceres and Proserpine, by representing in derision the holy mysteries, and showing them to his companions in his own house."

He was condemned as contumacious upon his not appearing, his property confiscated, and it was decreed that all the priests and priestesses should solemnly curse him.

Alcibiades, lying under these heavy decrees and sentences, when he fled from Thurii, passed over into Peloponnesus, and remained some time at Argos. But being there in fear of his enemies and seeing himself utterly hopeless of return to his native country, he sent to Sparta, desiring safe conduct, and assuring them that he would make them amends by his future services for all the mischief he had done them while he was their enemy. The Spartans giving him the security he desired, he went eagerly, was well received, and, at his very first coming, succeeded in inducing them, without any further caution or delay, to send aid to the Syracusans; and so roused and excited them, that they forthwith despatched Gylippus into Sicily, to crush the forces which the Athenians had in Sicily.

A second point was, to renew the war upon the Athenians at home. But the third thing, and the most important of all, was to make them fortify Decelea, which above everything reduced and wasted the recources of the Athenians.

The renown which he earned by these public services was equaled by the admiration he attracted to his private life; he captivated and won over everybody by his conformity to Spartan habits. People who saw him wearing his hair close cut, bathing in cold water, eating coarse meal, and dining on black broth, doubted, or rather could not believe, that he ever had a cook in his house, or had ever seen a perfumer, or had worn a mantle of Milesian purple. For he had, as it was observed, this peculiar talent for gaining men's affections, that he could at once comply with and really enter into their habits and ways of life, and change faster than the chameleon. One color, indeed, they say the chameleon cannot assume; it cannot make itself appear white; but Alcibiades, whether with good men or with bad, could adapt himself to his company, and equally wear the appearance of virtue or vice. At Sparta, he was devoted to athletic exercises, was frugal and reserved; in Ionia, luxurious, gay, and indolent; in Thrace, always drinking; in Thessaly, ever on horseback; and when he lived with Tissaphernes, the Persian satrap, he exceeded the Persians themselves in magnificence and pomp. Not that his natural disposition changed so easily, nor that his real character was so very variable, but, whenever he was sensible that by pursuing his own inclinations he might give offence to those with whom he had occasion to converse, he transformed himself into any shape, and adopted any fashion, that he observed to be most agreeable to them. So that to have seen him at Lacedæmon, a man, judging by the outward appearance, would have said, "'T is not Achilles' son, but he himself, the very man" that Lycurgus designed to form.

After the defeat which the Athenians received in Sicily. ambassadors were despatched to Sparta at once from Chios and Lesbos and Cyzicus, to signify their purpose of revolting from the Athenians. But the Lacedæmonians, at the persuasion of Alcibiades, chose to assist Chios before all others. He himself, also, went instantly to sea, procured the immediate revolt of almost all Ionia, and, co-operating with the Lacedæmonian generals, did great mischief to the Athenians. But King Agis was his enemy, and impatient of his glory, as almost every enterprise and every success was ascribed to Alcibiades. Others, also, of the most powerful and ambitious amongst the Spartans, were possessed with jealousy of him, and, at last, prevailed with the magistrates in the city to send orders into Ionia that he should be killed. Alcibiades, however, had secret intelligence of this, and, in apprehension of the result, while he communicated all affairs to the Lacedæmonians, yet took care not to put himself into their power. At last he retired to Tissaphernes, the satrap of the king of Persia, for his security, and immediately became the first and most influential person about him. For this barbarian, not being himself sincere, but a lover of guile and wickedness, admired his address and wonderful subtlety. And, indeed, the charm of daily intercourse with him was more than any character could resist or any disposition escape. Even those who feared and envied him could not but have a sort of kindness for him, when they saw him and were in his company. So that Tissaphernes, otherwise a cruel character, and, above all other Persians, a hater of the Greeks, was yet so won by the flatteries of Alcibiades, that he set himself even to exceed him in responding to them. The most beautiful of his parks, containing salubrious streams and meadows, where he had built pavilions, and places of retirement royally and exquisitely adorned, received by his direction the name of Alcibiades, and was always so called and so spoken of.

Thus Alcibiades, quitting the interests of the Spartans, whom he could no longer trust, because he stood in fear of Agis, endeavored to do them ill offices, and render them odious to Tissaphernes, who, by his means, was hindered from assisting them vigorously, and from finally ruining the Athenians. For his advice was to furnish them but sparingly with money, and so wear them out, and consume them insensibly; when they had wasted their strengh upon one another, they would both become ready to submit to the king.

At that time the whole strength of the Athenians was in Samos. Their fleet maintained itself here, and issued from these head-quarters to reduce such as had revolted, and protect the rest of their territories; in one way or other still contriving to be a match for their enemies at sea. What they stood in fear of, was Tissaphernes and the Phœnician fleet of one hundred and fifty galleys, which was said to be already under sail; if those came, there remained then no hopes for the commonwealth of Athens. Understanding this, Alcibiades sent secretly to the chief men of the Athenians, who were then at Samos, giving them hopes, that he would make Tissaphernes their friend; he was willing, he implied, to do some favor, not to the people, nor in reliance upon them, but to the better citizens, if only, like brave men, they would make the attempt to put down the insolence of the people, and, by taking upon them the government, would endeavor to save the city from ruin. All of them gave a ready ear to the proposal made by Alcibiades, except Phrynichus of the township of Dirades, despatched Pisander to Athens to attempt a change of government, and to encourage the aristocratical citizens to take upon themselves the government, and overthrow the democracy, representing to them, that, upon these terms, Aicibiades would procure them the friendship and alliance of Tissaphernes.

Those who were at Samos set sail for the Piræus; and, sending for Alcibiades declared him general. He, however, in that juncture did not, as it might have been thought a man would, on being suddenly exalted by the favor of a multitude, think himself under an obligation to gratify and submit to all the wishes of those who, from a fugitive and an exile, had created him general of so great an army and given him the command of such a fleet. But, as became a great captain, he opposed himself to the precipitate resolutions which their rage led them to, and, by restraining them from the great error they were about to commit, unequivocally saved the commonwealth. For if they had then sailed to Athens, all Ionia and the islands and the Hellespont would have fallen into the enemies' hands without opposition, while the Athenians, involved in civil war, would have been fighting with one another within the circuit of their own walls. It was Alcibiades alone, or, at least, principally, who prevented all this mischief; for he not only used persuasion to the whole army, and showed them the danger, but applied himself to them, one by one, entreating some, and constraining others. He was much assisted, however, by Thrasybulus of Stiria, who, having the loudest voice, as we are told, of all the Athenians, went along with him and cried out to those who were ready to go. A second great service which Alcibiades did for them was his undertaking that the Phœnician fleet, which the Lacedæmonians expected to be sent to them by the king of Persia, should either come in aid of the Athenians, or otherwise should not come at all. And now the people in the city not only desired, but commanded Alcibiades to return home from his exile. He, however, desired not to owe his return to the mere grace and commiseration of the people, and resolved to come back, not with empty hands, but with glory and after some service done. To this end, he sailed from Samos with a few ships, and cruised on the sea of Cnidos and about the isle of Cos; but receiving intelligence there that Mindarus, the Spartan admiral, had sailed with his whole army into the Hellespont, and that the Athenians had followed him, he hurried back to succor the Athenian commanders, and, by good fortune, arrived with eighteen galleys at a critical time. For both the fleets having engaged near Abydos, the fight between them had lasted till night, the one side having the advantage on one quarter, and the other on another. Upon his first appearance, both sides formed a false impression; the enemy was encouraged, and the Athenians terrified. But Alcibiades suddenly raised the Athenian ensign in the admiral ship, and fell upon those galleys of the Peloponnesians which had the advantage and were in pursuit. He soon put these to flight, and followed them so close that he forced them on shore, and broke the ships in pieces, the sailors abandoning them and swimming away, in spite of all the efforts of Pharnabazus, who had come down to their assistance by land, and did what he could to protect them from the shore. In fine, the Athenians, having taken thirty of the enemy's ships, and recovered all their own, erected a trophy. After the gaining of so glorious a victory his vanity made him eager to show himself to Tissaphernes, and, having furnished himself with gifts and presents, and an equipage suitable to his dignity, he set out to visit him. But the thing did not succeed as he had imagined, for Tissaphernes had long been suspected by the Lacedæmonians, and was afraid to fall into disgrace with his king upon that account, therefore thinking that Alcibiades had arrived very opportunely, he immediately caused him to be seized and sent away prisoner to Sardis; fancying, by this act of injustice, to clear himself from all former imputations.

But about thirty days after, Alcibiades escaped from his keepers, and, having got a horse, fled to Clazomenæ, where he procured Tissaphernes additional disgrace by professing that he was a party to his escape. From there he sailed to the Athenian camp, and, being informed that Mindarus and Pharnabazus were together at Cyzicus, he made a speech to the soldiers, telling them that sea-fighting, land-fighting, and, by the gods, fighting against fortified cities too, must be all one for them, as, unless they conquered everywhere, there was no money for them. As soon as he got them on ship-board, he hastened to Proconnesus, and gave command to seize all the small vessels they met, and guard them safely in the interior of the fleet, that the enemy might have no notice of his coming; and a great storm of rain, accompanied with thunder and darkness, which happened at the same time, contributed much to the concealment of his enterprise. Indeed, it was not only undiscovered by the enemy, but the Athenians themselves were ignorant of it, for he commanded them suddenly on board, and set sail when they had abandoned all intention of it. As the darkness presently passed away, the Peloponnesian fleet were seen riding out at sea in front of the harbor of Cyzicus. Fearing, if they discovered the number of his ships, they might endeavor to save themselves by land, he commanded the rest of the captains to slacken, and follow him slowly, whilst he, advancing with forty ships, showed himself to the enemy and provoked them to fight. The enemy, being deceived as to their numbers, despised them, and, supposing they were to contend with those only, made ready and began the fight. But as soon as they were engaged, they perceived the other part of the fleet coming down upon them, at which they were so terrified that they fled immediately. Upon that, Alcibiades, breaking through the midst of them with twenty of his best ships, hastened to the shore, disembarked, and pursued those who abandoned their ships and fled to land, and made a great slaughter of them. Mindarus and Pharnabazus, coming to their succor were utterly defeated. Mindarus was slain fighting valiantly; Pharnabazus saved himself by flight. The Athenians slew great numbers of their enemies, won much spoil, and took all their ships. They also made themselves masters of Cyzicus, which was deserted by Pharnabazus, and destroyed its Peloponnesian garrison, and thereby not only secured to themselves the Hellespont, but by force drove the Lacedæmonians out of all the rest of the sea. They intercepted some letters written to the ephors, which gave an account of this fatal overthrow, after their short, laconic manner. "Our hopes are at an end. Mindarus is slain. The men are starving. We know not what to do."

And now Alcibiades began to desire to see his native country again, or rather to show his fellow-citizens a person who had gained so many victories for them. He set sail for Athens, the ships that accompanied him being adorned with great numbers of shields and other spoils, and towing after them many galleys taken from the enemy, and the ensigns and ornaments of many others which he had sunk and destroyed; all of them together amounting to two hundred. Little credit, perhaps, can be given to what Duris the Samian, who professed to be descended from Alcibiades, adds, that Chrysogonus, who had gained a victory at the Pythian games, played upon his flute for the galleys, whilst the oars kept time with the music; and that Callippides, the tragedian, attired in his buskins, his purple robes, and other ornaments used in the theatre, gave the word to the rowers, and that the admiral's galley entered into the port with a purple sail. It is not credible, that one who had returned from so long an exile, and such a variety of misfortunes, should come home to his countrymen in the style of revelers breaking up from a drinking-party. On the contrary, he entered the harbor full of fear, nor would he venture to go on shore, till, standing on the deck, he saw Euryptolemus, his cousin, and others of his friends and acquaintance, who were ready to receive him, and invited him to land. As soon as he was landed, the multitude who came out to meet him scarcely appeared to see any of the other captains, but came in throngs about Alcibiades, and saluted him with loud acclamations, and followed him; those who could press near him crowned him with garlands, and they who could not come up so close yet stayed to behold him afar off, and the old men pointed him out to the young ones. Nevertheless, this public joy was mixed with some tears, and the present happiness was diminished by the remembrance of the miseries they had endured. They made reflections, that they could not have so unfortunately miscarried in Sicily, if they had left the management of their affairs and the command of their forces, to Alcibiades, since, upon his undertaking the administration, when they were absolutely driven from the sea, and could scarcely defend the suburbs of their city by land, and at the same time, were miserably distracted with intestine factions, he had raised them up from this low and deplorable condition, and had not only restored them to their ancient dominion of the sea, but had also made them everywhere victorious over their enemies on land.

The people being summoned to an assembly, Alcibiades came in among them, and first bewailed and lamented his own sufferings, and, in general terms complaining of the usage he had received, imputed all to his hard fortune, and some ill genius that attended him: then he spoke at large of their prospects, and exhorted them to courage and good hope. The people crowned him with crowns of gold, and created him general, both at land and sea, with absolute power. They also made a decree that his estate should be restored to him, and that the Eumolpidæ and the holy heralds should absolve him from the curses which they had solemnly pronounced against him by sentence of the people. All the rest obeyed, but Theodorus, the high-priest, excused himself, "For," said he, "if he is innocent, I never cursed him."

Certainly, if ever man was ruined by his own glory, it was Alcibiades. For his continual success had produced such an idea of his courage and conduct, that, if he failed in anything he undertook, it was imputed to his neglect, and no one would believe it was through want of power. For they thought nothing was too hard for him, if he went about it in good earnest. Now, having departed with a fleet of one hundred ships for the reduction of Chios, and of the rest of Ionia, the people grew impatient that things were not effected as fast and as rapidly as they could wish for them. They never considered how extremely money was wanting, and that, having to carry on war with an enemy who had supplies of all things from a great king, he was often forced to quit his armament, in order to procure money and provisions for the subsistence of his soldiers. This very thing gave occasion for the last accusation which was made against him. For Lysander, being sent from Lacedæmon with a commission to be admiral of their fleet, and being furnished by Cyrus with a great sum of money, gave every sailor four obols a day, whereas before they had but three. Alcibiades could hardly allow his men three obols, and therefore was obliged to go into Caria to furnish himself with money. He left the care of the fleet, in his absence, to Antiochus, an experienced seaman, but rash and inconsiderate, who had express orders from Alcibiades not to engage, though the enemy provoked him. But he slighted and disregarded these directions to such a degree that, having made ready his own galley and another, he stood for Ephesus, where the enemy lay, and, as he sailed before the heads of their galleys, used every provocation possible, both in words and deeds. Lysander manned out a few ships and pursued him. But all the Athenian ships coming in to his assistance, Lysander, also, brought up his whole fleet, which gained an entire victory. He slew Antiochus himself, took many men and ships, and erected a trophy.

As soon as Alcibiades heard this news, he returned to Samos, and loosing from thence with his whole fleet, came and offered battle to Lysander. But Lysander, content with the victory he had gained, would not stir. Amongst others in the army who hated Alcibiades, Thrasybulus, the son of Thrason, was his particular enemy, and went purposely to Athens to accuse him, and to exasperate his enemies in the city against him. Addressing the people, he represented that Alcibiades had ruined their affairs and lost their ships by mere self-conceited neglect of his duties, committing the government of the army, in his absence, to men who gained his favor by drinking and scurrilous talking, whilst he wandered up and down at pleasure to raise money, giving himself up to every sort of luxury in Abydos and Ionia, at a time when the enemy's navy were on the watch close at hand. It was also objected to him, that he had fortified a castle near Bisanthe in Thrace, for a safe retreat for himself, as one that either could not, or would not, live in his own country. The Athenians gave credit to these informations, and showed the resentment and displeasure which they had conceived against him, by choosing other generals.

As soon as Alcibiades heard of this, he immediately forsook the army, afraid of what might follow; and, collecting a body of mercenary soldiers, made war upon his own account against those Thracians who called themselves free, and acknowledged no king. By this means he amassed for himself considerable treasure, and, at the same time, secured the bordering Greeks from the incursions of the barbarians.

Tydeus, Menander, and Adimantus, the newly made generals, were at that time posted at Ægospotami, with all the ships which the Athenians had left. Whence they used to go out every morning, offer battle to Lysander, who lay near Lampsacus, and, returning back again, lie all the rest of the day, carelessly and without order, in contempt of the enemy. Alcibiades, who was not far off, did not think so lightly of their danger, nor neglect to let them know it, but, mounting his horse, came to the generals, and represented to them that they had chosen a very inconvenient station, where there was no safe harbor, and where they were distant from any town; so that they were constrained to send for their necessary provisions as far as Sestos. He also pointed out to them their carelessness in suffering the soldiers, when they went ashore, to disperse and wander up and down at their pleasure, while the enemy's fleet under the command of one general, and strictly obedient to discipline, lay so very near them. He advised them to remove the fleet to Sestos. But the admirals not only disregarded what he said, but Tydeus, with insulting expressions, commanded him to be gone saying, that now not he, but others, had the command of the forces. The event soon made it evident how rightly he had judged of the errors which the Athenians were committing. For Lysander fell upon them on a sudden, when they least suspected it, with such fury that Conon alone, with eight galleys, escaped him; all the rest, about two hundred, he took and carried away, together with three thousand prisoners, whom he put to death. And within a short time after, he took Athens itself, burnt all the ships which he found there, demolished their long walls and established the rule of the Thirty Tyrants.

After this, Alcibiades, standing in dread of the Lacedæmonians, who were now masters both at sea and land, retired into Bithynia. He sent there great treasure before him, took much with him, but left much more in the castle where he had before resided. But he lost a great part of his wealth in Bithynia, being robbed by some Thracians who lived in those parts, and thereupon determined to go to the court of Artaxerxes, not doubting but that the king, if he would make trial of his abilities, would find him not inferior to Themistocles, besides being recommended by a more honorable cause. For he went, not as Themistocles did, to offer his service against his fellow-citizens, but against their enemies, and to implore the king's aid for the defence of his country. The Athenians, in the meantime, miserably afflicted at their loss of empire and liberty, acknowledged and bewailed their former errors and follies, and judged this second ill-usage of Alcibiades to be of all the most inexcusable. For he was rejected, without any fault committed by himself; and only because they were incensed against his subordinate for having shamefully lost a few ships, they much more shamefully deprived the commonwealth of its most valiant and accomplished general.

Critias finally represented to Lysander that the Lacedæmonians could never securely enjoy the dominion of Greece, till the Athenian democracy was absolutely destroyed; and though now the people of Athens seemed quietly and patiently to submit to so small a number of governors, yet so long as

Alcibiades lived, the knowledge of this fact would never suffer them to acquiesce in their present circumstances.

Yet Lysander could not be prevailed upon by these representations, till at last he received secret orders from the magistrates of Lacedæmon, expressly requiring him to get Alcibiades despatched: whether it was that they feared his energy and boldness in undertaking what was hazardous, or that it was done to gratify king Agis. Upon receipt of this order, Lysander sent a messenger away to Pharnabazus, desiring him to put it in execution, Alcibiades resided at that time in a small villag in Phrygia. Those who were sent to assassinate him had not courage enough to enter the house, but surrounded it first, and set it on fire. Alcibiades, as soon as he perceived it, wrapped his cloak about his left arm, and holding his naked sword in his right, cast himself into the middle of the fire, and escaped securely through it, before his clothes were burnt. The barbarians, as soon as they saw him, retreated, and none of them durst engage with him, but, standing at a distance, they slew him with their darts and arrows.

CORIOLANUS.

The patrician house of the Marcii in Rome produced many men of distinction, and among the rest, Ancus Marcius, grandson to Numa by his daughter, and king after Tullus Hostilius. Of the same family were also Publius and Quintus Marcius, which two conveyed into the city the best and most abundant supply of water they have at Rome. But Caius Marcius, of whom I now write, being left an orphan, and brought up under the widowhood of his mother, has shown us by experience, that, although the early loss of a father may be attended with other disadvantages, yet it can hinder none from being either virtuous or eminent in the world, and that it is no obstacle to true goodness and excellence. Those who saw with admiration how proof his nature was against pleasure, hardships, and the allurements of gain, while allowing to that universal firmness of his the respective names of temperance, fortitude, and justice, yet, in the life of the citizen and the statesman, could not but be offended at the severity and ruggedness of his deportment, and with his overbearing, haughty, and imperious temper.

Those were times at Rome in which that kind of worth was most esteemed which displayed itself in military achievements; one evidence of which we find in the Latin word for virtue, which is properly equivalent to manly courage. But Marcius, having a more passionate inclination than any of that age for feats of war, began from his very childhood to handle arms; and feeling that adventitious implements and artificial arms would be of small use to such as have not their natural weapons well prepared for service, he so exercised and inured his body to all sorts of activity and encounter, that, besides the lightness of a racer, he had a weight in close seizures and wrestlings with an enemy, from which it was hard for anybody to disengage himself; so that his competitors at home in displays of bravery, loath to own themselves inferior in that respect, were wont to ascribe their deficiencies to his strength of body, which they said no resistance and no fatigue could exhaust.

The first time he went out to the wars, being yet a stripling, was when Tarquinius Superbus, who had been king of Rome and was afterwards expelled, after many unsuccessful attempts now entered upon his last effort, and proceeded to hazard all as it were upon a single throw. A great number of the Latins and other people of Italy joined their forces, and were marching with him toward the city, to procure his restoration; not, however, so much out of a desire to serve and oblige Tarquin, as to gratify their own fear and envy at the increase of the Roman greatness, which they were anxious to check. The armies met and engaged in a decisive battle, in the vicissitudes of which, Marcius, while fighting bravely in the dictator's presence, saw a Roman soldier struck down at a little distance, and immediately stepped in before him, and slew his assailant. The general, after having gained the victory, crowned him for this act with a garland of oak branches; it being the Roman custom thus to adorn those who had saved the life of a citizen; whether the law intended some special honor to the oak, in memory of the Arcadians, a people the oracle had made famous by the name of acorn-eaters; or, the oak wreath, being sacred to Jupiter, the guardian of the city, might, therefore, be thought a proper ornament for one who preserved a citizen. And the oak, in truth, is the tree which bears the most and the prettiest fruit of any that grow wild, and is the strongest of all that are under cultivation; its acorns were the principal diet of the first mortals, and the honey found in it gave them drink

In this battle it is stated that Castor and Pollux appeared, and, immediately after the battle, were seen at Rome just by the fountain where their temple now stands, with their horses foaming with sweat, and told the news of the victory to the people in the Forum. The fifteenth of July, being the day of this conquest, became consequently a solemn holiday sacred to the Twin Brothers.

It may be observed, in general, that when young men arrive early at fame and repute, if they are of a nature but slightly touched with emulation, this early attainment is apt to extinguish their thirst and satiate their small appetite; whereas the first distinctions of more solid and weighty characters only stimulate and quicken them, and take them away, like a wind, in the pursuit of honor; they look upon these marks and testimonies to their virtue not as a recompense received for what they have already done, but as a pledge given by themselves of what they will perform hereafter, ashamed now to forsake or underlive the credit they have won, or, rather, not to exceed and obscure all that is gone before by the lustre of their following actions. Marcius, having a spirit of this noble make, was ambitious always to surpass himself, and did nothing, how extraordinary soever, but he thought he was bound to outdo it at the next occasion; and ever desiring to give continual fresh instances of his prowess, he added one exploit to another, and heaped up trophies upon trophies, so as to make it a matter of contest also among his commanders, the latter still vying with the earlier, which should pay him the greatest honor and speak highest in his commendation. Of all the numerous wars and conflicts in those days, there was not one from which he returned without laurels and rewards. And, whereas others made glory the end of their daring, the end of his glory was his mother's gladness; the delight she took to hear him praised and to see him crowned, and her weeping for joy in his embraces, rendered him, in his own thoughts, the most honored and most happy person in the world. Epaminondas is similarly said to have acknowledged his feeling, that it was the greatest felicity of his whole life that his father and mother survived to hear of his successful generalship and his victory at Leuctra. And he had the advantage, indeed, to have both his parents partake with him, and enjoy the pleasure of his good fortune. But Marcius, believing himself bound to pay his mother Volumnia all that gratitude and duty which would have belonged to his father, had he also been alive, could never satiate himself in his tenderness and respect to her. He took a wife, also, at her request and wish, and continued, even after he had children, to live with his mother, without parting families.

The repute of his integrity and courage had, by this time, gained him considerable influence and authority in Rome, when the senate, favoring the wealthier citizens, began to be at variance with the common people, who made sad complaints of the rigorous and inhuman usage they received from the money-lenders.

There had been frequent assemblies of the whole senate within a small compass of time about this difficulty, but without any definite result; the poor commonalty, therefore, perceiving there was likely to be no redress of their grievances, collected in a body, and, encouraging each other in their resolution, forsook the city with one accord, and seizing the hill which is now called the Holy Mount, sat down by the river Anio, without committing any sort of violence or seditious outrage, but merely exclaiming, as they went along, that they had this long time past been expelled from the city by the cruelty of the rich; that Italy would everywhere afford them the benefit of air and water and a place of burial, which was all they could expect in the city, unless it were perhaps, the privilege of being wounded and killed in time of war for the defence of their creditors. The senate apprehending the consequences, sent the most moderate and popular men of their own order to treat with them.

Menenius Agrippa, their chief spokesman, after much entreaty to the people, concluded, at length, with this celebrated fable: "It once happened, that all the other members of a man mutinied against the stomach, which they accused as the only idle, uncontributing part in the whole body, while the rest were put to hardships and the expense of much labor to minister to its appetites. The stomach, however, merely ridiculed the silliness of the members, who appeared not to be aware that the stomach certainly does receive the general nourishment, but only to return it again, and redistribute it amongst the rest. Such is the case," he said, "citizens, between you and the senate. The counsels and plans that are there duly digested, secure to all of you, your proper benefit and support."

A reconciliation ensued, the senate acceding to the request of the people for the annual election of five protectors for those in need of succor, the same that are now called the tribunes of the people; and the first two they pitched upon were Junius Brutus and Sicinnius Vellutus, their leaders in the secession.

The city being thus united, the commons stood presently to their arms, and followed their commanders.

The Romans were now at war with the Volscian nation, whose principal city was Corioli; when, therefore, Cominius the consul had invested this important place, the rest of the Volscians, fearing it would be taken, mustered up whatever force they could from all parts, to relieve it, designing to give the Romans battle before the city, and so attack them on both sides. Cominius, to avoid this inconvenience, divided his army, marching himself with one body to encounter the Volscians on their approach from without, and leaving Titus Lartius, one of the bravest Romans of his time, to command the other and continue the siege. Those within Corioli, despising now the smallness of their number, made a sally upon them, and prevailed at first, and pursued the Romans into their trenches. Here it was that Marcius, flying out with a slender company, and cutting those in pieces that first engaged him, obliged the other assailants to slacken their speed; and then, with loud cries, called upon the Romans to renew the battle. For he had, what Cato thought a great point in a soldier, not only strength of hand and stroke, but also a voice and look that of themselves were a terror to an enemy. Some of his own party now rallying and making up to him, the enemies soon retreated; but Marcius, not content to see them draw off and retire, pressed hard upon the rear, and drove them, as they fled away in haste, to the very gates of their city; where, perceiving the Romans to fall back from their pursuit, beaten off by the multitude of darts poured in upon them from the walls, and that none of his followers had the hardiness to think of falling in pellmell among the fugitives and so entering a city full of enemies in arms, he, nevertheless, stood and urged them to the attempt, crying out, that fortune had now opened Corioli, not so much to shelter the vanquished, as to receive the conquerors. Seconded by a few that were willing to venture with him, he bore along through the crowd, made good his passage, and thrust himself into the gate through the midst of them, nobody at first daring to resist him. But when the citizens, on looking about, saw that a very small number had entered, they now took courage, and came up and attacked them. A combat ensued of the most extraordinary description, in which Marcius, by strength of hand, swiftness of foot, and daring of soul, overpowered every one that he assailed, succeeded in driving the enemy to seek refuge, for the most part, in the interior of the town, while the remainder submitted, and threw down their arms; thus affording Lartius abundant opportunity to bring in the rest of the Romans with ease and safety.

Corioli being thus surprised and taken, the greater part of the soldiers employed themselves in spoiling and pillaging it, while Marcius indignantly reproached them, and exclaimed that it was a dishonorable and unworthy thing, when the consul and their fellow-citizens had now perhaps encountered the other Volscians, and were hazarding their lives in battle, basely to mis-spend the time in running up and down for booty, and, under a pretence of enriching themselves, keep out of danger. Few paid him any attention, but, putting himself at the head of these, he took the road by which the consul's army had marched before him, encouraging his companions, and beseeching them, as they went along, not to give up, and praying often to the gods, too, that he might be so happy as to arrive before the fight was over, and come seasonably up to assist Cominius, and partake in the peril of the action.

It was customary with the Romans of that age, when they were moving into battle array, and were on the point of taking up their bucklers, and girding their coats about them, to make at the same time an unwritten will, or verbal testament, and to name who should be their heirs, in the hearing of three or four witnesses. In this precise posture Marcius found them at his arrival, the enemy having advanced within view.

They were not a little disturbed by his first appearance, seeing him covered with blood and sweat, and attended with a small train; but when he hastily made up to the consul with gladness in his looks, giving him his hand, and recounting to him how the city had been taken, and when they saw Cominius also embrace and salute him, every one took fresh heart; those that were near enough hearing, and those that were at a distance guessing, what had happened; and all cried out to be led to battle. First, however, Marcius desired to know of him how the Volscians had arrayed their army, and where they had placed their best men, and on his answering that he took the troops of the Antiates in the centre to be their prime warriors, that would yield to none in bravery, "Let me then demand and obtain of you," said Marcius, "that we may be posted against them." The consul granted the request, with much admiration of his gallantry. And when the conflict began by the soldiers darting at each other, and Marcius sallied out before the rest, the Volscians opposed to him were not able to make head against him; wherever he fell in, he broke their ranks, and made a lane through them; but the parties turning again, and enclosing him on each side with their weapons, the consul, who observed the danger he was in, despatched some of the choicest men he had for his rescue. The conflict then growing warm and sharp about Marcius, and many falling dead in a little space, the Romans bore so hard upon the enemies, and pressed them with such violence, that they forced them at length to abandon their ground, and to quit the field. And, going now to prosecute the victory, they besought Marcius, tired out with his toils, and faint and heavy through the loss of blood, that he would retire to the camp. He replied, however, that weariness was not for conquerors, and joined with them in the pursuit. The rest of the Volscian army was in like manner defeated, great numbers killed, and no less taken captive.

The day after, when Marcius, with the rest of the army, presented themselves at the consul's tent, Cominius rose, and having rendered all due acknowledgment to the gods for the success of that enterprise, turned next to Marcius, and first of all delivered the strongest encomium upon his rare exploits, of which he had partly been an eye-witness himself, in the late battle, and had partly learned from the testimony of Lartius. And then he required him to choose a tenth part of all the treasure and horses and captives that had fallen into their hands, before any division should be made to others; besides which, he made him the special present of a horse with trappings and ornaments, in honor of his actions. The whole army applauded; Marcius, however, stepped forth, and declaring his thankful acceptance of the horse, and his gratification at the praises of his general, said, that all other things, which he could only regard rather as mercenary advantages than any significations of honor, he must waive, and should be content with the ordinary proportion of such rewards. "I have only," said he "one special grace to beg, and this I hope you will not deny me. There was a certain hospitable friend of mine among the Volscians, a man of probity and virtue, who is become a prisoner, and from former wealth and freedom is now reduced to servitude. Among his many misfortunes let my intercession redeem him from the one of being sold as a common slave." Such a refusal and such a request on the part of Marcius were followed with yet louder acclamations; and he had many more admirers of this generous superiority to avarice, than of the bravery he had shown in battle. The very persons who conceived some envy and despite to see him so specially honored, could not but acknowledge, that one who so nobly could refuse reward, was beyond others worthy to receive it; and were more charmed with that virtue which made him despise advantage, than with any of those former actions that had gained him his title to it. It is a higher accomplishment to use money well than to use arms; but not to need it is more noble than to use it.

When the noise of approbation and applause ceased, Cominius, resuming, said, "It is idle, fellow-soldiers, to force those other gifts of ours on one who is unwilling to accept them; let us, therefore, give him one of such a kind that he cannot well reject it; let us pass a vote, I mean, that he shall hereafter be called Coriolanus, unless you think that his performance at Corioli has itself anticipated any such resolution." Hence, therefore, he had his third name of Coriolanus, making it all the plainer that Gaius was a personal proper name, and the second, or surname, Marcius, one common to his house and family; the third being a subsequent addition which used to be imposed either from some particular act or fortune, bodily characteristic, or good quality of the bearer.

Not long after Marcius stood for the consulship. It was usual for candidates for office to solicit personally the citizens, presenting themselves in the forum with the toga on alone and no tunic under it; either to promote their supplications by the humility of their dress, or that such as had received wounds might more readily display those marks of their fortitude.

Marcius, therefore, as the fashion of candidates was, showing the scars and gashes that were still visible on his body, from the many conflicts in which he had signalized himself during a service of seventeen years together, the people were affected at this display of merit, and told one another that they ought in common modesty to create him consul. But when the day of election had come, and Marcius appeared in the forum, with a pompous train of senators attending him, and the patricians all seemed to be exerting greater efforts than they had ever done before on a similar occasion, the commons then fell off again from the kindness they had conceived for him, and in the place of their late benevolence, began to feel something of indignation and envy; passions assisted by the fear they entertained, that if a man of such aristocratic temper, and so influential among the patricians, should be invested with the power which that office would give him, he might employ it to deprive the people of all that liberty which was yet left them. In conclusion, they rejected Marcius. Two other names were announced, to the great mortification of the senators, who felt as if the indignity reflected rather upon themselves than on Marcius. He, for his part, could not bear the affront with any patience. He had always indulged his temper, and had regarded the proud and contentious element of human nature as a sort of nobleness and magnanimity; reason and discipline had not imbued him with that solidity and equanimity which enter so largely into the virtues of the statesman. He had never learned how essential it is for any one who undertakes public business, and desires to deal with mankind, to avoid above all things that self-will, which, as Plato says, belongs to the family of solitude; and to pursue, above all things, that capacity so generally ridiculed, of submission to ill-treatment. Marcius, straightforward and direct, and possessed with the idea that to vanquish and overbear all opposition is the true part of bravery, and never imagining that it was the weakness and womanishness of his nature that broke out, so to say, in these ulcerations of anger, retired, full of fury and bitterness against the people.

In the midst of these distempers, a large quantity of corn reached Rome, a great part bought up in Italy, but an equal amount sent as a present from Syracuse, from Gelo, then reigning there. Many began now to hope well of their affairs, supposing the city, by this means, would be delivered at once, both of its want and discord. A council, therefore, being presently held, the people came flocking about the senate-house, eagerly awaiting the issue of that deliberation, expecting that the market-prices would now be less cruel, and that what had come as a gift, would be distributed as such. There were some within who so advised the senate; but Marcius, standing up, sharply inveighed against those who spoke in favor of the multitude, calling them flatterers of the rabble, traitors to the nobility, and alleging, that, by such gratifications, they did but cherish those bad seeds of boldness and petulance that had been sown among the people, to their own prejudice. "When things are come to such a pass, for us to sit here and decree largesses and bounties for them, like those Greeks where the populace is supreme, what else would it be," said he, "but to take their disobedience into pay, and maintain it for the common ruin of us all?"

Marcius, with much more to this purpose, succeeded, to an extraordinary degree, in inspiring the younger men with the same furious sentiments, and had almost all the wealthy on his side, who cried him up as the only person their city had, superior alike to force and flattery; some of the older men, however, opposed him, suspecting the consequences. And, indeed, there came no good of it; for the tribunes, who were present, perceiving how the proposal of Marcius took, ran out into the crowd with exclamations, calling on the plēbeians to stand together, and come in to their assistance. The assembly met, and soon became tumultuous. The sum of what Marcius had spoken, having been reported to the people, excited them to such fury, that they were ready to break in upon the senate. The tribunes prevented this, by laying all the blame on Coriolanus, and they accordingly cited him to come before them, and defend himself.

He came, therefore, as it were, to make his apology, and clear himself; in which belief the people kept silence, and gave him a quiet hearing. But when, instead of the submissive and deprecatory language expected from him, he began to use not only an offensive kind of freedom, seeming rather to accuse than apologize, but, as well by the tone of his voice as the expression of his countenance, displayed a security that was not far from disdain and contempt of them, the whole multitude then became angry, and gave evident signs of impatience and disgust; and Sicinnius, the most violent of the tribunes, after a little private conference with his colleagues, proceeded solemnly to pronounce before them all, that Marcius was condemned to die by the tribunes of the people, and bid the Ædiles take him to the Tarpeian rock, and without delay throw him headlong from the precipice. When they, however, in compliance with the order, came to seize upon his body, many, even of the plebeian party, felt it to be a horrible and extravagant act; the patricians, meantime, wholly beside themselves with distress and horror, hurried with cries to the rescue; and persuaded them not to despatch him by any sudden violence, but refer the cause to the general suffrage of the people. But when the people met together, the tribunes, contrary to all former practice, extorted first, that votes should be taken, not by centuries, but tribes; a change, by which the rabble, that had no respect for honesty and justice, would be sure to carry it against those who were rich and well known, and accustomed to serve the state in war. In the next place, whereas they had engaged to prosecute Marcius upon no other head but that of tyranny, which could never be made out against him, they relinquished this plea, and urged instead, his language in the senate against an abatement of the price of corn, and for the overthrow of the tribunician power; adding further, as a new impeachment, the distribution that was made by him of the spoil and booty he had taken from the Antiates, when he overran their country, which he had divided among those that had followed him, whereas it ought rather to have been brought into the public treasury; which last accusation did, they say, more discompose Marcius than all the rest, as he had not anticipated he should ever be questioned on that subject, and, therefore, was less provided with any satisfactory answer to it on the sudden. And when, by way of excuse, he began to magnify the merits of those who had been partakers with him in the action, those that had stayed at home, being more numerous than the other, interrupted him with outcries. In conclusion, when they came to vote, a majority of three tribes condemned him; the penalty being perpetual banishment.

Marcius himself, was neither stunned nor humiliated. In mien, carriage, and countenance, he bore the appearance of entire composure, and while all his friends were full of distress, seemed the only man that was not touched with his misfortune. On his return home, after saluting his mother and his wife, who were in tears and full of loud lamentations, and exhorting them to moderate the sense they had of his calamity, he proceeded at once to the city gates, whither all the nobility came to attend him; and not taking anything with him, or making any request to the company, he departed from them, having only three or four clients with him. He continued solitary for a few days in a place in the country, distracted with a variety of counsels, such as rage and indignation suggested to him; and proposing to himself no honorable or useful end, but only how he might best satisfy his revenge on the Romans, he resolved at length to arouse a heavy war against them from their nearest neighbors. He determined, first to make trial of the

Volscians, whom he knew to be still vigorous and flourishing, both in men and treasure, and he imagined their force and power was not so much abated, as their spite and anger increased, by the late overthrows they had received from the Romans.

There was a man of Antium, called Tullus Aufidius, who, for his wealth and bravery and the splendor of his family, had the respect and privilege of a king among the Volscians, but whom Marcius knew to have a particular hostility to himself, above all other Romans. Frequent menaces and challenges had passed in battle between them, and those exchanges of defiance to which their hot and eager emulation is apt to prompt young soldiers had added private animosity to their national feelings of opposition. Yet for all this, considering Tullus to have a certain generosity of temper, and knowing that no Volscian, so much as he, desired an occasion to requite upon the Romans the evils they had done, he put on a dress which completely disguised him and thus, like Ulysses,—

He entered the town of his mortal foes.

His arrival at Antium was about evening, and though several met him in the streets, yet he passed along without recognition, and went directly to the house of Tullus, and entering undiscovered, went up to the fire-hearth, and seated himself there without speaking a word, covering up his head. Those of the family could not but wonder, and yet they were afraid either to raise or question him, for there was a certain air of majesty both in his posture and silence, but they recounted to Tullus, then at supper, the strangeness of this accident. He immediately rose from table and came in, and asked him who he was, and for what business he came there; and then Marcius, unmuffling himself, and pausing awhile, said, "If you cannot yet call me to mind, Tullus, or do not believe your eyes concerning me, I must of necessity be my own accuser. I am Gaius Marcius, the author of so much mischief to the Volscians; of which, were I seeking to deny it, the surname of Coriolanus I now bear would be a sufficient evidence against me. The one recompense I received for all the hardships and perils I have gone through, was the title that proclaims my enmity to your nation, and this is the only thing which is still left me. Of all other advantages, I have been stripped and deprived by the envy of the Roman people, and the cowardice and treachery of the magistrates and those of my own order. I am driven out as an exile, and become an humble suppliant at your hearth, not so much for safety and protection (should I have come hither, had I been afraid to die?), as to seek vengeance against those that expelled me; which, methinks, I have already obtained, by putting myself into your hands. If, therefore, you have really a mind to attack your enemies, make use of that affliction you see me in to assist the enterprise, and convert my personal infelicity into a common blessing to the Volscians; as I am likely to be more serviceable in fighting for than against you, with the advantage, which I now possess, of knowing all the secrets of the enemy that I am attacking."

Tullus, on hearing this, was extremely rejoiced, and giving him his right hand, exclaimed, "Rise, Marcius, and be of good courage; it is a great happiness you bring to Antium, in the present you make us of yourself; expect everything that is good from the Volscians." He then proceeded to feast and entertain him with every display of kindness, and for several days after they were in close deliberation together on the prospects of a war.

Although the Volscians had sworn to a truce of arms for the space of two years, the Romans themselves soon furnished them with a pretence, by making proclamation, out of some jealousy or slanderous report, at an exhibition of games, that all the Volscians who had come to see them should depart from the city before sunset. Some affirm that this was a contrivance of Marcius, who sent a man privately to the consuls, falsely to accuse the Volscians of intending to fall upon the Romans during the games, and to set the city on fire. This public affront aroused their hostility to the Romans; and Tullus, perceiving it, took advantage of it, aggravating the fact, and working on their indignation, till he persuaded them, at last, to despatch ambassadors to Rome, requiring the Romans to restore that part of their country and those towns which they had taken from the Volscians in the late war. When the Romans heard the message, they indignantly replied, that the Volscians were the first that took up arms, but the Romans would be the last to lay them down. This answer being brought back, Tullus called a general assembly of the Volscians; and the vote passing for a war, he then proposed that they should call in Marcius, laying aside the remembrance of former grudges, and assuring themselves that the services they should now receive from him as a friend and associate, would abundantly outweigh any harm or damage he had done them when he was their enemy. Marcius was accordingly summoned, and having made his entrance, and spoken to the people, won their good opinion of his capacity, his skill, counsel, and boldness, not less by his present words than by his past actions. They joined him in commission with Tullus, to have full power as general of their forces in all that related to the war. And he, fearing lest the time that would be requisite to bring all the Volscians together in full preparation might be so long as to lose him the opportunity of action, left order with the chief persons and magistrates of the city to provide other things, while he himself, prevailing upon the readiest to assemble and march out with him as volunteers without staying to be enrolled, made a sudden inroad into the Roman confines, when nobody expected him, and possessed himself of so much booty, that the Volscians found they had more than they could either carry away or use in the camp. The abundance of provision which he gained, and the waste and havoc of the country which he made, were, however, the smallest results of that invasion;

the great mischief he intended, and his special object in all, was to increase at Rome the suspicions entertained of the patricians, and to make them upon worse terms with the people. With this view, while despoiling all the fields and destroying the property of other men, he took special care to preserve their farms and lands untouched, and would not allow his soldiers to ravage there, or seize upon any thing which belonged to them. Hence the quarrels broke out afresh, and rose to a greater height than ever; the senators reproaching those of the commonalty with their late injustice to Marcius; while the plebeians, on their side, did not hesitate to accuse them of having, out of spite and revenge, solicited him to this enterprise, and thus, when others were involved in the miseries of a war by their means, they sat like unconcerned spectators furnished with a guardian abroad of their fortunes, in the very person of the public enemy. After this incursion and exploit, which was of great advantage to the Volscians, since they learned by it to be more courageous and to despise their enemy, Marcius drew them off, and returned in safety.

But when the whole strength of the Volscians was brought together into the field, with great expedition, it appeared so considerable a body, that they agreed to leave part in garrison, for the security of their towns, and with the other part to march against the Romans. Marcius now desired Tullus to choose which of the two charges would be most agreeable to him. Tullus answered, that since he knew Marcius to be equally valiant with himself, and far more fortunate, he would have him take the command of those that were going out to the war, while he made it his care to defend their cities at home, and provide all conveniences for the army abroad. Marcius thus reinforced, and much stronger than before, moved first towards the city called Circæum, a Roman colony. He received its surrender, and did the inhabitants no injury; passing thence, he entered and laid waste the country of the Latins, where he expected the Romans would meet him, as the Latins were their confederates and allies, and had often sent to demand succor from them. The people, however, on their part, showing little inclination for the service, and the consuls themselves being unwilling to run the hazard of a battle, when the time of their office was almost ready to expire, they dismissed the Latin ambassadors without any effect; so that Marcius, finding no army to oppose him, marched up to their cities, and, having taken by force Toleria, Lavici, Peda, and Bola, all of which offered resistance, not only plundered their houses, but made a prey likewise of their persons. Meantime, he showed particular regard for all such as came over to his party, and, for fear they might sustain any damage against his will, encamped at the greatest distance he could, and wholly abstained from their property.

After, however, he had made himself master of Bola, a town not above ten miles from Rome, where he found great treasure, and put almost all the adults to the sword; the other Volscians that were ordered to stay behind and protect their cities, hearing of his achievements and success, had not patience to remain any longer at home, but came hastening in their arms to Marcius, saying that he alone was their general and the sole commander they would own; with all this, his name and renown spread throughout all Italy, and universal wonder prevailed at the sudden and mighty revolution in the fortunes of two nations which the loss and the accession of a single man had effected.

All at Rome was in great disorder; they were utterly averse from fighting, and spent their whole time in cabals and disputes and reproaches against each other; until news was brought that the enemy had laid close siege to Lavinium, where were the images and sacred things of their tutelar gods, and whence they derived the origin of their nation, that being the first city which Æneas built in Italy. These tidings produced a change as universal as it was extraordinary in the thoughts and inclinations of the people, but occasioned a yet stranger revulsion of feeling among the patricians. The people now were for repealing the sentence against Marcius, and calling him back into the city; whereas the senate, being assembled to consider the decree, opposed and finally rejected the proposal, either out of the mere humor of opposing the people in whatever they should desire, or because they were unwilling, perhaps, that he should owe his restoration to their kindness. When Marcius heard of this, he was more exasperated than ever, and, quitting the siege of Lavinium, marched furiously towards Rome, and encamped at a place called the Cluilian ditches, about five miles from the city. The nearness of his approach did, indeed, create much terror and disturbance, yet it also ended their dissensions for the present; as nobody now, whether consul or senator, durst any longer contradict the people in their design of recalling Marcius.

It was, therefore, unanimously agreed by all parties, that ambassadors should be despatched, offering him return to his country, and desiring him to free them from the terrors and distresses of the war. The persons sent by the senate with this message were chosen out of his kindred and acquaintance, who naturally expected a very kind reception at their first interview; in which, however, they were much mistaken. Being led through the enemy's camp, they found him sitting in state amid the chief men of the Volscians, looking insupportably proud and arrogant. He bade them declare the cause of their coming, which they did in the most gentle terms, and with a behavior suitable to their language. When they had made an end of speaking, he returned them a sharp answer, full of bitterness and angry resentment, as to what concerned himself, and the ill usage he had received from them but as general of the Volscians, he demanded restitution of the cities and the lands which had been seized upon during the late war, and that the same rights and franchises should be granted them at Rome, which had been before accorded to the Latins; since there could be no assurance that a peace would be firm and lasting, without just conditions on both sides. He allowed them thirty days to consider and resolve.

The ambassadors having departed, he withdrew his forces from the Roman territory. Those of the Volscians who had long envied his reputation, and could not endure to see the influence he had with the people, laid hold of this as a matter of complaint against him. Among them was Tullus himself, not for any wrong done him personally by Marcius, but through the weakness incident to human nature. He could not help feeling mortified to find his own glory totally obscured, and himself overlooked and neglected now by the Volscians, who had so great an opinion of their new leader. Yet Marcius spent no part of the time idly, but attacked the confederates of the enemy, ravaged their land, and took from them seven great and populous cities in that interval. The Romans, in the meanwhile, durst not venture out to their relief; but were utterly fearful, and showed no more disposition or capacity for action, than if their bodies had been struck with a palsy, and become destitute of sense and motion. But when the thirty days were expired, and Marcius appeared again with his whole army, they sent another embassy to beseech him that he would moderate his displeasure, and would withdraw the Volscian army, and then make any proposals he thought best for both parties, but if it were his opinion that the Volscians ought to have any favor shown them, upon laying down their arms they might obtain all they could in reason desire.

The reply of Marcius was, that he should make no answer to this as general of the Volscians, but in the quality still of a Roman citizen, he would advise them to return to him before three days were at an end, with a ratification of his previous demands.

When the ambassadors came back, and acquainted the senate with the answer, seeing the whole state now threatened as it were by a tempest, a decree was made, that the whole order of their priests should go in full procession to Marcius with their pontifical array, and the dress and habit which they respectively used in their several functions, and should urge him, as before, to withdraw his forces, and then treat with his countrymen in favor of the Volscians. He granted nothing at all, nor so much as expressed himself more mildly; but without capitulating or receding, bade them once for all choose whether they would yield or fight, since the old terms were the only terms of peace. In this great perplexity, the Roman women went, some to other temples, but the greater part, and the ladies of highest rank, to the altar of Jupiter Capitolinus. Among these suppliants was Valeria, sister to the great Poplicola, who happily lighting, not without divine guidance, on the right expedient, rose, and bade the others rise, and went directly with them to the house of Volumnia, the mother of Marcius. And coming in and finding her sitting with her daughter-in-law, and with her little grandchildren on her lap, Valeria, then surrounded by her companions, spoke in the name of them all:—

"We, O Volumnia, and Vergilia, are come as women to women, to request a thing on which our own and the common safety depends, and which, if you consent to it, will raise your glory above that of the daughters of the Sabines, who won over their fathers and their husbands from mortal enmity to peace and friendship. Arise and come with us to Marcius; join in our supplication, for your country's sake."

The words of Valeria were seconded by the acclamations of the other women, to which Volumnia made answer:—

"I and Vergilia, my countrywomen, have an equal share with you all in the common miseries, and we have the additional sorrow, which is wholly ours, that we have lost the merit and good fame of Marcius, and see his person confined, rather than protected by the arms of the enemy. Make use, however, of our service; and lead us, if you please, to him; we are able, if nothing more, at least to spend our last breath in making suit to him for our country."

Having spoken thus, she took Vergilia by the hand, and the young children, and so accompanied them to the Volscian camp. So lamentable a sight much affected the enemies themselves, who viewed them in respectful silence. Marcius, seeing the party of women advance, came down hastily to meet them, saluting his mother first, and embracing her a long time, and then his wife and children, sparing neither tears nor cares, but suffering himself to be borne away and carried headlong, as it were, by the impetuous violence of his passion.

When he had satisfied himself, and observed that his mother Volumnia was desirous to say something, the Volscian council being first called in, he heard her to the following effect: "Our dress and our very persons, my son, might tell you, though we should say nothing ourselves, in how forlorn a condition we have lived at home since your banishment and absence from us; and now consider with yourself, whether we may not pass for the most unfortunate of all women, to have that sight, which should be the sweetest that we could see, converted, through I know not what fatality, to one of all others the most formidable and dreadful,—Volumnia to behold her son, and Vergilia her husband, in arms against the walls of Rome. As for myself, if I cannot prevail with you to prefer amity and concord to quarrel and hostility, and to be the benefactor to both parties, rather than the destroyer of one of them, be assured of this, that you shall not be able to reach your country, unless you trample first upon the corpse of her that brought you into life. For it will be ill in me to loiter in the world till the day come wherein I shall see a child of mine, either led in triumph by his own countrymen, or triumphing over them."

Marcius listened to his mother while she spoke, without answering her a word; and Volumnia, seeing him stand mute also for a long time after she had ceased, resumed: "O my son, what is the meaning of this silence? Is it wrong to gratify a mother in a request like this? You have punished your country already; you have not yet paid your debt to me." Having said this, she threw herself down at his feet, as did also his wife and children; upon which Marcius, crying out, "O mother what is it you have done to me?" raised her from the ground, and pressing her right hand with more than ordinary vehemence said, "You have gained a victory, fortunate enough for the Romans, but destructive to your son; whom you, though none else, have defeated." And after a little private conference with his mother and his wife, he sent them back again to Rome, as they desired of him.

The next morning, he broke up his camp, and led the Volscians homeward, variously affected with what he had done. None, however, opposed his commands; they all obediently followed him, though rather from admiration of his virtue, than any regard they now had to his authority. The Roman people, meantime, began to crown themselves with garlands and prepare for sacrifice, as they were wont to do upon tidings brought of any signal victory. But the joy and transport of the whole city was chiefly remarkable in the honors and marks of affection paid to the women, as well by the senate as the people in general; every one declaring that they were, beyond all question, the instruments of the public safety. And the senate having passed a decree that whatsoever they would ask in the way of any favor or honor should be allowed and done for them by the magistrates, they demanded simply that a temple might be erected to the Goddess Fortuna, the expense of which they offered to defray out of their own contributions, if the city would be at the cost of sacrifices, and other matters pertaining to the due honor of the gods, out of the common treasury. The senate, much commending their public spirit, caused the temple to be built and a statue set up in it at the public charge; they, however, made up a sum among themselves, for a second image of Fortune, which the Romans say uttered these words as they were putting it up "Blessed of the gods, O women, is your gift."

When Marcius came back to Antium, Tullus, who thoroughly

hated and greatly feared him, proceeded at once to contrive how he might immediately despatch him; as, if he escaped now, he was never likely to give him such another advantage. Having, therefore, got together and suborned several partisans against him, he required Marcius to resign his charge, and give the Volscians an account of his administration.

An assembly was called, and popular speakers, as had been concerted, came forward to exasperate and incense the multitude; but when Marcius stood up to answer, even the most tumultuous part of the people became quiet on a sudden, and out of reverence allowed him to speak without the least disturbance; while all the better people, and such as were satisfied with a peace, made it evident by their whole behavior, that they would give him a favorable hearing, and judge and pronounce according to equity.

For these reasons, the conspirators judged it prudent not to test the general feeling; but the boldest of their faction fell upon Marcius in a body, and slew him there, none of those that were present offering to defend him. But it quickly appeared that the action was in nowise approved of by the majority of the Volscians, who hurried out of their several cities to show respect to his corpse; to which they gave honorable interment, adorning his sepulchre with arms and trophies, as the monument of a noble hero and a famous general. When the Romans heard tidings of his death, they gave no other signification either of honor or of anger toward him, but simply granted the request of the women, that they might put themselves into mourning and bewail him for ten months, as the usage was upon the loss of a father or a son or a brother; that being the period fixed for the longest lamentation by the laws of Numa Pompilius.

Marcius was no sooner deceased, than the Volscians felt the need of his assistance. They quarreled first with the Æquians, their confederates and friends, about the appointmen of the general of their joint forces, and carried their dispute to the length of bloodshed and slaughter; and were then defeated by the Romans in a pitched battle, where not only Tullus lost his life, but the flower of their whole army was cut to pieces; so that they were forced to submit and accept of peace upon very dishonorable terms, becoming subjects of Rome, and pledging themselves to submission.

COMPARISON OF ALCIBIADES AND CORIOLANUS.

Having described all their actions that seem to deserve commemoration, their military ones, we may say, incline the balance very decidedly upon neither side. They both, in pretty equal measure, displayed on numerous occasions the daring and courage of the soldier, and the skill and foresight of the general; unless, indeed, the fact that Alcibiades was victorious and successful in many contests both by sea and land, ought to gain him the title of a more complete commander. That so long as they remained and held command in their respective countries, they eminently sustained, and when they were driven into exile, yet more eminently damaged the fortunes of those countries, is common to both. All the sober citizens felt disgust at the petulance, the low flattery, and base seductions which Alcibiades, in his public life, allowed himself to employ with the view of winning the people's favor; and the ungraciousness, pride, and oligarchical haughtiness which Marcius, on the other hand, displayed in his, were the abhorrence of the Roman populace.

Marcius, according to our common conceptions of his character, was undoubtedly simple and straightforward; Alcibiades, unscrupulous as a public man, and false. He is more especially blamed for the dishonorable and treacherous way in

COMPARISON OF ALCIBIADES AND CORIOLANUS.

which, as Thucydides relates, he imposed upon the Lacedæmonian ambassadors, and disturbed the continuance of the peace. Yet this policy, which engaged the city again in war, nevertheless placed it in a powerful and formidable position, by the accession, which Alcibiades obtained for it, of the alliance of Argos and Mantinea. And Coriolanus also, Dionysius relates, used unfair means to excite war between the Romans and the Volscians, in the false report which he spread about the visitors at the Games; and the motive of this action seems to make it the worse of the two; since it was not done, like the other, out of ordinary political jealousy, strife and competition. Simply to gratify anger, from which, as Ion says, no one ever yet got any return, he threw whole districts of Italy into confusion, and sacrificed to his passion against his country numerous innocent cities. It is true, indeed, that Alcibiades, by his resentment, was the occasion of great disasters to his country, but he relented as soon as he found their feelings to be changed; and after he was driven out a second time, so far from taking pleasure in the errors and inadvertencies of their commanders, or being indifferent to the danger they were thus incurring, he did the very thing that Aristides is so highly commended for doing to Themistocles: he came to the generals who were his enemies, and pointed out to them what they ought to do. Coriolanus, on the other hand, first of all attacked the whole body of his countrymen, though only one portion of them had done him any wrong, while the other, the better and nobler portion, had actually suffered, as well as sympathized, with him. And, secondly, by the obduracy with which he resisted numerous embassies and supplications, addressed in propitiation of his personal anger, he showed that it had been to destroy and overthrow, not to recover and regain his country, that he had excited bitter and implacable hostilities against it. There is, indeed, one distinction that may be drawn. Alcibiades, it may be said, was not safe among the Spartans, and had the inducements at once of fear and of hatred to lead him again to Athens; whereas Marcius could not honorably have left the Volscians, when they were behaving so well to him: he, in the command of their forces and the enjoyment of their entire confidence, was in a very different position from Alcibiades, whom the Lacedæmonians did not so much wish to adopt into their service, as to use, and then abandon. Driven about from house to house in the city, and from general to general in the camp, the latter had no resort but to place himself in the hands of Tissaphernes; unless we are to suppose that his object in courting favor with him was to avert the entire destruction of his native city, whither he wished himself to return.

As regards money, Alcibiades, we are told, was often guilty of procuring it by accepting bribes, and spent it in luxury and dissipation. Coriolanus declined to receive it, even when pressed upon him by his commanders as an honor; and one great reason for the odium he incurred with the populace in the discussions about their debts was, that he trampled upon the poor, not for money's sake, but out of pride and insolence.

Antipater, in a letter written upon the death of Aristotle the philosopher, observes, "Amongst his other gifts he had that of persuasiveness;" and the absence of this in the character of Marcius made all his great actions and noble qualities unacceptable to those whom they benefited: pride, and self-will, the consort, as Plato calls it, of solitude, made him insufferable. With the skill which Alcibiades, on the contrary, possessed to treat every one in the way most agreeable to him, we cannot wonder that all his successes were attended with the most exuberant favor and honor; his very errors, at times, being accompanied by something of grace and felicity. And so, in spite of great and frequent hurt that he had done the city, he was repeatedly appointed to office and command; while Coriolanus stood in vain for a place which his great services had made his due.

Alcibiades never professed to deny that it was pleasant

to him to be honored and distasteful to him to be overlooked; and, accordingly, he always tried to place himself upon good terms with all that he met; Coriolanus's pride forbade him to pay attentions to those who could have promoted his advancement, and yet his love of distinction made him feel hurt and angry when he was disregarded. Such are the faulty parts of his character, which in all other respects was a noble one. For his temperance, continence, and probity, he might claim to be compared with the best and purest of the Greeks; not in any sort or kind with Alcibiades, the least scrupulous and most entirely careless of human beings in all these points.

ARISTIDES.

ARISTIDES, the son of Lysimachus, was of the tribe Antiochis and township of Alopece. Being the friend and supporter of that Clisthenes, who settled the government after the expulsion of the tyrants, and emulating and admiring Lycurgus the Lacedæmonian above all politicians, he adhered to the aristocratical principles of government; and had Themistocles, son to Neocles, his adversary on the side of the populace. Some say that, when boys together, they were always at variance in all their words and actions, serious as well as playful. One was ready, venturesome, and subtle, engaging readily and eagerly in every thing; the other of a staid and settled temper, intent on the exercise of justice, not admitting any degree of falsity, indecorum, or trickery, even at his play. Ariston of Ceos says that the first origin of the enmity which rose to so great a height, was a love affair; they were rivals for the affection of the beautiful Stesilaus of Ceos, and were passionate beyond all moderation, and did not lay aside their animosity when the beauty that had excited it passed away; but carried their heats and differences into public business.

Themistocles joined an association of partisans, and fortified himself with considerable strength; so that when some one told him that if he were impartial, he would make a good magistrate; "I wish," replied he, "I may never sit on that tribunal where my friends shall not plead a greater privilege than strangers." But Aristides walked alone on his path in politics, being unwilling to go with his associates in ill doing, or to cause them vexation by not gratifying their wishes

When he had once opposed Themistocles in some measures that were expedient, and had got the better of him, he could not refrain from saying, when he left the assembly, that unless they sent Themistocles and himself to the barathrum,* there could be no safety for Athens. Another time, when urging some proposal upon the people, although there was much opposition to it, yet he was gaining the day; but just as the president of the assembly was about to put it to the vote, perceiving by what had been said in debate the inexpediency of his advice, he let it fall. He often brought in his bills by other persons, lest Themistocles, through party spirit against him, should be any hindrance to the good of the public.

In all the vicissitudes of public affairs, the constancy he showed was admirable, not being elated with honors, and demeaning himself sedately in adversity. Once, at the recital of these verses of Æschylus in the theatre, relating to Amphiaraus,

> For not at seeming just, but being so
> He aims; and from his depth of soil below,
> Harvests of wise and prudent counsels grow,

the eyes of all the spectators were turned upon Aristides, as if this virtue in an especial manner belonged to him.

He was a most determined champion of justice, not only against feelings of friendship and favor, but wrath and malice. Thus it is reported of him that prosecuting one who was his enemy, when the judges after accusation refused to hear the criminal, and were proceeding immediately to pass sentence upon him, he rose in haste from his seat and joined in petition with him for a hearing, and that he might enjoy the privilege of the law. Another time, judging between two private persons, when the one declared his adversary had very much injured Aristides; "Tell me rather, good friend," he said,

---

* A pit into which the dead bodies of malefactors, or perhaps living malefactors themselves, were thrown. "The gallows" perhaps is the English term most nearly corresponding to the barathrum, as commonly spoken of in the Athenian popular language.

"what wrong he has done you: for it is your cause, not my own, which I now sit judge of." Being chosen to the charge of the public revenue, he made it appear, that not only those of his time, but the preceding officers, had alienated much treasure, and especially Themistocles:—

> Well known he was an able man to be,
> But with his fingers apt to be too free.

Therefore, Themistocles associating several persons against Aristides, and impeaching him when he gave in his accounts, caused him to be condemned of robbing the public; so Idomeneus states; but the best and chief men of the city much resented it, so that he was not only exempted from the fine imposed upon him, but again called to the same employment. Pretending now to repent of his former practice, and carrying himself with more remissness, he became acceptable to such as pillaged the treasury, by not detecting or calling them to an exact account. So that those who had their fill of the public money began highly to applaud Aristides, and sued to the people, to have him once more chosen treasurer. But when they were upon the point of election, he reproved the Athenians in these words: "When I discharged my office well and faithfully, I was insulted and abused; but now that I have countenanced the public thieves in a variety of malpractices, I am considered an admirable patriot. I am more ashamed, therefore, of this present honor than of the former sentence; and I pity your condition, with whom it is more praiseworthy to oblige bad men than to preserve the revenue of the public."

When Datis was sent by Darius under pretence of punishing the Athenians for their burning of Sardis, but in reality to reduce the Greeks under his dominion, and had landed at Marathon and laid waste the country, among the ten commanders appointed by the Athenians for the war, Miltiades was of the greatest name; but the second place, both for reputation and power, was possessed by Aristides: and when his opinion to join battle was added to that of Miltiades, it did much to incline the balance. Every leader by his day having the command in chief, when it came to Aristides' turn, he delivered it into the hands of Miltiades, showing his fellow officers, that it is not dishonorable to obey and follow wise and able men, but, on the contrary, noble and prudent. So appeasing their rivalry, and bringing them to acquiesce in the best advice, he confirmed Miltiades in the strength of an undivided and unmolested authority. And now every one, yielding his day of command, looked for orders only to him. During the fight the main body of the Athenians being the hardest pressed, the barbarians, for a long time, making opposition there against the tribes Leontis and Antiochis, Themistocles and Aristides being ranged together, fought valiantly; the one being of the tribe Leontis, the other of the Antiochis. But, after they had beaten the barbarians back to their ships, and perceived that they did not sail for the isles, but were driven in by the force of sea and wind towards the country of Attica, fearing lest they should take the city, they hurried away thither with nine tribes, and reached it the same day.

Of all the virtues of Aristides, the common people were most affected with his justice, because of its continual and common use; and thus, although of mean fortune and ordinary birth, he possessed himself of the most kingly and divine appellation of Just; which kings, however, and tyrants have never sought after; but have taken delight to be surnamed besiegers of cities, thunderers, conquerors, eagles and hawks; affecting, it seems, the reputation which proceeds from power and violence, rather than that of virtue.

Aristides, therefore, had at first the fortune to be beloved for this surname, but at length envied. Especially when Themistocles spread a rumor amongst the people, that, by determining and judging all matters privately, he had destroyed the courts of judicature, and was secretly making way for a monarchy in his own person, without the assistance of guards.

Moreover, the spirit of the people, now grown high, and confident with their late victory, naturally entertained feelings of dislike to all of more than common fame and reputation. Coming together, therefore, from all parts into the city, they banished Aristides by the ostracism, giving their jealousy of his reputation the name of fear of tyranny. For ostracism was not the punishment of any criminal act, but was speciously said to be the mere depression and humiliation of excessive greatness and power; and was in fact a gentle relief and mitigation of envious feeling, which was thus allowed to vent itself in inflicting no intolerable injury, only a ten years' banishment. But after it came to be exercised upon base and villanous fellows, they desisted from it; Hyperbolus, being the last whom they banished by the ostracism.

The cause of Hyperbolus's banishment is said to have been this. Alcibiades and Nicias, men that bore the greatest sway in the city, were of different factions. As the people, therefore, were about to vote the ostracism, and obviously to decree it against one of them, consulting together and uniting their parties, they contrived the banishment of Hyperbolus. Upon which the people, being offended, as if some contempt or affront was put upon the thing, left off and quite abolished it. It was performed, to be short, in this manner. Every one taking an *ostracon*, that is, a sherd, or piece of earthenware, wrote upon it the citizen's name he would have banished, and carried it to a certain part of the market-place surrounded with wooden rails. First, the magistrates numbered all the sherds in gross (for if there were less than six thousand, the ostracism was imperfect); then, laying every name by itself, they pronounced him whose name was written by the largest number, banished for ten years, with the enjoyment of his estate. As, therefore, they were writing the names on the sherds, it is reported that an illiterate clownish fellow, giving Aristides his sherd, supposing him a common citizen, begged him to write *Aristides* upon it; and he being surprised and asking if Aristides had ever done him any injury, "None at all," said he, "neither know I the man; but I am tired of hearing him everywhere called the Just." Aristides, hearing this, is said to have made no reply, but returned the sherd with his own name inscribed. At his departure from the city, lifting up his hands to heaven, he made a prayer (the reverse, it would seem, of that of Achilles), that the Athenians might never have any occasion which should constrain them to remember Aristides.

But three years afterwards, when Xerxes was marching through Thessaly and Bœotia into the country of Attica, they repealed the law, and decreed the return of the banished: chiefly fearing lest Aristides might join himself to the enemy, and bring over many of his fellow-citizens to the party of the barbarians; much mistaking the man, who, already before the decree, was exerting himself to excite and encourage the Greeks to the defence of their liberty.

After the battle of Salamis, Xerxes, much terrified, immediately hastened to the Hellespont. But Mardonius was left with the most serviceable part of the army, about three hundred thousand men, and was a formidable enemy, confident in his infantry, and writing messages of defiance to the Greeks: "You have overcome by sea men accustomed to fight on land, and unskilled at the oar; but there lies now the open country of Thessaly; and the plains of Bœotia offer a broad and worthy field for brave men, either horse or foot, to contend in." But he sent privately to the Athenians, both by letter and word of mouth from the king, promising to rebuild their city, to give them a vast sum of money, and constitute them lords of all Greece on condition they would not engage in the war. The Lacedæmonians receiving news of this, and fearing, despatched an embassy to the Athenians, entreating that they would send their wives and children to Sparta, and receive support from them for their superannuated. For, being despoiled both of their city and country, the people were suffering extreme distress. Having given audience to the ambassadors, they returned an answer, upon the motion of Aristides, worthy of the highest admiration; declaring, that they forgave their enemies if they thought all things purchasable by wealth, than which they knew nothing of greater value; but that they felt offended at the Lacedæmonians, for looking only to their present poverty, without any remembrance of their valor and magnanimity, and offering them their victuals, to fight in the cause of Greece. Aristides made this proposal, brought back the ambassadors into the assembly, and charged them to tell the Lacedæmonians that all the treasure on the earth or under it was of less value with the people of Athens than the liberty of Greece. And, showing the sun to those who came from Mardonius, "as long as that retains the same course, so long," said he, "shall the citizens of Athens wage war with the Persians for the country which has been wasted, and the temples that have been profaned and burnt by them." Moreover, he proposed a decree, that the priests should anathematize him who sent any herald to the Medes, or deserted the alliance of Greece.

When Mardonius made a second incursion into the country of Attica, the people passed over again into the isle of Salamis. Aristides himself went to Lacedæmon, and reproved them for their delay and neglect in abandoning Athens once more to the barbarians; and demanded their assistance for that part of Greece which was not yet lost. The Ephori, hearing this, made show of sporting all day, and of carelessly keeping holy day (for they were then celebrating the Hyacinthian festival), but in the night, selecting five thousand Spartans, each of whom was attended by seven Helots, they sent them forth unknown to those from Athens. And when Aristides again reprehended them, they told him in derision that he either doted or dreamed, for the army was already at Oresteum, in their march towards the *strangers;* as they calles the Persians. Aristides answered, that they jested unreasonably, deluding their friends, instead of their enemies.

Being chosen general for the war, he repaired to Platæa, with eight thousand Athenians, where Pausanias, generalissimo of all Greece, joined him with the Spartans; and the forces of the other Greeks came in to them. The encampment of the barbarians extended all along the bank of the river Asopus, their numbers being so great, there was no enclosing them all, but their baggage and most valuable things were surrounded with a square bulwark, each side of which was the length of ten furlongs.

The Tegeatans, contesting the post of honor with the Athenians, demanded, that according to custom, the Lacedæmonians being ranged on the right wing of the battle, they might have the left, alleging several matters in commendation of their ancestors. The Athenians being indignant at the claim, Aristides came forward and said: "To contend with the Tegeatans for noble descent and valor, the present time permits not: but this we say to you, O you Spartans, and you the rest of the Greeks, that place neither takes away nor contributes courage: we shall endeavor by maintaining the post you assign us, to reflect no dishonor on our former performances. For we are come, not to differ with our friends, but to fight our enemies; not to extol our ancestors, but to behave as valiant men. This battle will manifest how much each city, captain, and private soldier is worth to Greece." The council of war, upon this address, decided for the Athenians, and gave them the other wing of the battle.

At this juncture, Mardonius made trial of the Grecian courage, by sending his whole number of horse, in which he thought himself much the stronger, against them, while they were all, except the Megarians, encamped at the foot of Mount Cithæron, in strong and rocky places. They being three thousand in number, had pitched their tents on the plain, where the cavalry charged and made inroads upon them from all sides. They sent, therefore, in haste to Pausanias, demanding relief, not being able alone to sustain the great numbers of the barbarians. Pausanias, hearing this, and perceiving the tents of the Megarians almost hidden by the multitude of darts and arrows, and themselves driven together into a narrow space, was at a loss how to aid them with his battalions of heavy-armed Lacedæmonians. He asked, therefore, as a test of emulation in valor and love of distinction, to the commanders and captains who were around him, if any would voluntarily take upon them the defence and succor of the Megarians. The rest being backward, Aristides undertook the enterprise for the Athenians, and sent Olympiodorus, the most valiant of his inferior officers, with three hundred chosen men and some archers under his command. These were soon in readiness, and running upon the enemy, as soon as it was perceived by Masistius, who commanded the cavalry of the barbarians, a man of wonderful courage and of extraordinary bulk and comeliness of person, he turned his steed and made towards them. They sustained the shock and joined battle with him, as though by this encounter they were to try the success of the whole war. But after Masistius's horse received a wound, and flung him, and he falling, could hardly raise himself through the weight of his armor, the Athenians pressed upon him with blows, but could not easily get at his person, armed as he was, breast, head, and limbs all over, with gold and brass and iron; but one of them at last, running a javelin under the visor of his helmet, slew him; and the rest of the Persians, leaving the body, fled. The greatness of the Greek success was known, not by the multitude of the slain (for an inconsiderable number were killed), but by the sorrow the barbarians expressed. For they shaved themselves, their horses, and mules for the death of Masistius, and filled the plain with howling and lamentation; having lost a person, who, next to Mardonius himself, was by far the chief among them, both for valor and authority.

After this skirmish of the horse, they kept from fighting a long time; for the soothsayers, by the sacrifices, foretold the victory both to Greeks and Persians, if they stood upon the defensive part only, but if they became aggressors, the contrary. At length Mardonius, when he had but a few days' provision, and the Greek forces were increasing continually, impatient of delay, determined to lie still no longer, but, passing Asopus by daybreak, to fall unexpectedly upon the Greeks. This he signified the night before to the captains of his host. But about midnight, a certain horseman stole into the Greek camp, and coming to the watch, desired them to summon Aristides, the Athenian, to him. He came speedily, and the stranger said: "I am Alexander, king of the Macedonians, and have come here through the greatest danger in the world for the good-will I bear you, lest a sudden onset should dismay you, so as to behave in the fight worse than usual. For to-morrow Mardonius will give you battle, urged, not by any hope of success or courage, but by want of victuals: for the prophets prohibit him from the battle, the sacrifices and oracles being unfavorable; but the army is in despondency and consternation; and necessity forces him to try his fortune, or sit still and endure the last extremity of want." Alexander, thus saying, entreated Aristides to take notice and remember him, but not to tell any other. But he replied that it was not fair to conceal the matter from Pausanias (because he was general); as for any others he would keep it secret from them till the battle was fought; but if the Greeks obtained the victory, that then no one should be ignorant of Alexander's good-will and kindness towards them. After this, the king of the Macedonians rode back again, and Aristides went to Pausanias's tent and told him; and they sent for the rest of the captains and gave orders that the army should be in battle array.

Meantime, day came upon them; and Mardonius having his army in array, fell upon the Lacedæmonians with great shouting and noise of barbarous people, as if they were not about to join battle, but crush the Greeks in their flight—a thing which very nearly came to pass. For Pausanias, perceiving what was done, made a halt, and commanded every one to put themselves in order for the battle; but through the disturbance he was in, on account of the sudden approach of the enemy, he forgot to give the signal to the Greeks in general. Whence it was, that they did not come immediately, or in a body, to their assistance, but by small companies and straggling, when the fight was already begun. Pausanias, offering sacrifice, could not procure favorable omens, and so commanded the Lacedæmonians to set down their shields at their feet and quietly await for his directions, making no resistance to any of their enemies. At this time, Callicrates, who, we are told, was the most comely man in the army, being shot with an arrow and upon the point of expiring, said that he did not lament his death (for he came from home to lay down his life in the defence of Greece) but that he died without action. While Pausanias was thus in the act of supplication, the sacrifices appeared propitious, and the soothsayers foretold victory. The word being given, the Lacedæmonian battalion of foot seemed, on the sudden, like some fierce animal, setting up his bristles, and betaking himself to the combat; and the barbarians perceived that they encountered with men who would fight to the death. Therefore, holding their wicker shields before them, they shot their arrows amongst the Lacedæmonians. But they, keeping together in the order of a phalanx, and falling upon their enemies, forced their shields out of their hands, and, striking with their pikes at the breasts and faces of the Persians, overthrew many of them; they, however, fell neither unrevenged nor without courage. For taking hold of the spears with their bare hands, they broke many of them, and betook themselves with effect to the sword; and making use of their falchions and scimitars, and wresting the Lacedæmonians' shields from them, and grappling with them, for a long time stood their ground.

Meanwhile, the Athenians were standing still, waiting for

the Lacedæmonians to come up. But when they heard a great noise as of men engaged in fight, and a messenger came from Pausanias, to inform them of what was going on, they made haste to their assistance. And as they passed through the plain to the place where the noise was, the recreant Greeks, who took part with the enemy, came upon them. Aristides, as soon as he saw them, going a considerable space before the rest, cried out to them, by the guardian gods of Greece, not to enter the fight, and be no impediment to those who were going to succor the defenders of Greece. But when he perceived that they gave no attention to him, and had prepared themselves for the battle, then turning from the present relief of the Lacedæmonians, he engaged with them, being five thousand in number. But the greatest part soon gave way and retreated, as the barbarians also were put to flight.

The battle being thus divided, the Lacedæmonians first beat off the Persians; and a Spartan, named Arimnestus, slew Mardonius by a blow on the head with a stone, as the oracle in the temple of Amphiaraus had foretold to him. For Mardonius sent a Lydian thither, and another person, a Carian, to the cave of Trophonius. This latter, the priest of the oracle answered in his own language. But to the Lydian sleeping in the temple of Amphiaraus, it seemed that a minister of the divinity stood before him and commanded him to be gone; and on his refusing to do it, flung a great stone at his head, so that he thought himself slain with the blow. Such is the story. Of three hundred thousand of the enemy, forty thousand only are said to have escaped with Artabazus; while on the Greeks' side there perished in all thirteen hundred and sixty; of whom fifty-two were Athenians, all of the tribe Æantis, that fought, says Clidemus, with the greatest courage of all; and for this reason the men of this tribe used to offer sacrifice for the victory, as enjoined by the oracle, at the public expense; ninety-one were Lacedæmonians, and six teen Tegeatans. They engraved upon the altar this inscription:—

> The Greeks, when by their courage and their might,
> They had repelled the Persian in the fight,
> The common altar of freed Greece to be,
> Reared this to Jupiter who guards the free.

The battle of Platæa was fought on the fourth day of the month Boëdromion, on which day there is still a convention of the Greeks at Platæa, and the Platæans still offer sacrifice for the victory to "Jupiter of freedom."

After this, the Athenians, not yielding the honor of the day to the Lacedæmonians, nor consenting that they should erect a trophy, peace was well-nigh destroyed by a dissension among the armed Greeks; but Aristides, by soothing and counseling the commanders, especially Leocrates and Myronides, pacified and persuaded them to leave the thing to the decision of the Greeks. Cleocritus of Corinth rising up, made people think he would ask the palm for the Corinthians (for next to Sparta and Athens, Corinth was in greatest estimation); but he delivered his opinion, to the general admiration, in favor of the Platæans; and counseled to take away all contention by giving them the reward and glory of the victory, whose being honored could be distasteful to neither party. This being said, first Aristides gave consent in the name of the Athenians, and Pausanius, then, for the Lacedæmonians. So, being reconciled, they set apart eighty talents for the Platæans, with which they built the temple and dedicated the image to Minerva, and adorned the temple with pictures, which even to this very day retain their lustre. But the Lacedæmonians and Athenians each erected a trophy apart by themselves. On their consulting the oracle about offering sacrifice, Apollo answered that they should dedicate an altar to Jupiter of freedom, but should not sacrifice till they had extinguished the fires throughout the country, as having been defiled by the barbarians, and had kindled unpolluted fire at the common altar at Delphi. The magistrates of Greece, therefore, went forthwith and compelled such as had fire to put it out; and Euchidas, a Platæan, promising to fetch fire with all possible speed, from the altar of the god, ran to Delphi, and having sprinkled and purified his body, crowned himself with laurel; and taking the fire from the altar ran back to Platæa, arriving before sunset, and performing in one day a journey of a thousand furlongs; and saluting his fellow-citizens and delivering them the fire, he immediately fell down and a short time after expired. Then the Platæans, taking him up, interred him in the temple of Diana Euclia, setting this inscription over him: "Euchidas ran to Delphi and back again in one day."

A general assembly of all the Greeks being called, Aristides proposed a decree, that the deputies and religious representatives of the Greek states should assemble annually at Platæa, and every fifth year celebrate the Eleutheria, or games of freedom. And that there should be a levy upon all Greece, for the war against the barbarians, of ten thousand spearmen, one thousand horse, and a hundred sail of ships; but the Platæans to be exempt, and sacred to the service of the gods, offering sacrifice for the welfare of Greece. These things being ratified, the Platæans undertook the performance of annual sacrifice to such as were slain and buried in that place; which they still perform in the following manner. On the sixteenth day of Mæmacterion they make their procession, which, beginning by break of day, is led by a trumpeter sounding for onset; then follow chariots loaded with myrrh and garlands; and then a black bull; then come the young men of free birth carrying libations of wine and milk in large two-handed vessels, and jars of oil and precious ointments, none of servile condition being permitted to have any hand in this ministration, because the men died in defence of freedom; after all comes the chief magistrate of Platæa (for whom it is unlawful at other times for him either to touch iron, or wear any other colored garment but white), at that time appareled in a purple robe; and, taking a water-pot out of the city record-office, he proceeds, bearing a sword in his hand, through the middle of the town to the sepulchres. Then drawing water out of a spring, he washes and anoints the monuments, and sacrificing the bull upon a pile of wood, and making supplication to Jupiter and Mercury of the earth, invites those valiant men who perished in the defence of Greece, to the banquet and the libations of blood. After this, mixing a bowl of wine, and pouring out for himself, he says, "I drink to those who lost their lives for the liberty of Greece." These solemnities the Platæans observe to this day.

Theophrastus tells us that Aristides was, in his own private affairs, and those of his fellow-citizens, rigorously just, but that in public matters he acted often in accordance with his country's policy, which demanded, sometimes, not a little injustice. It is reported of him that he said in a debate, upon the motion of the Samians for removing the treasure from Delos to Athens, contrary to the league, that the thing indeed was not just, but was expedient.

In fine, having established the dominion of his city over so many people, he himself remained indigent; and always delighted as much in the glory of being poor, as in that of his trophies; as is evident from the following story. Callias, the torch-bearer, was related to him: and was prosecuted by his enemies in a capital cause, in which, after they had slightly argued the matters on which they indicted him, they proceeded, beside the point, to address the judges: "You know," said they, "Aristides, the son of Lysimachus, who is the admiration of all Greece. In what a condition do you think his family is at his house, when you see him appear in public in such a threadbare cloak? Is it not probable that one who, out of doors, goes thus exposed to the cold, must want food and other necessaries at home? Callias, the wealthiest of the

Athenians, does nothing to relieve either him or his wife and children in their poverty, though he is his own cousin, and has made use of him in many cases, and often reaped advantage by his interest with you." But Callias, perceiving that the judges were particularly moved by this, and were exasperated against him, called in Aristides, who testified that when Callias offered him divers presents, and entreated him to accept them, he had refused, answering, that it became him better to be proud of his poverty than Callias of his wealth. On Aristides deposing these facts in favor of Callias, there was not one who heard them that went not away desirous rather to be poor like Aristides, than rich as Callias. Thus Æschines, the scholar of Socrates, writes. But Plato declares, that of all the great and renowned men in the city of Athens, he was the only one worthy of consideration; for while Themistocles, Cimon, and Pericles filled the city with porticoes, treasure, and many other vain things, Aristides guided his public life by the rule of justice. He showed his moderation very plainly in his conduct towards Themistocles himself. For though Themistocles had been his adversary in all his undertakings, and was the cause of his banishment, yet when he afforded a similar opportunity of revenge, being accused by the city, Aristides bore him no malice; but while Alcmæon, Cimon, and many others, were prosecuting and impeaching him, Aristides alone, neither did, nor said any evil against him, and no more triumphed over his enemy in his adversity, than he had envied him his prosperity.

Some say Aristides died in Pontus, during a voyage upon the affairs of the public. Others that he died of old age at Athens, being in great honor and veneration among his fellow-citizens.

His monument is to be seen at Phalerum, which they say was built for him by the city, he not having left enough even to defray funeral charges. And it is stated, that his two daughters were publicly married out of the prytaneum, or state-house, by the city, which decreed each of them three thousand drachmas for her portion; and that upon his son Lysimachus, the people bestowed a hundred minas of money, and as many acres of planted land, and ordered him besides, upon the motion of Alcibiades, four drachmas a day.

MOUNTS OLYMPUS AND OSSA FROM THE PLAIN OF THESSALY

CIMON

Cimon was the son of Miltiades and Hegesipyle, who was by birth a Thracian, and daughter to the king Olorus. By this means the historian Thucydides was his kinsman by the mother's side; for his father's name also, in remembrance of this common ancestor, was Olorus, and he was the owner of the gold mines in Thrace, and met his death, it is said, by violence, in Scapte Hyle, a district of Thrace. Cimon was left an orphan very young, with his sister Elpinice, who was also young and unmarried. And at first he had but an indifferent reputation, being looked upon as disorderly in his habits, fond of drinking, and resembling his grandfather, also called Cimon, in character, whose simplicity got him the surname of Coalemus the simpleton. Stesimbrotus of Thasos, who lived about the same time with Cimon, reports of him that he had little acquaintance either with music, or any of the other liberal studies and accomplishments, then common among the Greeks; that he had nothing whatever of the quickness and the ready speech of his countrymen in Attica; that he had great nobleness and candor in his disposition, and in his character in general, resembled rather a native of Peloponnesus, than of Athens; as Euripides describes Hercules:—

———— Rude
And unrefined, for great things well-endued;

for this may fairly be added to the character which Stesimbrotus has given of him.

Almost all the points of Cimon's character were noble and good. He was as daring as Miltiades, and not inferior to Themistocles in judgment, and was incomparably more just and honest than either of them. Fully their equal in all military virtues, in the ordinary duties of a citizen at home he was immeasurably their superior. And this, too, when he was very young, his years not yet strengthened by any experience. For when Themistocles, upon the Median invasion, advised the Athenians to forsake their city and their country, and to carry all their arms on shipboard, and fight the enemy by sea, in the straits of Salamis; when all the people stood amazed at the confidence and rashness of this advice, Cimon was seen, the first of all men, passing with a cheerful countenance through the Ceramicus, on his way with his companions to the citadel, carrying a bridle in his hand to offer to the goddess, intimating that there was no more need of horsemen now, but of mariners. There, after he had paid his devotions to the goddess, and offered up the bridle, he took down one of the bucklers that hung upon the walls of the temple, and went down to the port; by this example giving confidence to many of the citizens. He was also of a fairly handsome person, according to the poet Ion, tall and large, and let his thick and curly hair grow long. After he had acquitted himself gallantly in this battle of Salamis, he obtained great repute among the Athenians, and was regarded with affection, as well as admiration. He had many who followed after him, and bade him aspire to actions not less famous than his father's battle of Marathon. And when he came forward in political life, the people welcomed him gladly, being now weary of Themistocles; in opposition to whom, and because of the frankness and easiness of his temper, which was agreeable to every one, they advanced Cimon to the highest employments in the government. The man that contributed most to his promotion was Aristides, who early discerned in his character his natural capacity, and purposely raised him, that he

PLAIN OF MARATHON.

might be a counterpoise to the craft and boldness of Themistocles.

After the Medes had been driven out of Greece, Cimon was sent out as admiral, when the Athenians had not yet attained their dominion by sea, but still followed Pausanias and the Lacedæmonians; and his fellow-citizens under his command were highly distinguished, both for the excellence of their discipline, and for their extraordinary zeal and readiness. And further, perceiving that Pausanias was carrying on secret communications with the barbarians, and writing letters to the king of Persia to betray Greece, and, puffed up with authority and success, was treating the allies haughtily, and committing many wanton injustices, Cimon, taking advantage, by acts of kindness to those who were suffering wrong, and by his general humane bearing, robbed him of the command of the Greeks, before he was aware, not by arms, but by his mere language and character.

Cimon, strengthened with the accession of the allies, went as general into Thrace. For he was told that some great men among the Persians, of the king's kindred, being in possession of Eion, a city situated upon the river Strymon, infested the neighboring Greeks. First he defeated these Persians in battle, and shut them up within the walls of their town. Then he fell upon the Thracians of the country beyond the Strymon, because they supplied Eion with victuals, and driving them entirely out of the country, took possession of it as conqueror, by which means he reduced the besieged to such straits, that Butes, who commanded there for the king, in desperation set fire to the town, and burned himself, his goods, and all his relations, in one common flame. By this means, Cimon got the town, but no great booty; as the barbarians had not only consumed themselves in the fire, but the richest of their effects. However, he put the country into the hands of the Athenians, a most advantageous and desirable situation for a settlement. For this action, the people permitted him to erect the stone Mercuries, upon the first of which was this inscription:—

> Of bold and patient spirit, too, were those
> Who, where the Strymon under Eion flows,
> With famine and the sword, to utmost need
> Reduced at last the children of the Mede.

Upon the second stood this:—

> The Athenians to their leaders this reward
> For great and useful service did accord;
> Others hereafter, shall, from their applause,
> Learn to be valiant in their country's cause.

And upon the third, the following:—

> With Atreus' sons, this city sent of yore
> Divine Menestheus to the Trojan shore;
> Of all the Greeks, so Homer's verses say,
> The ablest man an army to array;
> So old the title of her sons the name
> Of chiefs and champions in the field to claim.

Though the name of Cimon is not mentioned in these inscriptions, yet his contemporaries considered them to be the very highest honors to him; as neither Miltiades nor Themistocles ever received the like. When Miltiades claimed a garland, Sochares of Decelea stood up in the midst of the assembly and opposed it, using words which, though ungracious, were received with applause by the people. "When you have gained a victory by yourself, Miltiades, then you may ask to triumph so too."

One mark of Cimon's great favor with the people, was the judgment, afterwards so famous, upon the tragic poets. Sophocles, still a young man, had just brought forward his first plays; opinions were much divided, and the spectators had taken sides with some heat. So, to determine the case, Apsephion, who was at that time archon, would not cast lots who should be judges; but when Cimon, and his brother commanders with him, came into the theatre, after they had performed the usual rites to the god of the festival, he would not allow them to retire, but came forward and made them swear, being ten in all, one from each tribe, the usual oath; and so being sworn judges, he made them sit down to give sentence. The eagerness for victory grew all the warmer, from the ambition to get the suffrages of such honorable judges. And the victory was at last adjudged to Sophocles, which Æschylus is said to have taken so ill, that he left Athens shortly after, and went in anger to Sicily, where he died, and was buried near the city of Gela.

Ion relates that when he was a young man, and had recently come from Chios to Athens, he chanced to sup with Cimon, at Laomedon's house. After supper, when they had, according to custom, poured out wine to the honor of the gods, Cimon was desired by the company to give them a song, which he did with sufficient success, and received the commendations of the company, who remarked on his superiority to Themistocles, who, on a like occasion, had declared he had never learnt to sing, or to play, and only knew how to make a city rich and powerful. After talking of things incident to such entertainments, they entered upon the particulars of the several actions for which Cimon had been famous. And when they were mentioning the most signal, he told them they had omitted one, upon which he valued himself most for address and good contrivance. He gave this account of it. When the allies had taken a great number of the barbarians prisoners in Sestos and Byzantium, they gave him the preference to divide the booty; he accordingly put the prisoners in one lot, and the spoils of their rich attire and jewels in the other. This the allies complained of as an unequal division; but he gave them their choice to take which lot they would, saying that the Athenians should be content with that which they refused. Herophytus of Samos advised them to take the ornaments for their share, and leave the slaves to the Athenians; and Cimon went away, and was much laughed at for his ridiculous division. For the allies carried away the golden bracelets, and armlets, and collars, and purple robes, and the Athenians had only the naked bodies of the captives, which they could make no advantage of, being unused to labor. But a little while after, the friends and kinsmen of the prisoners coming from Lydia and Phrygia, redeemed every one his relations at a high ransom; so that by this means Cimon got so much treasure that he maintained his whole fleet of galleys with the money for four months; and yet there was some left to lay up in the treasury at Athens.

Cimon now grew rich, and what he gained from the barbarians with honor, he spent yet more honorably upon the citizens. For he pulled down all the enclosures of his gardens and grounds, that strangers, and the needy of his fellow-citizens, might gather of his fruits freely. At home, he kept a table, plain, but sufficient for a considerable number, to which any poor townsman had free access, and so might support himself without labor, with his whole time left free for public duties. Aristotle states, however, that this reception did not extend to all the Athenians, but only to his own fellow townsmen, the Laciadæ.* Besides this, he always went attended by two or three young companions, very well clad; and if he met with an elderly citizen in a poor habit, one of these would change clothes with the decayed citizen, which was looked upon as very nobly done. He enjoined them, likewise, to carry a considerable quantity of

---

* Every Athenian citizen belonged, as such, to a particular town or township, one of the *demi*, of which there were above a hundred in Attica, in the latest times one hundred and seventy-four, all distinct localities; but, as a man, wherever he lived, continued to belong to his father's township, the relation was not strictly a local, but rather a personal one. The town meetings were all held in Athens. Politically, the demi were, perhaps, hardly more than wards for registration, but socially, by connecting every man with a particular district, the institution seems to have exercised a good deal of practical influence. Cimon's town, Lacia, or the Laciadæ, was just out of Athens, on the road to Eleusis.

coin about them, which they were to convey silently into the hands of the better class of poor men, as they stood by them in the market-place. This, Cratinus, the poet, speaks of in one of his comedies, the Archilochi: —

> For I, Metrobius too, the scrivener poor,
> Of ease and comfort in my age secure,
> By Greece's noblest son in life's decline,
> Cimon, the generous-hearted, the divine,
> Well-fed and feasted hoped till death to be,
> Death which, alas! has taken him ere me.

Gorgias the Leontine gives him this character, that he got riches that he might use them, and used them that he might get honor by them. And Critias, one of the thirty tyrants, makes it, in his elegies, his wish to have

> The Scopads' wealth, and Cimon's nobleness,
> And king Agesilaus's success.

Lichas, we know, became famous in Greece, only because on the days of the sports, when the young boys ran naked, he used to entertain the strangers that came to see these diversions. But Cimon's generosity outdid all the old Athenian hospitality and good-nature. For though it is the city's just boast that their forefathers taught the rest of Greece to sow corn, and how to use springs of water, and to kindle fire, yet Cimon, by keeping open house for his fellow-citizens, and giving travelers liberty to eat the fruits which the several seasons produced in his land, seemed to restore to the world that community of goods, which mythology says existed in the reign of Saturn. Those who object to him that he did this to be popular, and gain the applause of the vulgar, are confuted by the constant tenor of the rest of his actions, which all tended to uphold the interests of the nobility and the Spartan policy, of which he gave instances, when, together with Aristides, he opposed Themistocles, who was advancing the authority of the people beyond its just limits, and resisted Ephialtes, who to please the multitude, was for abolishing the jurisdiction of the court of Areopagus. And when all the men of his time, except Aristides and Ephialtes, enriched themselves out of the public money, he still kept his hands clean and untainted, and to his last day never acted or spoke for his own private gain or emolument. They tell us that Rhœsaces, a Persian, who had traitorously revolted from the king his master, fled to Athens, and there, being harassed by sycophants, who were still accusing him to the people, he applied himself to Cimon for redress, and to gain his favor, laid down in his doorway two cups, the one full of gold, and the other of silver Darics. Cimon smiled and asked him whether he wished to have Cimon's hired service or his friendship. He replied, his friendship. "If so," said he, "take away these pieces, for being your friend, when I shall have occasion for them, I will send and ask for them."

The allies of the Athenians began now to be weary of war and military service, willing to have repose, and to look after their husbandry and traffic. For they saw their enemies driven out of the country, and did not fear any new vexations from them. They still paid the tax they were assessed at, but did not send men and galleys, as they had done before. This the other Athenian generals wished to constrain them to, and by judicial proceedings against defaulters, and penalties which they inflicted on them, made the government uneasy, and even odious. But Cimon practiced a contrary method; he forced no man to go that was not willing, but of those that desired to be excused from service he took money and vessels unmanned, and let them yield to the temptation of staying at home, to attend to their private business. Thus they lost their military habits, and luxury and their own folly quickly changed them into unwarlike husbandmen and traders; while Cimon, continually embarking large numbers of Athenians on board his galleys, thoroughly disciplined them in his expeditions, and ere long made them the lords of their own paymasters. The allies, whose indolence maintained them, while they thus went sailing about everywhere, and incessantly bearing arms and acquiring skill, began to fear and flatter them, and found themselves after a while allies no longer, but unwittingly become tributaries and slaves.

Nor did any man ever do more than Cimon did to humble the pride of the Persian king. He was not content with ridding Greece of him; but following close at his heels, before the barbarians could take breath and recover themselves, what with his devastations, and his forcible reduction of some places and the revolts and voluntary accession of others, in the end, from Ionia to Pamphylia, all Asia was clear of Persian soldiers. Word being brought him that the royal commanders were lying in wait upon the coast of Pamphylia, with a numerous land army, and a large fleet, he determined to make the whole sea on this side the Chelidonian islands so formidable to them that they should never dare to show themselves in it; and setting off from Cnidos and the Triopian headland, with two hundred galleys, which had been originally built with particular care by Themistocles, for speed and rapid evolutions, and to which he now gave greater width and roomier decks along the sides to move to and fro upon, so as to allow a great number of full-armed soldiers to take part in the engagements and fight from them, he shaped his course first of all against the town of Phaselis, which, though inhabited by Greeks, yet would not quit the interests of Persia, but denied his galleys entrance into their port. Upon this he wasted the country, and drew up his army to their very walls; but the soldiers of Chios, who were then serving under him, being ancient friends to the Phaselites, endeavoring to propitiate the general in their behalf, at the same time shot arrows into the town, to which were fastened letters conveying intelligence. At length he concluded peace with them, upon the conditions that they should pay down ten talents, and follow him against the barbarians. The Persian admiral lay waiting for him with the whole fleet at the mouth of the river Eurymedon, with no design to fight, but expecting a reinforcement of eighty Phœnician ships on their way from Cyprus. Cimon, aware of this, put out to sea, resolved, if they would not fight a battle willingly, to force them to it. The barbarians, seeing this, retired within the mouth of the river to avoid being attacked; but when they saw the Athenians come upon them, notwithstanding their retreat, they met them with six hundred ships, as Phanodemus relates, but according to Ephorus, with three hundred and fifty. However, they did nothing worthy such mighty forces, but immediately turned the prows of their galleys toward the shore, where those that came first threw themselves upon the land, and fled to their army drawn up thereabout, while the rest perished with their vessels, or were taken. By this, one may guess at their number, for though a great many escaped out of the fight, and a great many others were sunk, yet two hundred galleys were taken by the Athenians.

When their land army drew toward the seaside, Cimon was in suspense whether he should venture to try and force his way on shore; as he should thus expose his Greeks, wearied with slaughter in the first engagement, to the swords of the barbarians, who were all fresh men, and many times their number. But seeing his men resolute, and flushed with victory, he bade them land, though they were not yet cool from their first battle. As soon as they touched ground, they set up a shout and ran upon the enemy, who stood firm and sustained the first shock with great courage, so that the fight was a hard one, and some of the principal men of the Athenians in rank and courage were slain. At length, though with much ado, they routed the barbarians, and killing some, took others prisoners, and plundered all their tents and pavilions, which were full of rich spoil. Cimon, like a skilled athlete at the games, having in one day carried off two victories, wherein he surpassed that of Salamis by sea, and that of Platæa by land, was encouraged to try for yet another success. News being brought that the Phœnician succors, in number eighty sail, had come in sight at Hydrum, he set off with all speed to find them, while they as yet had not received any certain account of the larger fleet, and were in doubt what to think; so that thus surprised, they lost all their vessels, and most of their men with them. This success of Cimon so daunted the king of Persia, that he presently made that celebrated peace, by which he engaged that his armies should come no nearer the Grecian sea than the length of a horse's course; and that none of his galleys or vessels of war should appear between the Cyanean and Chelidonian isles. In the collection which Craterus made of the public acts of the people, there is a draft of this treaty given.

The people of Athens raised so much money from the spoils of this war, which were publicly sold, that, besides other expenses, and raising the south wall of the citadel, they laid the foundation of the long walls, not, indeed, finished till at a later time, which were called the Legs. And the place where they built them being soft and marshy ground, they were forced to sink great weights of stone and rubble to secure the foundation, and did all this out of the money Cimon supplied them with.

It was he, likewise, who first embellished the upper city with those fine and ornamental places of exercise and resort, which they afterward so much frequented and delighted in. He set the market-place with plane trees; and the Academy, which was before a bare, dry, and dirty spot, he converted into a well-watered grove, with shady alleys to walk in, and open courses for races.

When the Persians who had made themselves masters of the Chersonese, so far from quitting it, called in the people of the interior of Thrace to help them against Cimon, whom they despised for the smallness of his forces, he set upon them with only four galleys, and took thirteen of theirs; and having driven out the Persians, and subdued the Thracians, he made the whole Chersonese the property of Athens. Next, he attacked the people of Thasos, who had revolted from the Athenians; and, having defeated them in a fight at sea, where he captured thirty-three of their vessels, he took their town by siege, and acquired for the Athenians all the mines of gold on the opposite coast, and the territory dependent on Thasos.

GROVES OF THE ACADEMY

This opened him a fair passage into Macedon, so that he might, it was thought, have acquired a good portion of that country, and because he neglected the opportunity, he was suspected of corruption, and of having been bribed off by king Alexander. So, by the combination of his adversaries, he was accused of being false to his country. In his defence he told the judges, that he had always shown himself in his public life the friend, not, like other men, of rich Ionians and Thessalians, to be courted, and to receive presents, but of the Lacedæmonians; for as he admired, so he wished to imitate, the plainness of their habits, their temperance, and simplicity of living, which he preferred to any sort of riches; but that he always had been, and still was proud to enrich his country with the spoils of her enemies. Pericles proved the mildest of his prosecutors, and rose up but once all the while, almost as a matter of form, to plead against him. Cimon was acquitted.

In his public life after this, he continued, while at home, to control the common people, who would have trampled upon the nobility, and drawn all the power and sovereignty to themselves. But when he afterwards was sent out to war, the multitude broke loose, as it were, and overthrew all the ancient laws and customs they had hitherto observed, and, chiefly at the instigation of Ephialtes, withdrew the cognizance of almost all causes from the Areopagus; so that all jurisdiction now being transferred to them, the government was reduced to a perfect democracy, and this by the help of Pericles, who was already powerful, and had pronounced in favor of the common people.

He was indeed a favorer of the Lacedæmonians even from his youth, and gave the names of Lacedæmonius and Eleus to his two sons, twins.

Cimon was countenanced by the Lacedæmonians in opposition to Themistocles, whom they disliked; and while he was yet very young, they endeavored to raise and increase his credit in Athens. This the Athenians perceived at first with pleasure, and the favor the Lacedæmonians showed him was in various ways advantageous to them and their affairs; as at that time they were just rising to power, and were occupied in winning the allies to their side. So they seemed not at all offended with the honor and kindness showed to Cimon, who then had the chief management of all the affairs of Greece, and was acceptable to the Lacedæmonians, and courteous to the allies.

But afterwards the Athenians, grown more powerful, when they saw Cimon so entirely devoted to the Lacedæmonians, began to be angry, for he would always in speeches prefer them to the Athenians, and upon every occasion, when he would reprimand them for a fault, or incite them to emulation, he would exclaim, "The Lacedæmonians would not do thus." This raised the discontent, and got him in some degree the hatred of the citizens; but that which ministered chiefly to the accusation against him fell out upon the following occasion.

In the fourth year of the reign of Archidamus, the son of Zeuxidamus, king of Sparta, there happened in the country of Lacedæmon, the greatest earthquake that was known in the memory of man; the earth opened into chasms, and the mountain Taygetus was so shaken that some of the rocky points of it fell down, and except five houses, all the town of Sparta was shattered to pieces. They say that a little before any motion was perceived, as the young men and the boys just grown up were exercising themselves together in the middle of the portico, a hare, of a sudden, started out just by them, which the young men, though all naked and daubed with oil, ran after for sport. No sooner were they gone from the place, than the gymnasium fell down upon the boys who had stayed behind, and killed them all. Their tomb is to this day called Sismatias.* Archidamus, by the present danger made apprehensive of what might follow, and seeing the citizens intent upon removing the most valuable of their goods out of their houses, commanded an alarm to be sounded, as if an enemy were coming upon them, in order that they should collect about him in a body, with arms. It was this alone that saved Sparta at that time, for the Helots had come together from the country about, with design of surprising the Spartans, and overpowering those whom the earthquake had spared. But finding them armed and well prepared, they retired into the towns and

---

* From Seismos, or, as it is written in Latin, Sismus, an earthquake.

openly made war with them, gaining over a number of the Laconians of the country districts; while at the same time the Messenians, also, made an attack upon the Spartans, who therefore despatched Periclidas to Athens to solicit succor, of whom Aristophanes says in mockery that he came and

> In a red jacket, at the altars seated,
> With a white face, for men and arms entreated.

This Ephialtes opposed, protesting that they ought not to raise up or assist a city that was a rival to Athens; but that being down, it were best to keep her so, and let the pride and arrogance of Sparta be trodden under. But Cimon, as Critias says, preferring the safety of Lacedæmon to the aggrandizement of his own country, so persuaded the people, that he soon marched out with a large army to their relief. Ion records, also, the most successful expression which he used to move the Athenians. "They ought not to suffer Greece to be lamed, nor their own city to be deprived of her yoke fellow."

In his return from aiding the Lacedæmonians, he passed with his army through the territory of Corinth; whereupon Lachartus reproached him for bringing his army into the country, without first asking leave of the people. For he that knocks at another man's door ought not to enter the house till the master gives him leave. "But you, Corinthians, O Lachartus," said Cimon, "did not knock at the gates of the Cleonæans and Megarians, but broke them down and entered by force, thinking that all places should be open to the stronger." And having thus rallied the Corinthian, he passed on with his army. Some time after this, the Lacedæmonians sent a second time to desire succor of the Athenians against the Messenians and Helots, who had seized upon Ithome. But when they came, fearing their boldness and gallantry, of all that came to their assistance, they sent them only back, alleging that they were designing innovations. The Athenians returned home, enraged at this usage, and vented their anger upon all those who were favorers of the Lacedæmonians; and seizing some slight occasion, they banished Cimon for ten years, which is the time prescribed to those that are banished by the ostracism. In the mean time, the Lacedæmonians, on their return after freeing Delphi from the Phocians, encamped their army at Tanagra, whither the Athenians presently marched with design to fight them.

Cimon, also, came thither armed and ranged himself among those of his own tribe, which was the Œneis, desirous of fighting with the rest against the Spartans; but the council of five hundred being informed of this, and frightened at it, his adversaries crying out that he would disorder the army, and bring the Lacedæmonians to Athens, commanded the officers not to receive him. Wherefore Cimon left the army, conjuring Euthippus, the Anaphlystian, and the rest of his companions, who were most suspected as favoring the Lacedæmonians, to behave themselves bravely against their enemies, and by their actions make their innocence evident to their countrymen. These, being in all a hundred, took the arms of Cimon, and followed his advice; and making a body by themselves, fought so desperately with the enemy, that they were all cut off, leaving the Athenians deep regret for the loss of such brave men, and repentance for having so unjustly suspected them. Accordingly, they did not long retain their severity toward Cimon, partly upon remembrance of his former services, and partly, perhaps, induced by the juncture of the times. For being defeated at Tanagra in a great battle, and fearing the Peloponnesians would come upon them at the opening of the spring, they recalled Cimon by a decree, of which Pericles himself was author. So reasonable were men's resentments in those times, and so moderate their anger, that it always gave way to the public good. Even ambition, the least governable of all human passions, could then yield to the necessities of the State.

Cimon, as soon as he returned, put an end to the war, and

reconciled the two cities. Peace thus established, seeing the Athenians impatient of being idle, and eager for the honor and aggrandizement of war, lest they should set upon the Greeks themselves, or with so many ships cruising about the isles and Peloponnesus, they should give occasions for intestine wars, or complaints of their allies against them, he equipped two hundred galleys, with design to make an attempt upon Egypt and Cyprus; purposing, by this means, to accustom the Athenians to fight against the barbarians, and enrich themselves honestly by despoiling those who were the natural enemies to Greece. But when all things were prepared, and the army ready to embark, Cimon had this dream. It seemed to him that there was a furious female dog barking at him, and, mixed with the barking, a kind of human voice uttered these words:

> Come on, for thou shalt shortly be
> A pleasure to my whelps and me.

This dream was hard to interpret, yet Astyphilus of Posidonia, a man skilled in divinations, and intimate with Cimon, told him that his death was presaged by this vision, which he thus explained. A dog is enemy to him he barks at; and one is always most a pleasure to one's enemies, when one is dead; the mixture of human voice with barking signifies the Medes, for the army of the Medes is mixed up of Greeks and barbarians. After this dream, as he was sacrificing to Bacchus, and the priest cutting up the victim, a number of ants, taking up the congealed particles of the blood, laid them about Cimon's great toe. This was not observed for a good while, but at the very time when Cimon spied it, the priest came and showed him the liver of the sacrifice imperfect, wanting that part of it called the head. But he could not then recede from the enterprise, so he set sail. Sixty of his ships he sent toward Egypt; with the rest he went and fought the king of Persia's fleet, composed of Phœnician and Cilician galleys, recovered all the cities thereabout, and threatened Egypt; designing no less than the entire ruin of the Persian empire. And the more because he was informed that Themistocles was in great repute among the barbarians, having promised the king to lead his army, whenever he should make war upon Greece. But Themistocles, it is said, abandoning all hopes of compassing his designs, very much out of the despair of overcoming the valor and good-fortune of Cimon, died a voluntary death. Cimon, intent on great designs, which he was now to enter upon, keeping his navy about the isle of Cyprus, sent messengers to consult the oracle of Jupiter Ammon upon some secret matter. For it is not known about what they were sent, and the god would give them no answer, but commanded them to return again, for Cimon was already with him. Hearing this, they returned to sea, and as soon as they came to the Grecian army, which was then about Egypt, they understood that Cimon was dead; and computing the time of the oracle, they found that his death had been signified, he being then already with the gods.

He died, some say, of sickness, while besieging Citium, in Cyprus; according to others, of a wound he received in a skirmish with the barbarians. When he perceived that he was going to die, he commanded those under his charge to return, and by no means to let the news of his death be known by the way; this they did with such secrecy that they all came home safe, and neither their enemies nor the allies knew what had happened. Thus, as Phanodemus relates, the Grecian army was, as it were, conducted by Cimon thirty days after he was dead. But after his death there was not one commander among the Greeks that did any thing considerable against the barbarians, and instead of uniting against their common enemies, the popular leaders and partisans of war animated them against one another to such a degree, that none could interpose their good offices to reconcile them. And while, by their mutual discord, they ruined the power of Greece, they gave the Persians time to recover breath, and repair all their losses

It is true, indeed, Agesilaus carried the arms of Greece into Asia, but it was a long time afterwards; there were some brief appearances of a war against the king's lieutenants in the maritime provinces, but they all quickly vanished; before he could perform any thing of moment, he was recalled by fresh civil dissensions and disturbances at home. So that he was forced to leave the Persian king's officers to impose what tribute they pleased on the Greek cities in Asia, the confederates and allies of the Lacedæmonians. Whereas, in the time of Cimon, not so much as a letter-carrier, or a single horseman, was ever seen to come within four hundred furlongs of the sea.

The monuments, called Cimonian to this day, in Athens, show that his remains were conveyed home, yet the inhabitants of the city Citium pay particular honor to a certain tomb which they call the tomb of Cimon, according to Nausicrates the rhetorician, who states that in a time of famine, when the crops of their land all failed, they sent to the oracle, which commanded them not to forget Cimon, but give him the honors of a superior being.

GATE OF LIONS AT MYCENÆ.

POMPEY.

The people of Rome appear, from the first, to have been affected towards Pompey, much in the same manner as Prometheus, in Æschylus, was towards Hercules, when after that hero had delivered him from his chains, he says—

> The sire I hated, but the son I loved.

For never did the Romans entertain a stronger and more rancorous hatred for any general than for Strabo, the father of Pompey. While he lived, indeed, they were afraid of his abilities as a soldier, for he had great talents for war; but upon his death, which happened by a stroke of lightning, they dragged his corpse from the bier, on the way to the funeral pile, and treated it with the greatest indignity. On the other hand, no man ever experienced from the same Romans an attachment more early begun, more disinterested in all the stages of his prosperity, or more constant and faithful in the decline of his fortune, than Pompey.

The sole cause of their aversion to the father was his insatiable avarice; but there were many causes of their affection for the son; his temperate way of living, his application to martial exercises, his eloquent and persuasive address, his strict honor and fidelity, and the easiness of access to him upon all occasions; for no man was ever less importunate in asking favors, or more gracious in conferring them. When he gave, it was without arrogance; and when he received, it was with dignity.

In his youth he had a very engaging countenance, which

spoke for him before he opened his lips. Yet that grace of aspect was not unattended with dignity, and amidst his youthful bloom there was a venerable and princely air. His hair naturally curled a little before; which, together with the shining moisture and quick turn of his eye, produced a stronger likeness to Alexander the Great than that which appeared in the statues of that prince.

As to the simplicity of his diet, there is a remarkable saying of his upon record. In a great illness, when his appetite was almost gone, the physician ordered him a thrush. His servants, upon inquiry, found there was not one to be had for money, for the season was passed. They were informed, however, that Lucullus had them all the year in his menageries. This being reported to Pompey, he said, "Does Pompey's life depend upon the luxury of Lucullus?" Then, without any regard to the physician, he ate something that was easy to be had.

POMPEY.

After the death of Cinna, Carbo, a tyrant still more savage, took the reins of government. It was not long, however, before Sylla returned to Italy, to the great satisfaction of most of the Romans, who, in their present unhappy circumstances, thought the change of their master no small advantage.

Pompey, at the age of twenty-three, without a commission

from any superior authority, erected himself into a general; and having placed his tribunal in the most public part of the great city of Auximum, enlisted soldiers and appointed tribunes, centurions, and other officers, according to the established custom. He did the same in all the neighboring cities; for the partisans of Carbo retired and gave place to him; and the rest were glad to range themselves under his banners. So that in a little time he raised three complete legions, and furnished himself with provisions, beasts of burden, carriages; in short, with the whole apparatus of war.

In this form he moved towards Sylla, not by hasty marches, nor as if he wanted to conceal himself; for he stopped by the way to harass the enemy, and attempted to draw off from Carbo all the parts of Italy through which he passed. At last, three generals of the opposite party, Carinna, Cœlius, and Brutus, came against him all at once, not in front, or in one body, but they hemmed him in with their three armies, in hopes to demolish him entirely.

Pompey, far from being terrified, assembled all his forces, and charged the army of Brutus at the head of his cavalry. The Gaulish horse on the enemy's side sustained the first shock; but Pompey attacked the foremost of them, who was a man of prodigious strength, and brought him down with a push of his spear. The rest immediately fled and threw the infantry into such disorder that the whole was soon put to flight. This produced so great a quarrel among the three generals, that they parted and took separate routes. In consequence of which, the cities, concluding that the fears of the enemy had made them part, adopted the interest of Pompey.

Not long after, Scipio the consul advanced to engage him. But before the infantry were near enough to discharge their lances, Scipio's soldiers saluted those of Pompey, and came over to them. Scipio, therefore, was forced to fly. At last, Carbo sent a large body of cavalry against Pompey, near the river Arsis. He gave them so warm a reception, that they were soon broken, and in the pursuit drove them upon impracticable ground; so that finding it impossible to escape, they surrendered themselves with their arms and horses.

Sylla had not yet been informed of these transactions; but upon the first news of Pompey's being engaged with so many adversaries, and such respectable generals, he dreaded the consequence, and marched with all expedition to his assistance. Pompey, having intelligence of his approach, ordered his officers to see that the troops were armed and drawn up in such a manner as to make the handsomest and most gallant appearance before the commander-in-chief. For he expected great honors from him, and he obtained greater. Sylla no sooner saw Pompey advancing to meet him, with an army in excellent condition, both as to age and size of the men, and the spirits which success had given them, than he alighted; and upon being saluted of course by Pompey as *Imperator*, he returned his salutation with the same title: though no one imagined that he would have honored a young man not yet admitted into the senate with a title for which he was contending with the Scipios and the Marii. The rest of his behavior was as respectable as that in the first interview. He used to rise up and uncover his head, whenever Pompey came to him; which he was rarely observed to do for any other, though he had a number of persons of distinction about him.

While Pompey was in Sicily, he received a decree of the senate, and letters from Sylla, in which he was commanded to cross over to Africa and to carry on the war with the utmost vigor against Domitius, who had assembled a much more powerful army than that which Marius carried not long before from Africa to Italy, when he made himself master of Rome, and from a fugitive became a tyrant. Pompey soon finished his preparations for this expedition; and leaving the command in Sicily to Memmius, his sister's husband, he set sail with one hundred and twenty armed vessels, and eight hundred store-ships, laden with provisions, arms, money, and machines of war. Part of his fleet landed at Utica, and part at Carthage: immediately after which seven thousand of the enemy came over to him; and he had brought with him six legions complete.

On his arrival he met with a whimsical adventure. Some of his soldiers, it seems, found a treasure, and the rest of the troops concluded that the place was full of money, which the Carthaginians had hid there in some time of public distress. Pompey, therefore, could make no use of them for several days, as they were searching for treasures; and he had nothing to do but walk about and amuse himself with the sight of so many thousands digging and turning up the ground. At last, they gave up the point, and bade him lead them wherever he pleased, for they were sufficiently punished for their folly.

Domitius advanced to meet him, and put his troops in order of battle. There happened to be a channel between them, craggy and difficult to pass. Moreover, in the morning it began to rain, and the wind blew violently; insomuch that Domitius, not imagining there would be any action that day, ordered his army to retire. But Pompey looked upon this as his opportunity, and he passed the defile with the utmost expedition. The enemy stood upon their defence, but it was in a disorderly and tumultuous manner, and the resistance they made was neither general nor uniform. Besides, the wind and rain beat in their faces. The storm incommoded the Romans, too, for they could not well distinguish each other. Nay, Pompey himself was in danger of being killed by a soldier, who asked him the pass-word, and did not receive a speedy answer. At length, however, he routed the enemy with great slaughter; not above three thousand of them escaping out of twenty thousand. The soldiers then saluted Pompey, *Imperator*, but he said he would not accept that title while the enemy's camp stood untouched; therefore, if they chose to confer such an honor upon him, they must first make themselves masters of the intrenchments.

At that instant they advanced with great fury against them. Pompey fought without his helmet, for fear of such an accident as he had just escaped. The camp was taken, and Domitius slain; in consequence of which most of the cities immediately submitted, and the rest were taken by assault. He took Iarbas, one of the confederates of Domitius, prisoner, and bestowed his crown on Hiempsal. Advancing with the same tide of fortune, and while his army had all the spirits inspired by success, he entered Numidia, in which he continued his march for several days, and subdued all that came in his way. Thus he revived the terror of the Roman name, which the barbarians had begun to disregard. Nay, he chose not to leave the savage beasts in the deserts without giving them a specimen of the Roman valor and success. Accordingly he spent a few days in hunting lions and elephants. The whole time he passed in Africa, they tell us, was not above forty days; in which he defeated the enemy, reduced the whole country, and brought the affairs of its kings under proper regulations, though he was only in his twenty-fourth year.

Upon his return to Utica, he received letters from Sylla, in which he was ordered to send home the rest of his army, and to wait there with one legion only for a successor. This gave him a great deal of uneasiness, which he kept to himself, but the army expressed their indignation aloud; insomuch that when he entreated them to return to Italy, they launched out into abusive terms against Sylla, and declared they would never abandon Pompey, or suffer him to trust a tyrant. At first he endeavored to pacify them with mild representations: and when he found those had no effect, he descended from the tribunal, and retired to his tent in tears. However, they went and took him thence, and placed him again upon the tribunal, where they spent a great part of the day; they insisting that he should stay and keep the command, and he in persuading them to obey Sylla's orders, and to form no new faction. At last, seeing no end of their clamors and importunity, he as sured them, with an oath, that he would kill himself, if they attempted to force him. And even this hardly brought them to desist.

The first news that Sylla heard was, that Pompey had revolted; upon which he said to his friends, "Then it is my fate to have to contend with boys in my old age." This he said, because Marius, who was very young, had brought him into so much trouble and danger. But when he received true information of the affair, and observed that all the people flocked out to receive Pompey to conduct him home with marks of great regard, he resolved to exceed them in his regards, if possible. He, therefore, hastened to meet him, and embracing him in the most affectionate manner, saluted him aloud by the surname of *Magnus,* or *the Great:* at the same time he ordered all about him to give him the same appellation. Others say, it was given him by the whole army in Africa, but did not generally obtain till it was authorized by Sylla. It is certain, he was the last to take it himself, and he did not make use of it till a long time after, when he was sent into Spain with the dignity of pro-consul against Sertorius. Then he began to write himself in his letters and in all his edicts, *Pompey the Great;* for the world was accustomed to the name, and it was no longer invidious. In this respect we may justly admire the wisdom of the ancient Romans, who bestowed on their great men such honorable names and titles, not only for military achievements, but for the great qualities and arts which adorn civil life.

When Pompey arrived at Rome, he demanded a triumph, in which he was opposed by Sylla. The latter alleged that the laws did not allow that honor to any person who was not either consul or prætor. Hence it was that the first Scipio, when he returned victorious from greater wars and conflicts with the Carthaginians in Spain, did not demand a triumph; for he was neither consul nor prætor. He added, that if Pompey, who was yet little better than a beardless youth, and who was not of age to be admitted into the senate, should enter the city in triumph, it would bring an *odium* both upon the dictator's power, and those honors of his friend. These arguments Sylla insisted on, to show him that he would not allow of his triumph, and that, in case he persisted, he would chastise his obstinacy.

Pompey, not in the least intimidated, bade him consider, that more worshiped the rising than the setting sun; intimating that his power was increasing, and Sylla's upon the decline. Sylla did not hear well what he said, but perceiving by the looks and gestures of the company that they were struck with the expression, he asked what it was. When he was told it, he admired the spirit of Pompey and cried, " Let him triumph! Let him triumph!"

There is no doubt that he might then have been easily admitted a senator, if he had desired it; but his ambition was to pursue honor in a more uncommon track. It would have been nothing strange, if Pompey had been a senator before the age fixed for it; but it was a very extraordinary instance of honor to lead up a triumph before he was a senator. And it contributed not a little to gain him the affections of the multitude; the people were delighted to see him, after his triumph, class with the equestrian order.

The power of the pirates had its foundation in Cilicia. Their progress was the more dangerous, because at first it was little taken notice of. In the Mithridatic war they assumed new confidence and courage, on account of some services they had rendered the king. After this, the Romans being engaged in civil wars at the very gates of their capital, the sea was left unguarded, and the pirates by degrees attempted higher things; they not only attacked ships, but islands, and maritime towns. Many persons, distinguished for their wealth, their birth, and their capacity, embarked with them, and assisted in their depredations, as if their employment had been worthy the ambition of men of honor. They had in various places arsenals, ports, and watch-towers, all strongly fortified. Their fleets were not only extremely well manned, supplied with skilful pilots, and fitted for their business by their lightness and celerity; but there was a parade of vanity about them more mortifying than their strength, in gilded sterns, purple canopies, and plated oars; as if they took a pride and triumphed in their villany. Music resounded, and drunken revels were exhibited on every coast. Here generals were made prisoners; there the cities the pirates had taken were paying their ransom; all to the great disgrace of the Roman power. The number of their galleys amounted to one thousand, and the cities they were masters of to four hundred.

Temples which had stood inviolably sacred till that time, they plundered. They ruined the temple of Apollo at Claros, that of the Cabiri in Samothrace, of Ceres at Hermione, of Æsculapius at Epidaurus, those of Neptune in the Isthmus, at Tænarus and in Calauria, those of Apollo at Actium and in the isle of Leucas, those of Juno at Samos, Argos, and the promontory of Lacinium.

They likewise offered strange sacrifices; those of Olympus I mean; and they celebrated certain secret mysteries, among which those of Mithra continue to this day, being originally instituted by them. They not only insulted the Romans at sea but infested the great roads, and plundered the villas near the coast; they carried off Sextilius and Bellinus, two prætors, in their purple robes, with all their servants and *lictors*. They seized the daughter of Antony, a man who had been honored with a triumph, as she was going to her country house, and he was forced to pay a large ransom for her.

But the most contemptible circumstance of all was, that when they had taken a prisoner, and he cried out that he was a Roman, and told them his name, they pretended to be struck with terror, smote their thighs, and fell upon their knees to ask him pardon. The poor man, seeing them thus humble themselves before him, thought them in earnest, and said he would forgive them; for some were so officious as to put on his shoes, and others to help him on with his gown, that his quality might no more be mistaken. When they had carried on this farce, and enjoyed it for some time, they let a ladder down into the sea, and bade him go in peace; and if he refused to do it, they pushed him off the deck, and drowned him.

Their power extended over the whole Tuscan sea, so that the Romans found their trade and navigation entirely cut off. The consequence of which was, that their markets were not supplied, and they had reason to apprehend a famine. This at last led them to send Pompey to clear the sea of pirates. Gabinius, one of Pompey's intimate friends, proposed the decree, which created him not admiral, but monarch, and invested him with absolute power. The decree gave him the empire of the sea as far as the Pillars of Hercules, and of the land for 400 furlongs from the coasts. There were few parts of the Roman empire which this commission did not take in; and the most considerable of the barbarous nations, and most powerful kings, were moreover comprehended in it. Besides this he was empowered to choose out of the senators fifteen lieutenants, to act under him in such districts, and with such authority as he should appoint. He was to take from the quæstors, and other public receivers, what money he pleased, and equip a fleet of two hunderd sail. The number of marine forces, of mariners and rowers, was left entirely to his discretion.

When this decree was read in the assembly, the people received it with inconceivable pleasure. The most respectable part of the senate saw, indeed, that such an absolute and unlimited power was above envy, but they considered it as a real object of fear. They therefore all, except Cæsar, opposed its passing into a law. He was for it, not out of regard for Pompey, but to insinuate himself into the good graces of the people, which he had long been courting. The rest were very severe in their expressions against Pompey: and one of the consuls venturing to say, "If he imitates Romulus, he will not escape his fate," was in danger of being pulled in pieces by the populace.

It is true, when Catulus rose up to speak against the law, out of reverence for his person they listened to him with great attention. After he had freely given Pompey the honor that was his due, and said much in his praise, he advised them to spare him, and not to expose such a man to so many dangers; "for where will you find another," said he, "if you lose him?" They answered with one voice, "Yourself." Finding his arguments had no effect, he retired. Then Roscius mounted the rostrum, but not a man would give ear to him. However he made signs to them with his fingers, that they should not appoint Pompey alone, but give him a colleague. Incensed at the proposal, they set up such a shout, that a crow, which was flying over the *forum*, was stunned with the force of it, and fell down among the crowd. Hence we may conclude, that when birds fall on such occasions, it is not because the air is so divided with the shock as to leave a *vacuum*, but rather because the sound strikes them like a blow, when it ascends with force, and produces so violent an agitation.

The assembly broke up that day without coming to any resolution. When the day came that they were to give their suffrages, Pompey retired into the country; and, on receiving information that the decree was passed, he returned to the city by night, to prevent the envy which the multitudes of people coming to meet him would have excited. Next morning at break of day he made his appearance, and attended the sacrifice. After which, he summoned an assembly, and obtained a grant of almost as much more as the first decree had given him. He was empowered to fit out 500 galleys, and to raise an army of 120,000 foot, and 5,000 horse. Twenty-four senators were selected, who had all been generals or prætors.

and were appointed his lieutenants; and he had two quæstors given him. As the price of provisions fell immediately, the people were greatly pleased, and it gave them occasion to say that the very name of Pompey had terminated the war.

However, in pursuance of his charge, he divided the whole Mediterranean into thirteen parts, appointing a lieutenant for each, and assigning him a squadron. By thus stationing his fleet in all quarters, he inclosed the pirates as it were in a net, took great numbers of them, and brought them into harbor. Such of their vessels as had dispersed and made off in time, or could escape the general chase, retired to Cilicia, like so many bees into a hive. Against these he proposed to go himself, with sixty of his best galleys; but first he resolved to clear the Tuscan sea, and the coasts of Africa, Sardinia, Corsica, and Sicily, of all piratical adventurers; which he effected in forty days, by his own indefatigable endeavors and those of his lieutenants. But, as the consul Piso was indulging his malignity at home, in wasting his stores and discharging his seamen, he sent his fleet round to Brundusium, and went himself by land through Tuscany to Rome.

As soon as the people were informed of his approach, they went in crowds to receive him, in the same manner as they had done a few days before, to conduct him on his way. Their extraordinary joy was owing to the speed with which he had executed his commission, so far beyond all expectation, and to the superabundant plenty which reigned in the markets. For this reason Piso was in danger of being deposed from the consulship, and Gabinius had a decree ready drawn up for that purpose; but Pompey would not suffer him to propose it. On the contrary, his speech to the people was full of candor and moderation; and when he had provided such things as he wanted, he went to Brundusium, and put to sea again. Though he was straightened for time, and in his haste sailed by many cities without calling, yet he stopped at Athens. He entered the town and sacrificed to the gods; after which he addressed the people, and then prepared to reimbark immediately. As he went out of the gate he observed two inscriptions, each comprised in one line.

That within the gate was:

> But know thyself a man, and be a god.

That without:

> We wish'd, we saw; we loved, and we adored.

Some of the pirates, who yet traversed the seas, made their submission; and as he treated them in a humane manner, when he had them and their ships in his power, others entertained hopes of mercy, and avoiding the other officers, surrendered themselves to Pompey, together with their wives and children. He spared them all; and it was principally by their means that he found out and took a number who were guilty of unpardonable crimes, and therefore had concealed themselves.

Still, however, there remained a great number, and indeed the most powerful part of these corsairs, who sent their families, treasures, and all useless hands, into castles and fortified towns upon Mount Taurus. Then they manned their ships, and waited for Pompey at Coracesium, in Cilicia. A battle ensued, and the pirates were defeated; after which they retired into the fort. But they had not been long besieged before they capitulated, and surrendered themselves, together with the cities and islands which they had conquered and fortified, and which by their works as well as situation were almost impregnable. Thus the war was finished, and the whole force of the pirates destroyed, within three months at the farthest.

Besides the other vessels, Pompey took ninety ships with beaks of brass; and the prisoners amounted to 20,000. He did not choose to put them to death, and at the same time he thought it wrong to suffer them to disperse, because they were not only numerous, but warlike and necessitous, and therefore would probably knit again and give future trouble. He reflected, that man by nature is neither a savage nor an unsocial creature; and when he becomes so, it is by vices contrary to nature; yet even then he may be humanized by changing his place of abode, and accustoming him to a new manner of life; as beasts that are naturally wild put off their fierceness when they are kept in a domestic way. For this reason he determined to remove the pirates to a great distance from the sea, and bring them to taste the sweets of civil life, by living in cities, and by the culture of the ground. He placed some of them in the little towns of Cilicia, which were almost desolate, and which received them with pleasure, because at the same time he gave them an additional proportion of lands. He repaired the city of Soli, which had lately been dismantled and deprived of its inhabitants by Tigranes, king of Armenia, and peopled it with a number of these corsairs. The remainder, which was a considerable body, he planted in Dyma, a city of Achaia, which, though it had a large and fruitful territory, was in want of inhabitants.

Pompey, having secured the sea from Phœnicia to the Bosphorus, marched in quest of Mithridates, who had an army of 30,000 foot and 2,000 horse, but durst not stand an engagement. That prince was in possession of a strong and secure post upon a mountain, which he quitted upon Pompey's approach, because it was destitute of water. Pompey encamped in the same place; and conjecturing, from the nature of the plants and the crevices in the mountain, that springs might be found, he ordered a number of wells to be dug, and the camp was in a short time plentifully supplied with water. He was not a little surprised that this did not occur to Mithridates during the whole time of his encampment there.

After this, Pompey followed him to his new camp, and drew a line of circumvallation round him. Mithridates stood a siege of forty-five days, after which he found means to steal off with his best troops, having first killed all the sick, and such as could be of no service. Pompey overtook him near the Euphrates, and encamped over against him; but fearing he might pass the river unperceived, he drew out his troops at midnight. At that time Mithridates is said to have had a dream prefigurative of what was to befall him. He thought he was upon the Pontic Sea, sailing with a favorable wind, and in sight of the Bosphorus; so that he felicitated his friends in the ship, like a man perfectly safe, and already in harbor. But suddenly he beheld himself in the most destitute condition, swimming upon a piece of wreck. While he was in all the agitation which this dream produced, his friends awaked him, and told him that Pompey was at hand. He was now under a necessity of fighting for his camp, and his generals drew up the forces with all possible expedition.

Pompey, seeing them prepared, was loth to risk a battle in the dark. He thought it sufficient to surround them, so as to prevent their flight; and what inclined him still more to wait for daylight, was the consideration that his troops were much better than the enemy's. However, the oldest of his officers entreated him to proceed immediately to the attack, and at last prevailed. It was not indeed very dark; for the moon, though near her setting, gave light enough to distinguish objects. But it was a great disadvantage to the king's troops, that the moon was so low, and on the backs of the Romans; because she projected their shadows so far before them, that the enemy could form no just estimate of the distances, but thinking them at hand, threw their javelins before they could do the least execution.

The Romans, perceiving their mistake, advanced to the charge with all the alarm of voices. The enemy were in such a consternation, that they made not the least stand, and, in their flight, vast numbers were slain. They lost above 10,000 men, and their camp was taken. As for Mithridates, he broke through the Romans with 800 horse, in the beginning of the engagement. That corps, however, did not follow him far before they dispersed, and left him with only three of his people.

The pursuit of Mithridates was attended with great difficulties; for he concealed himself among the nations settled about the Bosphorus and the Palus Mæotis. Besides, news was brought to Pompey that the Albanians had revolted, and taken up arms again. The desire of revenge determined him to march back, and chastise them. But it was with infinite trouble and danger that he passed the Cyrnus again, the barbarians having fenced it on their side with palisades all along the banks. And when he was over, he had a large country to traverse, which afforded no water. This last difficulty he provided against, by filling 10,000 bottles; and pursuing his march, he found the enemy drawn up on the banks of the river Abas, to the number of 60,000 foot and 12,000 horse, but many of them ill-armed, and provided with nothing of the defensive kind but skins of beasts.

They were commanded by the king's brother, named Cosis; who, at the beginning of the battle, singled out Pompey, and rushing in upon him, struck his javelin into the joints of his breastplate. Pompey in return run him through with his spear, and laid him dead on the spot. It is said that the Amazons came to the assistance of the barbarians from the mountains near the river Thermodon, and fought in this battle. The Romans, among the plunder of the field, did, indeed, meet with bucklers in the form of a half-moon, and such buskins as the Amazons wore; but there was not the body of a woman found among the dead. They inhabit that part of Mount Caucasus which stretches toward the Hyrcanian Sea, and are not next neighbors to the Albanians; for Gelæ and Leges lie between; but they meet that people, and spend two months with them every year on the banks of the Thermodon; after which they retire to their own country.

Pompey had advanced near to Petra, and encamped, and was taking some exercise on horseback without the trenches, when messengers arrived from Pontus; and it was plain they brought good news, because the points of their spears were crowned with laurel. The soldiers seeing this, gathered about Pompey, who was inclined to finish his exercise before he opened the packet; but they were so earnest in their entreaties, that they prevailed upon him to alight and take it. He entered the camp with it in his hand; and as there was no tribunal ready, and the soldiers were too impatient to raise one of turf, which was the common method, they piled a number of pack-saddles one upon the other, upon which Pompey mounted, and gave them this information: "Mithridates is dead. He killed himself upon the revolt of his son Pharnaces. And Pharnaces has seized all that belonged to his father; which he declares he has done for himself and the Romans."

At this news the army, as might be expected, gave a loose rein to their joy, which they expressed in sacrifices to the gods, and in reciprocal entertainments, as if 10,000 of their enemies had been slain in Mithridates. Pompey having thus brought the campaign and the whole war to a conclusion so happy, and so far beyond his hopes, immediately quitted Arabia, traversed the provinces between that and Galatia with great rapidity, and soon arrived at Amisus. There he found many presents from Pharnaces, and several corpses of the royal family, among which was that of Mithridates. As for Pompey, he would not see the body, but to propitiate the avenging Nemesis, sent it to Sinope. However, he looked upon and admired the magnificence of his habit, and the size and beauty of his arms. The scabbard of his sword cost four hundred talents, and the diadem was of most exquisite workmanship.

Pompey having thoroughly settled the affairs of Asia, hoped to return to Italy the greatest and happiest of men.

People talked variously at Rome concerning his intentions. Many disturbed themselves at the thought that he would march with his army immediately to Rome and make himself sole and absolute master there. Crassus took his children and money, and withdrew; whether it was that he had some real apprehensions, or rather that he chose to countenance the calumny, and add force to the sting of envy; the latter seems the more probable. But Pompey had no sooner set foot in Italy, than he called an assembly of his soldiers, and, after a kind and suitable address, ordered them to disperse in their respective cities, and attend to their own affairs till his triumph, on which occasion they were to repair to him again.

Pompey's triumph was so great, that though it was divided into two days, the time was far from being sufficient for displaying what was prepared to be carried in procession; there remained still enough to adorn another triumph. At the head of the show appeared the titles of the conquered nations: Pontus, Armenia, Cappadocia, Paphlagonia, Media, Colchis, the Iberians, the Albanians, Syria, Cilicia, Mesopotamia, Phœnicia, Palestine, Judæa, Arabia; the pirates subdued both by sea and land. In these countries, it was mentioned that there were not less than 1,000 castles and 900 cities captured, 800 galleys taken from the pirates, and 39 desolate cities repeopled. On the face of the tablets it appeared besides, that whereas the revenues of the Roman empire before these conquests amounted but to 50,000,000 *drachmas*, by the new acquisitions they were advanced to 85,000,000; and that Pompey had brought into the public treasury in money, and in gold and silver vessels, the value of 20,000 talents, besides what he had distributed among the soldiers, of whom he that received least had 1,500 drachmas to his share. The captives who walked in the procession (not to mention the chiefs of the pirates) were the son of Tigranes, king of Armenia, together with his wife and daughter; Zosima, the wife of Tigranes himself; Aristobulus, king of Judæa; the sister of Mithridates, with her five sons, and some

Scythian women. The hostages of the Albanians and Iberians, and of the king of Commagene also appeared in the train; and as many trophies were exhibited as Pompey had gained victories, either in person or by his lieutenants, the number of which was not small.

But the most honorable circumstance, and what no other Roman could boast, was that his third triumph was over the third quarter of the world, after his former triumphs had been over the other two. Others before him had been honored with three triumphs; but his first triumph was over Africa, his second over Europe, and his third over Asia; so that the three seemed to declare him conqueror of the world.

Those who desire to make the parallel between him and Alexander agree in all respects, tell us he was at this time not quite thirty-four, whereas, in fact, he was entering upon his fortieth year.* Happy it had been for him, if he had ended his days while he was blessed with Alexander's good fortune! The rest of his life, every instance of success brought its proportion of envy, and every misfortune was irretrievable.

In the meantime the wars in Gaul lifted Cæsar to the first sphere of greatness. The scene of action was at a great distance from Rome, and he seemed to be wholly engaged with the Belgæ, the Suevi, and the Britons; but his genius all the while was privately at work among the people of Rome, and he was undermining Pompey in his most essential interests. His war with the barbarians was not his principal object. He exercised his army, indeed, in those expeditions, as he would have done his own body, in hunting and other diversions of the field, by which he prepared them for higher conflicts, and rendered them not only formidable but invincible.

---

* It should be the forty-sixth year. Pompey was born in the beginning of the month of August, in the year of Rome 647, and his triumph was in the same month in the year of Rome 692.

The gold and silver, and other rich spoils which he took from the enemy in great abundance, he sent to Rome; and by distributing them freely among the ædiles, prætors, consuls, and their wives, he gained a great party. Consequently when he passed the Alps and wintered at Lucca, among the crowd of men and women, who hastened to pay their respects to him, there were two hundred senators, Pompey and Crassus of the number; and there were no fewer than one hundred and twenty proconsuls and prætors, whose *fasces* were to be seen at the gates of Cæsar. He made it his business in general to give them hopes of great things, and his money was at their devotion; but he entered into a treaty with Crassus and Pompey, by which it was agreed that they should apply for the consulship, and that Cæsar should assist them, by sending a great number of his soldiers to vote at the election. As soon as they were chosen, they were to share the provinces, and take the command of armies, according to their pleasure, only confirming Cæsar in the possession of what he had for five years more.

Crassus, upon the expiration of his consulship, repaired to his province. Pompey remaining at Rome, opened his theatre; and to make the dedication more magnificent, exhibited a variety of gymnastic games, entertainments of music, and battles with wild beasts, in which were killed 500 lions; but the battle of elephants afforded the most astonishing spectacle.* These things gained him the love and admiration of the public; but he incurred their displeasure again, by leaving his provinces and armies entirely to his friends and lieutenants, and roving about Italy with his wife from one villa to another. The strong attachment of Julia appeared on the occasion of an election of ædiles. The people came to blows, and some were killed so

---

* Dio says the elephants fought with armed men. There were no less than eighteen of them; and he adds, that some of them seemed to appeal, with piteous cries to the people; who, in compassion, saved their lives. If we may believe him, an oath had been taken before they left Africa, that no injury should be done them.

near Pompey that he was covered with blood, and forced to change his clothes. There was a great crowd and tumult about his door, when his servants went home with a bloody robe; and Julia, happening to see it, fainted away and was with difficulty restored. Shortly after Julia died, and the alliance which had rather covered than restrained the ambition of the two great competitors for power was now no more. To add to the misfortune, news was brought soon after that Crassus was slain by the Parthians; and in him another great obstacle to a civil war was removed. Out of fear of him, they had both kept some measures with each other. But when fortune had carried off the champion who could take up the conqueror, we may say with the comic poet—

> High spirits of emprise
> Elates each chief; they oil their brawny limbs,
> And dip their hands in dust.

So little able is fortune to fill the capacities of the human mind; when such a weight of power, and extent of command, could not satisfy the ambition of two men. They had heard and read that the gods had divided the universe into three shares,* and each was content with that which fell to his lot, and yet these men could not think the Roman empire sufficient for two of them. Such anarchy and confusion took place that numbers began to talk boldly of setting up a dictator. Cato, now fearing he should be overborne, was of opinion that it were better to give Pompey some office whose authority was limited by law, than to intrust him with absolute power. Bibulus, though Pompey's declared enemy, moved in full senate, that he should be appointed sole consul. "For by that means,"

---

* Plutarch alludes here to a passage in the fifteenth book of the Iliad, where Neptune says to Iris—

> Assign'd by lot our triple rule we know;
> Infernal Pluto sways the shades below:
> O'er the wide clouds, and o'er the starry plain,
> Ethereal Jove extends his high domain:
> My court beneath the hoary waves I keep,
> And hush the roarings of the sacred deep.

said he, "the commonwealth will either recover from her disorder, or, if she must serve, will serve a man of the greatest merit." The whole house was surprised at the motion; and when Cato rose up, it was expected he would oppose it. A profound silence ensued, and he said, he should never have been the first to propose such an expedient, but as it was proposed by another, he thought it advisable to embrace it; for he thought any kind of government better than anarchy, and knew no man fitter to rule than Pompey, in a time of so much trouble. The senate came into his opinion, and a decree was issued, that Pompey should be appointed sole consul, and that if he should have need of a colleague, he might choose one himself, provided it were not before the expiration of two months.

Pompey being declared sole consul by the *Interrex* Sulpitius, made his compliments to Cato, acknowledged himself much indebted to his support, and desired his advice and assistance in the cabinet, as to the measures to be pursued in his administration. Cato made answer, that Pompey was not under the least obligation to him; for what he had said was not out of regard to him, but to his country. "If you apply to me," continued he, "I shall give you my advice in private; if not, I shall inform you of my sentiments in public." Such was Cato, and the same on all occasions.

Pompey then went into the city, and married Cornelia, the daughter of Metellus Scipio. She was a widow, having been married, when very young, to Publius the son of Crassus, who was lately killed in the Parthian expedition. This woman had many charms beside her beauty. She was well versed in polite literature; she played upon the lyre, and understood geometry; and she had made considerable improvements by the precepts of philosophy. What is more, she had nothing of that petulance and affectation which such studies are apt to produce in women of her age. And her father's family and reputation were unexceptionable.

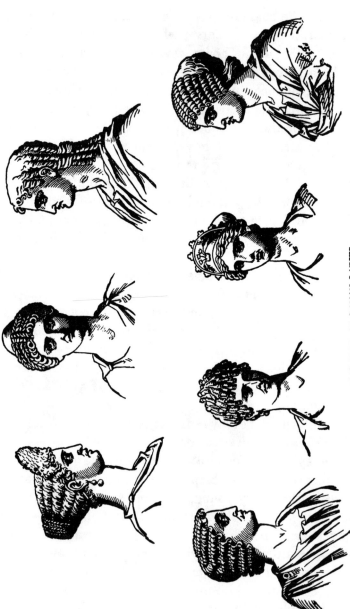

COIFFURES OF ROMAN LADIES.

Pompey's confidence made him so extremely negligent, that he laughed at those who seemed to fear the war. And when they said if Cæsar should advance in a hostile manner to Rome, they did not see what forces they had to oppose him, he bade them, with an open and smiling countenance, give themselves no pain: "For, if in Italy," said he, "I do but stamp upon the ground, an army will appear."

Meantime Cæsar was exerting himself greatly. He was now at no great distance from Italy, and not only sent his soldiers to vote in the elections, but by private pecuniary applications, corrupted many of the magistrates. Paulus the consul was of the number, and he had one thousand five hundred talents for changing sides. So also was Curio, one of the tribunes of the people, for whom he paid off an immense debt, and Mark Antony, who, out of friendship for Curio, had stood engaged with him for the debt.

It is said, that when one of Cæsar's officers, who stood before the senate-house, waiting the issue of the debates, was informed that they would not give Cæsar a longer term in his command, he laid his hand on his sword, and said, "But this shall give it." Indeed, all the preparations of his general tended that way; though Curio's demands in behalf of Cæsar seemed more plausible. He proposed, that either Pompey should likewise be obliged to dismiss his forces, or Cæsar suffered to keep his. "If they are both reduced to a private station," said he, "they will agree upon reasonable terms; or, if each retains his respective power, they will be satisfied. But he who weakens the one, without doing the same by the other, must double that force which he fears will subvert the government."

But now news was brought that Cæsar was marching directly towards Rome with all his forces. The last circumstance, indeed, was not true. He advanced with only three hundred horse and five thousand foot; the rest of his forces were on the other side of the Alps, and he would not wait for

ARCH OF CONSTANTINE.

them, choosing rather to put his adversaries in confusion by a sudden and unexpected attack, than to fight them when better prepared. When he came to the river Rubicon, which was the boundary of his province, he stood silent a long time, weighing with himself the greatness of his enterprise. At last, like one who plunges down from the top of a precipice into a gulf of immense depth, he silenced his reason, and shut his eyes against the danger; and crying out in the Greek language, "The die is cast," he marched over with his army.

Upon the first report of this at Rome, the city was in greater disorder and astonishment than had ever been known.

All Italy was in motion, with the stir of the coming storm. Those who lived out of Rome fled to it from all quarters, and those who lived in it abandoned it as fast. These saw, that in such a tempestuous and disorderly state of affairs, the well disposed part of the city wanted strength, and that the ill disposed were so refractory that they could not be managed by the magistrates. The terrors of the people could not be removed, and no one would suffer Pompey to lay a plan of action for himself. According to the passion wherewith each was actuated, whether fear, sorrow, or doubt, they endeavored to inspire him with the same; insomuch that he adopted different measures the same day. He could gain no certain intelligence of the enemy's motions, because every man brought him the report he happened to take up, and was angry if it did not meet with credit.

Pompey at last caused it to be declared by a formal edict, that the commonwealth was in danger, and no peace was to be expected. After which, he signified that he should look upon those who remained in the city as the partisans of Cæsar; and then quitted it in the dusk of the evening. The consuls also fled, without offering the sacrifices which their customs required before a war. However, in this great extremity, Pompey could not but be considered as happy in the affections of his countrymen. Though many blamed the war, there was not a man who hated the general. Nay, the number of those who followed him, out of attachment to his person, was greater than that of the adventurers in the cause of liberty.

A few days after, Cæsar arrived at Rome. When he was in possession of the city, he behaved with great moderation in many respects, and composed in a good measure the minds of its remaining inhabitants.

Pompey, who was the master of Brundusium, and had a sufficient number of transports, desired the consuls to embark without loss of time, and sent them before him with thirty cohorts to Dyrrhachium. But at the same time he sent his father-in-law Scipio and his son Cnæus into Syria, to provide ships of war. He had well secured the gates of the city, and planted the lightest of his slingers and archers upon the walls; and having now ordered the Brundusians to keep within doors, he caused a number of trenches to be cut, and sharp stakes to be driven into them, and then covered with earth, in all the streets, except two which led down to the sea. In three days all his other troops were embarked without interruption; and then he suddenly gave the signal to those who guarded the walls; in consequence of which, they ran swiftly down to the harbor, and got on board. Thus having his whole complement, he set sail, and crossed the sea to Dyrrhachium.

When Cæsar came and saw the walls left destitute of defence, he concluded that Pompey had taken to flight, and in his eagerness to pursue, would certainly have fallen upon the sharp stakes in the trenches, had not the Brundusians informed him of them. He then avoided the streets, and took a circuit round the town, by which he discovered that all the vessels had weighed anchor, except two that had not many soldiers aboard.

This manœuvre of Pompey was commonly reckoned among the greatest acts of generalship. Cæsar, however, could not help wondering, that his adversary, who was in possession of a fortified town, and expected his forces from Spain, and at the same time was master of the sea, should give up Italy in such a manner.

Cæsar thus made himself master of all Italy in sixty days without the least bloodshed, and he would have been glad to have gone immediately in pursuit of Pompey. But as he was in want of shipping, he gave up that design for the present, and marched to Spain, with an intent to gain Pompey's forces there.

In the meantime Pompey assembled a great army; and at sea he was altogether invincible. For he had five hundred ships of war, and the number of his lighter vessels was still greater.

HARBOR OF BRUNDUSIUM.

As for his land forces, he had seven thousand horse, the flower of Rome and Italy, all men of family, fortune, and courage. His infantry, though numerous, was a mixture of raw, undisciplined soldiers: he therefore exercised them during his stay at Berœa, where he was by no means idle, but went through the exercises of a soldier, as if he had been in the flower of his age. It inspired his troops with new courage, when they saw Pompey the Great, at the age of fifty-eight, going through the whole military discipline, in heavy armor, on foot; and then mounting his horse, drawing his sword with ease when at full speed, and as dexterously sheathing it again. As to the javelin, he threw it not only with great exactness, but with such force that few of the young men could dart it to a greater distance.

Many kings and princes repaired to his camp: and the number of Roman officers who had commanded armies was so great, that it was sufficient to make up a complete senate. Labienus, who had been honored with Cæsar's friendship, and served under him in Gaul, now joined Pompey.

Cæsar had now made himself master of Pompey's forces in Spain, and though it was not without a battle, he dismissed the officers, and incorporated the troops with his own. After this, he passed the Alps again, and marched through Italy to Brundusium, where he arrived at the time of the winter solstice. There he crossed the sea, and landed at Oricum; from whence he dispatched Vibullius, one of Pompey's friends, whom he had brought prisoner thither, with proposals of a conference between him and Pompey, in which they should agree to disband their armies within three days, renew their friendship, confirm it with solemn oath, and then both return to Italy.

Pompey took this overture for another snare, and therefore drew down in haste to the sea, and secured all the forts and places of strength for land forces, as well as all the ports and other commodious stations for shipping; so that there was not a wind that blew, which did not bring him either provisions, or troops, or money. On the other hand, Cæsar was reduced to such straits, both by sea and land, that he was under the necessity of seeking a battle. Accordingly, he attacked Pompey's intrenchments, and bade him defiance daily. In most of these attacks and skirmishes he had the advantage; but one day was in danger of losing his whole army. Pompey fought with so much valor, that he put Cæsar's whole detachment to flight, after having killed two thousand men upon the spot; but was either unable or afraid to pursue his blow, and enter their camp with them. Cæsar said to his friends on this occasion, "This day the victory had been the enemy's had their general known how to conquer."

Pompey's troops, elated with this success, were in great haste to come to a decisive battle. Nay, Pompey himself seemed to give in to their opinions by writing to the kings, the generals, and cities, in his interest, in the style of a conqueror. Yet all this while he dreaded the issue of a general action, believing it much better, by length of time, by famine and fatigue, to tire out men who had been ever invincible in arms, and long accustomed to conquer when they fought together. Besides, he knew the infirmities of age had made them unfit for the other operations of war, for long marches and countermarches, for digging trenches and building forts, and that, therefore, they wished for nothing so much as a battle. Pompey, with all these arguments, found it no easy matter to keep his army quiet.

After this last engagement, Cæsar was in such want of provisions, that he was forced to decamp, and he took his way through Athamania into Thessaly. This added so much to the high opinion Pompey's soldiers had of themselves, that it was impossible to keep them within bounds. They cried out with one voice, "Cæsar is fled." Some called upon the general to pursue: some to pass over into Italy. Others sent their friends and servants to Rome, to engage houses near the *forum*, for the convenience of soliciting the great offices of state. And not a few went of their own accord to Cornelia, who had been privately lodged in Lesbos, to congratulate her upon the conclusion of the war.

While he thus softly followed the enemy's steps, a complaint was raised against him, and urged with much clamor, that he was not exercising his generalship upon Cæsar, but upon the Senate and the whole commonwealth, in order that he might forever keep the command in his hands, and have those for his guards and servants who had a right to govern the world. Domitius Ænobarbus, to increase the *odium*, always called him Agamemnon, or king of kings. Favonius piqued him no less with a jest, than others by their unseasonable severity; he went about crying, "My friends, we shall eat no figs in Tusculum this year."

These and many other like sallies of ridicule had such an effect upon Pompey, who was ambitious of being spoken well of by the world, and had too much deference for the opinions of his friends, that he gave up his own better judgment, to follow them in the career of their false hopes and prospects. A thing which would have been unpardonable in the pilot or master of a ship, much more in the commander-in-chief of so many nations and such numerous armies. He had often commended the physician who gives no indulgence to the whimsical longings of his patients, and yet he humored the sickly cravings of his army, and was afraid to give them pain, though necessary for the preservation of their life and being. For who can say that army was in a sound and healthy state, when some of the officers went about the camp canvassing for the offices of consul and prætor; and others, namely, Spinther, Domitius, and Scipio, were engaged in quarrels and cabals about Cæsar's high-priesthood, as if their adversary had been only a Tigranes, a king of Armenia, or a prince of the Nabathæans; and not that Cæsar and that army who had stormed one thousand cities, subdued above three hundred nations, gained numberless battles of the Germans and Gauls, taken one million prisoners, and killed as many fairly in the field. Notwithstanding all this, they continued loud and tumultuous in their demands of a battle; and when they came to the plains of Pharsalia, forced Pompey to call a council of war. Labienus, who had the command of the cavalry, rose up first, and took an oath, that he would not return from the battle, till he had put the enemy to flight. All the other officers swore the same.

The night following, Pompey had this dream. He thought he entered his own theatre, and was received with loud plaudits; after which, he adorned the temple of Venus *the Victorious* with many spoils. This vision, on one side, encouraged him, and on the other alarmed him. He was afraid that Cæsar, who was a descendant of Venus, would be aggrandized at his expense. Besides, a panic* fear ran through the camp, the noise of which awakened him. And about the morning watch, over Cæsar's camp, where everything was perfectly quiet, there suddenly appeared a great light, from which a stream of fire issued in the form of a torch, and fell upon that of Pompey. Cæsar himself says he saw it as he was going his rounds.

Cæsar was preparing, at break of day, to march to Scotusa; his soldiers were striking their tents, and the servants and beasts of burden were already in motion, when his scouts brought intelligence that they had seen arms handed about in the enemy's camp, and perceived a noise and bustle, which indicated an approaching battle. After these, others came and assured him that the first ranks were drawn up.

Upon this Cæsar said: "The long-wished day is come, on which we shall fight with men, and not with want and famine." Then he immediately ordered the red mantle to be put up before his pavilion, which, among the Romans, is the signal of a battle. The soldiers no sooner beheld it, than they left their tents as they were, and ran to arms with loud shouts, and every expression of joy. And when the officers began to put them in order of battle, each man fell into his proper rank as quietly, and with as much skill and ease, as a *chorus* in a tragedy.

Pompey placed himself in his right wing over against Antony, and his father-in-law, Scipio, in the centre, opposite Domitius Calvinus. His left wing was commanded by Lucius Domitius, and supported by the cavalry; for they were almost all ranged on that side, in order to break in upon Cæsar, and cut off the tenth legion, which was accounted the bravest in his army, and in which he used to fight in person. Cæsar, seeing the enemy's left wing so well guarded with horse, and fearing the excellence of their armor, sent for a detachment of six

---

* A *Panic* was so called, from the terror which the god *Pan* is said to have struck the enemies of Greece with, at the battle of Marathon.

cohorts from the body of the reserve, and placed them behind the tenth legion, with orders not to stir before the attack, lest they should be discovered by the enemy; but when the enemy's cavalry had charged, to make up through the foremost ranks, and then not to discharge their javelins at a distance, as brave men generally do in their eagerness to come to sword in hand, but to reserve them till they came to close fighting, and to push them forward into the eyes and faces of the enemy. "For those fair young dancers," said he, "will never stand the steel aimed at their eyes, but will fly to save their handsome faces."

While Cæsar was thus employed, Pompey took a view on horseback of the order of both armies; and finding that the enemy kept their ranks with the utmost exactness, and quietly waited for the signal of battle, while his own men, for want of experience, were fluctuating and unsteady, he was afraid they would be broken up on the first onset. He therefore commanded the vanguard to stand firm in their ranks, and in that close order to receive the enemy's charge. Cæsar condemned this measure, as not only tending to lessen the vigor of the blows, which is always greatest in the assailants, but also to damp the fire and spirit of the men; whereas those who advance with impetuosity, and animate each other with shouts, are filled with an enthusiastic valor and superior ardor.

Cæsar's army consisted of twenty-two thousand men, and Pompey's was something more than twice that number. When the signal was given on both sides, and the trumpets sounded a charge, each common man attended only to his own concern. But some of the principal Romans and Greeks, who only stood and looked on, when the dreadful moment of action approached, could not help considering to what the avarice and ambition of two men had brought the Roman Empire. The same arms on both sides, the troops marshalled in the same manner, the same standards; in short, the strength and flower of one and the same city turned upon itself! What could be a stronger proof of the blindness and infatuation of human nature, when carried away by its passions? Had they been willing to enjoy the fruits of their labors in peace and tranquillity, the greatest and best part of the world was their own. Or, if they must have indulged their thirst of victories and triumphs, the Parthians and Germans were yet to be subdued; Scythia and India yet remained; together with a very plausible color for their lust of new acquisitions, the pretence of civilizing barbarians. And what Scythian horse, what Parthian arrows, what Indian treasures, could have resisted seventy thousand Romans, led on by Pompey and Cæsar. with whose names those nations had long been acquainted! Into such a variety of wild and savage countries had these two generals carried their victorious arms! Whereas now they stood threatening each other with destruction; not sparing even their own glory, though to it they sacrificed their country, but prepared, one of them, to lose the reputation of being invincible, which hitherto they had both maintained. So that the alliance which they had contracted by Pompey's marriage to Julia, was from the first only an artful expedient; and her charms were to form a self-interested compact, instead of being the pledge of a sincere friendship.

The plain of Pharsalia was now covered with men, and horses and arms; and the signal of battle being given on both sides, the first on Cæsar's side who advanced to the charge was Caius Crastinus, who commanded a corps of one hundred and twenty men, and was determined to make good his promise to his general. He was the first man Cæsar saw when he went out of the trenches in the morning; and upon Cæsar's asking him what he thought of the battle, he stretched out his hand, and answered in a cheerful tone, "You will gain a glorious victory, and I shall have your praise this day, either alive or dead." In pursuance of this promise, he advanced the foremost, and many follow·

ing to support him, he charged into the midst of the enemy. They soon took to their swords, and numbers were slain; but as Crastinus was making his way forward, and cutting down all before him, one of Pompey's men stood to receive him, and pushed his sword in at his mouth with such force, that it went through the nape of his neck. Crastinus thus killed, the fight was maintained with equal advantage on both sides.

Pompey did not immediately lead on his right wing, but often directed his eyes to the left, and lost time in waiting to see what execution his cavalry would do there. Meanwhile they had extended their squadrons to surround Cæsar, and prepared to drive the few horse he had placed in front, back upon the foot. At that instant Cæsar gave the signal; upon which his cavalry retreated a little; and the six cohorts, which consisted of 3000 men, and had been placed behind the tenth legion, advanced to surround Pompey's cavalry; and coming close up to them, raised the points of their javelins, as they had been taught, and aimed them at the face. Their adversaries, who were not experienced in any kind of fighting, and had not the least previous idea of this, could not parry or endure the blows upon their faces, but turned their backs, or covered their eyes with their hands, and soon fled with great dishonor. Cæsar's men took no care to pursue them, but turned their force upon the enemy's infantry, particularly upon that wing, which, now stripped of its horse, lay open to the attack on all sides. The six cohorts, therefore, took them in flank, while the tenth legion charged them in front; and they, who had hoped to surround the enemy, and now, instead of that, saw themselves surrounded, made but a short resistance, and then took to a precipitate flight.

By the great dust that was raised, Pompey conjectured the fate of his cavalry; and it is hard to say what passed in his mind at that moment. He appeared like a man moonstruck and distracted; and without considering that he was Pompey the Great, or speaking to any one, he quitted the ranks, and retired step by step toward his camp—a scene which cannot be better painted than in these verses of Homer :*

> But partial Jove, espousing Hector's part,
> Shot heaven-bred horror through the Grecian's heart;
> Confused, unnerv'd in Hector's presence grown,
> Amazed he stood with terrors not his own.
> O'er his broad back his moony shield he threw,
> And, glaring round, by tardy steps withdrew.

In this condition he entered his tent, where he sat down, and uttered not a word, till at last, upon finding that some of the enemy entered the camp with the fugitives, he said, "What! into my camp, too!" After this short exclamation, he rose up, and dressing himself in a manner suitable to his fortune, privately withdrew. All the other legions fled; and a great slaughter was made in the camp, of the servants and others who had the care of the tents. But Asinius Pollio, who then fought on Cæsar's side, assures us, that of the regular troops there were not above six thousand men killed. †

Upon the taking of the camp, there was a spectacle which showed, in strong colors, the vanity and folly of Pompey's troops. All the tents were crowned with myrtle; the beds were strewed with flowers; the tables covered with cups, and bowls of wine set out. In short, everything had the appearance of preparations for feasts and sacrifices, rather than for men going out to battle. To such a degree had their vain hopes corrupted them, and with such a senseless confidence they took to the field!

When Pompey had got at a little distance from the camp, he quitted his horse. He had very few people about him; and, as he saw he was not pursued, he went softly on, wrapped up in such thoughts as we may suppose a man to have, who had

---

* In the eleventh book of the Iliad, where he is speaking of the flight of Ajax before Hector.

† Cæsar says, that in all there were fifteen thousand killed, and twenty-four thousand taken prisoners.

been used for thirty-four years to conquer and carry all before him, and now in his old age first came to know what it was to be defeated and to fly. We may easily conjecture what his thoughts must be, when in one short hour he had lost the glory and the power which had been growing up amidst so many wars and conflicts; and he who was lately guarded with such armies of horse and foot, and such great and powerful fleets, was reduced to so mean and contemptible an equipage, that his enemies, who were in search of him, could not know him

RIVER PENEUS, LOOKING TOWARD MT. PINDUS.

He passed by Larissa, and came to Tempe, where, burning with thirst, he threw himself upon his face, and drank out of the river; after which, he passed through the valley, and went down to the sea-coast. There he spent the remainder of the night in a poor fisherman's cabin. Next morning, about break of day, he went on board a small river-boat, taking with him such of his company as were freemen. The slaves he dismissed, bidding them go to Cæsar, and fear nothing.

As he was coasting along, he saw a ship of burden just ready to sail; the master of which was Peticius, a Roman citizen, who, though not acquainted with Pompey, knew him by sight. Therefore, without waiting for any further application, he took him up, and such of his companions as he thought proper, and then hoisted sail. The persons Pompey took with him, were the two Lentuli and Favonius; and a little after, they saw king Deiotarus beckoning to them with great earnestness from the shore, and took him up likewise. The master of the ship provided them with the best supper he could, and when it was almost ready, Pompey, for want of a servant, was going to wash himself, but Favonius, seeing it, stepped up, and both washed and anointed him. All the time he was on board, he continued to wait upon him in all the offices of a servant, even to the washing of his feet and providing his supper; insomuch, that one who saw the unaffected simplicity and sincere attachment with which Favonius performed these offices, cried out—

> The generous mind adds dignity
> To every act, and nothing misbecomes it.

Pompey, in the course of his voyage, sailed by Amphipolis, and from thence steered for Mitylene, to take up Cornelia and his son. As soon as he reached the island, he sent a messenger to the town with news far different from what Cornelia expected. For, by the flattering accounts which many officious persons had given her, she understood that the dispute was decided at Dyrrhachium, and that nothing but the pursuit of Cæsar remained to be attended to. The messenger, finding her possessed with such hopes, had not power to make the usual salutations; but expressing the greatness of Pompey's misfortunes by his tears rather than words, only told her she must make haste if she had a mind to see Pompey with one ship only, and that not his own.

At this news Cornelia threw herself upon the ground, where she lay a long time insensible and speechless. At last, coming to herself, she perceived there was no time to be lost in tears and lamentations, and therefore hastened through the town to the sea. Pompey ran to meet her, and received her to his arms as she was just going to fall. While she hung upon his neck, she thus addressed him: "I see, my dear husband, your present unhappy condition is the effect of my ill fortune, and not yours. Alas! how are you reduced to one poor vessel, who, before your marriage with Cornelia, traversed the sea with 500 galleys! Why did you come to see me, and not rather leave me to my evil destiny, who have loaded you, too, with such a weight of calamities? How happy had it been for me to have died before I heard that Publius, my first husband, was killed by the Parthians! How wise, had I followed him to the grave, as I once intended! What have I lived for since, but to bring misfortunes upon Pompey the Great?"

Such, we are assured, was the speech of Cornelia; and Pompey answered: "Till this moment, Cornelia, you have experienced nothing but the smiles of fortune; and it was she who deceived you, because she stayed with me longer than she commonly does with her favorites. But, fated as we are, we must bear this reverse, and make another trial of her. For it is no more improbable that we may emerge from this poor condition and rise to great things again, than it was that we should fall from great things into this poor condition."

Cornelia then sent to the city for her most valuable movables and her servants.

As soon as his wife and his friends were embarked, he set sail, and continued his course without touching at any port, except for water and provisions, till he came to Attalia, a city of Pamphylia. There he was joined by some Cilician galleys; and beside picking up a number of soldiers, he found in a little time sixty senators about him. When he was informed that his fleet was still entire, and that Cato was gone to Africa with a considerable body of men which he had collected after their flight, he lamented to his friends his great error, in suffering himself to be forced into an engagement on land, and making no use of those forces, in which he was confessedly stronger; nor even taking care to fight near his fleet, that, in case of his meeting with a check on land, he might have been supplied from the sea with another army, capable of making head against the enemy. Indeed, we find no greater mistake in Pompey's whole conduct, nor a more remarkable instance of Cæsar's generalship, than in removing the scene of action to such a distance from the naval force.

However, as it was necessary to undertake something with the small means he had left, he sent to some cities, and sailed to others himself, to raise money, and to get a supply of men for his ships. But knowing the extraordinary celerity of the enemy's motions, he was afraid he might be beforehand with him, and seize all that he was preparing. He, therefore, began to think of retiring to some asylum, and proposed the matter in council. They could not think of any province in the Roman empire that would afford a safe retreat; and when they cast their eyes on the foreign kingdoms, Pompey mentioned Parthia as the most likely to receive and protect them in their present weak condition, and afterwards to send them back with a force sufficient to retrieve their affairs. Others were of opinion it was proper to apply to Africa, and to Juba in particular. But Theophanes of Lesbos observed it was madness to leave Egypt, which was distant but three days' sail. Besides, Ptolemy, who was growing towards manhood, had particular obligations to Pompey on his father's account. And so it was determined that they should seek for refuge in Egypt. Being informed that Ptolemy was with his army at Pelusium, where he was engaged in war with his sister, he proceeded thither, and sent a messenger before him to announce his arrival, and to entreat the king's protection.

Ptolemy was very young, fourteen years of age, and Photinus, his prime minister, called a council of his ablest officers; though their advice had no more weight than he was pleased to allow it. He ordered each, however, to give his opinion. But who can, without indignation, consider that the fate of Pompey the Great was to be determined by the wretch Photinus, by Theodotus, a man of Chios, who was hired to teach the prince rhetoric, and by Achillas, an Egyptian? For among the king's chamberlains and tutors these had the greatest influence over him and were the persons he most consulted. Pompey lay at anchor at some distance from the place waiting the determination of this respectable board; while he thought it beneath him to be indebted to Cæsar for his safety. The council were divided in their opinions, some advising the prince to give him an honorable reception, and others to send him an order to depart. But Theodotus, to display his eloquence, insisted that both were wrong. "If you receive him," said he, "you will have Cæsar for your enemy, and Pompey for your master. If you order him off, Pompey may one day revenge the affront and Cæsar resent your not having put him in his hands: the best method, therefore, is to send for him and put him to death. By this means you will do Cæsar a favor, and have nothing to fear from Pompey." He added with a smile, "Dead men do not bite."

This advice being approved of, the execution of it was committed to Achillas. In consequence of which he took with him Septimius, who had formerly been one of Pompey's officers, and Salvius, who had also acted under him as a centurion, with three or four assistants, and made up to Pompey's ship, where his principal friends and officers had assembled to see how the affair went on. When they perceived there was nothing magnificent in their reception, nor suitable to the hopes which Theophanes had conceived, but that a few men only in a fishing-boat came to wait upon them, such want of respect appeared a suspicious circumstance; and they advised Pompey, while he was out of the reach of missive weapons, to get out to the main sea.

Meantime, the boat approaching, Septimius spoke first, addressing Pompey in Latin by the title of *Imperator.* Then Achillas saluted him in Greek, and desired him to come into the boat, because the water was very shallow towards the shore, and a galley must strike upon the sands. At the same time they saw several of the king's ships getting ready, and the shore covered with troops, so that if they would have changed their minds it was then too late; besides, their distrust would have furnished the assassins with a pretence for their injustice. He therefore embraced Cornelia, who lamented his sad exit before it happened; and ordered two centurions, one of his enfranchised slaves, named Philip, and a servant called Scenes, to get into the boat before him. When Achillas had hold of his hand, and he was going to step in himself, he turned to his wife and son, and repeated that verse of Sophocles—

> Seek'st thou a tyrant's door? then farewell freedom!
> Though FREE as air before.

These were the last words he spoke to them.

As there was a considerable distance between the galley and the shore, and he observed that not a man in the boat showed him the least civility, or even spoke to him, he looked at Septimius, and said, "Methinks, I remember you to have been my fellow-soldier;" but he answered only with a nod, without testifying any regard or friendship. A profound silence again taking place, Pompey took out a paper, in which he had written a speech in Greek that he designed to make to Ptolemy, and amused himself with reading it.

When they approached the shore, Cornelia, with her friends in the galley, watched the event with great anxiety. She was a little encouraged, when she saw a number of the king's great officers coming down to the strand, in all appearance to receive her husband and do him honor. But the moment Pompey was taking hold of Philip's hand, to raise him with more ease, Septimius came behind, and ran him through the body;

after which Salvius and Achillas also drew their swords. Pompey took his robe in both hands and covered his face, and without saying or doing the least thing unworthy of him, submitted to his fate, only uttering a groan, while they despatched him with many blows. He was then just fifty nine years old, for he was killed the day after his birthday.

Cornelia, and her friends in the galley, upon seeing him murdered, gave a shriek that was heard to the shore, and weighed anchor immediately. Their flight was assisted by a brisk gale, as they got out more to sea; so that the Egyptians gave up their design of pursuing them. The murderers having cut off Pompey's head, threw the body out of the boat naked, and left it exposed to all who were desirous of such a sight. Philip stayed till their curiosity was satisfied, and then washed the body with sea-water, and wrapped it in one of his own garments, because he had nothing else at hand. The next thing was to look out for wood for the funeral pile; and casting his eyes over the shore, he spied the old remains of a fishing-boat; which, though not large, would make a sufficient pile for a poor naked body that was not quite entire.

While he was collecting the pieces of plank and putting them together, an old Roman, who had made some of his first campaigns under Pompey, came up and said to Philip, "Who are you that are preparing the funeral of Pompey the Great?" Philip answered, "I am his freedman." "But you shall not," said the old Roman, "have this honor entirely to yourself. As a work of piety offers itself, let me have a share in it; that I may not absolutely repent my having passed so many years in a foreign country; but, to compensate many misfortunes, may have the consolation of doing some of the last honors to the greatest general Rome ever produced." In this manner was the funeral of Pompey conducted.

Such was the end of Pompey the Great. As for Cæsar, he arrived not long after in Egypt, which he found in great disorder. When they came to present the head, he turned from it, and the person that brought it, as a sight of horror. He received the seal, but it was with tears. The device was a lion holding a sword. The two assassins, Achillas and Photinus, he put to death; and the king, being defeated in battle, perished in the river. Theodotus, the rhetorician, escaped the vengeance of Cæsar, by leaving Egypt; but he wandered about a miserable fugitive, and was hated wherever he went. At last, Marcus Brutus, who killed Cæsar, found the wretch, in his province of Asia, and put him to death, after having made him suffer the most exquisite tortures. The ashes of Pompey were carried to Cornelia, who buried them in his lands near Alba.*

---

* Langhorne has well remarked that Pompey has, in all appearance, and in all considerations of his character, had less justice done him by historians than any other man of his time. His popular humanity, his military and political skill, his prudence (which he sometimes unfortunately gave up), his natural bravery and generosity, his conjugal virtues, which (though sometimes impeached) were both naturally and morally great; his cause, which was certainly, in its original interests, the cause of Rome; all these circumstances entitled him to a more distinguished and more respectable character than any of his historians have thought proper to afford him.

THE ENGINES OF ARCHIMEDES.

FROM THE LIFE OF MARCELLUS.

MARCELLUS now moved with his whole army to Syracuse, and, encamping near the wall, proceeded to attack the city both by land and by sea. The land forces were conducted by Appius: Marcellus, with sixty galleys, each with five rows of oars, furnished with all sorts of arms and missiles, and a huge bridge of planks laid upon eight ships chained together, upon which was carried the engine to cast stones and darts, assaulted the walls, relying on the abundance and magnificence of his preparations, and on his own previous glory; all which, however, were, it would seem, but trifles for Archimedes and his machines.

These machines he had designed and contrived, not a matters of any importance, but as mere amusements it geometry; in compliance with king Hiero's desire and re quest, some little time before, that he should reduce to practice some part of his admirable speculations in science, and by accommodating the theoretical truth to sensation and ordinary use, bring it more within the appreciation of people in general. Eudoxus and Archytas had been the originators of this far-famed and highly prized art of mechanics, which they employed as an elegant illustration of geometrical truths, and as a means of sustaining experimentally, to the satisfaction of the senses, conclusions too intricate for proof by words and diagrams. As, for example, to solve the problem, so often required in constructing geometrical figures, given the two extreme, to find the two mean lines of a proportion, both these mathematicians had recourse to the aid of instruments, adapting to their purpose certain curves and sections of lines.* But what with Plato's indignation at it, and his invectives against it as the mere corruption and annihilation of the one good of geometry,—which was thus shamefully turning its back upon the unembodied objects of pure intelligence to recur to sensation, and to ask help (not to be obtained without base subservience and depravation) from matter; so it was that mechanics came to be separated from geometry, and, being repudiated and neglected by philosophers, took its place as a military art. Archimedes, however, in writing to king Hiero, whose friend and near relation he was, had stated, that given the force, any weight might be moved, and even boasted, we are told, relying on the strength of demonstration, that if there were another earth, by going into it he could remove this. Hiero being struck with amazement at this, and entreating him to make good this problem by actual experiment, and show some great weight moved by a small engine, he fixed accordingly upon a ship of burden out of the king's arsenal, which could not be drawn out of the dock without great labor and many men; and, loading her with many passengers and a full freight, sitting himself the while far off, with no great endeavor, but only holding the head of the pulley in his hand and drawing the cord by degrees, he drew the ship in a straight line, as smoothly and evenly as if she had been in the sea. The king, astonished at this, and convinced of the power of the art, prevailed upon Archimedes to make him engines accommodated to all the purposes, offensive and defensive, of a siege. These the king himself never made use of, because he spent almost all his life in a profound quiet, and the highest affluence. But the apparatus was, in a most opportune time, ready at hand for the Syracusans, and with it also the engineer himself.

When, therefore, the Romans assaulted the walls in two

---

* The *mesolábes* or *mesolabium*, was the name by which this instrument was commonly known.

places at once, fear and consternation stupefied the Syracusans, believing that nothing was able to resist that violence and those forces. But when Archimedes began to ply his engines, he at once shot against the land forces all sorts of missile weapons, and immense masses of stone that came down with incredible noise and violence, against which no man could stand; for they knocked down those upon whom they fell, in heaps, breaking all their ranks and files. In the mean time huge poles thrust out from the walls over the ships, sunk some by the great weights which they let down from on high upon them; others they lifted up into the air by an iron hand or beak like a crane's beak, and, when they had drawn them up by the prow, and set them on end upon the poop, they plunged them to the bottom of the sea; or else the ships, drawn by engines within, and whirled about, were dashed against steep rocks that stood jutting out under the walls, with great destruction of the soldiers that were aboard them. A ship was frequently lifted up to a great height in the air (a dreadful thing to behold), and was rolled to and fro, and kept swinging, until the mariners were all thrown out, when at length it was dashed against the rocks, or let fall. In the meantime, Marcellus himself brought up his engine upon the bridge of ships, which was called *Sambuca*, from some resemblance it had to an instrument of music, but while it was as yet approaching the wall, there was discharged at it a piece of a rock of ten talents' weight, then a second and a third, which, striking upon it with immense force and with a noise like thunder, broke all its foundation to pieces, shook out all its fastenings, and completely dislodged it from the bridge. So Marcellus, doubtful what counsel to pursue, drew off his ships to a safer distance, and sounded a retreat to his forces on land. They then took a resolution of coming up under the walls, if it were possible, in the night; thinking that as Archimedes used ropes stretched at length in playing his engines, the soldiers would now be under the shot, and the darts would, for want of sufficient distance to throw them, fly over their heads without effect. But he, it appeared, had long before framed for such occasion engines accommodated to any distance, and shorter weapons; and had made numerous small openings in the walls, through which, with engines of a shorter range, unexpected blows were inflicted on the assailants. Thus, when they who thought to deceive the defenders came close up to the walls, instantly a shower of darts and other missile weapons was again cast upon them. And when stones came tumbling down perpendicularly upon, their heads, and, as it were, the whole wall shot out arrows at them, they retired. And now, again, as they were going off, arrows and darts of a longer range inflicted a great slaughter among them, and their ships were driven one against another; while they themselves were not able to retaliate in any way; for Archimedes had fixed most of his engines immediately under the wall. The Romans, seeing that infinite mischiefs overwhelmed them from no visible means, began to think they were fighting with the gods.

Yet Marcellus escaped unhurt, and, deriding his own artificers and engineers, exclaimed "What! must we give up fighting with this geometrical Briareus, who plays pitch and toss with our ships, and, with the multitude of darts which he showers at a single moment upon us, really outdoes the hundred-handed giants of mythology?" The rest of the Syracusans were but the body of Archimedes' designs, one soul moving and governing all; for, laying aside all other arms, with his alone they infested the Romans, and protected themselves. In fine, when such terror had seized upon the Romans, that, if they did but see a little rope or a piece of wood from the wall, they instantly cried out, "There it is again! Archimedes is about to let fly another engine at us," and turned their backs and fled, Marcellus desisted from conflicts and assaults, putting all his hope in a long siege.

Yet Archimedes possessed so high a spirit, so profound a soul, and such treasures of scientific knowledge, that though these inventions had now obtained him the renown of more than human sagacity, he yet would not deign to leave behind him any commentary or writing on such subjects; but, repudiating as sordid and ignoble the whole trade of engineering, and every sort of art that lends itself to mere use and profit, he placed his whole affection and ambition in those purer speculations where there can be no reference to the vulgar needs of life; studies, the superiority of which to all others is unquestioned, and in which the only doubt can be, whether the beauty and grandeur of the subjects examined, or the precision and cogency of the methods and means of proof, most deserve our admiration. It is not possible to find in all geometry more difficult and intricate questions, or more simple and lucid explanations. Some ascribe this to his natural genius; while others think that incredible effort and toil produced these apparently easy and unlabored results. No amount of investigation of yours would succeed in attaining the proof, and yet, once seen, you immediately believe you would have discovered it; by so smooth and so rapid a path he leads you to the conclusion required. And thus it ceases to be incredible that (as is commonly told of him), the charm of his familiar and domestic Siren made him forget his food and neglect his person, to such a degree that when he was occasionally carried by absolute violence to bathe, or have his body anointed, he used to trace geometrical figures in the ashes of the fire, and diagrams in the oil on his body, being in a state of entire preoccupation, and, in the truest sense, divinely possessed with his love and delight in science. His discoveries were numerous and admirable; and he is said to have requested his friends and relations that when he was dead, they would place over his tomb a cylinder containing a sphere, inscribing it with the ratio of three to two which the containing solid bears to the contained.

DESCRIPTION OF CLEOPATRA.

FROM THE LIFE OF ANTONY.

When Antony was making preparation for the Parthian war, he sent to command Cleopatra to make her personal appearance in Cilicia, to answer an accusation, that she had given great assistance, in the late wars, to Cassius. Dellius, who was sent on this message, had no sooner seen her face, and remarked her adroitness and subtlety in speech, than he felt convinced that Antony would not so much as think of giving any molestation to a woman like this; on the contrary, she would be the first in favor with him. So he set himself at once to pay his court to the Egyptian, and gave her his advice, "to go," in the Homeric style, to Cilicia, "in her best attire," * and bade her fear nothing from Antony, the gentlest and kindest of soldiers. She had some faith in the words of Dellius, but more in her own attractions, which, having formerly recommended her to Cæsar and the young Gnæus Pompey, she did not doubt might prove yet more successful with Antony. Their acquaintance was with her when a girl, young, and ignorant of the world, but she was to meet Antony in the time of life when women's beauty is most splendid, and their intellects are in full maturity, for she was now about twenty-eight years of age. She made great preparation for her journey, of money, gifts, and ornaments of value, such as so wealthy a kingdom might afford, but she brought with her her surest hopes in her own magic arts and charms.

She received several letters, both from Antony and from

---

* "To go to Ida in her best attire" is the verse, in which Plutarch merely substitutes Cilicia for Ida. See the Iliad, Book XIV. 162, where Juno is described as setting forth to beguile Jupiter from his watch on Mount Ida, while Neptune shall check the Trojans.

his friends, to summon her, but she paid no attention to these orders; and at last, as if in mockery of them, she came sailing up the river Cydnus, in a barge with gilded stern and outspread sails of purple, while oars of silver beat time to the music of flutes and fifes and harps. She herself lay stretched along under a canopy of cloth of gold, dressed as Venus in a picture, and beautiful young boys, like painted Cupids, stood on each side to fan her. He maids were dressed like Sea Nymphs and Graces, some steering at the rudder, some working at the ropes. The perfumes diffused themselves from the vessel to the shore, which was covered with multitudes, part following the galley up the river on either bank, part running out of the city to see the sight. The market-place was quite emptied, and Antony at last was left alone sitting upon the tribunal; while the word went through all the mul-

LADY OF TANAGRA WITH CHITON AND HAT.

titude, that Venus had come to feast with Bacchus, for the common good of Asia. On her arrival, Antony sent to invite her to supper. She thought it fitter he should come to her; so, willing to show his good-humor and courtesy, he complied, and went. He found the preparations to receive him magnificent beyond expression, but nothing so admirable as the great number of lights; for on a sudden there were let down all together so great numbers of branches with lights in them so ingeniously disposed, some in squares, and some in circles, that the whole thing was a spectacle that has seldom been equaled for beauty.

The next day, Antony invited her to supper, and was very desirous to outdo her as well in magnificence as contrivance; but he found he was altogether beaten in both, and was so well convinced of it, that he was himself the first to jest and mock at his poverty of wit, and his rustic awkwardness. She, perceiving that his raillery was broad and gross, and savored more of the soldier than the courtier, rejoined in the same taste, and fell into it at once, without any sort of reluctance or reserve. For her actual beauty, it is said, was not in itself so remarkable that none could be compared with her, or that no one could see her without being struck by it, but the contact of her presence, if you lived with her, was irresistible; the attraction of her person, joining with the charm of her conversation, and the character that attended all she said or did, was something bewitching. It was a pleasure merely to hear the sound of her voice, with which, like an instrument of many strings, she could pass from one language to another; so that there were few of the barbarian nations that she answered by an interpreter; to most of them she spoke herself, as to the Æthiopians, Troglodytes, Hebrews, Arabians, Syrians, Medes, Parthians, and many others, whose language she had learnt; which was all the more surprising, because most of the kings her predecessors scarcely gave themselves the trouble to acquire the Egyptian tongue, and several of them quite abandoned the Macedonian.

Antony was so captivated by her, that, leaving his troops assembled in Mesopotamia, and ready to enter Syria, he suffered himself to be carried away by her to Alexandria, there to keep holiday, like a boy, in play and diversion, squandering and fooling away in enjoyments that most costly, as Antiphon says, of all valuables, time. They had a sort of company, to which they gave a particular name, calling it that of the "Inimitable Livers." The members entertained one another daily in turn, with an extravagance of expenditure beyond measure or belief. Philotas, a physician of Amphissa, who was at that time a student of medicine in Alexandria, used to tell my grandfather, Lamprias, that, having some acquaintance with one of the royal cooks, he was invited by him, being a young man, to come and see the sumptuous preparations for supper. So he was taken into the kitchen, where he admired the prodigious variety of all things; but particularly, seeing eight wild boars roasting whole, he exclaimed, "Surely you have a great number of guests." The cook laughed at his simplicity, and told him there were not more than twelve to sup, but that every dish was to be served up just roasted to a turn, and if anything was but one minute ill-timed, it was spoiled; "And," said he, "maybe Antony will sup just now, may be not this hour, maybe he will call for wine, or begin to talk, and will put it off. So that," he continued, "not one, but many, suppers must be had in readiness, as it is impossible to guess at his hour."

Plato admits four sorts of flattery, but Cleopatra had a thousand. Were Antony serious or disposed to mirth, she had at any moment some new delight or charm to meet his wishes. She played at dice with him, drank with him, hunted with him; and when he exercised in arms, she was there to see. At night she would go rambling with him to disturb and torment people at their doors and windows, dressed like a servant-woman, for Antony also went in servant's disguise, and from these expeditions he often came home very scurvily answered, and sometimes even beaten severely, though most people guessed who it was. It would be trifling without end to be particular in his follies, but his fishing must not be forgotten. He went out one day to angle with Cleopatra, and, being so unfortunate as to catch nothing in the presence of the queen, he gave secret orders to the fishermen to dive under water, and put fishes that had been already taken upon his hooks; and these he drew so fast that the Egyptian perceived it. But, feigning great admiration, she told everybody how dexterous Antony was, and invited them next day to come and see him again. So, when a number of them had come on board the fishing boats, as soon as he had let down his hook, one of her servants was beforehand with his divers, and fixed upon his hook a salted fish from Pontus. Antony, feeling his line give, drew up the prey, and when, as may be imagined, great laughter ensued, Cleopatra said, " Leave the fishing-rod, general, to us poor sovereigns of Pharos and Canopus; your game is cities, provinces, and kingdoms."

AGESILAUS, KING OF SPARTA.

Agesilaus is said to have been a little man, of a contemptible presence; but the goodness of his humor, and his con

GREEK WARRIOR.

stant cheerfulness and playfulness of temper, always free from anything of moroseness or haughtiness, made him more attractive, even to his old age, than the most beautiful and youthful men of the nation. Theophrastus writes, that the Ephors laid a fine upon Archidamus for marrying a little wife, "For," said they, "she will bring us a race of kinglets, instead of kings."

Agesilaus was excessively fond of his children; and it is to him the story belongs, that when they were little ones, he used to make a horse of a stick, and ride with them; and being caught at this sport by a friend, he desired him not to mention it, till he himself should be the father of children.

When the Mantineans revolted from Thebes to Sparta, and Epaminondas understood that Agesilaus had come to their assistance with a powerful army, he privately in the night quitted his quarters at Tegea, and unknown to the Mantineans, passing by Agesilaus, marched toward Sparta, insomuch that he failed very little of taking it empty and unarmed. Agesilaus had intelligence sent him by Euthynus, the Thespian, as Callisthenes says, but Xenophon says by a Cretan,

GREEK WARRIOR.

and immediately despatched a horseman to Lacedæmon, to apprise them of it, and to let them know that he was hastening to them. Shortly after his arrival the Thebans crossed the Eurotas. They made an assault upon the town, and were received by Agesilaus with great courage, and with exertions beyond what was to be expected at his years. For he did not now fight with that caution and cunning which he formerly made use of, but put all upon a desperate push; which, though not his usual method, succeeded so well, that he rescued the city out of the very hands of Epaminondas, and forced him to retire, and, at the erection of a trophy, was able, in the presence of their wives and children, to declare that the Lacedæmonians had nobly paid their debt to their country, and particularly his son Archidamus, who had that day made himself illustrious, both by his courage and agility of body, rapidly passing about by the short lanes to every endangered point, and everywhere maintaining the town against the enemy with but few to help him. Isadas, too, the son of Phœbidas, must have been, I think, the admiration of the enemy as well as of his friends. He was a youth of remarkable beauty and stature, in the very flower of the most attractive time of life, when the boy is just rising into the man. He had no arms upon him, and scarcely clothes; he had just anointed himself at home, when, upon the alarm, without further waiting, in that undress, he snatched a spear in one hand, and a sword in the other, and broke his way through the combatants to the enemies, striking at all he met. He received no wound, whether it were that a special divine care rewarded his valor with an extraordinary protection, or whether his shape being so large and beautiful, and his dress so unusual, they thought him more than a man. The Ephors gave him a garland; but as soon as they had done so, they fined him **a thousand drachmas, for going out to battle unarmed.**

THE BROTHERS

FROM THE LIFE OF TIMOLEON.

TIMOLEON had an elder brother, whose name was Timophanes, who was every way unlike him, being indiscreet and rash and infected by the suggestions of some friends and foreign soldiers, whom he kept always about him, with a passion for absolute power. He seemed to have a certain force and vehemence in all military service, and even to delight in dangers, and thus he took much with the people, and was advanced to the highest charges as a vigorous and effective warrior; in the obtaining of which offices and promotions Timoleon much assisted him, helping to conceal or at least to extenuate his errors, embellishing by his praise whatever was commendable in him, and setting off his good qualities to the best advantage.

It happened once in the battle fought by the Corinthians against the forces of Argos and Cleonæ, that Timoleon served among the infantry, when Timophanes, commanding their cavalry, was brought into extreme danger; for his horse being wounded fell forward, and threw him headlong amidst the enemies, while part of his companions dispersed at once in a panic, and the small number that remained, bearing up against a great multitude, had much ado to maintain any resistance. As soon, therefore, as Timoleon was aware of the accident, he ran hastily to his brother's rescue, and covering the fallen Timophanes with his buckler, after having received an abundance of darts and several strokes by the sword upon his body and his armor, he at length with much difficulty obliged the enemies to retire, and brought off his brother alive and safe. But when the Corinthians, for fear of losing their city a second time, as they had once before, by admitting their allies, made a decree to maintain four hundred mercenaries for its security, and gave Timophanes the command over them, he, abandoning all regard for honor and equity, at once proceeded to put into execution his plans for making himself absolute, and bringing the place under his own power; and having cut off many principal citizens, uncondemned and without trial, who were most likely to hinder his design, he declared himself tyrant of Corinth; a procedure that infinitely afflicted Timoleon, to whom the wickedness of such a brother appeared to be his own reproach and calamity. He undertook to persuade him by reasoning to desist from that wild and unhappy ambition, and bethink himself how he could make the Corinthians some amends, and find out an expedient to remedy the evils he had done them. When his single admonition was rejected and contemned by him, he made a second attempt, taking with him Æschylus his kinsman, brother to the wife of Timophanes, and a certain diviner, that was his friend, whom Theopompus in his history calls Satyrus. This company coming to his brother, all three of them surrounded and earnestly importuned him upon the same subject, that now at length he would listen to reason and be of another mind. But when Timophanes began first to laugh at the men's simplicity, and presently broke out into rage and indignation against them, Timoleon stepped aside from him and stood weeping with his face covered, while the other two, drawing out their swords, despatched him in a moment.

When the rumor of this act was spread about, the better and more generous of the Corinthians highly applauded Timoleon for the hatred of wrong and the greatness of soul that had made him, though of a gentle disposition and full of love and kindness for his family, think the obligations to his country stronger than the ties of consanguinity, and prefer that which is good and just before gain and interest and his own particular advantage. For the same brother, who with so much bravery had been saved by him when he fought valiantly in the cause of Corinth, he had now as nobly sacrificed for enslaving her afterward by a base and treacherous usurpation. But when he came to understand how heavily his mother took it, and that she likewise uttered the saddest complaints and most terrible imprecations against him, he went to satisfy and comfort her, but he found that she would not endure so much as to look upon him, but caused her doors to be shut that he might have no admission into her presence, and with grief at this he grew so disordered in mind and disconsolate, that he determined to put an end to his perplexity with his life, by abstaining from all manner of sustenance. But through the care and diligence of his friends, who were very persistent with him, and added force to their entreaties, he promised at last that he would endure living, provided it might be in solitude, and remote from company; so that, quitting all civil transactions and commerce with the world, for a long while after his first retirement he never came into Corinth, but wandered up and down the fields, full of anxious and tormenting thoughts, and for almost twenty years did not offer to concern himself in any honorable or public action.

THE WOUND OF PHILOPŒMEN.

CLEOMENES, king of the Lacedæmonians, surprised Megalopolis by night, forced the guards, broke in, and seized the market-place.

Awhile after, king Antigonus coming down to succor the Achæans, they marched with their united forces against Cleomenes; who, having seized the avenues, lay advantageously posted on the hills of Sellasia. Antigonus drew up close by him, with a resolution to force him in his strength. Philopœmen, with his citizens, was that day placed among the horse, next to the Illyrian foot, a numerous body of bold fighters, who completed the line of battle, forming, together with the Achæans, the reserve. Their orders were to keep their ground, and not engage till they should see a red coat lifted up on the point of a spear from the other wing, where the king fought in person. The Achæans obeyed their order and stood fast; but the Illyrians were led on by their commanders to the attack. Euclidas, the brother of Cleomenes; seeing the foot thus severed from the horse, detached the best of his light-armed men, commanding them to wheel about and charge the unprotected Illyrians in the rear. This charge put things into confusion, and Philopœmen, considering that those light-armed men could be easily repelled, went first to the king's officers to make them sensible of what the occasion required. But when they did not mind what he said, slighting him as a hare-brained fellow (as indeed he was not yet of any repute sufficient to give credit to a proposal of such importance), he charged with his own citizens, and at the first encounter disordered, and soon after put the troops to flight with great slaughter. Then, to encourage the king's army further, to bring them all upon the enemy while he was in confusion, he quitted his horse, and fighting with extreme difficulty in his heavy horseman's dress, in rough, uneven ground, full of water-courses and hollows, had both his thighs struck through with a thonged javelin. It was thrown with great force, so that the head came out on the other side, and made a severe though not a mortal wound. There he stood awhile, as if he had been shackled, unable to move. The fastening which joined the thong to the javelin made it difficult to get it drawn out, nor would anybody about him venture to do it. But the fight being now at the hottest, and likely to be quickly decided, he was transported with the desire of partaking in it, and struggled and strained so violently, setting one leg forward, the other back, that at last he broke the shaft in two, and thus got the pieces pulled out. Being in this manner set at liberty he caught up his sword, and running through the midst of those who were fighting in the first ranks, animated his men, and set them afire with emulation. Antigonus, after the victory, asked the Macedonians, to try them, how it happened that the cavalry had charged without orders before the signal? and when they answered that they were forced to it against their wills by a young man of Megalopolis, who had fallen in before it was time, Antigonus replied, smiling, "**That young man acted like an experienced commander.**"

A ROMAN TRIUMPH.

FROM THE LIFE OF PAULUS ÆMILIUS.

Paulus Æmilius, advanced in years, being nearly threescore, yet vigorous in his own person, and rich in valiant sons and sons-in-law, besides a great number of influential relations and friends, all of whom joined in urging him to yield to the desires of the people, who called him to the consulship. He at first manifested some shyness of the people, and withdrew himself from their importunity, professing reluctance to hold office; but, when they daily came to his doors, urging him to come forth to the place of election, and pressing him with noise and clamor, he acceded to their request. When he appeared amongst the candidates, it did not look as if it were to sue for the consulship, but to bring victory and success, that he came down into the Campus; with such hopes and such gladness did they all receive him there, unanimously choosing him a second time consul; nor would they suffer the lots to be cast, as was usual, to determine which province should fall to his share, but immediately decreed him the command of the Macedonian war. It is told, that when he had been proclaimed general against Perseus, and was honorably accompanied home by great numbers of people, he found his daughter Tertia, a very little girl, weeping, and taking her to him asked her why she was crying. She, catching him about the neck and kissing him, said, "O father, do you not know that Perseus is dead?" meaning a little dog of that name who had been brought up in the house with her; to which Æmilius replied, "Good fortune, my daughter; I embrace the omen." This Cicero, the orator, relates in his book on divination.

* * * * * * * *

The triumph of Æmilus over Perseus was performed after this manner.

The people erected scaffolds in the Forum, in the circuses, as they call their buildings for horse-races, and in all other parts of the city where they could best behold the show. The spectators were clad in white garments; all the temples were open, and full of garlands and perfumes; the ways were cleared and kept open by numerous officers, who drove back all who crowded into or ran across the main avenue. This triumph lasted three days. On the first, which was scarcely long enough for the sight, were to be seen the statues, pictures, and colossal images, which were taken from the enemy, drawn upon two hundred and fifty chariots. On the second, was carried in a great many wagons the finest and richest armor of the Macedonians, both of brass and steel, all newly polished and glittering; the pieces of which were piled up and arranged purposely with the greatest art, so as to seem to be tumbled in heaps carelessly and by chance; helmets were thrown upon shields, coats of mail upon greaves; Cretan targets, and Thracian bucklers and quivers of arrows, lay huddled amongst horses' bits, and through these there appeared the points of naked swords, intermixed with long Macedonian sarissas. All these arms were fastened together with just so much looseness that they struck against one another as they were drawn along, and made a harsh and alarming noise, so that, even as spoils of a conquered enemy, they could not be beheld without dread. After these wagons loaded with armor, there followed three thousand men who carried the silver that was coined, in seven hundred and fifty vessels, each of which weighed three talents, and was carried by four men. Others brought silver bowls and goblets and cups, all disposed in such order as to make the best show.

and all curious as well for their size as the solidity of their embossed work.

On the third day, early in the morning, first came the trumpeters, who did not sound as they were wont in a procession or solemn entry, but such a charge as the Romans use when they encourage the soldiers to fight. Next followed young men wearing frocks with ornamented borders, who led to the sacrifice a hundred and twenty stalled oxen, with their horns gilded, and their heads adorned with ribbons

WINE JUGS OR OINOCHOI.

and garlands; and with these were boys that carried basins for libation, of silver and gold. After this was brought the gold coin, which was divided into vessels that weighed three talents, like those that contained the silver; they were in number seventy-seven. These were followed by those that brought the consecrated bowl which Æmilius had caused to be made, that weighed ten talents, and was set with precious stones. Then were exposed to view the cups of Antigonus and Seleucus, and those of the Thericlean* make, and all the gold plate that was used at Perseus' table. Next to these

---

* Thericles, according to the more probable supposition, was a Corinthian potter: the first maker of a particular kind of cup, which long continued to bear his name.

came Perseus' chariot, in which his armor was placed, and on that his diadem. And, after a little intermission, the king's children were led captives, and with them a train of their attendants, masters, and teachers, all shedding tears, and stretching out their hands to the spectators, and making the children themselves also beg and entreat their compassion. There were two sons and a daughter whose tender age made them but little sensible of the greatness of their misery, which

MIXING BOWLS OR KROTERES.

very insensibility of their condition rendered it the more deplorable; insomuch that Perseus himself was scarcely regarded as he went along, whilst pity fixed the eyes of the Romans upon the infants; many of them could not forbear tears, and all beheld the sight with a mixture of sorrow and pleasure, until the children had passed.

After his children and their attendants came Perseus himself, clad all in black, and wearing the boots of his country; and looking like one altogether stunned and deprived of reason, through the greatness of his misfortunes. Next followed a great company of his friends and familiars, whose countenances were disfigured with grief, and who let the spectators see, by their tears and their continual looking upon Perseus, that it was his fortune they so much lamented, and that they were regardless of their own. Perseus sent to Æmilius to entreat that he might not be led in pomp, but be left out of the triumph; who, deriding, as was but just, his cowardice and fondness of life, sent him this answer, that as for that, it had been before, and was now, in his own power; giving him to understand that the disgrace could be avoided by death; which the faint-hearted man not having the spirit for, and made effeminate by I know not what hopes, allowed himself to appear as a part of his own spoils. After these were carried four hundred crowns, all made of gold, sent from the cities by their respective deputations to Æmilius, in honor of his victory. Then he himself came, seated on a chariot magnificently adorned (a man well worthy to be looked at, even without these ensigns of power), dressed in a robe of purple, interwoven with gold, and holding a laurel branch in his right hand. All the army, in like manner, with boughs of laurel in their hands, divided into their bands and companies, followed the chariot of their commander; some singing verses, according to the usual custom, mingled with raillery; others, songs of triumph, and the praise of Æmilius's deeds; who, indeed, was admired and accounted happy by all men, and unenvied by every one that was good; except so far as it seems the province of some god to lessen that happiness which is too great and inordinate, and so to mingle the affairs of human life that no one should be entirely free from calamities; but, as we read in Homer,* only those should think themselves truly blessed to whom fortune has given an equal share of good and evil.

---

* "Grief is useless; cease to lament," says Achilles to Priam, his suppliant for the body of Hector. "For thus have the gods appointed for mortal men; that they should live in vexation, while the gods themselves are untroubled. Two vessels are set upon the threshold of Zeus, of the gifts that he dispenses; one of evil things, the other of good; he who receives from both at the hand of thundering Zeus, meets at one time with evil, and at another with good; he who receives from only one, is a miserable wretch."

THE NOBLE CHARACTER OF CAIUS FABRICIUS.

FROM THE LIFE OF PYRRHUS.

CAIUS FABRICIUS, a man of highest consideration among the Romans as an honest man and a good soldier, but extremely poor, went upon an embassy to Pyrrhus to treat about prisoners that had been taken. Pyrrhus received him with much kindness, and privately would have persuaded him to accept of his gold, not for any evil purpose, but as a mark of respect and hospitable kindness. Upon Fabricius's refusal, he pressed him no further, but the next day, having a mind to discompose him, as he had never seen an elephant before, he commanded one of the largest, completely armed, to be placed behind the hangings, as they were talking together. This being done, at a given signal the hanging was drawn aside, and the elephant, raising his trunk over the head of Fabricius, made a horrid and ugly noise. He gently turned about and, smiling, said to Pyrrhus, "neither your money yesterday, nor this beast to-day make any impression upon me." At supper, amongst all sorts of things that were discoursed of, but more particularly Greece and the philosophers there, Cineas, by accident, had occasion to speak of Epicurus, and explained the opinions his followers hold about the gods and the commonwealth, and the object of life, who place the chief happiness of man in pleasure, and decline public affairs as an injury and disturbance of a happy life, and remove the gods afar off both from kindness or anger or any concern for us at all, to a life wholly without business and flowing in pleasures. Before he had done speaking, Fabricius cried out to Pyrrhus, "O Hercules! may Pyrrhus and the Samnites entertain themselves with this sort of opinions as long as they are at war with us." Pyrrhus, admiring the wisdom and gravity of the man, was the more transported with desire to make friendship instead of war with the city, and entreated him, personally, after the peace should be concluded, to accept of living with him as the chief of his ministers and generals. Fabricius answered quietly, "Sir, this will not be for your advantage, for they who now honor and admire you, when they have had experience of me, will rather choose to be governed by me, than by you." And Pyrrhus received his answer without any resentment or tyrannic passion; nay, among his friends he highly commended the great mind of Fabricius, and intrusted the prisoners to him alone, on condition that if the senate should not vote a peace, after they had conversed with their friends and celebrated the festival of Saturn, they should be remanded. And, accordingly, they were sent back after the holidays; death being decreed for any that stayed behind.

After this, when Fabricius had taken the consulate, a person came with a letter to the camp written by the king's principal physician, offering to take Pyrrhus off by poison, and so end the war without further hazard to the Romans, if he might have a reward proportionable to his service. Fabricius, despising the villany of the man, and disposing the other consul to the same opinion, sent despatches immediately to Pyrrhus to caution him against the treason. His letter was to this effect: "Caius Fabricius and Quintus Æmilius, consuls of the Romans, to Pyrrhus the king, health. You seem to have made a bad judgment both of your friends and your enemies; you will understand by reading this letter sent to us, that you are at war with honest men, and trust villains and knaves. Nor do we disclose this out of any favor to you, but lest your ruin might bring a reproach upon us, as if we had ended the war by treachery because not able to do it by force." When Pyrrhus had read the letter, and made inquiry into the treason, he punished the physician, and as an acknowledgment to the Romans sent to Rome the prisoners without ransom. But they, regarding it as at once too great a kindness from an enemy, and too great a reward for not doing a mean act to accept their prisoners so, released in return an equal number of the Tarentines and Samnites, but would admit of no debate of alliance or peace until Pyrrhus had removed his arms and forces out of Italy, and sailed back to Epirus with the same ships that brought him over.

FROM THE LIFE OF QUINTUS FABIUS MAXIMUS.

HANNIBAL was within five miles of Tarentum, when he was informed that the town had been taken by Fabius. He said openly, "Rome, then, has also got a Hannibal; as we won Tarentum, so have we lost it." And, in private with some of his confidants, he told them, for the first time, that he always thought it difficult, but now he held it impossible, with the forces he then had, to master Italy.

Upon this success, Fabius had a triumph decreed him at Rome, much more splendid than his first; they looked upon him now as a champion who had learned to cope with his antagonist, and could now easily foil his arts and prove his best skill ineffectual. And, indeed the army of Hannibal was at this time partly worn out with continual action, and partly weakened and become dissolute with over abundance and luxury. Marcus Livius, who was governor of Tarentum when it was betrayed to Hannibal, and had then retired into the citadel, which he kept till the town was retaken, was annoyed at these honors and distinctions, and, on one occasion, openly declared in the senate, that by his resistance, more than by any action of Fabius, Tarentum had been recovered; on which Fabius laughingly replied: "What you say is very true, for if Marcus Livius had not lost Tarentum, Fabius Maximus had never recovered it." The people, among other marks of gratitude, gave his son the consulship of the next year; shortly after whose entrance upon his office, there being some business on foot about provision for the war, his father, either on account of age and infirmity, or perhaps out of design to try his son, came up to him on horseback. While he was still at a distance, the young consul observed it, and bade one of his lictors command his father to alight, and tell him that, if he had any business with the consul, he should come on foot. The bystanders seemed offended at the imperiousness of the son towards a father so venerable for his age and his authority, and turned their eyes in silence towards Fabius. He, however, instantly alighted from his horse, and with open arms came up, almost running, and embracing him said, "Yes, my son, you do well, and understand what authority you have received, and over whom you are to use it. This was the way by which we and our forefathers advanced the dignity of Rome, preferring ever her honor and service to our own fathers and children."

And, in fact, it is told that the great-grandfather of Fabius, who was undoubtedly the greatest man of Rome in his time, both in reputation and authority, who had been five times consul, and had been honored with several triumphs for victories obtained by him, took pleasure in serving as lieutenant under his own son, when he went as consul to his command. And when afterwards his son had a triumph bestowed upon him for his good service, the old man followed his triumphant chariot, on horseback, as one of his attendants; and made it his glory, that while he really was, and was acknowledged to be, the greatest man in Rome, and held a father's full power over his son, he yet submitted himself to the laws and the magistrate.

THE CRUELTY OF LUCIUS CORNELIUS SYLLA.

Sylla's general personal appearance may be known by his statues; only his blue eyes, of themselves extremely keen and glaring, were rendered all the more forbidding and terrible by the complexion of his face, in which white was mixed with rough blotches of fiery red. Hence, it is said, he was surnamed Sylla, and in allusion to it one of the scurrilous jesters at Athens made the verse upon him,

> Sylla is a mulberry sprinkled o'er with meal.

Sylla being wholly bent upon slaughter, filled the city with executions without number or limit, many wholly uninterested persons falling a sacrifice to private enmity, through his permission and indulgence to his friends. At last Caius Metellus, one of the younger men, made bold in the senate to ask him what end there was of these evils, and at what point he might be expected to stop? "We do not ask you," said he, "to pardon any whom you have resolved to destroy, but to free from doubt those whom you are pleased to save." Sylla answering, that he knew not as yet whom to spare, he asked: "Will you then tell us whom you will punish?" This Sylla said he would do. These last words, some authors say, were spoken not by Metellus, but by Afidius, one of Sylla's fawning companions. Immediately upon this, without communicating with any of the magistrates, Sylla proscribed eighty persons, and notwithstanding the general indignation, after one day's respite, he posted two hundred and twenty more, and on the third again, as many. In an address to the people on this occasion, he told them he had put up as many names as he could think of; those which had escaped his memory, he would publish at a future time. He issued an edict likewise, making death the punishment of humanity, proscribing any who should dare to receive and cherish a proscribed person, without exception to brother, son, or parents. And to him who should slay any one proscribed person, he ordained two talents' reward, even were it a slave who had killed his master, or a son his father. And what was thought most unjust of all, he caused the attainder to pass upon their sons, and sons' sons, and made open sale of all their property. Nor did the proscription prevail only at Rome, but throughout all the cities of Italy the effusion of blood was such that neither sanctuary of the gods nor hearth of hospitality nor ancestral home escaped. Men were butchered in the embraces of their wives, children in the arms of their mothers. Those who perished through public animosity, or private enmity, were nothing in comparison to the numbers of those who suffered for their riches. Even the murderers began to say, that "his fine house killed this man, a garden that, a third, his hot baths." Quintus Aurelius, a quiet, peaceable man, and one who thought all his part in the common calamity consisted in condoling with the misfortunes of others, coming into the forum to read the list, and finding himself among the proscribed, cried out, "Woe is me, my Alban farm has informed against me." He had not gone far, before he was despatched by a ruffian, sent on that errand.

In the meantime Marius, on the point of being taken, killed himself; and Sylla, coming to Præneste, at first proceeded judicially against each particular person, till at last, finding it a work of too much time, he cooped them up together in one place, to the number of twelve thousand men

and gave order for the execution of them all, his own host*
alone excepted. But he, brave man, telling him he could not
accept the obligation of life from the hands of one who had
been the ruin of his country, went in among the rest, and
submitted willingly to the stroke.

---

* The friend, that is, with whom he always stayed when he happened to be at Præneste
his *xenos;* a relationship much regarded in the Greek and Roman world.

THE LUXURY OF LUCULLUS.

LUCULLUS's life, like the Old Comedy, presents us at the commencement with acts of policy and of war, and at the end offers nothing but good eating and drinking, feastings and revelings, and mere play. For I give no higher name to his sumptuous buildings, porticos and baths, still less to his paintings and sculptures, and all his industry about these curiosities, which he collected with vast expense, lavishly bestowing all the wealth and treasure which he got in the war upon them, insomuch that even now, with all the advance of luxury, the Lucullean gardens are counted the noblest the emperor has. Tubero, the stoic, when he saw his buildings at Naples, where he suspended the hills upon vast tunnels, brought in the sea for moats and fish-ponds round his house, and pleasure-houses in the waters, called him Xerxes in a gown. He had also fine seats in Tusculum, belvederes, and large open balconies for men's apartments, and porticos to walk in, where Pompey coming to see him, blamed him for making a house which would be pleasant in summer, but uninhabitable in winter; whom he answered with a smile, "You think me, then, less provident than cranes and storks, not to change my home with the season." When a prætor, with great expense and pains, was preparing a spectacle for the people, and asked him to lend him some purple robes for the performers in a chorus, he told him he would go home and see, and if he had any, would let him take them; and the next day asking how many he wanted, and being told that a hundred would suffice,

WALL DECORATION FROM POMPEII.

bade him take twice as many: on which the poet Horace observes, that a house is indeed a poor one, where the valuables unseen and unthought of do not exceed all those that meet the eye.

Lucullus's daily entertainments were ostentatiously extravagant, not only in purple coverlets, and plate adorned with precious stones, and dancings, and interludes, but with the greatest diversity of dishes and the most elaborate cookery, for the vulgar to admire and envy. It was a happy thought of Pompey in his sickness, when his physician prescribed a thrush for his dinner, and his servants told him that in summer time thrushes were not to be found anywhere but in Lucullus's fattening coops, that he would not suffer them to fetch one thence, but observed to his physician, "So if Lucullus had not been an epicure, Pompey had not lived," and ordered something else that could easily be got to be prepared for him. Cato was his friend and connection, but, nevertheless, so hated his life and habits, that when a young man in the senate made a long and tedious speech in praise of frugality and temperance, Cato got up and said, "How long do you mean to go making money like Crassus, living like Lucullus, and talking like Cato?"

It is plain from the anecdotes on record of him, that Lucullus was not only pleased with, but even gloried in his way of living. For he is said to have feasted several Greeks upon their coming to Rome day after day, who, out of a true Grecian principle, being ashamed, and declining the invitation, where so great an expense was every day incurred for them, he with a smile said to them, "Some of this, indeed, my Grecian friends, is for your sakes, but more for that of Lucullus." Once when he supped alone, there being only one course, and that but moderately furnished, he called his steward and reproved him, who, professing to have supposed that there would be no need of any great entertainment, when nobody was invited, was answered, "What, did you not know, then, that to-day Lucullus was to dine with Lucullus?" This being much spoken of about the city, Cicero and Pompey one day met him loitering in the forum, the former his intimate friend and familiar, and, though there had been some ill-will between Pompey and him about the command in the war, still they used to see each other and converse on easy terms together. Cicero accordingly saluted him, and asked him whether to-day was a good time for asking a favor of him, and on his answering, "Very much so," and begging to hear what it was, Cicero said, "then we should like to dine with you to-day, just on the dinner that is prepared for yourself." Lucullus being surprised, and requesting a day's time, they refused to grant it, and would not allow him to talk with his servants, for fear he should give orders for more than was appointed before. But this they consented to, that before their faces he might tell his servant, that to-day he would sup in "the Apollo" (for so one of his best dining-rooms was called), and by this evasion he outwitted his guests. For every room, as it seems, had its own assessment of expenditure, dinner at such a price, and all else in accordance; so that the servants, on knowing where he would dine, knew also how much was to be expended, and in what style and form dinner was to be served. The expense for the Apollo was fifty thousand drachmas, and such a sum being that day laid out, the greatness of the cost did not so much amaze Pompey and Cicero, as the rapidity of the outlay. One might believe that Lucullus thought his money really captive and barbarian, so wantonly and contumeliously did he treat it.

His furnishing of a library, however, deserves praise and record, for he collected very many choice manuscripts; and the use they were put to was even more magnificent than the purchase, the library being always open, and the walks and reading-rooms about it free to all Greeks, whose delight it was to leave their other occupations and hasten thither as to the habitation of the Muses, there walking about, and diverting one another. He himself often passed his hours there, disputing with the learned in the walks, and giving his advice to statesmen who required it, insomuch that his house was altogether a home, and, in a manner. a Greek prytaneum for those that visited Rome.

FROM THE
LIFE OF SERTORIUS THE ROMAN

WHO ENDEAVORED TO ESTABLISH A SEPARATE GOVERNMENT FOR HIMSELF IN SPAIN.

SERTORIUS was highly honored for his introducing discipline and good order among the Spaniards, for he altered their furious and savage manner of fighting, and brought them to make use of the Roman armor, taught them to keep their ranks, and observe signals and watchwords; and out of a confused horde of thieves and robbers, he constituted a regular, well-disciplined army. He bestowed silver and gold upon them liberally to gild and adorn their helmets, he had their shields worked with various figures and designs, he brought them into the mode of wearing flowered and embroidered cloaks and coats, and by supplying money for these purposes, and joining with them in all improvements, he won the hearts of all. That, however, which delighted them most, was the care that he took of their children. He sent for all the boys of noblest parentage out of all their tribes, and placed them in the great city of Osca, where he appointed masters to instruct them in the Grecian and Roman learning, that when they came to be men, they might, as he professed, be fitted to share with him in authority, and in conducting the government, although under this pretext he really made them hostages. However, their fathers were wonderfully pleased to see their children going daily to the schools in good order, hand somely dressed in gowns edged with purple, and that Sertorius paid for their lessons, examined them often, distributed rewards to the most deserving, and gave them the golden bosses to hang around their necks, which the Romans called "bullæ."

All the cities on this side of the river Ebro finally united their forces under his command, and his army grew very great, for they flocked together and flowed in upon him from all quarters. But when they continually cried out to attack the enemy, and were impatient of delay, their inexperienced, disorderly rashness caused Sertorius much trouble, who at first strove to restrain them with reason and good counsel, but when he perceived them refractory and unseasonably violent, he gave way to their impetuous desires, and permitted them to engage with the enemy, in such a way that they might be repulsed, yet not totally routed, and so become more obedient to his commands for the future. This happening as he had anticipated, he soon rescued them, and brought them safe into his camp. And after a few days, being willing to encourage them again, when he had called all his army together, he caused two horses to be brought into the field, one an old, feeble, lean animal, the other a lusty, strong horse, with a remarkably thick and long tail. Near the lean one he placed a tall, strong man, and near the strong, young horse a weak, despicable-looking fellow; and at a given signal the strong man took hold of the weak horse's tail with both his hands, and drew it to him with his whole force, as if he would pull it off; the other, the weak man, in the meantime, set to work to pluck off hair by hair the great horse's tail. And when the strong man had given trouble enough to himself in vain, and sufficient diversion to the company, and had abandoned his attempt, whilst the weak, pitiful fellow in a short time and with little pains had left not a hair on the great horse's tail, Sertorius arose and said to his army, "You see, fellow-soldiers, that perseverance is more prevailing than violence, and that many things which cannot be overcome when they are together, yield readily when taken little by little. Assiduity and persistence are irresistible, and in time overthrow and destroy the greatest powers. Time being the favorable friend and assistant of those who use their judgment to await his occasions, and the destructive enemy of those who are unseasonably urging and pressing forward."

Of all his remarkable exploits, none raised greater admiration than that which he put in practice against the Characitanians. These are a people beyond the river Tagus, who inhabit neither cities nor towns, but live in a vast, high hill, within the deep dens and caves of the rocks, the mouths of which all open towards the north. The country below is of a soil resembling a light clay, so loose as easily to break into powder, and is not firm enough to bear any one that treads upon it, and if you touch it in the least, it flies about like ashes or unslaked lime. In any danger of war, these people enter their caves, and carrying in their booty and prey along with them, stay quietly within, secure from every attack. And when Sertorius, leaving Metellus some distance off, had placed his camp near this hill, they slighted and despised him, imagining that he retired into these parts to escape being overthrown by the Romans. And whether out of anger and resentment, or out of his unwillingness to be thought to fly from his enemies, early in the morning he rode up to view the situation of the place. But finding there was no way to come at it, as he rode about, threatening them in vain and disconcerted, he took notice that the wind raised the dust and carried it up towards the caves of the Characitanians, and the northerly wind, which some call Cæcias, prevailing most in those parts, coming up out of moist plains or mountains covered with snow, at this particular time, in the heat of summer, being further supplied and increased by the melting of the ice in the northern regions, blew a delightful, fresh gale, cooling and refreshing the Characitanians and their cattle all the day long. Sertorius, considering well all circumstances in which either the information of the inhabitants, or his own experience had instructed him, commanded his soldiers to shovel up a great quantity of this light, dusty earth, to heap it together, and make a mound of it over against the hill in which these barbarous people lived, who, imagining that all this preparation was for raising a mound to get at them, only mocked and laughed at it. However, he continued the work till the evening, and brought his soldiers back into their camp. The next morning a gentle breeze at first arose, and moved the lightest parts of the earth, and dispersed it about as the chaff before the wind; but when the sun got higher, and the strong, northerly wind had covered the hills with the dust, the soldiers came and turned this mound of earth over and over, and broke the hard clods in pieces, whilst others on horseback rode through it backward and forward, and raised a cloud of dust into the air; then with the wind the whole of it was carried away and blown into the dwellings of the Characitanians, all lying open to the north. And there being no other vent or breathing-place than that through which the Cæcias rushed in upon them, it quickly blinded their eyes, and filled their lungs, and all but choked them, whilst they strove to draw in the rough air mingled with dust and powdered earth. Nor were they able, with all they could do, to hold out more than two days, but surrendered on the third, adding, by their defeat, not so much to the power of Sertorius, as to his renown, in proving that he was able to conquer places by art, which were impregnable by the force of arms.

THE SCROLL.

FROM THE LIFE OF LYSANDER.

THE scroll is made up thus: when the Ephors send an admiral or general on his way, they take two round pieces of wood, both exactly of a length and thickness, and cut even to one another; they keep one themselves, and the other they give to the person they send forth; and these pieces of wood they call Scytales. When, therefore, they have occasion to communicate any secret or important matter, making a scroll of parchment long and narrow like a leathern thong, they roll it about their own staff of wood, leaving no space void between, but covering the surface of the staff with the scroll all over. When they have done this, they write what they please on the scroll, as it is wrapped about the staff; and when they have written, they take off the scroll, and send it to the general without the wood. He, when he has received it, can read nothing of the writing, because the words and letters are not connected, but all broken up; but taking his own staff, he winds the slip of the scroll about it, so that this folding, restoring all the parts into the same order that they were in before, and putting what comes first into connection with what follows, brings the whole consecutive contents to view round the outside. And this scroll is called a *staff*, after the name of the wood, as a thing measured is by the name of the measure

THE CHARACTER OF MARCUS CATO.

Marcus Cato grew so powerful by his eloquence that he was commonly called the Roman Demosthenes; but his manner of life was yet more famous and talked of. For oratorical skill was, as an accomplishment, commonly studied and sought after by all young men; but he was a rare man who would cultivate the old habits of bodily labor, or prefer a light supper, and a breakfast which never saw the fire; or be in love with poor clothes and a homely lodging, or could set his ambition rather on doing without luxuries than on possessing them. For now the state, unable to keep its purity by reason of its greatness, and having so many affairs, and people from all parts under its government, was fain to admit many mixed customs, and new examples of living. With reason, therefore, everybody admired Cato, when they saw others sink under labors, and grow effeminate by pleasures, but beheld him unconquered by either; and that, too, not only when he was young and desirous of honor, but also when old and grayheaded, after a consulship and triumph; like some famous victor in the games, persevering in his exercise and maintaining his character to the very last. He himself says, that he never wore a suit of clothes which cost more than a hundred drachmas; and that, when he was general and consul, he drank the same wine which his workmen did; and that the meat or fish which was bought in the market for his dinner, did not cost above thirty *asses*. All which was for the sake of the commonwealth, that his body might be the hardier for the war. Having a piece of embroidered Babylonian tapestry left him, he sold it; because none of his farm-houses were so much as plastered. Nor did he ever buy a slave for above fifteen hundred drachmas; as he did not seek for effeminate and handsome ones, but able, sturdy workmen, horse-keepers, and cow-herds; and these he thought ought to be sold again, when they grew old, and no useless servants fed in a house. In short, he reckoned nothing a good bargain, which was superfluous; but whatever it was, though sold for a farthing, he would think it a great price, if you had no need of it.

Yet, in my judgment, it marks an over-rigid temper for a man to take the work out of his servants as out of brute beasts, turning them off and selling them in their old age. A kind-natured man will keep even worn-out horses and dogs, and not only take care of them when they are foals and whelps, but also when they are grown old. The Athenians, when they built their Hecatompedon,* turned those mules loose to feed freely, which they had observed to have done the hardest labor. One of these came once of itself to offer its service, and ran along with, nay, went before, the teams which drew the wagons up to the Acropolis, as if it would incite and encourage them to draw more stoutly; upon which a vote was passed that the creature should be kept at the public charge till it died. The graves of Cimon's horses, which thrice won the Olympian races, are yet to be seen close by his own monument. Old Xanthippus, too, the father of Pericles, entombed his dogs which swam after his galley to Salamis, when the people fled from Athens, on the top of a cliff, which they call the dogs' tomb to this day.

For his general temperance, however, and self-control, Cato really deserves the highest admiration. For when he commanded the army, he never took for himself, and those that belonged to him, more than three bushels of wheat for a month,

---

* The Parthenon; built on the site of an older temple which had borne the name of Hecatompedon, or a "hundred feet long." The name was retained for the new building.

and somewhat less than a bushel and a half a day of barley for his baggage-cattle. And when he entered upon the government of Sardinia, where his predecessors had been used to require tents, bedding, and clothes upon the public account, and to charge the state heavily with the cost of provisions and entertainments for a great train of servants and friends, the difference he showed in his economy was something incredible. There was nothing of any sort for which he put the public to expense; he would walk, instead of taking a carriage to visit the cities, with only one of the common town officers, who carried his dress, and a cup to offer libation with. Yet, on the other hand, he showed most inflexible severity and strictness, in what related to public justice, and was rigorous, and precise in what concerned the ordinances of the commonwealth; so that the Roman government never seemed more terrible, nor yet more mild, than under his administration.

His very manner of speaking seemed to have such a kind of idea with it; for it was courteous, and yet forcible; pleasant, yet overwhelming; facetious, yet austere; sententious, and yet vehement: like Socrates, in the description of Plato, who seemed outwardly to those about him to be but a simple, talkative, blunt fellow; whilst at the bottom he was full of such gravity and matter, as would even move tears, and touch the very hearts of his auditors. Reproving on one occasion the sumptuous habits of the Romans, he said: "It is hard to preserve a city, where a fish is sold for more than an ox." He had a saying, also, that the Roman people were like sheep; for they, when single, do not obey, but when altogether in a flock, they follow their leaders: "So you," said he, "when you have got together in a body, let yourselves be guided by those whom singly you would never think of being advised by."

The Romans having sent three ambassadors to Bithynia, of whom one was gouty, another had his skull trepanned, and the other seemed little better than a fool; Cato, laughing, gave out, that the Romans had sent an embassy, which had neither feet, head, nor heart.*

Cato also said that in his whole life he most repented of three things; one was, that he had trusted a secret to a woman; another, that he went by water when he might have gone by land; the third, that he had remained one whole day without doing any business of moment.

He was a good father, an excellent husband to his wife, and an extraordinary economist; and as he did not manage his affairs of this kind carelessly, and as things of little moment, I think I ought to record a little further whatever was commendable in him in these points. He married a wife more noble than rich; being of opinion that the rich and the high-born are equally haughty and proud; but that those of noble blood would be more ashamed of base things, and consequently more obedient to their husbands in all that was fit and right. A man who beat his wife or child, laid violent hands, he said, on what was most sacred; and a good husband he reckoned worthy of more praise than a great senator; and he admired the ancient Socrates for nothing so much, as for having lived a temperate and contented life with a wife who was a scold, and children who were half-witted.

When his son began to come to years of discretion, Cato himself would teach him to read, although he had a servant, a very good grammarian, called Chilo, who taught many others; but he thought not fit, as he himself said, to have his son reprimanded by a slave, or pulled, it may be, by the ears when found tardy in his lesson: nor would he have him owe to a servant the obligation of so great a thing as his learning; he himself, therefore, taught him his grammar, his law, and his gymnastic exercises. Nor did he only show him, too, how to

---

* Both the Romans and the Greeks conceived of the region of the heart, the chest, as the seat not of emotion, nor of will and courage merely, but more especially of judgment, deliberation, and practical sense. Thus the Greeks derived their word for moral wisdom from *phren*, the diaphragm, and the Romans by *egregie cordatus homo* meant a wise statesman.

throw a dart, to fight in armor, and to ride, but to box also and to endure both heat and cold, and to swim over the most rapid and rough rivers. He says, likewise, that he wrote histories, in large characters, with his own hand, that so his son, without stirring out of the house, might learn to know about his countrymen and forefathers: nor did he less abstain from speaking any thing improper before his son, than if it had been in the presence of the sacred virgins, called vestals. Nor would he ever go into the bath with him; which seems indeed to have been the common custom of the Romans.

Thus, like an excellent work, Cato formed and fashioned his son to virtue.

THE SACRED THEBAN BAND.

FROM THE LIFE OF PELOPIDAS.

Gorgidas, according to some, first formed the Sacred Band of three hundred chosen men, to whom, as being a guard for the citadel, the State allowed provision, and all things necessary for exercise: and hence they were called the city band, as citadels of old were usually called cities. Others say that it was composed of young men attached to each other by personal affection, and a pleasant saying of Pammenes is current, that Homer's Nestor was not well skilled in ordering an army, when he advised the Greeks to rank tribe and tribe, and family and family together, that

> So tribe might tribe, and kinsmen kinsmen aid,

but that he should have joined lovers and their beloved. For men of the same tribe or family little value one another when dangers press; but a band cemented by friendship grounded upon love, is never to be broken, and invincible; since all, ashamed to be base in sight of their beloved, willingly rush into danger for the relief of one another. Nor can that be wondered at; since they have more regard for their absent loving friends than for others present; as in the instance of the man who, when his enemy was going to kill him, earnestly requested him to run him through the breast, that his lover might not blush to see him wounded in the back. It is a tradition likewise, that Iolaüs, who assisted Hercules in his labors and fought at his side, was beloved of him; and

FROM THE
LIFE OF TITUS FLAMININUS,
THE CONQUEROR OF PHILIP.

AMONG the songs written after the battle of Cynos Cephalas (the Dog-heads), was the following epigram, composed by Alcæus in mockery of Philip, exaggerating the number of the slain:

> Naked and tombless see, O passer-by,
> The thirty thousand men of Thessaly,
> Slain by the Ætolians and the Latin band,
> That came with Titus from Italia's land:
> Alas for mighty Macedon! that day,
> Swift as a roe, king Philip fled away.

Titus himself thought more highly of his liberation of Greece than of any other of his actions, as appears by the inscription upon some silver targets, dedicated together with his own shield, to Apollo at Delphi:

> Ye Spartan Tyndarids, twin sons of Jove,
> Who in swift horsemanship have placed your love,
> Titus, of great Æneas' race, leaves this
> In honor of the liberty of Greece.

And a golden crown, also offered to Apollo, bore this inscription:

> This golden crown upon thy locks divine,
> O blest Latona's son, was set to shine

> By the great captain of the Ænean name,
> O Phœbus, grant the noble Titus fame!

When the ambassadors of Antiochus were recounting to those of Achæa, the various multitudes composing their royal master's forces, and ran over a long catalogue of hard names, "I supped once," said Titus, "with a friend, and could not forbear expostulating with him at the number of dishes he had provided, and said I wondered where he had furnished himself with such a variety; 'Sir,' replied he, 'to confess the truth, it is all hog's flesh differently cooked.' And so, men of Achæa, when you are told of Antiochus's lancers, and pikemen, and foot-guards, I advise you not to be surprised; since in fact they are all Syrians differently armed."

The Chalcidians, who owed their lives to Titus, dedicated to him all the best and most magnificent of their sacred buildings, inscriptions upon which, like the following, may be seen to this day: THE PEOPLE DEDICATE THIS GYMNASIUM TO TITUS AND TO HERCULES; so again: THE PEOPLE CONSECRATE THE DELPHINIUM TO TITUS AND TO HERCULES; and what is yet more remarkable, even in our time, a priest of Titus was formally elected and declared; and after sacrifice and libation, they sang a set song, of which these are the closing verses:—

> The Roman Faith, whose aid of yore,
> Our vows were offered to implore,
> We worship now and evermore.
> To Rome, to Titus, and to Jove,
> O maidens, in the dances move.
> Dances and Io-Pæans too
> Unto the Roman Faith are due,
> O Savior Titus, and to you.

ALEXANDER.

It must be borne in mind that my design has been not to write histories, but lives. And the most glorious exploits do not always furnish us with the clearest discoveries of virtue or vice in men; sometimes a matter of less moment, an expression or a jest, informs us better of their characters and inclinations, than the most famous sieges, the greatest armaments, or the bloodiest battles whatsoever. Therefore as portrait-painters are more exact in the lines and features of the face, in which the character is seen, than in the other parts of the body, so I must be allowed to give my more particular attention to the marks and indications of the souls of men, in my portrayal of their lives.

It is agreed on by all hands, that on the father's side, Alexander descended from Hercules by Caranus, and from Æacus by Neoptolemus on the mother's side. His father Philip, being in Samothrace, when he was quite young, fell in love there with Olympias, in company with whom he was initiated in the religious ceremonies of the country, and her father and mother being both dead, soon after, with the consent of her brother Arymbas, he married her.

Alexander was born on the sixth of Hecatombæon, the same day that the temple of Diana at Ephesus was burnt. The statues that gave the best representation of Alexander's person, were those of Lysippus, those peculiarities which many of his successors afterwards and his friends used to affect to imitate,—the inclination of his head a little on one side towards his left shoulder, and his melting eye,—having been expressed by this artist with great exactness. But Apelles, who drew him with thunderbolts in his hand, made his complexion browner and darker than it was naturally; for he was fair and of a light color, passing into ruddiness in his face and upon his breast. His temperance, as to all pleasures, was apparent in him in his very childhood, as he was with much difficulty incited to them, and always used them with great moderation; though in other things he was extremely eager and vehement, and in his love of glory and the pursuit of it, he showed a solidity of high spirit and magnanimity far above his age. For he neither sought nor valued it upon every occasion, as his father Philip did (who affected to show his eloquence almost to a degree of pedantry, and took care to have the victories of his racing chariots at the Olympic games engraved on his coin), but when he was asked by some about him, whether he would run a race in the Olympic games, as he was very swift-footed, he answered, that he would, if he might have kings to run with him.

While he was yet very young, he entertained the ambassadors from the king of Persia, in the absence of his father, and entering much into conversation with them, gained so much upon them by his affability, and the questions he asked them, which were far from being childish or trifling (for he inquired of them the length of the ways, the nature of the road into inner Asia, the character of their king, how he carried himself toward his enemies, and what forces he was able to bring into the field), that they were struck with admiration of him, and looked upon the ability so much famed of Philip, to be nothing in comparison with the forwardness and high purpose that appeared thus early in his son. Whenever he heard that Philip had taken any town of importance, or won any signal victory, instead of rejoicing at it altogether, he would tell his companions that his father would anticipate every thing, and leave him and them no opportunities of performing great and illustrious actions. For being more bent upon action and glory than upon either pleasure or riches, he esteemed all that he should receive from his father as a diminution of his own future achievements; and would have chosen rather to succeed to a kingdom involved in troubles and wars, which would have afforded him frequent exercise of his courage, and a large field of honor, than to one already flourishing and settled, where his inheritance would be an inactive life, and the mere enjoyment of wealth and luxury.

The care of his education, as it might be presumed, was committed to a great many attendants, preceptors, and teachers, over the whole of whom Leonidas, a near kinsman of Olympias, a man of an austere temper, presided, who did not indeed himself decline the name of what in reality is a noble and honorable office,* but in general his dignity, and his near relationship, obtained him from other people the title of Alexander's fosterfather and governor. But he who took upon him the actual place and style of his "pedagogue," was Lysimachus the Acarnanian.

Philonicus the Thessalian brought the horse Bucephalas† to Philip, offering to sell him for thirteen talents; but when they went into the field to try him, they found him so very vicious and unmanageable, that he reared up when they endeavored to mount him, and would not so much as endure the voice of any of Philip's attendants. Upon which, as they were leading him away as wholly useless and untractable, Alexander, who stood by, said, "What a magnificent horse they lose, for want of address and boldness to manage him!" Philip at first took no notice of what he said, but when he heard him repeat the same thing several times, and perceived that he was much vexed to see the horse sent away, he said

---

* The paidagogus or pædagogus, was usually a slave, who *took the boy about.*

† Bucephalas, not Bucephalus, appears to be the correct form, though authority is not wanting for the latter

to him, "Do you reproach those who are older than yourself, as if you knew more, and were better able to manage him than they?" "I could manage this horse," replied he, "better than others do." "And if you fail," said Philip, "what will you forfeit for your rashness?" "I will pay," answered Alexander, "the whole price of the horse." At this the whole company fell to laughing; and as soon as the wager was settled amongst them, he immediately ran to the horse, and taking hold of the bridle, turned him directly towards the sun, having, it seems, observed that he was disturbed at and afraid of the motion of his own shadow; then letting him go forward a little, still keeping the reins in his hand, and stroking him gently when he found him beginning to grow eager and fiery, he let fall his upper garment softly, and with one nimble leap securely mounted him, and when he was seated, little by little drew in the bridle, and curbed him without either striking or spurring him. Presently, when he found him free from all rebelliousness, and only impatient for the course, he let him go at full speed, inciting him now with a commanding voice, and urging him also with his heel. Philip and his friends looked on at first in silence and anxiety for the result, till seeing him turn at the end of his career, and come back rejoicing and triumphing for what he had performed, they all burst out into acclamations of applause; and his father, shedding tears, it is said, for joy, kissed him as he came down from his horse, and in his tran-

ALEXANDER THE GREAT.

sport, said, "O my son, seek out a kingdom worthy of thyself for Macedonia is too little for thee."

After this, considering him to be of a temper easy to be led to his duty by reason, but by no means to be compelled, he always endeavored to persuade rather than to command or force him to any thing; and now looking upon the instruction and tuition of his youth to be of greater difficulty and importance, than to be wholly trusted to the ordinary masters in music and poetry, and the common school subjects, and to require, as Sophocles says,

> The bridle and the rudder too,

he sent for Aristotle, the most learned and most celebrated philosopher of his time, and rewarded him with a munificence proportionable to and becoming the care he took to instruct his son. For he repeopled his native city Stagira, which he had caused to be demolished a little before, and restored all the citizens who were in exile or slavery, to their habitations. As a place for the pursuit of their studies and exercises, he assigned the temple of the Nymphs, near Mieza, where, to this very day, they show you Aristotle's stone seats, and the shady walks which he was wont to frequent. It would appear that Alexander received from him not only his doctrines of Morals, and of Politics, but also something of those more abstruse and profound theories which these philosophers, by the very names they gave them, professed to reserve for oral communication to the initiated, and did not allow many to become acquainted with. For when he was in Asia, and heard Aristotle had published some treatises of that kind, he wrote to him, using very plain language to him in behalf of philosophy, the following letter: "Alexander to Aristotle greeting. You have not done well to publish your books of oral doctrine, for what is there now that we excel others in, if those things which we have been particularly instructed in be laid open to all? For my part, I assure you, I had rather excel others in the knowledge of what is excellent, than in the extent of my power and dominion. Farewell." And Aristotle, soothing this passion for pre-eminence, speaks, in his excuse for himself, of these doctrines, as in fact both published and not published. To tell the truth, his books on metaphysics are written in a style which makes them useless for ordinary teaching, and instructive only in the way of memoranda, for those who have been already conversant with that sort of learning.

Doubtless also it was to Aristotle, that he owed the inclination he had, not to the theory only, but also to the practice of the art of medicine. For when any of his friends were sick, he would often prescribe for them their course of diet, and medicines proper to their disease, as we may find in his epistles. He was naturally a great lover of all kinds of learning and reading; and Onesicritus informs us, that he constantly laid Homer's Iliads, according to the copy corrected by Aristotle, called "the casket copy," with his dagger under his pillow, declaring that he esteemed it a perfect portable treasure of all military virtue and knowledge. When he was in the upper Asia, being destitute of other books, he ordered Harpalus to send him some; who furnished him with Philistus's History, a great many of the plays of Euripides, Sophocles, and Æschylus, and some dithyrambic odes, composed by Telestes and Philoxenus.

While Philip went on his expedition against the Byzantines, he left Alexander, then sixteen years old, his lieutenant in Macedonia, committing the charge of his seal to him; who, not to sit idle, reduced the rebellious Mædi, and having taken their chief town by storm, drove out the barbarous inhabitants, and planting a colony of several nations in their room, called the place after his own name, Alexandropolis. At the battle of Chæronea, which his father fought against the Greeks, he is said to have been the first man that charged the Thebans' sacred band. And even in my remembrance, there stood an old oak near the river Cephisus, which people called Alexander's oak, because his tent was pitched under it. And not far off are to be seen the graves of the Macedonians who fell in that battle. This early bravery made Philip so fond of him, that nothing pleased him more than to hear his subjects call himself their general and Alexander their king.

But later on, through an unfortunate marriage of Philip with Cleopatra, the niece of Attalus, an estrangement grew up between them. And not long after the brother of Alexander, Pausanias, having had an insult done to him at the instance of Attalus and Cleopatra, when he found he could get no reparation for his disgrace at Philip's hands, watched his opportunity and murdered him.

Alexander was but twenty years old when his father was murdered, and succeeded to a kingdom beset on all sides with great dangers, and rancorous enemies. Hearing the Thebans were in revolt, and the Athenians in correspondence with them, he immediately marched through the pass of Thermopylæ, saying that to Demosthenes, who had called him a child while he was in Illyria, and a youth when he was in Thessaly, he would appear a man before the walls of Athens.

When he came to Thebes, to show how willing he was to accept of their repentance for what was past, he only demanded of them Phœnix and Prothytes, the authors of the rebellion, and proclaimed a general pardon to those who would come over to him. But when the Thebans merely retorted by demanding Philotas and Antipater to be delivered into their hands, he applied himself to make them feel the last extremities of war. The Thebans defended themselves with a zeal and courage beyond their strength, being much outnumbered by their enemies. But when the Macedonian garrison sallied out upon them from the citadel, they were so hemmed in on all sides, that the greater part of them fell in the battle; the city itself being taken by storm, was sacked and razed, Alexander's hope being that so severe an example might terrify the rest of Greece into obedience. So that, except the priests, and a few who had heretofore been the friends and connections of the Macedonians, the family of the poet Pindar, and those who were known to have opposed the public vote for the war, all the rest, to the number of thirty thousand, were publicly sold for slaves; and it is computed that upwards of six thousand were put to the sword. Among the other calamities that befell the city, it happened that some Thracian soldiers having broken into the house of a matron of high character and repute named Timoclea, their captain, to satisfy his avarice, asked her if she knew of any money concealed; to which she readily answered that she did, and bade him follow her into a garden, where she showed him a well, into which, she told him, upon the taking of the city she had thrown what she had of most value. The greedy Thracian presently stooping down to view the place where he thought the treasure lay, she came behind him, and pushed him into the well, and then flung great stones in upon him, till she had killed him. After which, when the soldiers led her away bound to Alexander, her very mien and gait showed her to be a woman of dignity and high mind, not betraying the least sign of fear or astonishment. And when the king asked her who she was, she said, "I am the sister of Theagenes, who fought at the battle of Chæronea with your father Philip, and fell there in command for the liberty of Greece." Alexander was so surprised, both at what she had done, and what she said, that he could not chose but give her and her children their freedom to go whither they pleased.

After this he received the Athenians into favor. Whether it were, like the lion, that his passion was now satisfied, or that after an example of extreme cruelty, he had a mind to appear merciful, it happened well for the Athenians. Certain it is, too, that in after-time he often repented of his severity to the Thebans, and his remorse had such influence on his temper as to make him ever after less rigorous to all others.

And it was observed that whatsoever any Theban, who had the good fortune to survive this victory, asked of him, he was sure to grant without the least difficulty.

Soon after, the Greeks being assembled at the Isthmus, declared their resolution of joining with Alexander in the war against the Persians, and proclaimed him their general. While he stayed here, many public ministers and philosophers came from all parts to visit him, and congratulated him on his election, but contrary to his expectation, Diogenes of Sinope, who then was living at Corinth, thought so little of him,

THERAMENES DRAGGED FROM THE ALTAR BY ORDER OF CRITIAS.

that instead of coming to compliment him, he never so much as stirred out of the suburb called the Cranium, where Alexander ran across him lying at full length in the sun. When he saw so much company near him, he raised himself a little, and vouchsafed to look upon Alexander; and when he kindly asked him whether he wanted any thing, "Yes," said he, "I would have you stand from between me and the sun." Alexander was so struck at this answer, and surprised at the greatness of the man, who had taken so little notice of him, that as he went away, he told his followers who were laughing at the moroseness of the philosopher, that if he were not Alexander, he would choose to be Diogenes.

His army consisted of about thirty thousand foot, and four thousand horse; and Aristobulus says, he had not a fund of over seventy talents for their pay, nor more than thirty days' provision, if we may believe Duris. However narrow the beginnings of so vast an undertaking might seem to be, yet he would not embark his army until he had informed himself particularly what means his friends had to enable them to follow him, and supplied what they wanted, by giving good farms to some, a village to one, and the revenue of some hamlet or harbor town to another. So that at last he had portioned out or engaged almost all the royal property; which giving Perdiccas an occasion to ask him what he would leave himself, he answered, " My hopes." " Your soldiers," replied Perdiccas, "will be your partners in those," and refused to accept of the estate he had assigned him.

With such vigorous resolutions, and his mind thus disposed, he passed the Hellespont, and at Troy sacrificed to Minerva, and honored the memory of the heroes who were buried there, with solemn libations; especially Achilles, whose gravestone he anointed, and with his friends, as the ancient custom is, ran naked about his sepulchre, and crowned it with garlands, declaring how happy he esteemed him, in having, while he lived, so faithful a friend, and when he was dead, so famous a poet to proclaim his actions. While he was viewing the rest of the antiquities and curiosities of the place, being told he might see Paris's harp, if he pleased, he said, he thought it not worth looking at, but he should be glad to see that of Achilles,[*] to which he used to sing the glories and great actions of brave men.

In the meantime Darius's captains having collected large

---

[*] Iliad, IX. 189. When Ajax, Ulysses, and Phœnix came with the offers of reconciliation from Agamemnon, they found Achilles seated with Patroclus in the tent, singing to his harp " the glories of men."

forces, were encamped on the further bank of the river Granicus, and it was necessary to fight, as it were, in the gate of Asia for an entrance into it. And when Parmenio advised him not to attempt anything that day, because it was late, he told him that he should disgrace the Hellespont, should he fear the Granicus. And so without saying more, he immediately took the river with thirteen troops of horse, and advanced against whole showers of darts thrown from the steep opposite side, which was covered with armed multitudes of the enemy's horse and foot, notwithstanding the disadvantage of the ground and the rapidity of the stream; so that the action seemed to have more of frenzy and desperation in it, than of prudent conduct. However, he persisted obstinately to gain the passage, and at last with much ado making his way up the banks, which were extremely muddy and slippery, he had instantly to join in a mere confused hand-to-hand combat with the enemy, before he could draw up his men, who were still passing over, into any order. For the enemy pressed upon him with loud and warlike outcries; and charging horse against horse, with their lances, after they had broken and spent these, they fell to it with their swords. And Alexander, being easily known by his buckler, and a large plume of white feathers on each side of his helmet, was attacked on all sides, yet escaped without a wound, though his cuirass was pierced by a javelin in one of the joinings. And Rhœsaces and Spithridates, two Persian commanders, falling upon him at once, he avoided one of them, and struck at Rhœsaces, who had a good cuirass on, with such force, that his spear breaking in his hand, he was glad to betake himself to his dagger. While they were thus engaged, Spithridates came up on the other side of him, and raising himself upon his horse, gave him such a blow with his battle-axe on the helmet, that he cut off the crest of it, with one of his plumes, and the helmet was only just so far strong enough to save him, that the edge of the weapon touched the hair of his head. But as he was about to repeat his stroke, Clitus, called the black Clitus, prevented him, by running him through the body with his spear. At the same time Alexander despatched Rhœsaces with his sword. While the horse were thus dangerously engaged, the Macedonian phalanx passed the river, and the foot on each side advanced to fight. But the enemy hardly sustaining the first onset, soon gave ground and fled, all but the mercenary Greeks, who, making a stand upon a rising ground, desired quarter, which Alexander, guided rather by passion than judgment, refused to grant, and charging them himself first, had his horse (not Bucephalas, but another) killed under him. And this obstinacy of his to cut off these experienced, desperate men, cost him the lives of more of his own soldiers than all the battle before, besides those who were wounded. The Persians lost in this battle twenty thousand foot, and two thousand five hundred horse. On Alexander's side, Aristobulus says there were not over four and thirty missing, of whom nine were foot-soldiers; and in memory of them he caused as many statues of brass, of Lysippus's making, to be erected. And that the Greeks might participate in the honor of his victory, he sent a portion of the spoils home to them, particularly to the Athenians three hundred bucklers, and upon all the rest he ordered this inscription to be set : " Alexander the son of Philip, and the Greeks, except the Lacedæmonians, won these from the barbarians who inhabit Asia." All the plate and purple garments, and other things of the same kind that he took from the Persians, except a very small quantity which he reserved for himself, he sent as a present to his mother.

This battle presently made a great change of affairs to Alexander's advantage. For Sardis itself, the chief seat of the barbarians' power in the maritime provinces, and many other considerable places, were surrendered to him ; only Halicarnassus and Miletus stood out, which he took by force, together with the territory about them. After which he was a little unsettled in his opinion how to proceed. Sometimes he thought it best to find out Darius as soon as he could, and put all to the hazard of a battle; at another time he looked upon it as a more prudent course to make an entire reduction of the sea-coast, and not to seek the enemy till he had first exercised his power here and made himself secure of the resources of these provinces. While he was thus deliberating what to do, it happened that a spring of water near the city of Xanthus in Lycia, of its own accord swelled over its banks, and threw up a copper plate upon the margin, in which was engraven in ancient characters, that the time would come, when the Persian empire should be destroyed by the Greeks. Encouraged by this incident, he proceeded to reduce the maritime parts of Cilicia and Phœnicia, and passed his army along the sea-coasts of Pamphylia with such expedition that many historians have described and extolled it with a height of admiration, as if it were no less than a miracle, and an extraordinary effect of divine favor, that the waves which usually come rolling in violently from the main, and hardly ever leave so much as a narrow beach under the steep, broken cliffs at any time uncovered, should on a sudden retire to afford him passage. Menander, in one of his comedies alludes to this marvel when he says,

> Was Alexander ever favored more?
> Each man I wish for meets me at my door,
> And should I ask for passage through the sea,
> The sea, I doubt not, would retire for me.

Then he subdued the Pisidians who made head against him, and conquered the Phrygians, at whose chief city Gordium, which is said to be the seat of the ancient Midas, he saw the famous chariot fastened with cords made of the rind of the cornel-tree, about which the inhabitants had a tradition, that for him who should untie it, was reserved the empire of the world. Most authors tell the story that Alexander, finding himself unable to untie the knot, the ends of which were secretly twisted round and folded up within it, cut it asunder with his sword. But Aristobulus tells us it was easy for him to undo it, by only pulling the pin out of the pole, to which the yoke was tied, and afterwards drawing off the yoke itself from below.

Darius was by this time upon his march from Susa, very confident, in the number of his men, which amounted to six hundred thousand. But Alexander was detained in Cilicia by a sickness, which some say he contracted from his fatigues, others from bathing in the river Cydnus, whose waters were exceedingly cold. None of his physicians would venture to give him any remedies, they thought his case so desperate, and were so afraid of the suspicions and ill-will of the Macedonians if they should fail in the cure; till Philip, the Acarnanian, seeing how critical his case was, but relying on his own well-known friendship for him, resolved to try the last efforts of his art, and rather hazard his own credit and life, than suffer him to perish for want of physic, which he confidently administered to him, encouraging him to take it boldly, if he desired a speedy recovery, in order to prosecute the war. At this very time, Parmenio wrote to Alexander from the camp, bidding him have a care of Philip, as one who was bribed by Darius to kill him, with great sums of money, and a promise of his daughter in marriage. When he had perused the letter, he put it under his pillow, without so much as showing it to any of his most intimate friends, and when Philip came in with the -potion, he took it with great cheerfulness and assurance, giving him meantime the letter to read. This was a spectacle well worth being present at, to see Alexander take the draught, and Philip read the letter at the same time, and then turn and look upon one another, but with different sentiments; for Alexander's looks were cheerful and open, to show his kindness to and confidence in his physician, while the other was full of surprise and alarm at the accusation, appealing to the gods to witness his innocence, sometimes lifting up his hands to heaven, and then throwing himself down by the bedside, and beseeching Alexander to lay aside all fear, and follow his directions without apprehension. For the medicine at first worked so strongly as to drive, as it were, the vital forces into the interior; he lost his speech, and falling into a swoon, had scarcely any sense or pulse left. However, in a very short time, by Philip's means, his health and strength returned, and he showed himself in public to the Macedonians, who were in continual fear and dejection until they saw him abroad again.

Darius, in the meantime marched into Cilicia, at the same time that Alexander advanced into Syria to meet him; and missing one another in the night, they both turned back again. Alexander, greatly pleased with the event, made all the haste he could to fight in the defiles, and Darius to recover his former ground, and draw his army out of so disadvantageous a place. For now he began to see his error in engaging himself too far in a country in which the sea, the mountains, and the river Pinarus running through the midst of it, would force him to divide his forces, render his horse almost unserviceable, and only cover and support the weakness of the enemy. Fortune was not kinder to Alexander in the choice of the ground, than he was careful to improve it to his advantage. For being much inferior in numbers, so far from allowing himself to be outflanked, he stretched his right wing much further out than the left wing of his enemies, and fighting there himself in the very foremost ranks, put the barbarians to flight. In this battle he was wounded in the thigh, Chares says by Darius, with whom he fought hand to hand. But in the account which he gave Antipater of the battle, though he owns he was wounded in the thigh with a sword, though not dangerously, he does not mention who it was that wounded him.

Nothing was wanting to complete this victory, in which he overthrew above a hundred and ten thousand of his enemies, but the taking of the person of Darius, who escaped very narrowly by flight. However, having captured his chariot and his bow, he returned from pursuing him, and found his own men busy in pillaging the barbarians' camp, which (though to disburden themselves, they had left most of their baggage at Damascus) was exceedingly rich. But Darius's tent, which was full of splendid furniture, and quantities of gold and silver, they reserved for Alexander himself, who after he had put off his arms, went to bathe himself, saying, "Let us now cleanse ourselves from the toils of war in the bath of Darius." "Not so," replied one of his followers, "but in Alexander's rather, for the property of the conquered is, and should be called, the conqueror's." Here, when he beheld the bathing vessels, the water-pots, the pans, and the ointment boxes, all of gold, curiously wrought, and smelt the fragrant odors with which the whole place was exquisitely perfumed, and from thence passed into a pavilion of great size and height, where the couches and tables and preparations for an entertainment were perfectly magnificent, he turned to those about him and said, "This, it seems, is royalty."

But as he was going to supper, word was brought him that Darius's mother and wife and two unmarried daughters, being taken among the rest of the prisoners, were all in mourning and sorrow upon the sight of his chariot and bow, imagining him to be dead. After a little he sent Leonnatus to them, to let them know Darius was not dead, and that they need not fear any harm from Alexander, who made war upon him only for dominion. But the noblest and most royal part of their usage was, that he treated these illustrious prisoners according to their virtue and character, not suffering them to hear, or receive, or so much as to apprehend any thing that was unbecoming. So that they seemed rather lodged in some temple, or some holy chambers, where they enjoyed their privacy sacred and uninterrupted, than in the camp of an enemy. Yet Darius's wife was accounted the most beautiful princess then living, as her husband the tallest and handsomest man of his time, and the daughters were not unworthy of their parents.

In his diet Alexander was most temperate, as appears, omitting many other circumstances, by what he said to Ada, whom he adopted, with the title of mother, and afterwards created queen of Caria. For when she out of kindness sent him every day many curious dishes, and sweetmeats, and would have furnished him with some cooks and pastry-men, who were thought to have great skill, he told her he wanted none of them, his preceptor, Leonidas, having already given him the best, which were "a night march to prepare for breakfast, and a moderate breakfast to create an appetite for supper." Leonidas also, he added, used to open and search the furniture of his chamber, and his wardrobe, to see if his mother had left him any thing that was delicate or superfluous. He was much less addicted to wine than was generally believed; that which gave people occasion to think so of him was, that when he had nothing else to do, he loved to sit long and talk, rather than drink, and over every cup hold a long conversation. For when his affairs called upon him, he would not be detained, as other generals often were, either by wine, or sleep, nuptial solemnities, spectacles, or any other diversion whatsoever; a convincing argument of which is, that in the short time he lived, he accomplished so many and so great actions. When he was free from employment, after he was up, and had sacrificed to the gods, he used to sit down to breakfast, and then spend the rest of the day in hunting, or writing memoirs, giving decisions on some military questions, or reading. In marches that required no great haste, he would practice shooting as he went along, or to mount a chariot, and alight from it in full speed. Sometimes, for sport's sake, as his journals tell us, he would hunt foxes and go fowling. When he came in for the evening, after he had bathed and was anointed, he would call for his bakers and chief cooks, to know if they had his dinner ready. He never cared to dine till it was pretty late and beginning to be dark, and was wonderfully circumspect at meals that every one who sat with him should be served alike and with proper attention; and his love of talking, as was said before, made him delight to sit long at his wine. And no prince's conversation was ever so agreeable, yet he would at times fall into a temper of ostentation and soldierly boasting, which gave his flatterers a great advantage to ride him, and made his better friends very uneasy. After such an entertainment, he was wont to bathe, and then perhaps he would sleep till noon, and sometimes all day long. He was so very temperate in his eating, that when any rare fish or fruits were sent him, he would distribute them among his friends, and often reserve nothing for himself. His table, however, was always magnificent, the expense of it still increasing with his good fortune, till it amounted to ten thousand drachmas a day, to which sum he limited it, and beyond this he would suffer none to lay out in any entertainment where he himself was the guest.

Among the treasures and other booty that was taken from Darius, there was a very precious casket, which being brought to Alexander for a great rarity, he asked those about him what they thought fittest to be laid up in it; and when they had delivered their various opinions, he told them he should keep Homer's Iliad in it. Nor did Homer prove an unprofitable companion to him in his expeditions. For, after he had become master of Egypt he determined to found a great and populous city, and give to it his own name. And when he had measured and staked out the ground with the advice of the best architects, he chanced one night in his sleep to see a wonderful vision; a gray-headed old man, of a venerable aspect, appeared to stand by him, and pronounce these verses:

> An island lies, where loud the billows roar,
> Pharos they call it, on the Egyptian shore.

Alexander upon this immediately rose up and went to Pharos, which, at that time, was an island lying a little above the Canobic mouth of the river Nile, though it has now been joined to the main land by a mole. As soon as he saw the commodious situation of the place, it being a long neck of land, stretching like an isthmus between large lagoons and shallow waters on one side, and the sea on the other, the latter at the end of it making a spacious harbor, he said, Homer, besides his other excellences, was a very good architect, and ordered the plan of a city to be drawn out answerable to the place. To do which, for want of chalk, the soil being black, they laid out their lines with flour, taking in a pretty large compass of ground in a semicircular figure, and drawing into the inside of the circumference equal straight lines from each end, thus giving it something of the form of a cloak or cape. While he was pleasing himself with his design, on a sudden an infinite number of great birds of several kinds, rising like a black cloud out of the river and the lake, came and devoured every morsel of the flour that had been used in setting out the lines; at which omen even Alexander himself was troubled, till the augurs restored his confidence again by telling him it was a sign that the city he was about to build would not only abound in all things within itself, but also be the nurse and feeder of many nations.

The great battle of all that was fought with Darius, was not, as most writers tell us, at Arbela, but at Gaugamela, which, in their language, signifies the camel's house, forasmuch as one of their ancient kings having escaped the pursuit of his enemies on a swift camel, in gratitude to his beast settled him at this place, with an allowance of certain villages and rents for his maintenance. It came to pass that in the month Boëdromion, about the beginning of the Feast of Mysteries at Athens, there was an eclipse of the moon, the eleventh night after which, the two armies being now in view of one another, Darius kept his men in arms, and by torchlight took a general review of them. But Alexander, while his soldiers slept, spent the night before his tent with his diviner Aristander, performing certain mysterious ceremonies, and sacrificing to the god Fear.

In the meanwhile the oldest of his commanders, and chiefly Parmenio, when they beheld all the plain between Niphates and the Gordyæan mountains shining with the lights and fires which were made by the barbarians, and heard the uncertain and confused sound of voices out of their camp, like the distant roaring of a vast ocean, were so amazed at the thoughts of such a multitude, that after some conference among themselves, they concluded it an enterprise too difficult and hazardous for them to engage so numerous an enemy in the day, and therefore meeting the king as he came from sacrificing, besought him to attack Darius by night, that the darkness might conceal the danger of the ensuing battle. To this he gave them the celebrated answer, "I will not steal a victory," which, though some at the time thought it a boyish and inconsiderate speech, as if he played with danger, others regarded as an evidence that he confided in his present condition, and acted on a true judgment of the future, not wishing to leave Darius, in case he were worsted, the pretext of trying his fortune again, which he might suppose himself to have, if he could impute his overthrow to the disadvantage of the night, as he did before to the mountains, the narrow passages, and the sea. For while he had such numerous forces and large dominions still remaining, it was not any want of men or arms that could induce him to give up the war, but only the loss of all courage and hope upon the conviction of an undeniable and manifest defeat.

After they were gone from him with this answer, he laid himself down in his tent and slept the rest of the night more soundly than was usual with him, to the astonishment of the commanders. Not only before the battle, but in the height of the danger, he showed himself great, and manifested the self-possession of a just foresight and confidence. For the battle for some time fluctuated and was dubious. The left wing, where Parmenio commanded, was so impetuously charged by the Bactrian horse that it was disordered and forced to give ground, at the same time that Mazæus had sent a detachment around to fall upon those who guarded the baggage, which so disturbed Parmenio, that he sent messengers to acquaint Alexander that the camp and baggage would be all lost unless he immediately relieved the rear by a considerable reinforcement drawn out of the front. This message being brought him just as he was giving the signal to those about him for the onset, he bade them tell Parmenio that he must have surely lost the use of his reason, and had forgotten, in his alarm, that soldiers, if victorious, become masters of their enemies' baggage; and if defeated, instead of taking care of their wealth or their slaves, have nothing more to do but to fight gallantly and die with honor. When he had said this, he put on his helmet, having the rest of his arms on before he came out of his tent, which were a coat of the Sicilian make, girt close about him, and over that a breastpiece of thickly quilted linen, which was taken among other booty at the battle of Issus. The helmet, which was made by Theophilus, though of iron, was so well wrought and polished, that it was as bright as the most refined silver. To this was fitted a gorget of the same metal, set with precious stones. His sword, which was the weapon he most used in fight, was given him by the king of the Citieans, and was of an admirable temper and lightness. The belt which he also wore in all engagements, was of much richer workmanship than the rest of his armor. It was the work of the ancient Helicon, and had been presented to him by the Rhodians, as a mark of their respect to him. So long as he was engaged in drawing up his men, or riding about to give orders or directions, or to view them, he spared Bucephalas, who was now growing old, and made use of another horse; but when he was actually to fight, he sent for him again, and as soon as he was mounted, commenced the attack.

He made the longest address that day to the Thessalians and other Greeks, who answered him with loud shouts desiring him to lead them on against the barbarians, upon which he shifted his javelin into his left hand, and with his right lifted up towards heaven, besought the gods, as Callisthenes tells us, that if he was of a truth the son of Jupiter, they would be pleased to assist and strengthen the Grecians. At the same time the augur Aristander, who had a white mantle about him, and a crown of gold on his head, rode by and showed them an eagle that soared just over Alexander, and directed his flight towards the enemy; which so animated the beholders, that after mutual encouragements and exhortations, the cavalry charged at full speed, and were followed in a mass by the whole phalanx of the foot. But before they could well come to blows with the first ranks, the barbarians shrunk back, and were hotly pursued by Alexander, who drove those that fled before him into the middle of the battle, where Darius himself was in person, whom he saw from a distance over the foremost ranks, conspicuous in the midst of his lifeguard, a tall and fine-looking man, drawn in a lofty chariot, defended by an abundance of the best cavalry who stood close in order about it, ready to receive the enemy. But Alexander's approach was so terrible, forcing those who gave back upon those who yet maintained their ground, that he beat down and dispersed them almost all. Only a few of the bravest and valiantest opposed the pursuit, who were slain in their king's presence, falling in heaps upon one another, and in the very pangs of death striving to catch hold of the horses. Darius now seeing all was lost, that those who were placed in front to defend him were broken and beaten back upon him, that he could not turn or disengage his chariot without great difficulty, the wheels being clogged and entangled among the dead bodies, which lay in such heaps as not only stopped, but almost covered the horses, and made them rear and grow so unruly, that the frighted charioteer could govern them no longer, in this extremity was glad to quit his chariot and his arms, and mounting, it is said, upon a mare that had been taken from her foal, betook himself to flight.

This battle being thus over, seemed to put a period to the Persian empire; and Alexander, who was now proclaimed king of Asia, returned thanks to the gods in magnificent sacrifices, and rewarded his friends and followers with great sums of money, and places, and governments of provinces.

From here he marched through the province of Babylon, which immediately submitted to him, and was much surprised at the sight in one place where fire issues in a continuous stream, like a spring of water, out of a cleft in the earth, and the stream of naphtha, which, not far from this spot, flows out so abundantly as to form a sort of lake. This naphtha, in other respects resembling bitumen, is so subject to take fire, that before it touches the flame, it will kindle at the very light that surrounds it, and often inflame the intermediate air also. The barbarians, to show the power and nature of it, sprinkled the street that led to the king's lodgings with little drops of it, and when it was almost night, stood at the further end with torches, which being applied to the moistened places, the first at once taking fire, instantly, as quick as a man could think of it, it caught from one end to another, in such a manner that the whole street was one continuous flame.

Alexander, in his own letters, has given us an account of his war with Porus. He says the two armies were separated by the river Hydaspes, on whose opposite bank Porus continually kept his elephants in order of battle, with their heads towards their enemies, to guard the passage; that he, on the other hand, made every day a great noise and clamor in his camp, to dissipate the apprehensions of the barbarians; that one stormy, dark night he passed the river, at a distance from the place where the enemy lay, into a little island, with part of his foot, and the best of his horse. Here there fell a most violent storm of rain accompanied with lightning and whirlwinds, and although he saw some of his men burnt and dying with the lightning, he nevertheless quitted the island and made over to the other side. Here, apprehending the multitude of the enemy, and to avoid the shock of their elephants, he divided his forces, and attacked their left wing himself, commanding Cœnus to fall upon the right, which was performed with good success. By this means both wings being broken, the enemies fell back in their retreat upon the centre, and crowded in upon their elephants. There rallying, they fought a hand to hand battle, and it was the eighth hour of the day before they were entirely defeated.

Almost all the historians agree in relating that Porus was four cubits and a span high, and that when he was upon his elephant, which was of the largest size, his stature and bulk were so answerable, that he appeared to be proportionably mounted, as a horseman on his horse. This elephant, during the whole battle, gave many singular proofs of sagacity and of particular care of the king, whom as long as he was strong and in a condition to fight, he defended with great courage, repelling those who set upon him; and as soon as he perceived him overpowered with his numerous wounds and the multitude of darts that were thrown at him, to prevent his falling off, he softly knelt down and began to draw out the darts with his proboscis. When Porus was taken prisoner, and Alexander asked him how he expected to be used, he answered, "As a king." And Alexander, accordingly, not only suffered him to govern his own kingdom as satrap under himself, but gave him also the additional territory of various independent tribes whom he subdued.

Some little time after the battle with Porus, Bucephalas died, as most of the authorities state, under cure of his wounds, or as Onesicritus says, of fatigue and age, being thirty years old. Alexander was no less concerned at his death, than if he had lost an old companion or an intimate friend, and built a city, which he named Bucephalia, in memory of him, on the bank of the river Hydaspes.

Aristobulus tells us that Alexander died of a raging fever, having, in a violent thirst, taken a copious draught of wine, upon which he fell into delirium, and died on the thirtieth day of the month Dæsius.

But the journals give the following record. On the eighteenth of the month, he slept in the bathing-room on account of his fever. The next day he bathed and removed into his chamber, and spent his time in playing at dice with Medius. In the evening he bathed and sacrificed, and ate freely, and had the fever on him through the night. On the twenty-fourth he was much worse, and was carried out of his bed to assist at the sacrifices, and gave order that the general officers should wait within the court, whilst the inferior officers kept watch without doors. On the twenty-fifth he was removed to his palace on the other side the river, where he slept a little, but his fever did not abate, and when the generals came into his chamber, he was speechless, and continued so the following day. The Macedonians, therefore, supposing he was dead, came with great clamors to the gates, and menaced his friends so that they were forced to admit them, and let them all pass through unarmed along by his bedside. The same day Python and Seleucus were despatched to the temple of Serapis to inquire if they should bring Alexander thither, and were answered by the god, that they should not remove him. On the twenty-eighth, in the evening, he died.

TEMPLE OF POSEIDON AT PÆSTUM.

THE DEATH OF CÆSAR.

THE place destined for the scene of this murder, in which the senate met that day, was the same in which Pompey's statue stood, and was one of the edifices which Pompey had raised and dedicated with his theatre to the use of the public, plainly showing that there was something of a supernatural influence which guided the action, and ordered it to that particular place. Cassius, just before the act, is said to have looked towards Pompey's statue, and silently implored his assistance, though he had been inclined to the doctrines of Epicurus. But this occasion and the instant danger, carried him away out of all his reasonings, and filled him for the time with a sort of inspiration. As for Antony, who was firm to Cæsar, and a strong man, Brutus Albinus kept him outside the house, and delayed him with a long conversation contrived on purpose. When Cæsar entered, the senate stood up to show their respect to him, and of Brutus's confederates, some came about his chair and stood behind it, others met him, pretending to add their petitions to those of Tillius Cimber, in behalf of his brother, who was in exile; and they followed him with their joint supplications till he came to his seat. When he had sat down, he refused to comply with their requests, and upon their urging him further, began to reproach them severally for their importunities, when Tillius, laying hold of his robe with both his hands, pulled it down from his neck, which was the signal for the assault. Casca gave him the first cut, in the neck, which was not mortal nor dangerous, coming as it did, from one who at the beginning of such a bold action was probably very much disturbed. Cæsar immediately turned about, and laid his hand upon the dagger and kept hold of it. And both of them at the same time cried out, he that received the blow, in Latin, "Vile Casca, what does this mean?" and he that gave it, in Greek, to his brother, "Brother, help!" Upon this first onset, those who were not privy to the design were astounded, and their horror and amazement at what they saw were so great, that they durst not fly nor assist Cæsar, nor so much as speak a word. But those who came prepared for the business inclosed him on every side, with their naked daggers in their hands. Which way soever he turned, he met with blows, and saw their swords leveled at his face and eyes, and was encompassed, like a wild beast in the toils, on every side. For it had been agreed that they should each make a thrust at him, and flesh themselves with his blood; for which reason Brutus also gave him one stab in the groin. Some say that he fought and resisted all the rest, shifting his body to avoid the blows, and calling out for help, but that when he saw Brutus's sword drawn, he covered his face with his robe and submitted, letting himself fall, whether it were by chance, or that he was pushed in that direction by his murderers, at the foot of the pedestal on which Pompey's statue stood, and which was thus wet with his blood. So that Pompey himself seemed to have presided, as it were, over the revenge done upon his adversary, who lay here at his feet, and breathed out his soul through his multitude of wounds, for they say he received three and twenty. And the conspirators themselves were many of them wounded by each other, whilst they all leveled their blows at the same person.

When Cæsar's will was opened, and it was found that he had left a considerable legacy to each one of the Roman citizens, and when his body was seen carried through the market-place all mangled with wounds, the multitude could no longer contain themselves within the bounds of tranquillity and order, but heaped together a pile of benches, bars, and tables, upon which they placed the corpse, and setting fire to it, burnt it on them.

Then they took brands from the pile, and ran some to fire the houses of the conspirators, others up and down the city, to find out the men and tear them to pieces, but met, however, with none of them, they having taken effectual care to secure themselves.

Cæsar died in his fifty-sixth year, not having survived Pompey above four years. That empire and power which he had pursued through the whole course of his life with so much hazard, he did at last with much difficulty compass, but reaped no other fruits from it than the empty name and invidious glory. But the great genius which attended m through his lifetime, even after his death remained as the avenger of his murder, pursuing through every se d land all those who were concerned in it, and suffering none to escape, but reaching all who in any sort or kind were either actually engaged in the fact, or by their counsels any way promoted it.

The most remarkable of mere human coincidences was that which befell Cassius, who, when he was defeated at Philippi, killed himself with the same dagger which he had made use of against Cæsar. The most signal preternatural appearances were the great comet, which shone very bright for seven nights after Cæsar's death, and then disappeared, and the dimness of the sun, whose orb continued pale and dull for the whole of that year, never showing its ordinary radiance at its rising, and giving but a feeble heat. The air consequently was damp and gross, for want of stronger rays to open and rarefy it. The fruits, for that reason, never properly ripened, and began to wither and fall off for want of heat, before they were fully formed.

THEATRICAL MASKS.

WEIGHTS, MEASURES, ETC.,

MENTIONED BY PLUTARCH.

From the Tables of Dr. Arbuthnot.

WEIGHTS.

	lb.	oz.	p.wt.	gr.
The Roman libra or pound	0	10	18	$13\frac{4}{7}$
The Attic mina or pound	0	11	7	$16\frac{2}{7}$
The Attic talent, equal to 60 minæ	56	11	0	$17\frac{1}{7}$

DRY MEASURES OF CAPACITY.

	peck.	gal.	pints.
The Roman modius	1	0	$0\frac{2}{9}$
The Attic chœnix, one pint, 15, $705\frac{1}{8}$ solid inches	0	0	$1\frac{1}{2}$ nearly.
The Attic medimnus	4	0	$6\frac{1}{10}$

LIQUID MEASURES OF CAPACITY.

	pints.	solid inches.
The cotyle	$\frac{1}{2}$	$2,141\frac{1}{2}$
The cyathus	$1\frac{1}{2}$	$356\frac{1}{12}$
The chus	6	25,698

MEASURES OF LENGTH.

	Eng. ft.	in.
The Roman foot	0	$11\frac{3}{5}$
The Roman cubit	1	$5\frac{2}{3}$
The Roman pace	4	10
The Roman furlong	604	4[illegible]
The Roman mile	4835	0
The Grecian cubit	1	$6\frac{1}{3}$
The Grecian furlong	504	$4\frac{1}{8}$
The Grecian mile	4030	0

MONEY.

The quadrans, about	$ 0.001
The as	0.0015
The sestertius	0.04
The sestertium, equal to 1000 sestertii	40.00
The denarius	0.157
The Attic obolus	0.025
The drachma (= the denarius)	0.157
The mina, equal to 100 drachmæ	15.70
The talent, equal to 60 minæ	950.00
The stater-aureus of the Greeks, weighing two Attic drachms	4.00
The stater-darius	8.00
The Roman aureus was of different value at different periods. According to the proportion mentioned by Tacitus, when it exchanged for 25 denarii, it was of the same value as the Grecian stater	4.00

NAMES OF THE ATTIC MONTHS.

The year began with the summer solstice, June 21st of our year. The months were alternately twenty-nine and thirty days in length, so that it was necessary every third year to intercalate a month which was called a second Posideon, to make up the annual loss of eleven days. This, again, had to be omitted every thirtieth year.

Hecatombaeon = a part of June and July.
Metageitnion = a part of July and August.
Boedromion = a part of Aug. and September.
Pyanepsion = a part of Sept. and October.
Maemacterion = a part of Oct. and November.
Posideon = a part of Nov. and December.
Gamelion = a part of December and January.
Anthesterion = a part of Jan'y and February.
Elaphebolion = a part of Feb'y and March.
Munychion = a part of March and April.
Thargelion = a part of April and May.
Scirophorion = a part of May and June.

A CHRONOLOGICAL TABLE

FROM DACIER AND OTHER WRITERS.

Years of the world.	Years before the first Olympiad.		Years before the building of Rome.	Years before Christ.	Years of the world.	Olympiads.		Years of Rome.	Years before Christ.
2437	737	Deucalion's deluge.	761	1511			NUMA.		
2547	627	Minos I. son of Jupiter and Europa.	651	1401	3236	xvi. 3.	Numa elected king..	39	712
2698	486	Minos II. grandson of the first.	500	1250	3279	xxvii. 2.	Numa dies.........	82	669
		THESEUS.					SOLON.		
2720	454	The expedition of the Argonauts. Theseus attended Jason in it.	473	1228	3350	xlv. 1.	Solon flourishes.....	153	598
					3350	—	Cylon's conspiracy..	—	—
					3354	xlvi. 1.	Epimenides goes to Athens, and expiates the city. He dies soon after at the age of 154. The seven wise men : Æsop and Anacharsis flourish.	157	594
2768	406	Troy taken. Demophoon the son of Theseus was at the siege.	430	1180					
2847	327	The return of the Heraclidone to Peloponnesus.	351	1101					
2880	294	The first war of the Athenians against Sparta. Codrus devotes himself.	318	1068	3356	xlvi. 3.	Solon Archon......	159	592
							Crœsus, king of Lydia.		
					3370	l. 1.	Pythagoras goes into Italy. Pisistratus sets up his tyranny.	173	578
2894	288	The Helots subdued by Agis.	304	1055					
					3391	lv. 2.	Cyrus, king of Persia.	194	557
2908	266	The Ionic migration.	290	1040					
3045	129	Lycurgus flourishes..	153	904	3401	lvii. 4.	Crœsus taken.......	204	547
	Olympiads.								
3174	I.	*The First Olympiad.*	25	774			PUBLICOLA.		
		ROMULUS.	Years of Rome		3442	lxviii. 1.	Is chosen consul in the room of Collatinus.	245	509
3198	vii. 1.	Rome built........	—	750					
3201	vii. 4.	The rape of the Sabine virgins.	4	747			Brutus fights Aruns, the eldest son of Tarquin. Both are killed.		
3235	xvi. 1.	The death of Romulus.	38	713					

A CHRONOLOGICAL TABLE. 451

Years of the world.	Olympiads.		Years of Rome.	Years before Christ.	Years of the world.	Olympiads.		Years of Rome.	Years before Christ.
3444	lxviii. 3.	Publicola consul the third time. His colleague Horatius Pulvillus dedicates the temple of Jupiter Capitolinus. Horatius Cocles defends the Sublician bridge against the Tuscans.	247	504	3500	lxxxii. 3.	Cimon dies. Alcibiades born the same year. Herodotus and Thucydides flourish; the latter is 12 or 13 years younger than the former. Pindar dies, 80 years old.	303	448
								—	440
3448	lxix. 3.	Publicola dies...... Zeno Eleates flourished.	251 —	500 499			PERICLES		
3459	lxxii. 1.	The battle of Marathon.	262	489	3519	lxxxvii. 2.	Stirs up the Peloponnesian war, which lasts 27 years. He was very young when the Romans sent the Decemviri to Athens for Solon's laws.	322	429
		CORIOLANUS							
3461	lxxii. 2.	Is banished and retires to the Volsci.	263	488					
3462	lxxiii. 1.	Herodotus is born...	265	486					
3463	lxxiii. 2.	Coriolanus besieges Rome; but being prevailed upon by his mother to retire, is stoned to death by the Volsci.	266	485	3521	lxxxvii. 4.	Pericles dies........	324	427
					3522	lxxxviii. 1.	Plato born......... Xerxes killed by Artabanus.	325	426
		ARISTIDES					NICIAS.		
3467	lxxiv. 2.	Is banished for ten years, but recalled at the expiration of three.	270	481	3535	xci. 2.	The Athenians undertake the Sicilian war.	338	413
					3537	xci. 4.	Nicias beaten and put to death in Sicily.	340	411
		THEMISTOCLES.							
3470	lxxv. 1.	The battle of Salamis	273	478			ALCIBIADES		
3471	lxxv. 2.	The battle of Platæa..	274	477					
3474	lxxvi. 1.	Thucydides is born..	277	474					
3479	lxxvii. 2.	Themistocles is banished by the Ostracism.	282	469	3538	xcii. 1.	Takes refuge at Sparta, and afterward amongst the Persians.	—	—
		CIMON			3539	xcii. 2.	Dionysius the elder, now tyrant of Sicily.	342	409
3480	lxxvii. 3.	Beats the Persians both at sea and land.	283	468	—	—	Sophocles dies, aged 91.	—	407
3481	lxxvii. 4.	Socrates is born. He lived 71 years.	284	467	—	—	Euripides dies, aged 75.	—	406

Years of the world.	Olympiads.		Years of Rome.	Years before Christ.	Years of the world	Olympiads.		Years of Rome.	Years before Christ.
		LYSANDER					PELOPIDAS,		
3545	xciii. 4.	Puts an end to the Peloponnesian war, and establishes the thirty tyrants at Athens.	348	403	3580	cii. 3.	General of the Thebans. He headed the sacred band the year before at Leuctra, where Epaminondas commanded in chief.	383	368
—	—	Thrasybulus expels them.	—	401					
3546	xciv. 1.	Alcibiades put to death by order of Pharnabazus.	349	402	3582	ciii. 1.	Dionysius the elder, tyrant of Sicily, dies, and is succeeded by his son.	385	366
					3584	ciii. 3.	Isocrates flourishes..	387	364
		ARTAXERXES MNEMON					TIMOLEON		
3549	xciv. 4.	Overthrows his brother Cyrus in a great battle. The retreat of the 10,000 Greeks, conducted by Xenophon.	352	399	3585	ciii. 4.	Kills his brother Timophanes, who was setting himself up tyrant in Corinth.	388	363
					3586	civ. 1.	Pelopidas defeats Alexander the tyrant of Pheræ, but falls in the battle.	—	—
3550	xcv. 1.	Socrates dies	353	398					
					3587	civ. 2.	The famous battle of Mantinea, in which Epaminondas, though victorious, is killed by the son of Xenophon.	390	361
		AGESILAUS							
3553	xcv. 4.	Ascends the Spartan throne.	356	395					
3554	xcvi. 1.	Lysander sent to the Hellespont.	357	394	3588	civ. 3.	Camillus dies......	391	360
					3589	civ 4.	Artaxerxes dies. So does Agesilaus.	392	359
3555	xcvi. 2.	Agesilaus defeats the Persian cavalry. Lysander dies.	—	—					
							DION		
3561	xcvii. 4.	The Romans lose the battle of Allia.	364	387					
					3593	cv. 4.	Expels Dionysius the younger.	396	355
		CAMILLUS			3594	cvi. 1.	Alexander the Great born.	397	354
3562	xcviii. 4.	Retires to Ardea....	365	386					
3566	xcix. 1.	Aristotle born	369	382	3596	cvi. 3.	Dion is killed by Calippus.	399	352
3569	xcix. 4.	Demosthenes born ..	372	379					
3574	ci. 1.	Chabrias defeats the Lacedæmonians.	377	374					
							DEMOSTHENES		
3579	cii. 2.	Peace between the Athenians and Lacedæmonians. The important battle of Leuctra.	382	369	3598	cvii. 1.	Begins to thunder against Philip. Xenophon dies, aged 90.	401	350

A CHRONOLOGICAL TABLE.

Years of the world.	Olympiads.		Years of Rome.	Years before Christ.	Years of the world.	Olympiads.		Years of Rome.	Years before Christ.
3602	cviii. 1.	Plato dies, aged 80 or 81.	405	346			DEMETRIUS,		
3605	cviii. 4.	Timoleon sent to assist the Syracusans.	408	343	3636	cxvi. 4.	Surnamed Poliorcetes, permitted by his father Antigonus to command the army in Syria, when only 22 years of age. He restores the Athenians to their liberty, but they choose to remain in the worst of chains, those of servility and meanness.	439	312
3607	cix. 2.	Dionysius the younger sent off to Corinth.	410	341					
3609	cix. 4.	Epicurus born......	412	339	3643	cxviii. 2.		446	305
3612	cx. 3.	The battle of Chæronea, in which Philip beats the Athenians and Thebans.	415	336					
3613	cx. 4.	Timoleon dies......	416	335					
		ALEXANDER THE GREAT					Dionysius, the tyrant, dies at Heraclea, aged 55.		
3614	cxl. 1.	Is declared general of all Greece against the Persians, upon the death of his father Philip.	417	334			In the year before Christ 288, died Theophrastus, aged 85.		
3616	cxi. 3.	The battle of the Granicus.	419	332			And in the year before Christ 285, Theocritus flourished.		
3619	cxii. 2.	The battle of Arbela.	422	329					
3623	cxiii. 2.	Porus beaten.......	426	325					
3627	cxiv. 1.	Alexander dies, aged 33.	430	321					
		Diogenes dies, aged 90.					PYRRHUS,		
—	—	Aristotle dies, aged 63	—	319					
		PHOCION			3670	cxxv. 1.	King of Epirus, passes over into Italy, where he is defeated by Lævinus.	473	272
3632	cxv. 3.	Retires to Polyperchon, but is delivered up by him to the Athenians, who put him to death.	435	316					
					3685	cxxviii. 4.	The first Punic war, which lasted 24 years.	488	263
		EUMENES,			3696	cxxxi. 3.	Philopœmen born...	499	252
3634	cxvi. 1.	Who had attained to a considerable rank amongst the successors of Alexander the Great, is betrayed to Antigonus, and put to death.	437	314			ARATUS,		
					3699	cxxxii. 1.	Of Sicyon, delivered his native city from the tyranny of Nicocles.	502	249

Years of the world.	Olympiads.		Years of Rome.	Years before Christ.	Years of the world.	Olympiads.		Years of Rome.	Years before Christ.
		AGIS AND CLEOMENES,					CATO THE CENSOR		
3723	cxxxviii. 2.	Contemporaries with Aratus, for Aratus being beaten by Cleomenes, calls in Antigonus from Macedonia, which proves the ruin of Greece.	526	225	3754	cxlvi. 1.	Was 21 or 22 years old when Fabius Maximus took Tarentum. See above. All Greece restored to her liberty, by T. Q. Flamininus. Flamininus triumphs; Demetrius, the son of Philip, and Nabis, tyrant of Lacedemon, follow his chariot.	557	194
		PHILOPŒMEN							
3727	cxxxix. 2.	Thirty years old when Cleomenes took Megalopolis. About this time lived Hannibal, Marcellus, Fabius Maximus, and Scipio Africanus.	530	221	3755	cxlvi. 2.	Cato triumphs for his conquests in Spain.	558	193
					3766	cxlix. 1.	Scipio Africanus dies.	569	182
					3767	cxlix. 2.	Philopœmen dies the same year.	570	181
							PAULUS ÆMILIUS,		
3731	cxl. 2.	The second Punic war, which lasted 18 years.	534	217			Then first consul, was beaten by Hannibal at Cannæ. When consul the second time he conquered Persius, and brought him in chains to Rome. Now Terence flourished.		
3733	cxl. 4.	Hannibal beats the consul Flaminius at the Thrasymenean lake;	536	215	3782	cliii. 1.		585	166
3734	cxli. 1.	And the consuls Varro and Æmilius at Cannæ.	537	214					
3736	cxli. 3.	He is beaten by Marcellus at Nola.	539	212					
3738	cxlii. 1.	Marcellus takes Syracuse.	541	210	3790	clv. 1.	Paulus Æmilius dies.	593	158
					3794	clvi. 1.	Marius born........	597	154
3741	cxlii. 4.	Fabius Maximus seizes Tarentum.	544	207	3801	clvii. 4.	The third Punic war, which continued four years	604	147
3747	cxliv. 2.	Fabius Maximus dies	550	201					
3749	cxliv. 4.	Scipio triumphs for his conquests in Africa.	552	199	3804	clviii. 3.	Cato the Censor dies. Scipio Æmilianus destroys Carthage; and Mummius sacks and burns Corinth.	607	144
		TITUS QUINCTIUS FLAMININUS					Carneades dies, aged 85.	—	129
3752	cxlv. 3.	Elected consul at the age of 30.	555	196	—	—	Polybius dies, aged 81.	—	123

A CHRONOLOGICAL TABLE.

Years of the world.	Olympiads.		Years of Rome.	Years before Christ.	Years of the world.	Olympiads.		Years of Rome.	Years before Christ.
		TIBERIUS AND CAIUS GRACCHUS.					POMPEY,		
3827	clxiv. 2.	The laws of Caius Gracchus.	630	121	3869	clxxiv. 4.	At the age of 25, is sent into Africa against Domitius, and beats him.	672	79
		MARIUS					CATO OF UTICA		
3843	clxviii. 2.	Marches against Jugurtha. Cicero born.	646	105			Was younger than Pompey; for he was but 14 years old when Sylla's proscriptions were in their utmost rage.		
3844	clxviii. 3.	Pompey born......	647	104					
3846	clxix. 1.	Marius, now consul the second time, marches against the Cimbri.	649	102					
3850	clxxi. 2.	Julius Cæsar is born in the sixth consulship of Marius.	653	98			CICERO		
—	—	Lucretius born......	—	94	3870	clxxv. 1.	Defends Roscius against the practices of Sylla. This was his first public pleading. After this he retires to Athens to finish his studies.	673	78
		SYLLA,							
3855	clxxii. 2.	After his prætorship, sent into Cappadocia.	658	93					
3862	clxxiii. 1.	Makes himself master of Rome.	665	86					
3863	clxxiii. 2.	Takes Athens...... Marius dies the same year.	666	85	3871	clxxv. 2.	Sylla, after having destroyed above 100,000 Roman citizens, proscribed 90 senators, and 2,600 knights, resigns his dictatorship, and dies the year following.	674	77
		SERTORIUS							
3867	clxxiv. 2.	Sent into Spain.....	670	81					
3868	clxxiv. 3.	The younger Marius beaten by Sylla; yet soon after he defeats Pontius Telesinus at the gates of Rome. Sylla enters the city, and being created dictator, exercises all manner of cruelties.	671	80					
					3874	clxxvi. 1.	Pompey manages the war in Spain against Sertorius.	677	74
							LUCULLUS,		
					3877	clxxvi. 4.	After his consulship, is sent against Mithridates.	680	71
		CRASSUS			3879	clxxvii. 2.	Sertorius assassinated in Spain. Crassus consul with Pompey.	682	69
		Enriches himself with buying the estates of persons proscribed.			3881	clxxvii. 4.	Tigranes conquered by Lucullus.	684	67

Years of the world.	Olympiads.		Years of Rome.	Years before Christ.	Years of the world.	Olympiads.		Years of Rome.	Years before Christ.
3887	clxxix. 2.	Mithridates dies. Pompey forces the temple of Jerusalem. Augustus Cæsar born.	690	61	3907	clxxxiv. 2.	Brutus passes into Macedonia.	710	41
		JULIUS CÆSAR					MARK ANTONY		
3891	clxxx. 2.	Appointed consul with Bibulus, obtains Illyria, and the two Gauls, with four legions. He marries his daughter Julia to Pompey.	694	57			Beaten the same year by Augustus at Modena. He retires to Lepidus. The triumvirate of Augustus, Lepidus, and Antony, who divide the empire amongst them.		
3897	clxxxi. 4.	Crassus is taken by the Parthians and slain.	700	51	3908	clxxxiv. 3.	The battle of Philippi, in which Brutus and Cassius being overthrown by Augustus and Antony, lay violent hands on themselves.	711	40
3902	clxxxiii. 1.	Cæsar defeats Pompey at Pharsalia. Pompey flies into Egypt and is assassinated there.	705	46					
3903	clxxxiii. 2.	Cæsar makes himself master of Alexandria, and subdues Egypt; after which he marches into Syria, and soon reduces Pharnaces.	706	45	3909	clxxxiv. 4.	Antony leagues with Sextus the son of Pompey against Augustus.	712	39
					3910	clxxxv. 1.	Augustus and Antony renew their friendship after the death of Fulvia, and Antony marries Octavia.	713	38
3904	clxxxiii. 3.	He conquers Juba, Scipio, and Petreius, in Africa, and leads up four triumphs. Previous to which, Cato kills himself.	707	44					
					3918	clxxxvii. 1.	Augustus and Antony again embroiled.	721	30
3905	clxxxiii. 4.	Cæsar defeats the sons of Pompey at Munda. Cneius falls in the action, and Sextus flies into Sicily. Cæsar triumphs the fifth time.	708	43	3919	clxxxvii. 3.	The battle of Actium. Antony is beaten, and flies into Egypt with Cleopatra.	722	29
					3920	clxxxvii. 4.	Augustus makes himself master of Alexandria. Antony and Cleopatra destroy themselves.	723	28
		BRUTUS.							
3906	clxxxiv. 1.	Cæsar is killed by Brutus and Cassius	709	42					

A CHRONOLOGICAL TABLE.

Years of the world.	Olympiads.		Years of Rome.	Era of the Incarnation.	Years of the world.	Olympiads.		Years of Rome.	Era of the Incarnation.
		GALBA					OTHO		
3920	clxxxvii. 4.	Born.	723	28	4019	ccxii. 1.	Revolts and persuades the soldiers to despatch Galba; upon which he is proclaimed emperor; and three months after, being defeated by Vitellius, despatches himself.	821	71
3947	cxciv. 2.	Otho born..........	750	—					
3981	ccii. 4.	Galba appointed consul.	784	34					
3982	cciii. 1.	The revolt of Vindex.	785	35					
4018	ccxi. 4.	Nero killed.	820	70					
—	—	Galba declared emperor.	—	—					

INDEX

FOR REFERENCE AS TO THE PRONUNCIATION OF PROPER NAMES

Aban'tidas.
Abde'ra.
Abœoc'ritus
Ab'olus.
Abri'orix.
Abrot'onon.
Abule'tes.
Aby'dos.
Academi'a.
Acestodo'rus.
Achelo'ūs.
Achradi'na.
Acrop'olis.
Acrot'atus.
Acu'phis.
Adju'trix.
Adme'tus.
Ado'nis.
Adrani'tans.
Adra'num.
Adra'nus.
Adria'nus.
Adrume'tum.
Æac'idæ.
Æac'ides.
Æ'acus
Ægiali'a.
Æ'gias.
Ægic'ores.
Ægi'na.
Æ'gium.
Ægos-pot'ami.
Æne'as.
Æ'olus.
Aër'opus.
Æs'chines.
Æs'chylus
Æ'sion

Æso'pus.
Agathocle'a.
Aga've.
Age'sias.
Agesila'ūs.
Agesip'olis.
Agesis'trata.
Agi'adæ.
A'gias.
Agia'tis.
Agnon'ides.
Aha'la.
Aïdo'neus.
Albi'nus.
Al'cetas.
Alcibi'ades.
Alcid'amas.
Alcim'enes.
Al'cimus.
Alcme'na
Alcy'oneus.
A'leäs.
Alexandrop'olis.
Alexic'rates.
Alfe'nus.
Allob'roges
Alo'pece.
Alo'pecus.
Al'ycus.
Ama'nus.
Amar'syas.
Ambi'orix.
Ambro'nes.
Ame'ria.
Ami'sus
Amœ'beäs.
Amomphar'etus.
Ampha'res.

Amphiara'ūs.
Amphic'rates.
Amphilo'chia.
Amphip'olis.
Amphith'eūs.
Amphit'rope.
Amphit'ryon.
Am'ycla.
Am'yclas.
An'aces.
Anac'reon.
Ana'pus.
Anaxag'oras.
Anazan'drides.
Anaxe'nor.
Anaxida'mus
Anax'ilas.
Anaxila'ūs.
Anaxim'enes.
Andoc'ides.
Androc'leon.
An'drocles.
Androcli'des.
Androc'rates.
Androcy'des.
Andro'geūs.
Androm'ache.
Androm'achus.
Androni'cus.
Androt'ion.
An'gelus.
Anie'nus.
Antag'oras.
Antal'cidas.
Ante'nor.
Anthe'don.
Anthe'mion.
Anthemoc'ritus.

An'tias.
Antia'tes.
Anticli'des.
Antic'rates.
Antic'yra.
Antig'enes.
Antigen'idas.
Antig'one.
Antig'onus.
Antilib'anus.
Antil'ochus.
Antim'achus.
Anti'ochis.
Anti'ochus.
Anti'ope.
Antio'rus.
Antip'ater.
Antiph'anes.
Antiph'ates.
Antiph'ilus.
An'tiphon.
Antis'thenes.
Ao'üs.
Ap'ama.
Apel'licon.
Aph'ytæ.
Apolloc'rates.
Apollodo'rus.
Apollon'ides.
Apolloph'anes.
Apolloth'emis.
Apoth'etæ.
Apseph'ion.
Ap'tera.
Aqui'num.
Aqui'nus.
Ar'acus.
Ara'tus.
Arbe'la.
Arcesila'üs.
Archede'mus.
Archela'üs.
Archep'tolis.
Arches'tratus.
Ar'chias.
Archibi'ades.
Archib'ius.
Archida'mia.
Archidam'idas.
Archida'mus.
Archil'ochus.

Archime'des.
Archit'eles.
Archon'ides.
Archy'tas.
Ar'dea.
Areop'agus.
Ar'ete.
A'reas.
Argileo'nis.
Arginu'sæ.
Ariam'enes.
Ariara'thes.
Ari'us.
Arim'inum.
Ariobarza'nes.
Aris'teäs.
Aristi'des.
Aris'tion.
Aristobu'le.
Aristobu'lus.
Aristocli'tus.
Aristoc'rates.
Aristoc'ritus.
Aristode'mus.
Aristogi'ton.
Aristom'ache.
Aristom'achus
Aristom'enes.
Aristoni'cus.
Aris'tonus.
Aristoph'anes.
Aristot'eles.
Aristox'enus.
Aris'tratus.
Ar'naces or Arna'ces.
Ar'pates or Arpa'tes.
Arpi'num.
Arrhen'ides.
Ar'saces or Arsa'ces.
Artaba'nus.
Artax'ata.
Artemido'rus.
Ar'temis.
Ar'temon.
Arthmi'adas.
Aruve'ni.
Ar'ybas.
Asbolom'eni.
As'calis.
As'calon.
Asclepi'ades.

As'culum.
A'sea.
Asiat'icus.
Asin'arus.
Aso'pus.
As'petus.
Astero'pus.
Astu'ra.
Asty'anax.
Asty'ochus.
Astyph'ilus.
Asy'lum.
Athama'nes.
Ath'anis.
Athenodo'rus.
Athenoph'anes
Ath'esis.
Atropate'ne.
Attali'a.
At'talus.
At'ticus.
Autocli'des.
Auto'leon.
Autol'ycus.
Aux'imum.
Axi'ochus.
Ax'ius.

Bab'yca.
Bacchi'adæ.
Bac'chides.
Bacchyl'ides.
Bago'äs.
Bali'nus.
Bamby'ce.
Barsi'ne.
Bat'aces.
Bat'alus.
Bata'vi or Bat'avi
Batia'tes.
Bedri'acum.
Belbi'na.
Beller'ophon.
Belli'nus.
Bello'na.
Belu'ris.
Bereni'ce.
Bery'tus or Ber'ytu.
Bib'ulus.
Boccho'ris.
Boëdrom'ion.

INDEX.

Bœo'rix.
Bos'porus.
Bras'idas.
Bri'areus.
Buceph'alas.
Busi'ris.
Buthro'tum.

Cabi'ra.
Cabi'ri.
Cadme'a.
Cæci'na.
Cæsa'rion.
Caie'ta.
Calauri'a, correctly Calaure'a.
Cale'nus.
Calli'ades.
Cal'lias.
Callib'ius.
Callic'rates.
Callicrat'idas.
Callid'romon.
Callim'achus.
Callim'edon.
Callini'cus.
Cal'liphon.
Callip'pides.
Callis'thenes.
Callis'tratus.
Calvi'nus.
Cal'ydon.
Camby'ses.
Cameri'num.
Came'rium.
Cami'rus.
Cane'thus.
Cano'pus.
Can'tharus.
Cap'aneus.
Cape'na.
Capena'tes.
Ca'phyæ.
Cap'itæ.
Cap'ito.
Capitoli'nus.
Caprifi'cus.
Caproti'næ.
Car'anus.
Cari'næ.
Carne'ades.

Carnu'tes.
Carnuti'ni.
Caryat'ides.
Casili'num.
Casi'num.
Cas'tulo.
Cat'ana.
Catili'na.
Cat'ulus.
Cau'casus.
Cebali'nus.
Cel'eres.
Cen'chrea.
Censori'nus.
Ceph'alon.
Ceph'alus.
Cephi'sodorus.
Cephisod'otus.
Cephi'sus or Cephis'sus.
Cerami'cus.
Cerci'na.
Cer'cyon.
Cerea'te.
Cer'malus.
Cethe'gus.
Chærone'a.
Chalce'don.
Chalco'don.
Charide'mus.
Charila'üs.
Charim'enes.
Chari'nus.
Charoni'tæ.
Chersone'sus.
Chilo'nis.
Chœr'ilus.
Chrysog'onus.
Cin'eas.
Circe'um.
Cissu'sa.
Clazom'enæ.
Cleæ'netus.
Clean'drides.
Cle'obis.
Cleoc'ritus.
Cleom'brotus.
Cleome'des.
Cleom'edon.
Cleom'enes.
Cleo'næ.
Cleoni'ce.

Cleon'ides.
Cleon'ymus.
Cleop'ater.
Cleopa'tra.
Cleoph'anes.
Cleoptol'emus.
Cle'ora.
Clep'sydra.
Clide'mus.
Clis'thenes.
Clitom'achus.
Clodo'nes.
Clym'ene.
Cna'cion.
Coäl'emus.
Co'lias.
Collati'nus.
Colo'nis.
Col'ophon.
Co'mias.
Commage'ne.
Con'nidas.
Cono'pion.
Corace'sium.
Corcy'ra.
Cor'duba.
Cori'oli.
Cornu'tus.
Corvi'nus.
Coryne'tes.
Cot'ylo.
Cra'nium or **Crane'um**.
Crat'erus.
Cratesicle'a.
Cratesip'olis.
Crati'nus.
Cremo'na.
Creophy'lus.
Crime'sus.
Crispi'nus.
Critola'idas.
Critola'üs.
Cro'bylus.
Crom'myon.
Crustume'rium.
Ctesib'ius.
Ctes'iphon.
Cya'nean Islands.
Cyc'lades.
Cynægy'rus.
Cynosceph'alæ.

Cyp′selus.
Cyre′ne and Cyrene′ans.
Cythe′ra.
Cythe′ris.
Cyz′icus.

Dæd′alus.
Daïm′achus.
Damag′oras.
Damara′tus.
Damoch′ares.
Damocli′das.
Damoc′rates.
Damon′ides.
Damot′eles.
Damyr′ias.
Dan′aüs.
Da′ochus.
Dar′danus.
Dari′us.
Dascyli′tis.
Dassare′tis.
Decele′a.
Deïani′ra.
Deïdami′a.
Deïm′achus.
Deï′oneus.
Deïot′arus.
Dem′ades.
Demæ′netus.
Demara′tus.
Demar′etus.
De′meas.
Democli′des.
Democh′ares.
Democ′rates.
Democ′ritus.
Demo′leon.
Demo′nax.
Demoph′anes.
Demoph′ilus.
Dem′ophon.
Demop′olis.
Demos′tratus
Dercyl′lidas.
Dexith′ea.
Diade′matus.
Diam′peres.
Dicæarche′a.
Dic′omes.
Did′yma.

Did′ymus.
Dieutych′idas.
Dindyme′ne.
Dinoc′rates.
Dinom′ache.
Diocli′des.
Diodo′rus.
Diog′enes.
Diogi′ton.
Diome′des.
Dionysodo′rus.
Dioph′anes.
Diopi′thes.
Dioscor′ides.
Dioscu′ri.
Diphil′ides.
Diph′ilus.
Dip′ylon.
Di′rades.
Doc′imus.
Dodo′na.
Doryla′üs.
Dromocli′des.

Ecbat′ana.
Ecde′lus.
Ecde′mus.
Echec′rates.
Echecrat′ides.
Echede′mus and Echedemi′a.
Ec′nomum.
Elate′a.
El′atus.
E′lea.
Elephe′nor.
Ele′üs.
Elpini′ce.
Em′pylus.
Enar′sphorus.
Ende′is.
Epaphrodi′tus.
Epe′ratus.
Eph′orus.
Epic′rates.
Epicu′rus.
Epicy′des.
Epicyd′idas.
Epige′thes.
Epig′onus.
Epil′ycus.

Epimen′ides.
Epip′olæ.
Epi′rus.
Epita′deus. (?)
Epiti′mus.
Epix′yës.
Erasis′tratus.
Eratos′thenes.
Er′gades.
Ergi′nus.
Ergot′eles.
Eri′neüs.
Es′quiline.
Etym′ocles.
Eubu′lus.
Eu′chidas.
Eucli′a.
Eucli′das.
Eucli′des.
Eudam′idas.
Euda′mus.
Eude′mus.
Euer′getes.
Eume′lus.
Eu′menes.
Eu′neos.
Eu′nomus.
Euphem′ides.
Eupho′rion.
Euphran′tides
Euphra′tes.
Eupol′emus.
Eupo′lia.
Eu′polis.
Eurip′ides.
Euro′tas.
Eurybi′ades.
Eu′rycles.
Eurycli′das.
Euryd′ice.
Euryl′ochus.
Eurym′edon.
Eu′rypon.
Euryptol′emus.
Eurys′aces.
Eu′rytus.
Euthyde′mus.
Euthy′mus.
Euthy′nus.
Eu′tychus.
Evag′oras.

INDEX.

Evan'gelus.
Execes'tides.

Fau'stulus.
Fecia'les.
Ferenti'na.
Fide'næ.
Flam'ines.
Flamini'nus.

Gabe'ni.
Gæ'satæ.
Gæsy'lus.
Gal'ate.
Gandari'tans.
Gaugame'la.
Gela'nor.
Ger'adas.
Gerane'a.
Gergi'thus.
German'icus.
Gon'atas.
Gon'gylus.
Gordye'ne.
Gor'gias.
Gor'gidas.
Gorgo'leon.
Graci'nus.

Hagnon'ides.
Hagnoth'emis.
Hal'imus.
Halone'sus.
Hal'ycus.
Har'palus.
Has'drubal.
Hec'ale.
Hecale'ne.
Hecatom'pedon.
Hec'uba.
Hedyl'ium.
Hege'mon.
Hege'sias.
Hegesip'yle.
Heges'tratus.
Hel'enus.
Hel'icon.
Hel'icus.
Heliop'olis.
He'lius.
Hellan'icus.

Heni'ocha.
Hephæs'tion.
Heracle'a.
Heracli'des.
Heracli'tus.
Her'cules.
He'reäs.
Hermag'oras.
Hermi'one.
Hermoc'rates.
Hermola'üs.
Hermoti'mus.
Hero'des.
Herod'otus.
Heroph'ytus.
Heros'tratus.
He'siod.
Hesych'ia.
Hexap'yla.
Hic'etes.
Hid'rieus.
Hi'eræ.
Hierap'olis.
Hi'ero.
Hieron'ymus.
Him'era.
Hip'pada.
Hippar'ete.
Hippari'nus.
Hip'pias.
Hip'pitas.
Hippob'otæ.
Hip'poclus.
Hippoc'oön.
Hippoc'rates.
Hippodami'a.
Hippol'yta.
Hippol'ytus.
Hippom'achus.
Hippom'edon.
Hipponi'cus.
Hipposthen'idas.
Homolo'ïchus.
Hopli'tæ.
Hopli'tes.
Horcomos'ium.
Hyb'reas.
Hyc'cara.
Hyp'ates.
Hyper'batas.
Hyper'bolus.

Hyperi'des.
Hypos'tates.
Hypse'chidas.
Hypsicra'tia.
Hyp'sion.
Hyro'des.
Hy'siæ.

Iacche'um.
Ialy'sus.
Iapyg'ia.
Ib'ycus.
Ic'elus.
Icti'nus.
Idom'eneus.
I'ëtæ.
Illyr'icum.
Ino'ra.
Iola'üs.
I'ope.
I'ophon.
Iphic'rates.
Iph'itus.
Isau'ricus.
Is'ias.
Is'idas.
Isido'rus.
Isme'nias.
Isme'nus.
Isoc'rates.
Isod'ice.
Isso'rion.
It'alus.
Ithag'enes.
Itho'me.
Ithoma'tas.
Iu'lis.
Ixi'on.

Janic'ulum.

La'beo.
Labie'nus.
Laccoplu'ti
Lach'ares.
La'cia.
Laci'adæ.
Lam'prias.
Lamp'sacus.
Langobri'tæ. (?)
Laod'ice.
Laodice'a.

Laom'edon.
Lacrat'idas.
Lac'ritus.
Lævi'nus.
La'ïs.
Lam'achus.
La'mia.
Lam'pido.
Lap'ithæ.
Lath'yrus.
Lati'nus.
Lato'na.
Lattam'yas.
Lau'rium or Lauri'um.
Lavi'ci.
Lebade'a.
Len'tulus.
Leob'otes.
Leoch'ares.
Leoc'rates.
Leon'idas.
Leonna'tus.
Leon'tidas.
Leonti'ni.
Leos'thenes.
Leotych'ides.
Lep'idus.
Lep'tines.
Leucas'pides.
Leucon'oë.
Leucoth'eä.
Leuc'trides.
Libe'thra.
Libiti'na.
Licto'res.
Lin'gones.
Lipare'ans.
Lit'uus.
Longim'anus.
Loth'ronus.
Lu'ceres.
Luci'na.
Luci'nus.
Lu'cumo.
Lycao'nia.
Lyce'um.
Lycome'dæ or Lycom'-idæ.
Lydi'adas.
Lyg'damis.
Lysan'dridas.

Lysanor'idas.
Lys'ias.
Lysid'ice.
Lysim'achus.

Maca'ria.
Mac'edon.
Macedon'icus.
Machan'idas.
Macha'res. (?)
Macha'tas.
Machærio'nes.
Macri'nus.
Mæce'nas.
Mæ'dica.
Mæmacte'rion.
Mæo'tis.
Majo'res.
Mal'aca.
Mal'citas.
Ma'lea.
Manci'nus.
Mandrocli'das.
Manip'uli.
Manipula'res.
Mantine'a.
Mar'athon.
Mar'athus.
Marcelli'nus.
Margi'tes.
Mar'ica.
Marphada'tes.
Marruci'ni.
Mar'syas.
Martia'nus.
Masaba'tes.
Massil'ia.
Matu'ta.
Mau'ricus.
Max'imus.
Mede'a.
Mediola'num.
Medu'sa.
Megaba'tes.
Megaby'zus.
Meg'acles.
Mega'leäs.
Megaloph'anes.
Megalop'olis.
Meg'ara.
Megis'tonus.

Melano'pus.
Melea'ger.
Mele'sias.
Melesip'pidas.
Mel'ita.
Melite'a.
Menecli'das.
Menec'rates.
Menede'mus.
Menela'üs.
Menem'achus.
Mercedi'nus.
Meri'ones.
Mer'ope.
Mer'ula.
Mesol'abes.
Mesola'bium.
Messa'la.
Messa'na.
Messe'na.
Messi'na.
Metag'enes.
Metagit'nion.
Metro'bius.
Metrodo'rus.
Mic'ion.
Mid'ias.
Milesi'aca.
Mile'tus.
Milti'ades.
Mimallo'nes.
Min'darus.
Mino'a.
Mise'num.
Mithrida'tes.
Mithrobarza'nes.
Mityle'ne.
Mnasith'eüs.
Mne'sicles.
Mnesiph'ilus.
Mnesiptol'ema.
Mo'dena.
Mœ'rocles.
Molpa'dia.
Mone'ta.
Mon'ime.
Motho'ne.
Munych'ia.
Munych'ion.
Mu'nychus.
Mure'na.

INDEX.

Muse'um.
Mu'tina.
Myc'ale.
Myce'næ.
Myla'sa.
Myron'ides.
Myr'silus.
Myr'tilus.
Mystago'gus.
My'üs.

Nar'nia.
Nartha'cius.
Nasi'ca.
Nau'plia.
Nausic'rates.
Nausith'oüs.
Neal'ces.
Neäp'olis.
Nectan'abis.
Ne'leus.
Ne'mea.
Neme'an.
Nem'esis.
Neocho'rus.
Ne'ocles.
Neoptol'emus.
Nicag'oras.
Nica'nor.
Nica'tor.
Nicera'tus.
Nic'ias.
Nic'ocles.
Nicoc'reon.
Nicode'mus.
Nicog'enes.
Nicola'üs.
Nicom'ache.
Nicom'achus.
Nicome'des.
Nicon'idas.
Nicop'olis.
Nicos'trata.
Nipha'tes.
Nis'ibis.
Non'acris.
Norba'nus.
Nor'ici.
Nume'rius.
Numid'icus.
Nu'mitor.

Nun'dinæ.
Nur'sia.
Nymphid'ia.

Oä'ses.
Ob'olus.
Oce'anus.
Ode'üm.
Œd'ipus.
Œn'arus.
Œne'ïs.
Œni'adæ.
Œno'pion.
Oli'zon.
Ol'ocrus.
Ol'orus.
Ol'thacus.
Olym'pias.
Olympiodo'rus.
Omi'ses.
Om'phale.
On'arus.
One'a.
Onesic'ritus.
Opi'ma.
Opisthod'omus.
Op'lacus.
Op'tilus.
Optil'etis.
Orchal'ides.
Orchom'enus.
Orci'ni.
Orcyn'ii.
Oreste'üm.
O'reüs.
Or'icum.
Or'icus.
Ori'tæ.
Or'neüs.
Or'nytus.
Oroba'zes.
Oro'pus.
Orsoda'tes.
Orthag'oras.
Orthop'agus.
Osta'nes.
Ot'ryæ.
Ovic'ula.
Oxyd'racæ. (?)

Pachy'nus.

Pacia'nus.
Pac'orus.
Pad'ua.
Pædago'gus.
Pædare'tus.
Pag'asæ.
Pal'atine.
Pala'tium.
Pallan'tidæ.
Pallan'tium.
Palle'ne.
Pam'menes.
Pam'philus.
Pamphyl'ia.
Pandi'on.
Pando'sia.
Pan'emus.
Pan'ope.
Pan'opeus.
Panta'leon.
Pantho'ides.
Papy'rus.
Paræto'nium.
Par'alus.
Parapota'miana.
Parmen'ides.
Parme'nio.
Parrha'sius.
Par'thenon.
Parys'atis. (?)
Pas'acas. (?)
Pasar'gadæ.
Pa'seäs.
Pasic'rates.
Pasiph'aë.
Pas'iphon.
Pasiti'gris.
Pas'saro.
Patare'ans.
Pata'vium.
Patro'bius.
Patro'clus.
Patro'nis.
Pauli'nus.
Pausa'nias.
Peda'lium.
Pel'agon.
Pe'lias.
Pelop'idas.
Peloponne'sus.
Pelu'sium.

Penel'ope.
Pentacosiomedim'ni.
Pentap'yla.
Pentel'ican.
Pentele'um.
Pepare'thus.
Per'gamus.
Per'icles.
Pericli'das.
Perigu'ne.
Peripatet'ic.
Periphe'mus.
Periphe'tes.
Periphore'tus.
Per'itas.
Perseph'one.
Pes'sinus.
Pete'lia.
Pet'eüs.
Peti'nus.
Pet'rochus.
Phæd'imus.
Phænar'ete.
Phænomer'ides.
Pha'ëthon.
Phale'rum.
Phali'nus.
Phanode'mus.
Pharmacu'sa.
Pharmu'thi.
Pharnaba'zus.
Phar'naces.
Pharnapa'tes.
Pharsa'lia.
Pharsa'lus.
Phar'ygæ.
Phase'lis.
Phayl'lus.
Phe'neus.
Pher'ecles.
Pher'eclus.
Pherecy'des.
Pherenda'tes.
Phereni'cus.
Phidit'ia.
Phila'idæ.
Philag'rus.
Philar'gyrus.
Phil'arus.
Phile'tas.
Phil'ides.
Philip'pides.

Phil'lidas.
Philobœo'tus.
Philoch'orus.
Phil'ocles.
Philoc'rates.
Philocte'tes.
Philoc'yprus.
Philol'acon.
Philol'ogus.
Philom'brotus.
Philome'des.
Philome'lus.
Philome'tor.
Philoni'cus.
Philop'ator.
Philopoli'tes.
Philosteph'anus.
Philos'tratus.
Philo'tas.
Philox'enus.
Philo'tis.
Phli'us.
Phlog'idas.
Phlo'gius.
Phly'a.
Pho'cion.
Phœb'idas.
Phor'mion.
Phraä'tes.
Phras'icles.
Phrear'rhi.
Phryn'ichus.
Phthi'a.
Phthio'tis.
Phyla'cia.
Phyla'cion.
Phy'le.
Phytal'idæ.
Pice'num.
Pië'rion.
Pin'arus.
Pin'darus.
Pirith'oüs.
Pisis'tratus.
Pissuth'nes.
Pit'ane.
Pit'tacus.
Pixodo'rus.
Plemmyr'ium.
Plisti'nus.
Plisto'änax.
Ploti'nus.

Pœ'cile.
Pol'emarch.
Pol'emon.
Poliorce'tes.
Pol'lichus.
Pol'lio.
Polyæ'nus.
Polyal'ces.
Polyb'ius.
Polycle'tus.
Polycli'tus.
Polyc'rates.
Polycrat'idas.
Polyc'rite.
Polyc'ritus.
Polyd'amas.
Polydec'tes.
Polydo'rus.
Polyeuc'tus.
Polygno'tus.
Polyï'dus. (?)
Polym'achus.
Polyme'des.
Polyni'ces.
Pol'yphron.
Polys'tratus.
Polyx'enus.
Polyze'lus.
Pomaxath'res.
Pon'ticus.
Pontif'ices.
Poplic'ola.
Posi'deon.
Posido'nius.
Pos'tuma.
Pos'tumus.
Pot'amon.
Pot'amus.
Pothi'nus.
Poti'tus.
Pran'ichus.
Praxag'oras.
Praxier'gidæ.
Pria'pus.
Pri'ene.
Proconne'sus.
Procule'ius.
Proc'ulus.
Prod'icus.
Prol'yta.
Prom'achus.
Proma'thion.

INDEX.

Prome'theus.
Proser'pina.
Protag'oras.
Pro'teäs.
Proth'ous.
Proth'ytes.
Protog'enes.
Prox'enus.
Pru'sias.
Pryt'anis.
Prytane'üm.
Pseno'phis.
Pseudom'enos
Psiltu'cis.
Psy'che.
Psyttale'a.
Ptœodo'rus.
Ptolema'ïs.
Public'ola.
Pute'oli.
Pyanep'sion.
Pyl'ades.
Pyl'ius.
Pyra'mia.
Pyr'rhidæ.
Pythag'oras.
Pyth'eas.
Pyth'ocles
Pythocli'des.
Pythodo'rus.
Pythola'üs.
Pythoni'ce.
Pythop'olis.

Quadran'tia.
Quinti'lis.
Quiri'nal.
Quiri'nus.
Quiri'tes.

Ratu'mena.
Rhe'a.
Rhe'gium.
Rhene'a.
Rhodogu'ne.
Rhœ'saces.
Rhœte'um.
Rhyn'dacus.
Roma'nus.
Rom'ulus.
Roxa'na.
Roxa'nes.

Ru'bicon.
Rufi'nus.
Rumina'lis.

Sab'aco.
Sabi'nus.
Saccu'lio.
Sad'alas. (?)
Sa'ïs.
Sal'amis.
Salina'tor.
Sali'næ.
Sambu'ca.
Samos'ata.
Sandau'ce.
Sarpe'don.
Satibarza'nes.
Sat'ricum.
Saturni'nus.
Sat'yrus.
Scæv'ola.
Scambon'idæ.
Scande'a.
Scap'-te-Hy'le.
Scar'phia or Scarphe'a.
Sced'asus.
Schinoceph'alus.
Sci'athus.
Scira'dium.
Sciraph'idas.
Scirophor'ion.
Scyt'ale.
Seleu'cia or Seleuce'a.
Seli'nus.
Sem'ele.
Sene'cio.
Senectu'te.
Seno'nes.
Seq'uani.
Sera'pion.
Sera'pis.
Seri'phus.
Sexti'lis.
Sic'yon.
Sila'nus.
Sile'nus.
Sil'laces.
Simon'ides.
Sim'ylus.
Sin'naca.
Sino'pe.
Sino'ra.

Sisachthe'a.
Sisimith'res.
Sisma'tias.
So'chares.
Soc'rates.
Sol'oön.
So'phanes.
Sophe'ne.
Soph'ocles.
Sophros'yne.
Sora'nus.
Sosib'ius.
Sos'icles.
Sosig'enes.
Sosis'tratus.
So'tion.
So'üs.
Sparami'zes.
Spar'tacus.
Sperchi'us.
Sphacte'ria.
Sphi'nes.
Sphod'rias.
Sphragit'ides.
Spic'ulus.
Spithrida'tes.
Stagi'ra or Stagi'ru
Staph'ylus.
Stasic'rates.
Statia'nus.
Stati'ra.
Steph'anus.
Stesila'us.
Stesim'brotus
Sthen'elus.
Stil'bides.
Stir'ia.
Strate'gus.
Strat'ocles.
Stratoni'ce.
Stratoni'cus.
Su'nium.
Sure'na.
Susamith'res.
Syb'aris.
Sym'bolum.
Syn'alus.

Tac'ita.
Tæn'arus.
Tala'sius.
Tam'ynæ.

INDEX

Tan'agra.
Tan'aïs.
Taphosi'ris.
Tarconde'mus.
Tarraci'na.
Tau'reäs.
Tau'rion.
Taurome'nium.
Tax'iles.
Taÿg'etus.
Tectos'ages.
Teg'ea.
Tegea'tans.
Teg'yræ.
Tel'amon.
Telecl'ides.
Telem'achus.
Tel'ephus.
Teles'ides.
Telesi'nus.
Teleu'tias.
Temeni'tid.
Ten'edos.
Tenteri'tæ.
Ter'merus.
Ter'minus.
Terraci'na.
Tetrap'olis.
Teu'tamis.
Teu'tones.
Tha'ïs.
Thal'amæ.
Thap'sacus.
Tharge'lion.
Thar'rhypas.
Theag'enes.
Theän'gela.
Theä'no.
Theär'idas.
Theär'ides.
Themiscy'ra.
Themis'tocles.
Theoc'ritus.
Theodo'rus.
Theod'otes.
Theod'otus.
Theogi'ton.
Theoph'anes.
Theoph'ilus.
Theo'ris.
Theo'rus.

Theram'enes.
Thermo'don.
Thermop'ylæ.
Theryc'ion.
Thesmoth'etæ.
Thes'piæ.
Thessaloni'ca.
Thes'salus.
Thetid'ium.
Thetide'um.
Tho'äs.
Thra'sea.
Thrasybu'lus.
Thras'ymene.
Thucyd'ides.
Thu'rii.
Thyati'ra.
Thymœt'adæ.
Thyr'ea.
Thyrea'tis.
Tigelli'nus.
Tigra'nes.
Tiguri'ni.
Tilphos'sium.
Timag'enes.
Timag'oras.
Timesil'eüs.
Timesith'eüs.
Timocle'a.
Timocli'des.
Timoc'rates.
Timoc'reon.
Timode'mus.
Timola'üs.
Timo'leon.
Timoleonte'üm.
Timone'um.
Timon'ides.
Timoph'anes.
Timo'theüs.
Timox'enus.
Tisam'enus.
Ti'sias.
Tisiph'onus.
Tith'ora.
Titu'rius.
Tit'yüs.
Tole'ria.
Tol'mides.
Tor'yne.
Tra'gia

Trape'zus.
Tre'bia.
Trip'ylus.
Tro'äs.
Tro'ädes.
Tu'bero.
Tudita'nus.
Tus'culum.
Tu'tula.
Tyn'darus.
Tyran'nion.

Uli'ades.
U'sipes.
Usip'etes.
U'tica.

Vagi'ses.
Vargunti'nus.
Vari'nus.
Vela'brum.
Velatu'ra.
Vel'esus.
Ve'lia.
Vel'itræ.
Vellu'tus.
Venu'sia.
Vera'nia.
Vercingen'torī
Vergen'torix.
Verruco'sus.
Vet'erem.
Viridoma'rus.

Xanthip'pides.
Xenag'oras.
Xena'res.
Xen'ocles.
Xenoc'rates.
Xenod'ochus.
Xenoph'ilus.
Xen'ophon.
Xyp'ete.

Zare'tra.
Zenodo'tia.
Zenod'otus.
Zeugi'tæ.
Zeuxida'mi.
Zo'ïlus.
Zo'pyrus.
Zos'ime.